A COMPLETE GUIDE TO THE BOOK
PUBLISHERS' WORLD OF SPECIAL SALES

HOW TO MAKE REAL MONEY SELLING BOOKS

(without worrying About Returns)

D0191459

BRIAN JUD

SQUAREONE
PUBLISHERS

Please note that all company names, addresses, telephone numbers, and websites, while accurate at the time of publication, are subject to change as the book industry continues to evolve. Before contacting any business or organization, please make sure the contact information is still correct. This will save you both time and money.

Cover Designer: Jeannie Tudor
Editor: Anna Comstock
Indexer: Danielle Burby
Typesetter: Gary A. Rosenberg

Square One Publishers
Garden City Park, NY 11040
(516)535-2010
www.squareonepublishers.com

Library of Congress Cataloging-in-Publication Data

Jud, Brian.
    How to make real money selling books (without worrying about returns) : a complete guide to the book publishers' world of solid sales / Brian Jud.
        p. cm.
    Includes index.
    ISBN 978-0-7570-0213-7
    1. Books—United States—Marketing. 2. Booksellers and bookselling—United States. 3. Selling—Books—United States.
I. Title.
Z471.J833   2009
381'.45002—dc22
                                                                2009020471

Printed in Canada.

10   9   8   7   6   5   4   3   2   1

Contents

Introduction, 1

This book is dedicated to my grandchildren—
Jordan, Sydney, and Kevin.

Their love of words, respect for books,
and continuous search for knowledge
are an inspiration.

Acknowledgments

This book would not have been possible without the help and cooperation of literally hundreds of people giving me their time and providing me with information and insights. In particular, I would like to thank the following people:

Guy Achtzehn, Mark Amtower, Chris Anderson, Robin Bartlett, Connie Bennett, Gloria Boileau, Judith Briles, Dick Bruso, Sharon Buck, Lynda Burch, Gordon Burgett, Peggy Butler, Sheila Clapkin, Charlene Costanza, Bill Creed, Patty Crowe, Jim Donovan, Michelle Yozzo Drake, Elaine Dumler, Ken Dwight, Grace Easely, Paulette Ensign, Megan Feeney, Rick Fisher, Scott Flora, Rick Frishman, Dan Gordon, Barbara Florio Graham, Wes Green, David Hancock, John Harnish, Shel Horowitz, Rita Ippoliti, Lynn C. Johnston, Nicki Jud, Eric Kampmann, Ben Kaplan, Sarah Keeney, Wanda C. Keesey, Hill Kemp, Antoinette Kuritz, Jerry Labriola, Brenda Lee, Jim Leisy, Nolan Lewis, Pam Lontos, Ken Majer, Jane Martin, David Marx, Pam Matthews, Steve Meyerhoff, Nanette Miner, Dorothy Molstad, Nerissa Moran, Kasper Nielsen, Michelle Olvera, Amanda Packer, Curtis Patrick, Dan Poynter, Jay Quickel, Yelba Quinn, Ellen Reid, Mark Resnick, Denise Richardson, Terry Roberts, Mitch Rogatz, Arlene Sachitano, Chris Salditt, Amy Schoen, Jacqueline Seewald, Linda Semmler, Kathleen Shaputis, Rudy Shur, D. K. Simoneau, Marcella Smith, Michael Andrew Smith, Patrick Snow, Charles Stahler, Heather Steenrod, John Styron, Michael Van Meter, Molly Walker, Martin Warzala, Ed White, Jerry Wigen, Randy Yarbrough, Amy Zenn

If I have left anyone out, I apologize. Know, though, that your influence on this book is much appreciated. To all of you, my heartfelt thanks.

Introduction

Book marketing is not what it used to be, nor what it could be. Publishers of all sizes are learning that limiting sales to bookstores—also called trade channels—may be the least effective and most costly way to sell books. This understanding has spawned a better way to market books—one that increases sales, revenue, and profits for those who take their products to people where they buy, rather than waiting for consumers to come to them. This technique is the essence of non-trade book marketing.

Whether you are thinking about writing a book, have already written a book but have not yet started selling it, or are already selling your book to bookstores, *How To Make Real Money Selling Books* will help you understand all of the different non-trade marketplaces that exist. You will also learn that selling to non-trade markets should not be a separate or new way of doing business. Rather, it should be an integral part of your overall sales strategy.

Non-trade marketing is put into practice in all three stages of the publishing process: writing, production, and marketing. First, you write information that consumers' need and publish it in the form in which they want it. Then, you make it available where they shop (pet stores, gift shops, online, etc.), gather (seminars, libraries, etc.), or work (offices, schools, hospitals, etc.).

The purpose of this book is to get you to think about how to sell your book to non-trade markets, and then to help you actually get started doing it. It begins by answering the question—What is non-trade marketing? It then goes into in-depth discussions about all of the different non-trade marketplaces—retail and non-retail—including what buyers look for and how to contact them. That information is followed by sales preparation advice, promotional ideas, and strategies for putting everything together.

In short, this book provides information, strategies, examples, case studies, tips, and more that will make non-trade marketing accessible and profitable for you. You will read about new markets in which to sell your books, and also discover tried-and-true ways to reach them. To paraphrase Robert Kennedy, the most important thing to remember is to "Look where everyone else has been looking, but see what no one else has seen." It sounds simple, and it is. But it is not easy. Persistence and determination are a must. The following list includes a few tips that will jump-start your non-trade sales journey:

■ *Focus on content and form.* Some publishers believe the key to increased income is to publish as many books as possible. However, instead of worrying about the quantity of *books* you produce, find out how the people in your target audience want the information you have delivered—do they want it in a book, booklet, three-ring binder, DVD, or something else? Then, manipulate your existing content into those desired forms. A book may be the best way to communicate your information, but at least be open to considering new product ideas. An open book and an open mind have a lot in common—they can both stimulate your thinking in unknown areas.

■ *Work toward long-term results.* The sales process for a large order to a non-trade outlet may take several years. Buyers may initially test your title, and then wait several months or even a year before placing an order. Rarely are people in as much of a hurry to buy your book as you are to sell it, so be patient. You may be thinking, "If I don't make it through the short term, there won't be a long term." However, consider these points before hitting the panic button:

- There is more at stake for buyers purchasing in large quantities, and corporate buyers in particular want to buy from people they know. It takes time to build the relationships that lead to large orders.

- As you prioritize your list of potential buyers, a process that is described in *29. Qualify, Classify, and Prioritize Your List of Potential Buyers* (page 225), plan to frequently sell small quantities to retailers while you work on the larger orders. This will hopefully generate some interim cash flow, but the axiom still holds true that people buy on their timelines, not yours.

- Eliminate the "Ready. Go. Get Set." philosophy that can lead to failure. Instead, take the time to plan your marketing actions before you implement them; then evaluate their results and make any necessary changes in strategy or action. The "Ready. *Get Set.* Go." philosophy will get you more profitable, long-term results.

- Media exposure is important to selling in non-trade markets, and it takes time to establish relationships and create awareness of your book in the media outlets that are relevant to your title.

- Research and test marketing, described in *26. Conduct Simple Market Research* (page 210) and *27. Perform Basic Test Marketing* (page 215), can increase the likelihood of your success; however, both take time. In the end, though, your sales efforts will prove to be more profitable if you do both, rather than if you proceed without any pre-sales feedback.

- In the trade market, books need to show sales results quickly or they are removed from the shelves. On the contrary, in non-trade markets the focus is on long-term profit optimization, rather than on short-term profit maximization. This makes for a better all-around business strategy.

■ *It is not necessary to choose between marketing to trade and non-trade markets.* It actually makes good sense to do both. If you are already distributing to bookstores and your books are listed on Amazon.com, do not abandon those outlets in search of other markets. Instead, maintain those sales outlets, but keep an open mind and look for new places to sell your books at the same time. If you are just beginning, educate yourself about trade and non-trade marketplaces, and combine both into your overall marketing strategy.

Beginning on the path of non-trade sales can be intimidating, but it will almost certainly increase your revenue and you will not have to worry about returns. This book will give you all of the tools you will need to educate yourself, build your confidence, and start selling to non-trade markets.

Chapter One

What Is Non-Trade Marketing?

M any authors and independent publishers are frustrated because they have 5,000 books in storage, but have no way to get rid of them. Their original dreams of selling large quantities of books in bookstores are shattered. However, even if you find yourself in a similar situation, there is still hope. You can sell your books to new buyers in non-trade markets at any stage of a book's life cycle.

Hesitation in pursuing new sources of revenue in non-trade markets is typically caused by thinking bookstores are the only places to sell books, and also by not knowing where or how to find new buyers in new markets. This book addresses both of these issues, and gives you the impetus and knowledge to sell more books, more profitably. As you will discover over the following chapters, selling to non-trade markets is not that different from selling to bookstores, particularly in the non-trade retail sector, which includes mass merchandisers and specialty shops.

For now, simply acknowledge that there is a potential opportunity to sell large quantities of books in marketplaces other than brick-and-mortar and online bookstores. These cash mines are all around you, but until now you have probably overlooked them, because unlike bookstores, they do not have canyons of bookshelves. Instead, these non-trade sales outlets are disguised as corporations, associations, home shopping networks, book clubs, schools, catalogs, gift shops, retail stores, government agencies, military bases, supermarkets, drug stores, and so many more.

This chapter begins by comparing and contrasting non-trade marketing to trade marketing. It then discusses books' life-cycle phases, which will give you an idea as to how long your book will sell. Next, you will learn about the retail and non-retail sectors of the non-trade market, as well as the importance of your book's content in sales to each. You will then discover that the best results come from a dual distribution strategy. And finally, you will learn how to conduct an effective marketing brainstorm session. In short, this chapter will introduce you to the world of non-trade sales.

1. TRADE VERSUS NON-TRADE BOOK MARKETING

Publishers sometimes overlook hidden, non-trade sales opportunities because they are blinded by tradition. "I have always done it this way," has become their mantra, and they are stuck in a trade sales rut. However, hesitation to enter new markets, which is usually caused by uncertainty, can be overcome by reading this book. Hidden markets are everywhere, and they reveal themselves if you know they exist. Soon you will have more ideas for new sales opportunities than you will know what to do with.

Publishers tend to see the obvious places to sell their books—national super-stores, online bookstores, independent booksellers, and regional chains—and then console themselves with the thought that those channels represent their entire book-selling opportunity. Instead of stopping there, however, stimulate your thinking by asking new questions such as, "How many other places could I sell my book?" Or, "Where else do my target readers look for information on my topic?" Or, "Who else could be a prospective buyer?" Such questions force you to seek additional possibilities in places where your competitors will not be found. For a question-and-answer technique that will help you generate ideas to increase your revenue, see *6. Ask the Right Questions* (page 29).

WHAT IS THE DIFFERENCE?

The differences between marketing to the trade and non-trade book markets are not huge, but they are hugely important. According to Chris Anderson in his book *The Long Tale,* "The average Borders bookstore carries 100,000 titles. Yet about a quarter of Amazon.com's book sales come from outside the top 100,000 titles." Consider the implication: If the Amazon.com statistics are any guide, the market for books that are not even sold in average bookstores is already one forth the size of the existing trade market—and what is more, it is growing quickly. Bookstores do not have space to carry any more books, so if these growth trends continue, more and more books will have to be sold through non-trade outlets.

Furthermore, bookstores have been losing ground as *the place* to sell books. Over the past few years, sales of books to buyers in non-trade market segments have exceeded those in the trade segment. Still, non-trade and trade distribution are not mutually exclusive approaches to book marketing. In fact, there is some overlap in definition, strategy, and implementation between the two. For instance, both sales in the trade and the non-trade retail sectors may require a distribution partner and its subsequent discount; books are also typically returnable in both marketplaces and you may not be paid for ninety days or more. Additionally, in some cases the channels of distribution to trade and non-trade markets are actual-ly identical. In other words, sometimes a trade distributor like Baker and Taylor will not only represent your titles to bookstores, but will also sell it to non-trade marketplaces such as libraries, airport stores, or discount stores. Understand the

UNDERSTANDING THE TRADITIONAL AND NON-TRADITIONAL BOOK MARKETS

The book publishing industry has gone through many phases since the time of Johann Guttenberg (1400–1468) and his revolutionary press. Originally, up until the eighteenth century, printers were the publishers of their times. Like Guttenberg, if Bibles sold, then printers would produce Bibles. By the late eighteenth century, writers had begun contracting printers to publish their own works, and they joined the ranks of the book business by selling their own titles. By the nineteenth century, bookstores had joined the publishing business, as well. By the mid-1800s, a small group of independent entrepreneurs, without presses or bookstores, created stand-alone publishing houses. These houses relied on existing and developing systems of distribution to get their products to the public. For nearly all of these publishers, their buyers constituted what we now call the traditional book market.

THE TRADITIONAL BOOK MARKET

For nearly two hundred years, the majority of book publishers around the world have sold their goods to similar marketplaces, and these marketplaces have been consistent in the way they purchase books. The markets were relatively easy to find, and they continually grew in size. Publishers established their companies' successes based upon their ability to sell to them. These traditional book markets include the following retail and non-retail outlets:

- The Trade (Independent and Chain Bookstores)
- Public Libraries
- Religious Markets
- Educational Outlets (Including Elementary, High School, and College Textbooks)
- Book Clubs

Over time, each of these marketplaces developed its own method of distribution, its own standardized discount policy, and its own promotional vehicles. Up until the end of the 1920s, that system worked reasonably well. When the Great Depression hit, however, bookstores required a new strategy to make it through those hard times. To help sustain many of the hard hit bookshops, publishers established a returns policy that allowed stores to give unsold titles back to their publishers for full credit. While the Great Depression eventually passed, the returns policy that it brought forth has remained in place in the trade market. Unfortunately, this policy has become a pitfall for most independent publishers.

THE NON-TRADITIONAL BOOK MARKET

Within the last fifty years or so, new and exciting marketplaces emerged that offered more opportunities for publishers to increase book sales. While some of these outlets developed as offshoots from the traditional markets, many others developed with the growth of specialty shops. New promotional programs also opened avenues of book sales. All of these newer markets have become known as non-traditional book markets, and they include:

- Mass Merchandisers (Wal-Mart, Kmart, Target, etc.)
- Specialty Shops (Hospital Gift Shops, Culinary Stores, Knitting Shops, etc.)
- Specialty Libraries
- Book Fairs
- Promotional Sales
- Special-Sales
- Niche Marketplaces (Child Birth Centers, Clinics, Hobbyists, RV Enthusiasts, etc.)

As these markets grew and matured, they too developed their own systems of distribution, discount schedules, and promotional opportunities. In addition, this portion of the market allowed for the possibility of selling to previously untapped and hidden marketplaces.

WHERE YOU NEED TO GO TO SELL BOOKS

As an independent publisher, you will discover that there are many potential pitfalls that can wreak havoc with your business. One of the biggest pitfalls is running headlong into the problem of returned books. When most people think of becoming publishers, they immediately think of bookstores as their prime place to sell books. To the uninitiated, this seems to be where all the glitz and glamour is. With their long lines for book-signings, their filled-to-capacity lectures, and their millions of copies of bestsellers, bookstores are what the public thinks is the essence of the book publishing industry. While this may be true for a relatively small number of authors and an even smaller number of big publishing houses, it is quicksand for most new publishers.

This book has been written for those individuals interested in surviving and thriving in the book business. Instead of heading your operation into the deep and uncertain waters of the trade market, this book will provide you with information about marketplaces that will not sink your boat because they have little or no returns attached to them. This book removes the trade market, and then gives a detailed discussion of all of the other markets, both traditional and non-traditional, that exist in which to sell books.

similarities between trade and non-trade markets before looking into the differences; you may already be farther along the path to selling to additional markets than you know.

FOCUS POINTS

Non-trade marketing is basically the process of taking a book that was written in response to an identified need and published in a desired form, and selling it to people in defined groups of prospective customers. The following list contains points you should focus on when you are first beginning to think about non-trade marketing:

■ *Focus on the content of your book, not the book itself.* A recurring theme throughout this book is that what your book contains is more important to buyers than the book itself. This means that successful non-trade marketing begins with content that satisfies an unmet need in the marketplace. Content is king in marketing outside of bookstores, and the old adage, "find a need and fill it," has never been more relevant. For more information on the importance of content in the non-trade marketplace, see *4. Content is King* (page 26).

■ *Focus on people rather than on markets.* It has been said that good doctors treat people and mediocre doctors treat diseases. If you adapt this saying to non-trade marketing, successful publishers market to people and average publishers market to stores. Many publishers talk about selling books to schools, the military, or corporations, and sometimes forget that it is the *people* in each of those groups to whom they are actually marketing. People buy books for their own reasons and they use them for their own purposes. Find out what those are and market to them.

■ *Focus on the marketing end of the business more than on the production end of the business.* The concepts of frontlists and backlists are irrelevant in non-trade markets. Publishing more titles to keep your frontlist current is not nearly as profitable as concentrating on selling the titles you already have. For example, "Booklet Queen" Paulette Ensign has made a business and a career out of selling one title over sixteen years in non-trade markets.

■ *Focus on getting people to buy, rather than selling to them.* This may seem like a minor difference, and it may just be a matter of degree. But today's business buyers are more astute than those of the past. They are not simply looking for ways to reduce costs; they are looking for ways to create value for their organizations. Discover what customers' need, which will probably be some combination of products and services, and then describe to them how your book can help improve their revenues, margins, or brand images. In other words, tell them how your book will add value to their way of doing business. For example, you may be trying to sell a barbeque cookbook to Lowe's or Home Depot, except they do not want to sell cookbooks as much as they want to sell high-priced, more profitable barbeque grills. However, you could sell your cookbook to them by demonstrating how they could use it as an enticement to get people to buy their grills. They could *use* your book as a premium—rather than *sell* it on its own—by giving one away with each grill purchased.

■ *Focus on the differences of your content, not on its sameness.* Authors, particularly of fiction, sometimes describe their books as being similar to a current trend leader by saying, "It's the next *Harry Potter*," or, "It's like *The Da Vinci Code*, but better." However, non-trade buyers do not want more of what they already have. They want to hear how your information is different from the better-known titles, and why it is better.

■ *Focus on both push and pull marketing. Push* marketing is marketing that you direct toward your distributors and wholesalers. It involves giving them information that supports your book, which will in turn help them sell it. Some examples include providing them with incentives, communicating with them regularly, and sending them updated sales literature. This type of marketing is the preferred strategy in non-trade, non-retail markets.

On the other hand, *pull* marketing is marketing that you direct toward the ultimate consumer. Its purpose is to create a demand for your book by making people aware it exists and encouraging them to buy it. Examples include media performances, bookstore events, and personal presentations. Pull marketing is the strategy of choice in non-trade, retail marketing. You should do a little of both in order to achieve the best results.

■ *Focus on what you can control.* There are four primary activities you can control in book marketing:

- Product control: You can control the book's content and form. Remember that the form does not have to be a book. It can be a booklet, a series of podcasts, or many other things.

- Distribution Control: In non-trade marketing you can devise and control your own sales channels to various segments. For example, you might sell your business books to schools or airport stores; your book about dogs to Petco or animal shelters; your book about car safety to driver-training companies or automobile manufacturers; or your romance novel to supermarkets, chocolate companies, or cruise ships and limousine services.

- Price control: Competitive titles are usually not on a shelf next to yours in non-trade outlets, so immediate price comparisons are unlikely. Therefore, the price ceiling is raised, if not eliminated. At the same time, distribution discounts may be eliminated as well, and your print run could be higher resulting in a lower unit cost. A strategy of pricing your titles based upon the value they offer customers as opposed to setting your price based upon the competition is more the rule in non-trade marketing, which results in a greater amount of control for you. The effect is increased pricing flexibility and more leeway in offering price incentives such as discounts, two-for-ones, or coupons. It is entirely possible that you could lower your list price and still be more profitable.

- Promotion control: You can create and communicate your story, in your way, directly to your non-trade market buyers. You have the freedom to directly contact people by mail order, telephone, or personal visit to make your case and negotiate the terms of sale.

The responsibility for success falls squarely upon your shoulders as you direct and control the journey of your title from manuscript to its ultimate buyers in non-trade markets.

■ *Focus on market segments instead of the mass market.* Some people looked at Goliath and thought he was too big to hit. David, however, looked at him and thought he was too big to miss. You might look at non-trade marketing the same way and think, "Is the non-trade market too big to hit, or too big to miss?" The answer to *both* is actually yes. A market of $16 billion is too big to pass up, but it is also too big to compete in profitably if you look at it as one, goliath market. However, if you break the non-trade market into smaller segments to make it more manageable, it is definitely too big to miss.

The essence of non-trade marketing is this concept of *segmentation*—the act of breaking the mass market down into smaller pieces that are relevant to your particular title. The following inset entitled, "Breaking down the Mass Market" provides three examples of how this can be done. Once you have selected the appropriate niches for your title, you can then create and implement a separate marketing strategy for each. The more carefully you define each niche, the more successful you will be in penetrating it with information people in that particular niche find important.

BREAKING DOWN THE MASS MARKET

Looking at the mass market as one big entity can certainly be overwhelming. It becomes much more manageable once it is broken down into smaller segments. Furthermore, once the mass market has been segmented, the marketing strategies you direct toward each niche become much more effective than a general marketing scheme directed at the total market. The following are three examples of how the mass market could be broken down into smaller segments for three different types of books.

EXAMPLE ONE: GOLF TITLE

Michael Andrew Smith's *Business-to-Business Golf: How to Swing Your Way to Business Success* is a book that helps sales people develop successful business relationships while playing golf with their clients. Michael could market to companies that sell sporting goods and also appear on television and radio shows; however, by going after the entire sports products market like that, much of his efforts would be wasted on people who are not interested in his subject.

The total market for sports products is actually made up of several unique, smaller segments. These include school athletic programs, sporting-goods stores, discount retailers like Target and Wal-Mart, and others. Since Michael's book targets one specific group—sales people interested in using golf as a means to improve relationships and sales—only a few of the people in the total sports products market would actually be interested in it. Therefore, instead of creating a mass marketing program, it would be much more effective for Michael to target only the smaller market segments that include people who could use the specific information in his book.

To reach those people, Michael could sell his book through online stores such as www.golfwarehouse.com, as well as through golf pro shops. He could also barter for advertising space in golf magazines like *Golf* and *Golf Digest*, airline magazines, and magazines whose readers include sales people and business executives. Furthermore, niche online and mail-order catalogs that sell golf-related books and products, like www.golfsmart.com, would also be good outlets. Additionally, Michael could approach business sales managers because they might want purchase his book to give to their sales people as an educational resource. Companies that manufacture golf equipment and accessories could use it as a premium or as a self-liquidator, as well. Furthermore, the national Professional Golfers' Association (PGA) and state PGAs might want to use his book as a promotional tool to promote golf as a business sport. Finally, Michael could approach associations like the National Association of Sales Professionals, the Hospitality Sales and Marketing Association International, or the Canadian Professional Sales Association to speak at their conferences or have them use his book as a premium.

EXAMPLE TWO: HEALTH TITLE

Suppose you have a book on health for people in the 50+ age bracket. Instead of taking out an advertisement for it in the *New York Times* and calling it a day, you should reconsider and instead think about smaller, more relevant market-ing outlets. For example, you could target pharmacies, supermarkets, boat stores, senior centers, hospital gift shops, and health-food stores. Additional-ly, you could target corporate libraries, associations like the National Council on Teacher Retirement or the Retired Officers Association, alumni associations, the Baby Boomer Headquarters, or even promote on the air via the Seniors Connection—a radio show dedicated to helping senior adults become educat-ed consumers. Pursuing these smaller, niche markets will allow you to more efficiently and economically reach people interested in your book then your first instinct advertisement in the *New York Times* would have.

EXAMPLE THREE: CHILDREN'S TITLE

A person could spend a lifetime attempting to make contact with every busi-ness, institution, and media outlet that reaches children and their parents. For-tunately for publishers, though, they do not have to. There is a broad range of children's titles, and not every title is appropriate for all children. Similarly, not every outlet that reaches children necessarily reaches those that your book tar-gets. Thus, depending on the topic of the book and the age level it is geared toward, the mass market can be broken down into a less overwhelming and more relevant list of potential sales outlets.

Examples of smaller segments to which children's books could be sold include toy stores, children's museums, children's libraries, children's hospitals, daycare centers, restaurants, and clothing stores. The list goes on to include gift shops like Restoration Hardware, craft stores like Michaels, and specialty stores like Gymboree. Children's books could also be sold to Parent Teacher Organiza-tions to be used as fundraisers, or to schools for use as recreational or supple-mental reading. Additionally, they might be sold to corporations such as Mattel, Hasbro, Fisher Price, or Gerber to be used as premiums, or to members of groups such as the International Mom's Club or Working Mom's Refuge. Cre-ating a list of only those outlets that reach the children your book is geared toward will significantly reduce the time and cost of your marketing actions.

As you can see, breaking down the mass market makes it much more man-ageable. It also saves you time and makes your marketing efforts more economical, because you end up only targeting the people who might be interested in your book. If you apply the ideas behind each of these exam-ples to your own title, the non-trade mass market will not seem quite so intimidating.

With a little strategy and imagination, you can find sales opportunities for almost any title—fiction or non-fiction—in the non-trade marketplace. Think in terms of who *else* could be in your target market, including who else buys books for your target readers and where else your target readers shop. Then find out how to get your books into their hands.

BENEFITS OF EXPANDING YOUR MARKETPLACES

Expanding the number and variety of marketplaces in which you sell your books will almost certainly increase your revenue. But everyone has to start somewhere. The following are priorities you should set for yourself when you first begin selling books:

■ Establish yourself as an ongoing business in a marketplace of your choosing—trade or non-trade—in which you develop a cash flow for your books.

■ Expand your list of products to increase your revenue flow.

■ Expand your sales into more non-trade market segments.

■ Continually increase the intrinsic value of your company for potential future sale.

Significant benefits accrue to the astute publishers that set and meet these priorities. The bottom line is an improved bottom line, since these priorities translate into greater profitability for your business. The following are some of the benefits you will see when you begin expanding your marketplaces in the non-trade segment:

■ *Increased revenue.* Some estimates have shown that the non-trade market is 5 to 10 percent larger than the trade market. Therefore, you could potentially double your sales with additional marketing efforts directed to non-trade markets. Or, to look at it from a different perspective, if you do not seek book sales outside of bookstores, then you may be missing over half of your potential sales.

■ *Recurring revenue.* In non-trade marketing, your customers may place a standing order (a given number of books to be shipped automatically on some predetermined schedule) if, for example, your book is used as a textbook required by students every semester, or as a successful premium with an ongoing sales promotion. This recurring revenue improves the velocity of your cash flow.

■ *Lower acquisition costs.* Selling to an existing customer is less expensive than acquiring new customers. The more frequently people reorder your book, the more profitable each sale becomes. Furthermore, an audience presold on your existing content may greet a second edition—or new, related titles—warmly.

■ *Lower unit costs.* The greater the quantity of books you print, the lower your unit cost will be. Therefore, some publishers print a large number of books at one time, and then have to hold them in inventory to meet the just-in-time shipping requirements of some bookstores. On the other hand, non-trade marketing permits you to hold low (or no) inventory and fill small orders through digital printing, which allows you to print a single copy of a book on demand. Then you can print longer runs to fill orders for large quantities of books.

■ *Increased profitability.* The lower your unit cost, the greater your profitability at the same selling price. In non-trade marketing you print to fill orders, because buyers—particularly non-retail buyers—usually buy in advance of promotions and are willing to wait for delivery. Not only do you print to order (with no inventory costs), but the quantities are typically larger than you might produce to hold for potential trade sales. If you want some books to keep on hand, simply tack on a quantity to the special print run—at a much lower price than if that quantity were printed alone. This tactic could increase your gross profit. Figure 1.1 demonstrates this, using a 6 x 9 inch soft-cover book with 240 pages as an example (Actual printing costs as determined on the website www.booksjustbooks.com).

■ *Greater total sales.* You can increase your total sales and sell more books to an entirely new market segment simply by using a little creativity. For example, Amy Schoen's title *Get it Right This Time* is about helping single people meet their life-long partner. By thinking beyond the bookstore, Amy found opportunities selling her book to cruise ship lines, florists, and online dating services for use as a premium to attract new business.

■ *Less competition.* When you promote a book, you may tell people to go to the bookstore to buy it. However, when the buyers get there they see your title among

Figure 1.1. Profit Benefits of Non-Trade Sales

Trade Order: Print 1,000 books for a unit printing cost of $3.04, and sell them to a bookstore through a distribution partner with a 65 percent discount off the list price.

List price:	$19.95
Distribution Partner's Discount:	−$12.97
Publisher's Revenue:	$6.98
Unit Printing Cost:	−$ 3.04
Publisher's Unit Gross Profit:	**$3.94**
Publisher's Total Gross Profit:	**$3,940.00** (Before Returns)

Non-Trade Order: Print 10,000 books—9,000 to fill a non-returnable non-trade order, and 1,000 for inventory—for a unit printing cost of $1.06 and sell the additional 1,000 to a bookstore through a distribution partner with a 65 percent discount off the list price.

List price:	$19.95
Distribution Partner's Discount:	−$12.97
Publisher's Revenue:	$ 6.98
Unit Printing Cost:	−$1.06
Publisher's Unit Gross Profit:	**$5.92**
Publisher's Total Gross Profit:	**$5,920.00** (Before Fewer Returns)

all of your competitors' titles and may not end up choosing yours. On the other hand, when you make personal sales calls to corporations, government agencies, or small gift shops, you have the buyers' undivided attention, because most likely no other author or publisher has tried to contact them.

■ *Less discounting.* When you sell to non-trade markets, buyers may not have immediate access to competitive pricing. For example, product or brand managers look for premiums to boost the sales of their products, and they often do not know if yours is priced above or below competitors' titles. They are only concerned with your book's potential to increase the sales and profitability of their company's products. Therefore, there is not as much pressure on you to discount the price of your book in order to keep up with the competition.

■ *Fewer returns.* Although some retail buyers (discount stores, supermarkets, airport stores, etc.) buy books on a returnable basis, most non-retail buyers (book clubs, niche marketplaces, schools, etc.) almost never expect to return books.

■ *More effective and efficient media exposure.* Pinpointing promotions to carefully selected target market segments can reduce waste in your marketing expenditures and lead to more sales. For example, if you are selling a title about improving someone's tennis serve, a review or article in *Tennis* magazine will more efficiently reach prospective buyers and be more cost effective than a review or article in *The New York Times*.

■ *Negotiable terms.* You may increase your flexibility in sales negotiations because unlike trade markets, discounts are not fixed in non-trade markets and are typically based on the number of books purchased. Even if you negotiate a 50 percent discount with a non-trade buyer, you are still 5 to 20 percent better off than you would be by selling that same book through the trade where discounts are set at 55 to 70 percent. There are also other variables open to negotiation in non-trade sales, such as shipping expenses and payment terms.

■ *Improved cash flow.* In non-trade markets, many orders are for multiple copies or for standing orders. Both of these minimize your cost of filling orders, and therefore result in a greater profit. Furthermore, some non-trade buyers purchase your products at list price and pay you in less than ninety days. For example, government agencies are obligated to pay you interest if your uncontested invoice is not paid within thirty days.

As you can see, the more you expand your sales into non-trade marketplaces, the more your business will grow and succeed.

T
I
P
If you are an author, check with your publisher to find out which buyers you may contact and which are precluded before contacting any non-trade market buyers, because your contract may prevent you from selling to certain segments such as libraries, warehouse clubs, or airport stores. Work with your publisher to increase your sales to all markets.

A QUICK COMPARISON

There are some similarities but also several differences between selling your book in the trade market as opposed to the non-trade market. Figure 1.3 on the next page provides you with a quick overview of what you can expect when marketing your book to each.

At first glance, non-trade marketing may seem daunting, or even impossible. However, once you have educated yourself about these hidden marketplaces, reaching them is not as difficult as it may first appear. Furthermore, the benefits you will accrue from expanding your book sales into non-trade market sectors will make your efforts worthwhile. The following sections will teach you more about non-trade marketplaces, and also demonstrate how you can get started selling your book to them.

2. HOW LONG WILL YOUR BOOK SELL?

All products go through a series of phases based on the revenue they produce (if any) over a period of time; however, there is no predetermined time-frame for each phase. A book begins with an *introduction phase,* which occurs when it is first introduced to the market. It then enters a *growth phase,* during which sales increase. As the sales grow, profits increase. Then at some point, growth slows and begins to level off; this is the book's *maturity phase.* Eventually, the book reaches its *decline phase* and sales begin to fall. Figure 1.2 below depicts this concept. It shows the revenue from a product's bookstore sales going through the traditional life-cycle phases of introduction, growth, maturity, and decline.

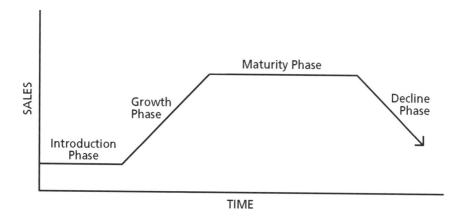

Figure 1.2. Life-Cycle Phases

Figure 1.3.   Quick Overview of Trade and
Non-Trade Book Marketing

Characteristic	Trade Book Marketing	Non-Trade Book Marketing
Sales Demand for Books	Sales decrease during slow economic periods and increase during holiday or gift-giving periods.	Sales remain stable or increase during slow economic periods and there are fewer seasonal variations.
Publishing Decisions	A publisher's choice of titles is literary and depends on the manuscript's quality and fit with the publisher's line.	A publisher's choice of titles is marketing based and depends upon a need for the information by buyers in a target market.
Publishing Process	Books may be hurried through the publishing process to meet artificial deadlines or to reach an imposed number of titles to publish annually.	The emphasis is on selling content, not on publishing a set number of titles, and the need for a separate frontlist and backlist is eliminated.
Segmentation of Buyers	Buyers are generally dispersed, with some geographical and regional differences.	Prospective buyers are concentrated in industrial, geographic, or demographic segments.
Contact with Buyers	Publishers rely on distributors' sales representatives to sell their titles.	Publishers directly contact prospective buyers, particularly in the non-retail sector.
Learn About Titles	Buyers learn about titles through publicity and media appearances.	Buyers learn about titles through personal selling, advertising, direct marketing, and publicity.
Buyers' Motives	Buyers choose books more and more subjectively as the degree of similarity among titles increases.	Buyers are trained and experienced, and seek good returns on investments; buying decisions are more rational and objective.
Buyers' Decision Making Process	Buyers decide which books they want quickly—usually during two or three selling periods per year; the emphasis is on the frontlist.	Buyers' decisions are deliberate— large companies may take a year or more to make a decision; the emphasis is on content rather than on copyright date.
Distribution	Books are distributed through distributors, wholesalers, and sales representative groups.	In the retail sector, books are distributed through distributors and wholesalers; in the non-retail sector, books are distributed directly to buyers by the publisher, or through sales representative groups.

Characteristic	Trade Book Marketing	Non-Trade Book Marketing
Distribution Discounts	Standard distribution discounts range from 55 to 70 percent of retail price.	Buyers in the retail sector require substantial discounts; in the non-retail sector, however, there are opportunities for negotiated discounts and sales at list price.
Pricing	Books are priced competitively.	Prices are less competitive and more value-based.
Returns	Returns are common and return rates are high; the return rate for hardcover bestsellers could be as much as 35 percent.	Most sales in the retail sector are made on a returnable basis, but non-retail sales usually do not allow returns.
Break Even Point (BEP)	The BEP for unit sales is high due to distribution discounts, returns, and delayed payments.	The BEP for unit sales is low due to few (if any) distribution discounts and returns.
Product Line	Product lines are standardized.	Product lines are customized to meet the needs of buyers.
Customer Acquisition Costs	Customer acquisition costs are high because of the need to sell single books to many different customers.	Customer acquisition costs are low because of the ability to sell many books to few customers.
Promotion	Publishers broadly promote their books to large populations and rely on uncontrollable public relations and media appearances.	Publishers promote their books to specific groups of people with pinpoint accuracy and have more control over how their book is promoted.
Promotional Material	Books are promoted with press kits, reviews, and press releases for the media, and fact sheets for distributors.	Books are promoted with creative material that connects the benefits of the titles to the buyers' needs.
Control Over the Book's Life Cycle	Control of a title's life cycle is left to others who decide if sales are sufficient to maintain market presence.	Author's have the opportunity to extend the growth phase of their books with sales to new markets and buyers.
Length of Time a Book Will Sell	Books will only sell for a short period of time and must show sales results quickly or they pulled from the shelves.	There are opportunities to sell your book for a long time and your backlist is as important as your frontlist.

EXTENDING THE GROWTH PHASE

Since the period of greatest profitability lies in the growth phase, it behooves the publisher to extend this period as long as possible. Selling more books to new markets is certainly one way to do this. In Figure 1.4 below, the growth phase is extended by selling to new markets, thereby maximizing the profits generated from this particular title.

Expanding the number and variety of marketplaces to which you sell books is a business-growth strategy. For instance, if you are able to produce your title in different forms aimed at new users for new uses, you can extend the title's growth phase almost indefinitely. In essence, that is what Mark Victor Hansen and Jack Canfield did with their *Chicken Soup for the Soul* line.

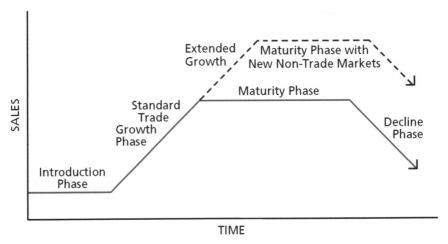

Figure 1.4. Extending the Growth Phase

MANIPULATING MARKET VARIABLES

As a book marketing strategist, you have three major variables with which to deal: the products you offer, customer needs, and competition. These variables overlap in different ways, as demonstrated in Figure 1.5 on page 22. The way you manipulate and exploit these three components defines the degree to which you will be successful.

T I P A discussion beginning with the words, "I received a great manuscript today," will rarely be as effective as one beginning with, "I was reading about a new consumer trend for which there are no current titles available. What if we . . ."

THE LIFE-CYCLE PHASES OF FRONTLIST VERSUS BACKLIST BOOKS

Traditionally, books were sold to the trade by salesmen. During the fall and spring selling seasons they would go around to different bookstores and show the owners a catalog. The front of these catalogs displayed new books, whereas the older books got pushed to the back—hence the terms frontlist and backlist. That same language is now used in the industry in a more general way, and it is important to understand its meaning.

Books are considered frontlist titles for the first three to six—sometimes nine—months after their publication date. Backlist titles, then, are those books that are typically nine months old and older. Many of the large publishing companies are frontlist driven, meaning that they place most of their attention on their new titles. Pushing their frontlist titles allows these companies to grow; however, their backlists actually support them. On the other hand, smart, small- and mid-sized companies are backlist driven. They market new and old books equally, knowing that their older lists are what continue to drive sales forward.

Because of their different natures, frontlist and backlist books have different life-cycle phases. Frontlist books typically have a big burst of sales during their introduction phase, and then quickly cycle through the remainder of the phases, leading to a quick decline. This is especially true for fiction and current event non-fiction titles. Large publishers may initially sell 5,000 to 20,000 copies of these books, but then see sales abruptly drop off. The trade's attention to books' copyright dates typically forces their demise at the end of the copyright year, as well. Additionally, eventual returns can shrink those initial sales numbers.

Backlist titles on the other hand, particularly non-fiction books, generally move more slowly through the life-cycle phases. They are often presold, so the publishers have a nice sale during their introduction phase. Then, three or four months later the book may start getting good reviews, leading to increased sales during the growth phase. The title then becomes a backlist book, but sales can continue to increase for another six months to a year. Next the title enters its maturity phase, and sales can stay stable at 1,000 to 3,000 copies per year for an additional one to three years through the use of non-trade market sales. At that point, some books get revised and updated, thus prolonging their growth and maturity phases, and others enter the decline phase.

Finally, there are those titles that are considered evergreen. Evergreen titles can stay in their maturity phase for twenty years, and they can sell between 3,000 and 10,000 copies during each of them. Since marketing costs are reduced, these titles become almost purely profit and are therefore the gems of any publishing company.

Remember that all publishing companies and all books are different; they do not necessarily fit this mold. In almost every case, though, pushing a big frontlist can be at the expense of backlist books that could have potentially been big sellers. Thus, especially for smaller publishers, it is important not to neglect your backlist titles. This concept is particularly relevant in the non-trade marketplace. Non-trade buyers are less concerned with the copyright dates of books and the concepts of frontlists and backlists than they are with the applicability of the content to their employees, students, customers, or members. In effect, if the information in your book is current and relevant to a segment of buyers, your title can enter the growth and maturity phases and remain there for as long as you follow the principles described in this book.

Publishers that produce books based on literary criteria rather than market need, compete in *Area A,* as shown in Figure 1.5. They spend time trying to get their books placed on retail shelves and then wonder why they do not sell. The simple answer is that their books do not sell because people do not want them.

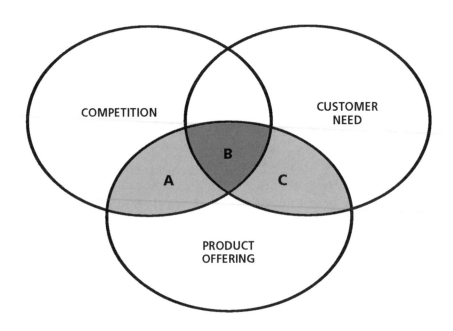

Figure 1.5. Market Variables

Publishing a book based on market need but in a highly competitive environment may be equally as frustrating. These publishers deal in *Area B* of Figure 1.5, trying to sell a quality book based on market need, but among several competitive titles. This could be in a bookstore, an airport shop, a supermarket, or a discount store. Because so many titles are available right next to each other in these venues, interested buyers immediately weigh the value of your book (the degree to which the information you provide is applicable to them at the price you are asking) against that of the competition's.

The intention of this book is to help you market your books in *Area C* of Figure 1.5—meeting the needs of prospective buyers while circumventing competition. of course, you should not ignore the buyers in *Area B*, but by using the concept of dual distribution described in *5. Dual Distribution* (page 27), you can sell through these retail outlets without relying on them for the bulk of your revenue. Then in addition, you should pursue revenue and profits in non-retail, non-trade markets, which will increase your book's growth phase. The differences between the retail and non-retail sectors of the non-trade market are described in the next section.

3. THE SECTORS OF NON-TRADE MARKETS

The non-trade sales market is made up of two (almost) mutually exclusive sectors. The first is the retail sector, which is similar to the trade market in that it utilizes distributors and wholesalers to reach retail outlets. The second is the non-retail sector, which is made up of groups of people who have an identifiable need for the information in your book, or that can use your book as a promotional device.

RETAIL SECTOR

The non-trade retail sector includes mass merchandisers and specialty shops. Its distribution system utilizes many of the distribution channels that are used to sell to bookstores. The most common chain of retail distribution goes from the publisher, to distribution partners, to retailers, and ultimately, to consumers. However, there are also retail distribution systems in which the middleman sells directly to the consumer. These include book fairs, book clubs, mail-order catalogs, and home-shopping networks. Figure 1.6 on page 24 demonstrates both of these retail distribution chains.

The similarities between retail distribution channels and trade distribution channels do not end there. In both, the retailer's choice of titles is a marketing decision, not a literary one. Additionally, returns are endemic, the discount schedule can reach 70 percent, and payment terms may exceed ninety days. Conversely, the rewards of immediate national distribution can be significant.

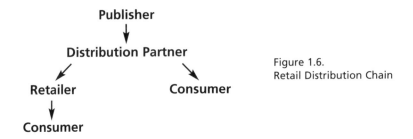

Figure 1.6.
Retail Distribution Chain

Chapter Two. Non-Trade Retail Markets (page 35) details each segment of the non-trade retail market. Additionally, there are several retail associations that can help you learn more about selling to the retail sector.

○ For a complete list of state and local retail associations, go to www.boogar.com/resources/associations/retail_trade.htm

In addition to the state and local associations you will find on the above website, there are also four national associations that can provide you with valuable information. They are included in the following list:

■ *National Association for Retail Marketing Services.* NARMS is the only legal forum that brings together all facets of the retail services industry—retailer, manufacturer, and retail service company—to network and discuss common issues and solutions. Over 500 companies are currently members, including merchandising service organizations, event marketing, mystery shopping, demonstration companies, independent food brokers, consumer goods manufacturers, and retailers.

❑ NARMS; P.O. Box 906, Plover, Wisconsin 54467
Tel: 715-342-0948; Website: www.narms.com

■ *National Retail Federation.* NRF is the world's largest retail trade association. Its membership comprises all retail formats and channels of distribution, including department stores, specialty stores, discount stores, catalogs, online websites, independent stores, chain restaurants, drug stores, and grocery stores, as well as the industry's key trading partners of retail goods and services. NRF represents an industry that has more than 1.6 million retail companies in the United States. As the industry's umbrella group, NRF also represents over 100 state, national, and international retail associations.

❑ National Retail Federation; 325 7th St., N.W., Ste. 1100, Washington, DC 20004
Tel: 202-783-7971, 800-673-4692; Website: www.nrf.com

■ *National Retail Hardware Association.* This association helps member retailers become better and more profitable merchants. In doing so, it provides them with educational and training programs, financial management resources, and human resource tools such as books.

❑ National Retail Hardware Association; 5822 W. 74th St., Indianapolis, IN 46278
Tel: 317-290-0338, 800-772-4424; Website: www.nrha.org

■ *Retail Merchants Association.* The mission of the Retail Merchants Association is to enhance the image and profitability of member companies through advocacy, information, and networking opportunities.

❑ Retail Merchants Association; 5101 Monument Ave., Richmond, Virginia 23230
Tel: 804-662-5500, 866-750-2532; Website: www.retailmerchants.com

Before you begin selling your books in the retail sector, learn as much as you can about it through these associations. Find out the preferred terminology so you can deal with buyers using their language. Also become familiar with the top distribution partners and the typical terms of sale, so you will be prepared to sell profitably to these buyers.

NON-RETAIL SECTOR

The non-trade non-retail sector contains organizations that use books in different ways—to motivate employees, to increase membership, or to market their products and services. Some examples of ways in which different organizations might use your book include the following: a corporation may purchase it to sell as an advertising specialty; an association may use it as a premium to increase attendance at its annual conference; schools may use it as a textbook; or government agencies may purchase it to give to their constituents. *Chapter Three. Non-Trade Non-Retail Markets* (page 111) goes into more detail about each segment in the non-trade non-retail market.

Distribution in the non-retail sector differs from the retail sector, because here you contact, negotiate with, ship directly to, and bill the people representing each individual organization. As Figure 1.7 depicts below, there are rarely distribution partners to deal with. Furthermore, in the non-retail sector you can bargain for buying terms, returns are uncommon, and payment is generally made in less than sixty days.

As long as your content is current and relevant, both non-trade market sectors give you the flexibility to increase your sales by changing the form of your product from a book to something else, and then to deliver it for use as a

Publisher
↓
Non-Retail Buyer
↓
Consumer

Figure 1.7.
Non-Retail Distribution Chain

fundraising item, premium, incentive, or gift, even though the majority of non-trade buyers will purchase your books as they are. The next section provides you with a more in-depth discussion about the importance of content in the non-trade marketplace.

4. CONTENT IS KING

Content is king in non-trade marketplaces. You will achieve the most success not by selling non-trade buyers your book, but by selling them the benefits they will get from your book's content. In other words, the form in which your content is presented is of less consequence than the content itself in the non-trade marketplace.

Both non-trade retail and non-trade non-retail stores, companies, institutions, and organizations want to use the information in your book to help them sell more of the products or services they offer, or to help them train and educate their employees. They may repurpose your content for use as a premium, a fundraiser, or any number of other devices. For example, in the case of schools, your content could help the teachers improve the education they provide their students. Furthermore, government agencies purchase books, but they also seek publishers to create and deliver content that does not already exist in the form in which they need it. These are just two of the many prospective sales opportunities you will discover in this book. The opportunity to increase your revenue is limited only by your creativity.

Frank Fochetta, the Vice President and Director of Special Sales and Custom Publishing at Simon and Schuster, agrees. According to Frank, "There is only one way to increase your sales, revenue, and profits in the non-trade segment. That is, sell *content.*" Businesses are less concerned about the place your title holds in your frontlist or backlist than bookstores are. Instead, they want to know how the information contained in your product line can help their business more than that of some other marketing tool. The following list contains three areas that signify the importance of your book's content in the non-trade marketplace:

■ *Brand association.* A book should have the same image as the outlet through which it is associated. For example, a book sold through dollar stores will have a much different image than a book offered as a premium for a $300 suede coat from Eddie Bauer. Additionally, the concept of product placement functions as much and as well in the publishing industry as it does in television shows and movies. If a brand name is mentioned in a book, the owner of that brand becomes a likely sales prospect. Furthermore, the capabilities of print-on-demand publishing make it easier to change the name of the product if it is necessary to sell to a different buyer.

■ *Repackaged content.* When selling to non-trade market buyers, the starting place for your negotiations is the information that your book provides. If a prospective buyer decides that your content has value, then you settle on the form in which the content will be disseminated. This may be as a book, booklet, DVD, audio book, or other form. Even if you do choose a book as the final form, it can still be customized by changing its size, reducing its paper weight to lower shipping costs, creating a custom version using the client's product as the hero of the story, changing the binding to meet a specific function, or many other options.

■ *Value for the customer.* Books are valuable to non-trade market buyers for two reasons. First, the information in your book can help them improve, educate, or entertain their customers in some way. Second, they can purchase books inexpensively in relation to their perceived value. People generally hold books in high esteem and are reluctant to throw them away. They keep books, giving them long shelf lives in customers' homes, schools, libraries, and offices. In the best case, this will stimulate positive word-of-mouth advertising, leading to more sales for you and your clients.

The non-trade sales process is not about you or your book. Rather, it is about providing your customers and readers with valuable information. Learn how to sell what your content will do for your readers by looking at it from their perspectives. Once you change your marketing focus from "me" to "them," you will go a long way in increasing your sales, revenue, and profits. There are numerous opportunities for you to sell your books out there. The next section will show you why it is beneficial for you to attempt sales to several outlets simultaneously.

5. DUAL DISTRIBUTION

You now know that you have three possible avenues in which to sell your books: trade outlets, non-trade retail outlets, and non-trade non-retail outlets. As a general rule, however, it is not necessary to choose only one of the three options, because some combination of them will most likely optimize your profitability. This is the concept of dual distribution.

CREATIVE MARKETING EXAMPLE

By understanding your options, you can choose the best marketing strategy for each of your titles. For example, refer back to Figure 1.1 on page 15. The book it describes is a 6 x 9 inch soft-cover book, with 240 pages and a list price of $19.95. If you printed 1,000 of those books at $3.04 each and sold all 1,000 to bookstores with a distribution discount of 65 percent off the list price, your revenue would be $3,943. If instead you sold all 1,000 to a discount store like Wal-Mart at a 70 percent discount, your revenue would only be $2,945, which is $1,000 less. Figure 1.8 demonstrates both of these situations. Furthermore, in both of these cases the books are returnable.

Figure 1.8.   Revenue from Trade and Discount Store Sales

Bookstore Distributor	Discount Stores	Revenue
1,000		$3,943
	1,000	$2,945

On the other hand, if you apply a creative marketing strategy you will most likely be able to increase your revenue. For instance, you could sell the same 1,000 books through a library wholesaler at a 55 percent discount and make $2,000 to $3,000 more than you would by selling them all to a bookstore. Or, you could sell them directly to end users at a 20 percent discount and maximize your revenue, as shown in Figure 1.9. You might complete this analysis and decide you want to market all of your books directly to end-users. However, you will quickly learn that your gross revenue will be diminished by the increased costs of doing all the selling work yourself, which is why dual distribution is often best. Also, you may not have the time or skill to successfully conduct such an intense direct marketing campaign and fulfill every order manually.

Figure 1.9.   Revenue from Creative Marketing

Bookstore Distributor	Library Wholesaler	Direct	Discount Stores	Net Revenue
1,000				$ 3,943
	1,000			$ 5,938
		1,000		$12,920
			1,000	$ 2,945

OPTIMIZE YOUR REVENUE

Your overall sales goal should be to *optimize*, rather than *maximize* your revenue. As Figure 1.10 shows, if you divide your sales among several distribution channels—employing the concept of dual distribution—you can find the distribution combination that will lead to the most revenue given your available time and talents; thus, optimizing your profits.

For example, Combination B in Figure 1.10 eliminates the hassle of direct marketing, but minimizes your potential revenue. However, this may optimize your revenue if you disdain selling. Combinations A, C, and D may not maximize your

Figure 1.10. Using Different Creative Marketing Strategies to Optimize Revenue

Distribution Channel	Bookstore Distributor	Library Wholesaler	Direct	Discount Stores	Total Sales	Net Revenue
Distributor only	1,000				1,000	$ 3,943
Wholesaler only		1,000			1,000	$ 5,938
Direct only			1,000		1,000	$12,920
Discount Stores				1,000	1,000	$ 2,945
Combination A	250	250	250	250	1,000	$ 6,436
Combination B	250	500		250	1,000	$ 4,691
Combination C	125	125	500	250	1,000	$ 8,431
Combination D	150	250	350	250	1,000	$ 7,334

revenue, but they do demonstrate how a strategy of dual distribution can optimize and strengthen your revenue streams, which will protect you against competitive actions and deviations in the general economy.

○ You can purchase an Excel spreadsheet that will automatically calculate your own distribution options at www.bookmarketingworks.com

Not all dual distribution strategies and combinations yield the same results. Manipulate your non-trade marketing strategy to generate the most lucrative distribution combination for your circumstances. Your answers to the questions in the following section will help you determine the best combination for your book.

6. ASK THE RIGHT QUESTIONS

Many independent publishers ignore non-trade sales because they do not know where to start. Their definition of non-trade marketing is selling books "outside of the bookstore." However, that only suggests where *not* to sell books; it offers no direction, insight, or instruction about where or how to actually do it. Many publishers who choose to sell in non-trade markets feel uncomfortable because it is either something they do not know how to do, or it is something at which they may have failed in the past. Let us say you recognize the need to increase your revenue and profits in non-trade markets, but are nervous to get started. Asking and answering the types of questions discussed in this section can help you overcome these initial anxieties about entering the world of non-trade sales. After all, if you do not ask the right questions, you will never get the right answers.

GUIDELINES FOR SUCCESSFUL QUESTION-ASKING SESSIONS

When first entering the world of non-trade sales, the best way to begin is by conducting an idea-generating, question and answer session. The idea that two heads are better than one is definitely applicable here, so try to get some people together to help you brainstorm. The following six guidelines will help your question-asking sessions become more productive:

■ Properly formulate your questions. Instead of asking, "Where else can we sell this title?" which may only elicit one response, ask, "In how many places can we sell this title, and what are they?" thereby generating additional possibilities.

■ Limit your discussion to one topic before moving on to the next. In other words, fully exhaust all of your ideas on how to improve your product before beginning your discussion about different ways you can distribute, price, and promote it. Then in turn, discuss each of those topics before moving on to the next.

■ Stimulate as many responses as possible. Think quantity, not quality early in the process. Always ask, "What else can we do?" before moving on to the next topic. This last probing question may uncover a big idea that will help you make real money selling your books.

■ Use a flip chart, chalkboard, or some other means of recording all responses that is visible to all participants. Something you write down might trigger another idea in someone else's mind.

■ Have fun and be creative. Encourage far-fetched responses even though many of them will not be practical. One of these implausible ideas may lead to a more realistic and lucrative one.

■ Do not judge any idea during your brainstorming session, so people feel completely free to contribute. Then go back and decide which of the responses are not applicable after the idea-generating portion of the meeting is finished.

Following these guidelines will contribute to the success of your question-asking sessions. However, do not feel like you have to limit it to these six. Be open to suggestions and do what works best for you.

STARTER QUESTIONS

To make it easier for you to conduct your own question-asking sessions, you should use the following list of basic questions about different topics as a jumping-off point. Hopefully once you get your creative juices flowing with these, you will then be able to expand upon them. Remember to fully exhaust your ideas for each topic before moving on to the next, and always finish each topic with the question, "What else can we do?"

■ In how many ways can we change our book to make it more marketable?

Should we make it smaller or larger? Increase the spine width or make the type-face on the spine more legible for better visibility on the shelf? Come up with a new title, color combination, or cover design? What else can we do?

■ In how many ways can we work more successfully with our distributors? Can we communicate better? Share our marketing plans? Participate in cooperative advertising? Provide the distributor's sales people with more and better sales liter-ature or information about our title's top sales handles? What else can we do?

■ In how many ways can we improve our pricing? If we lower our production costs could we make more money at the same list price, or even at a lower list price? What else can we do?

■ In how many ways can we improve the quality and quantity of our promotion? Should we try to appear on targeted television and radio shows? Improve our per-formance on each by taking media training courses? Improve our press release and kits? Hire a publicist? Create more and better sales promotion items? Improve our website? Make a personal selling kit? Conduct more personal presentations? What else can we do?

Again, these questions do not represent an exhaustive list. Let your conversa-tion lead the way and when you least expect it, you just might stumble upon that one great idea.

ADDITIONAL QUESTIONS AND EXAMPLE ANSWERS

The following are some additional questions you can ask to generate insight into your business, as well as find new ways to sell your books and new places in which people can buy them. The questions themselves are universal and apply to all subject areas; however, this example focuses on how they relate to a publisher trying to market a career or job-search title.

■ *Who could use the information in your book?* The answer to this question should direct you to broad market segments. In this case, it is people seeking employment for the first time, looking for a career change, or trying to find new employment after being laid off.

■ *Where do people generally look for the information in your book?* Your first answer is most likely bookstores, but do not stop there. Keep adding places like colleges and high schools, churches, state employment departments, employment agencies, outplacement firms, and networking groups to your list until you cannot think of anything else.

■ *Who else could use the information in your book?* Here is where you should think beyond the broad market segments you came up with in answer to the first ques-tion. Finding new niches in which to sell existing titles may be the most efficient way to increase your sales and revenue. You might be able to sell your content to high school or college students, people who are over fifty years old, women, blue-collar workers, and more.

■ *Who could use your content in generally over-looked segments?* This question should get you thinking about very specific groups of people. In this case, prisoners who are released or paroled must be trained to find new jobs, so could potentially have a need for your book. The same concept applies to military personnel who are discharged and need job-search information.

■ *Where do the people in these generally over-looked segments look for the information in your book?* This answer will tell you how to reach those specific groups of people. Prisoners may go to their prison libraries, search online for career information, or ask their parole officers for advice. Military bases, posts, and installations provide books and courses for people in the armed services who are about to reenter civilian life.

■ *Is there anyone that might want your content presented in a different form?* Not everyone uses information in the same way, so you may need to publish your information in different forms to make it more accessible to different groups of people. For example, blind job-seekers need the same information as people with sight, but they need it delivered in an audible format.

■ *Who influences the people that use your content?* Instead of marketing directly to prospective customers, you may want to market to people who can influence them. You could potentially sell your book to career development officers atcolleges, to guidance counselors in high schools, or to the parents of graduating seniors.

■ *Do people use the information in your book in any unusual ways?* If the content of your book could be used in an unusual way, think about different ways to disseminate your information to make it easier to use in that particular way. For example, bound books do not lie flat, so a three-ring binder might be the preferred format for use during a seminar or workshop. The person in charge may be more willing to buy your book if you provide it with a spiral or comb binding.

■ *How might you lower your costs without negatively effecting quality?* The four-color cover is typically the most expensive part of the book-printing process. If you print in large quantities the unit cost is substantially reduced, but it is not always logical to produce a large quantity of books. Therefore, you might consider printing a large number of covers, but a smaller number of books. That way, you would have covers readily available for your next print run.

■ *What is the biggest hassle for people purchasing your content?* Books are not always easy to transport. Heavy and oversized books do not sell well in airport stores, for example, because people do not want the aggravation of carrying them through the airport and onto planes. If your content can be delivered in a more portable form, it may be purchased in larger quantities. This might lead you to creating podcasts that can be downloaded to iPods or making CDs.

■ *Who spends money to adapt your content to their specific needs?* Informal research may disclose an absence of career information available for the Hispanic market. You might find that Hispanics are spending time and money translating English written job-search information into Spanish. Thus, you could have your content translated into Spanish for them, giving yourself the opportunity to sell many more books to a whole new market.

■ *Who uses (or could use) your book in large quantities?* You can sell 10,000 books to 10,000 different people one at a time, or you can sell 10,000 books to one person at one time. Clearly, the latter option would be more profitable. Find people who can buy in large quantities. They may be in government offices, corporations, schools, or many other places. In this case, you might get meeting planners to buy books for everyone in the audience of your job-search presentation.

■ *Who could purchase your book without large discounts?* When people buy your book in order to resell it, they obviously want to buy it from you at a discount so their sales are profitable. To avoid having to grant steep discounts, sell your book at list price or short discounts to people who use it themselves instead of reselling it. For example, you could sell your book to college career-development offices at list price because they would keep it for their own use.

■ *Is there an aspect of your content that could lead to a new product form?* Sometimes certain things are difficult to verbalize. In this case, it may be difficult to adequately portray in writing certain interview skills like body language, eye communication, and facial expression. This might lead to demonstrating those skills in a video or DVD.

■ *What information about your customers could lead to a new product form?* Once you determine who your target audience is, find out how they like to get their information. Research among college students may uncover the need for job-search information in a more easy-to-use format. Instead of one long book, a series of booklets could be created, each devoted to one traditional job-search tactic such as writing a resume or interviewing. With a little rewriting, the booklets could easily be adapted to meet the needs of other markets, such as state unemployment offices.

■ *How could your information lead to a by-product that could be the key to entering another business?* Some aspect of your book might transcend its original purpose and extend into different markets. For example, your information about interview skills for job-seekers is also relevant for anyone who is going to be a guest on a television or radio show. Therefore, you could refocus and repackage that part of your book and sell it to an entirely new market.

■ *Which technologies underlying your production processes have changed the most since you last published this content?* Technology is constantly advancing, so instead of blindly reprinting books, take a look at what else is out there and see if any new platforms would work with your information. You might reach more people through webinars or podcasts than you would through books, and your previously published videos might be more profitable in DVD format.

■ *Does your book need to be updated?* It is important to make sure your material is updated with each reprint. For example, the ways in which people look for employment have changed over the years. Newspaper advertising was historically the primary source of available job listings. The advent of the Internet changed the entire job-search process, though. Social networking has also made an impact. You want to make sure your book reflects these changes.

■ *In how many ways can you use the information in your book to extend your product line, exploit new opportunities, and enter new markets?* Seek new opportunities with a clear eye and an alert imagination. Be open to at least evaluating a different way of reaching the goals you have set for your business. Non-trade marketing is like electricity. It gives energy and power to the publisher, author, and title. It brings good books to life.

Asking and answering these questions for your own book will help you formulate ideas about how to take your title to new markets—possibly in different formats—to meet the needs of new groups of people. In short, these questions, along with the other information you gathered in this chapter, will help you find new ways to make real money selling your book without worrying about returns.

Chapter Two

Non-Trade Retail Markets

The non-trade retail market is made up of several different outlets that sell goods directly to consumers. These outlets include everything from airport stores, to home shopping networks, to museums, and more. All retail buyers purchase products for many of the same reasons—they want items that identify with their stores' images and meet the needs of their clientele. Books are typically only one part of the product selection that these outlets offer, and are usually not their primary focus. However, this does not mean that you will not have success in this market. In fact, the opposite is true—retail outlets can be incredibly profitable places to sell books.

Non-trade retail buyers purchase books under conditions comparable to those of trade buyers. Buyers in each retail market segment operate a little differently, but most rarely purchase directly from publishers, and instead, often go through a wholesaler or distributor. This means that when you sell to them you have to find the right distribution partner, and that the distribution discounts may be in the 60 to 70 percent range, which means you net 30 to 40 percent. Therefore, your cost structure must be able to support these fees. Furthermore, retail buyers typically buy on a returnable basis, and you will be paid in 90 to 120 days.

The good news is that if you have a quality book with content appropriate to a particular store's customers' needs, you can get into these outlets and profitably sell numerous books. But remember—just like with bookstores, these retail outlets only *display* books. It is up to you to make them move off the shelves with your promotional efforts, such as media performances, personal events, direct mailings, and publicity—processes which are described in *Chapter Six. Promoting to Non-Trade Buyers* (page 259).

This chapter is composed of sections that discuss in detail the retail outlets in which you could potentially sell your book. Each section tells you what types of books buyers in that particular market look for, what information and materials you should include in your submission packages, and how you should contact the buyers and store owners. Additionally, each section also provides you with selling strategies and information, as well as the names, addresses, telephone numbers, and websites of the relevant businesses in that particular market segment. When you finish reading this chapter, you will be armed with all of the information you need to successfully sell to non-trade retail markets.

7. DISCOUNT STORES AND WAREHOUSE CLUBS

A discount store is a type of department store that sells products at prices lower than those asked by other retail outlets. They commonly sell branded goods and prices vary widely between different products. Most discount stores and warehouse clubs offer a wide assortment of goods; however, others specialize in a certain type of merchandise, such as jewelry, electronic equipment, or electrical appliances.

DOLLAR STORES

Dollar stores are ultra-discount outlets. They are not conducive to selling frontlist titles, but they are great if you have a title you want to abandon. Before you contact a remainder company or give your unsold books away, contact Symak Sales Company. Symak is a wholesaler and distributor of dollar store items, discount merchandise, and general merchandise for discount stores, dollar stores, variety stores, grocery stores, and pharmacies throughout the United States and Canada. Symak has warehouses in Plattsburgh, New York and in Montreal, Canada.

❏ Symak Sales Co.; 4747 Cote Vertu, Saint-Laurent, QC, H4S 1C9
   Tel: 514-336-8780; Website: www.symaksales.com

BOOK SELECTION CRITERIA

Discount store and warehouse club buyers have several criteria for selecting the products they sell, as do most retailers. They want more frequent inventory turns, maximum profitability per square foot, and products that will attract more people to their stores. Books are discounted heavily in these stores and do not offer the margins that some larger-ticket products do; therefore, their limited shelf space is generally restricted to well-known authors and top-selling books. Since customers are already familiar with those authors and titles, they pick them up impulsively and no additional selling by store personnel is necessary.

SELLING TO THE DISCOUNT SEGMENT

Getting your book into discount stores and warehouse clubs like Sam's, Costco, Wal-Mart, Kmart, Target, and others is the jackpot of non-trade marketing. Many publishers imagine quick, national celebrity as tens of thousands of their books fly

THE DIFFERENCE BETWEEN WHOLESALERS AND DISTRIBUTORS

The classic definitions of book wholesalers and book distributors have become confused over the past thirty years or so, and thus, are now confusing. Traditionally speaking, wholesalers—sometimes called jobbers—are pipelines that get products into stores. Many wholesalers have buyers that select their products, including books, for them. It can sometimes be very difficult for small, independent publishers to get past these buyers; however, it is not impossible. Finally, wholesalers do not require exclusive selling rights from publishers. This means that you can sell to different marketplaces through many different wholesalers at the same time.

Distributors, on the other hand, normally require exclusivity, so you cannot use more than one distributor at once. Distributors inventory your books, do all of your invoicing, and handle all of your returns for you. Furthermore, they often employ sales people to sell your books. Today, even though many distributors still require exclusive agreements with publishers and wholesalers do not, the terms wholesaler and distributor are used interchangeably. In order to know which type of company you are dealing with, make sure you ask about their terms before signing a contract. For ease of reference throughout this book, know that the term "distribution partners" refers to both wholesalers and distributors.

off the shelves and tables of these outlets. This can be true; however, there are several reasons why sales to this segment may not be the best place to start your non-trade activities.

In order to sell tens of thousands of books in discount and warehouse outlets, you must first get them into the stores. This means you have to print tens of thousands of books, as well as arrange a channel of distribution. Since the books are returnable, some of these outlets may require you to maintain an escrow in the amount of potential returns. Others may require expensive product-liability insurance coverage. See the inset entitled "Liability Insurance vs. Errors and Omissions Insurance" (page 38) for more information about required insurance. Furthermore, if buyers agree to sell your book in their stores, then you are expected to keep enough books in stock and ready to ship during the promotion month(s). For example, a discount store or warehouse club buyer may order 10,000 copies of your book to be shipped immediately, and also expect you to be able to provide 10,000 more on demand. In this case, you would have to print 20,000 books and warehouse 10,000 of them. If your books end up not selling and are returned, you could be left with all 20,000 copies on your hands, which could place significant pressure on your finances and cash flow.

That is the bad news. The good news is that if you have a good book, an established platform, and consistent publicity exposure, you can sell a lot of books through these outlets. Moreover, there is a safeguard, so to speak, for publishers in this market—discount store and warehouse club buyers will not purchase your books in the first place if they do not think they can sell them.

By starting locally, you may be able to get some of the rewards of selling to this market without as much risk. Go to your nearby discount stores and warehouse clubs and contact the department managers. Describe how the content of your book is appropriate for their store's customers, and tell them about your plans to create local publicity to build store traffic. You should also demonstrate your ability and willingness to conduct in-store events to further attract attention and store traffic, which will lead to increased sales for you and their store.

LIABILITY INSURANCE VS. ERRORS AND OMISSIONS INSURANCE

Many large retail chains require the suppliers of the goods they sell in their stores to be covered by liability insurance. People often confuse this required liability insurance with errors and omissions insurance, usually referred to as E&O insurance, which is actually a completely different and more expensive policy. Therefore, it is important to distinguish between the two.

Liability insurance provides protection against third party lawsuits. In other words, if your product injures a consumer and they file a lawsuit, your liability insurance will cover the legal fees and potential damages up to a certain amount. These large retail outlets often require liability coverage because they carry a wide variety of products in their stores, and some of them can be potentially harmful. Most books are safe from a liability perspective and will never injure a consumer; however, books that have movable parts have hazardous potential, because there is a risk that a child may swallow a piece and get injured. Thus, even though books are almost always safe items, publishers are still sometimes required to carry this insurance. When selling to a retail outlet that requires it, the buyer will let you know.

The entity that needs the liability coverage is the entity that owns the book. If your book is owned by an insured company, chances are that liability is already included in the company's policy. If that is the case, when a retail store asks for proof of coverage, all you need to do is call the insurance provider and have them send the retailer a certificate of liability insurance, which they will do at no

SUBMITTING YOUR BOOK

Although buyers in this market will sometimes entertain submissions directly from publishers, they typically forward them on to their distribution partners so you might have better luck just going directly to the middlemen. As you will notice throughout this book, several distributors and wholesalers sell books to many different markets. The two top middlemen in this particular market are Anderson Merchandisers and Levy Home Entertainment.

■ *Anderson Merchandisers.* Anderson Merchandisers is a distributor of prerecorded music, movies, and books for retail stores in the United States. It is part of Anderson Media and has 4,000 employees throughout all fifty states and Puerto Rico.

❏ Anderson Merchandisers Book Purchasing Dept., 421 E. 34th St., Amarillo, TX 79103
  Tel: 806-376-6251, 800-999-0904; Website: www.amerch.com

additional cost to you. This certificate details your coverage plan and proves to the retailer that you are insured. If, however, you individually own a book, then you need to call an insurance company and set up a liability policy of your own. The typical coverage amount required of publishers by these retailers is somewhere around $2 million. You should check with your insurance provider to find out the details of your liability policy.

On the other hand, E&O insurance is something totally different. United States citizens are guaranteed various freedoms including freedom of speech and freedom of press under the First Amendment to the United States Constitution. This means that people can say or print practically anything—as long as it does not slander or libel another person. Both slander and libel involve making false or malicious statements that damage someone's reputation; the only difference is that slander is *spoken* and libel is *written.* E&O insurance helps fight slander, libel, and breach of contract in the event of a lawsuit. However, unlike liability insurance which should be no additional cost to you if your company has a preexisting general insurance policy, E&O insurance will cost you thousands of extra dollars each year.

Generally speaking, no retailers will require you to have E&O insurance, so save yourself some money and do not confuse their liability requirement for an E&O requirement. If your titles are exposé or memoir oriented, though, you should always make sure that all of your information is based on provable fact to avoid potential lawsuits. Because of the high price of E&O policies, you should carefully consider whether or not your company really needs this type of coverage before purchasing it.

■ *Levy Home Entertainment.* Levy Home Entertainment is a distributor of paperback and hardcover books to retailers in the United States. Levy buys from over 300 different publishers and provides books and services surrounding books to BJ's, Kmart, Meijer, Rite Aid, ShopKo, Stop and Shop, Target, Toys"R"Us, Wal-Mart, and others.

❑ Levy Home Entertainment Book Buyer, 4201 Raymond Dr., Hillside, IL 60162
   Tel: 708-547-4400; Website: www.levybooks.com

Before you send any materials to either of these distribution partners, call to find out the name of the proper buyer for your topic so you know to whom to address your submission. In most cases, you will receive a voicemail message that will give you this information, as well as the company's submission guidelines. Usually you will be asked to send a cover letter with a sample of your book, your terms, a sell sheet, and a one-page marketing plan. See the inset entitled "Create Professional Sales-Promotional Materials" (page 260), as well as the example materials beginning on page 325 to learn more about creating these items. Be sure your materials demonstrate why it is in the company's best interest to carry your title. If the message does not tell you the submission guidelines, you can always find them on the company website. It is important to stick to these guidelines and send everything they ask for.

You should always include a summary marketing plan with your materials even if the submission guidelines do not request one. Half of this plan should be about what promotions you intend to do, and the other half should be about what you have already done. Anyone can make grandiose statements about their intentions, but buyers are only interested in those that are realistic. For example, if you submit a plan with the statement that your sole promotional tactic is to get on the *Oprah Winfrey Show,* you will immediately label yourself as someone who is not realistic in your expectations. However, if you say the same thing but can prove that you have done something similar in the past and that you have connections with people who can help you obtain that goal, your plans will be more believable and get you better results. Your previous actions give your statements credibility and demonstrate that you are experienced, dependable, and realistic.

Finally, for scanning and accounting purposes, many of these stores require all merchandise to have a UPC label. You must first become a member of the Uniform Code Council (UCC) before you can obtain a UCC company prefix, which is part of the UPC label. When contacting these stores, you should enclose a copy of your UCC membership letter reporting your firm's actual UPC number, along with a sample of your book.

❑ Uniform Code Council; GS1 US, Princeton Pike Corporate Center, 1009 Lenox
   Dr., Ste. 202, Lawrenceville, NJ 08648
   Tel: 609-620-0200; Website: www.uc-council.org

MINORITY OR WOMEN-OWNED BUSINESSES

Many discount stores and warehouse clubs offer programs through outside councils that help develop the potential of minority- and women-owned businesses that provide retail goods or services. Through these programs, assistance in locating resources, as well as guidance and consultation are available to help participants develop their individual businesses. If your business is minority- or women-owned and you are interested in participating in one of these programs, you must first become certified by one of the participating councils listed below:

❑ National Minority Suppliers Development Council; 15 W. 39th St., NY, NY 10018
Tel: 212-944-2430; Website: www.nmsdc.org

❑ Women's Business Enterprise National Council; 1710 H St., N.W., 7th Fl.,
Washington, DC 20006
Tel: 202-872-5515; Website: www.wbenc.org

MAJOR DISCOUNT STORE AND WAREHOUSE CLUB CHAINS

There are several national and regional discount stores and warehouse clubs. Since each one works a little differently, be sure to do your research on their submission guidelines before contacting buyers in order to achieve the most successful results possible. The largest national discount stores and warehouse clubs include the following:

■ *Best Buy Co., Inc.* Since its inception in 1966, Best Buy has become a specialty retailer of consumer electronics, personal computers, entertainment software, and appliances. Best Buy has over 500 stores in the United States, and primarily buys books from Levy Home Entertainment (See previous page). Fiction and non-fiction bestsellers make up 60 to 70 percent of their book sales, and the remaining book sales are comprised of juvenile, craft, and reference titles. The products sold through Best Buy stores attract more of a male than female audience, and the company also has an affiliate program available.

❑ Best Buy; P.O. Box 9312, Minneapolis, MN 55440
Tel: 612-291-1000; Website: www.bestbuy.com

To be considered for future business with Best Buy, you must submit preliminary information about your product(s) and company. Their buyers are looking for product vendors who are willing to partner with them, and you are expected to sign a Vendor Master Agreement as a prerequisite for a business relationship.

○ Complete the form at www.extendingthereach.com/bestbuyusa.html, and email it to NewVendorInquiry@BestBuy.com to begin your business relationship with Best Buy.

■ *BJ's Wholesale Club.* BJ's introduced the warehouse club concept to New England in 1984, and has since expanded throughout the eastern United States with operations in sixteen states from Maine to Florida. BJ's is dedicated to providing its members with high-quality, brand-name merchandise at prices that are significantly lower than the prices found at supermarkets, department stores, drug stores, and specialty retail stores.

❑ BJ's Wholesale Club; Book Buyer, P.O. Box 9601, Natick, MA 01760
   Phone: 800-257-2582; Website: www.bjs.com

■ *Cost-U-Less.* Cost-U-Less opened its first retail warehouse store in 1989 on the Hawaiian island of Maui. Today, Cost-U-Less operates mid-sized warehouse clubs in the United States Territories, the Hawaiian Islands, and foreign island countries in the Pacific and the Caribbean. They predominately offer United States branded goods.

❑ Cost-U-Less; 8160 304th Ave., S.E., Bldg. 3, Ste. A, Preston, WA 98050
   Tel: 425-222-5022; Website: www.costuless.com

■ *Costco Wholesale Corporation.* Costco operates an international chain of membership warehouses that carry brand name merchandise at low prices for small- and medium-sized businesses. Costco clubs sell a wide range of products including groceries, appliances, automotive supplies, toys, sporting goods, jewelry, office supplies, and books. The books are carried in Costco's stores and on its website, and the major genres are best sellers, non-fiction, juvenile, mystery and crime, health and fitness, reference, self improvement, relationships, and cookbooks. Costco has 533 warehouses in 40 states and Puerto Rico, and it has over 50 million cardholders. Costco uses two sets of buyers—one for its stores in the United States and one for its stores in Canada.

❑ Costco; P.O. Box 34331, Seattle, WA 98124
   Tel: 613-221-2000, 800-607-6861; Website: www.costco.com

❑ Costco Canada; 415 W. Hunt Club Rd., Ottawa, ON, K2E 1C5, Canada
   Tel: 800-463-3783; Website: www.costco.ca

■ *Kmart.* Kmart is a mass merchandising company and a wholly owned subsidiary of Sears Holdings Corporation. It operates more than 1,400 stores across 49 states, Guam, Puerto Rico, and the Virgin Islands that carry a wide assortment of general merchandise, including books. Kmart Super Centers are combination full-service grocery and general merchandise stores. Most of these Centers operate twenty-four hours a day and carry between 100,000 and 150,000 stock-keeping units (SKUs).

❑ Kmart; Sears Holdings Corp., 3333 Beverly Rd., Hoffman Estates, IL 60179
   Tel: 847-286-2500; Websites: www.kmart.com, www.searsholdings.com

■ *PriceSmart.* PriceSmart owns and operates United States-style membership shopping warehouse clubs selling basic consumer goods to both individuals and businesses in Latin America and the Caribbean. With the addition of locations in Mexico and Jamaica, PriceSmart operates twenty-five warehouse clubs in eleven countries and one United States territory.

❏ PriceSmart; 4649 Morena Blvd., San Diego, CA 92117
   Tel: 858-581-4530; Website: www.pricesmart.com/Corporate/Buying-Team.aspx

■ *Sam's Club.* Sam's Club is the nation's largest members-only warehouse club. It has 46 million members—both individuals and businesspeople. Its goal is to provide its members with quality products, including books, at low prices. You should submit your book to Sam's Club using the same steps as described for Wal-Mart on page 44. However, before you do it is important to note that Sam's Club requires its vendors to carry commercial liability insurance with a minimum limit of $2 million. Refer back to the liability inset on page 38 for more information.

Sam's Club has two programs that can help authors sell more books. The first is its Road Shows program, which offers special discounts on various products—including books—in Sam's Club locations around the country. The second is in-store author events, which are encouraged. If Sam's Club buyers select your book, be sure to inquire about these opportunities.

❏ Sam's Club; 608 S.W. 8th St., Benonville, AR 72716
   Tel: 888-746-7726; Website: www.samsclub.com

■ *Target Corporation.* Target's first store opened in Roseville, Minnesota, in 1962. Today, Target operates approximately 1,500 stores in 47 states, including more than 175 Super Target stores that present an upscale grocery shopping experience. Target projects a middle class image, so its customers' demographics are skewed more upscale than Wal-Mart's, and lean toward women with families. Category buyers at Target are more "book friendly" than most discounters due to a corporate commitment to reading and learning. The literacy program Reading Is Fundamental (RIF) partnered with Target to encourage children to stay engaged in reading activities throughout the summer. Children who complete the challenge receive a ten dollar Target gift card and a summer reading bookmark.

❏ Target Corporation; 777 Nicollet Mall, Minneapolis, MN 55402
   Tel: 612-304-6073; Website: www.targetcorp.com

Target believes in careful vendor selection and education, and conducts vendor education classes for both United States and non-United States vendors. These classes are offered in Minneapolis and regionally throughout the world to teach vendors Target's standards of engagement and requirements.

○ For more information, go to www.partnersonline.com/web-app/pol/home/entryHome.jsp

SUBMITTING AN ONLINE PROPOSAL TO WAL-MART

Follow these steps in order to electronically submit your proposal to Wal-Mart:

1. Go to www.walmartstores.com.

2. Click on the "Suppliers" tab.

3. Choose "Proposal Packet."

4. Choose "Online Product Submission."

5. Complete and submit the application.

6. Your application will then be reviewed and if it is accepted, you will receive an email that gives instructions on filling out the long-form questionnaire. If it is rejected, you will receive an email explaining the reason for the decision.

7. If your long-form questionnaire is successful, you will receive an email from Retail Link, giving you a user ID and password.

8. Before any purchase is made, you will receive an email requesting that you complete the vendor agreement. The assigned user ID and password gives you access to a retail link where you can access the vendor agreement.

While the application process is relatively easy to complete, the approval process may take weeks, if not months. For this reason, you should submit your application well before you want to see your book on the shelf. Furthermore, do not get your hopes up too high—acceptance is limited to only the top titles in each category.

■ *Toys"R"Us, Inc.* Toys"R"Us is a toy and baby-products retailer with more than 1,550 toy and baby specialty stores worldwide. The company currently sells merchandise online, and through nearly 600 Toys"R"Us stores and more than 250 Babies"R"Us stores in the United States. It also operates more than 700 international stores in 34 countries. Toys"R"Us buyers purchase books both directly from publishers and from Levy Home Entertainment (See page 40). Stores average up to thirty-two linear feet of shelf space for books, which is about three times more than most mass merchandisers. Toy"R"Us stores fill these shelves with 300 to 400 titles for kids of all age groups. The top 100 titles account for almost 85 percent of their book sales. Their sell-through rate is higher than other discount retailers at 75 to 85 percent, so returns are generally lower than their competitors. In order to sell well in Toys"R"Us stores, your book should be a softcover or board book, and be priced at less than nine dollars.

❑ Toys"R"Us, Inc. Headquarters; One Geoffrey Way, Wayne, NJ 07470
   Tel: 973-617-3500; Website: www.toysrusinc.com

■ *Wal-Mart Stores, Inc.* The birth of discount retailing is believed to be 1962—the first year of operation for Kmart, Target, and Wal-Mart. Today, Wal-Mart Stores, Inc. is the largest retailer in the United States with nearly 6,500 stores, Super Centers, and Sam's Clubs across thirteen countries. Sales at these stores are discounted heavily, addressing a target audience with low income demographics. Books are not a high priority and are typically grouped with paper products. Topics that do well in Wal-Mart stores are romance, mystery, juvenile, and cooking. Bibles also sell well in most Wal-Mart locations. The hot buttons with Wal-Mart's buyers are price and inventory turns. Wal-Mart purchases books through Levy Home Entertainment and Anderson Merchandisers (See pages 39 and 40). Publishers are encouraged to contact local stores with regional titles.

❑ Wal-Mart Stores, Inc; Book Buyer, 702 S.W. 8th St., Bentonville, AR 72716
   Tel: 501-273-4000; Website: www.walmarstores.com

If you have the right book, discount stores and warehouse clubs can help you sell thousands of copies. The more you learn about these outlets and the processes they use to select books, the greater the advantage you will have over other publishers who are also trying to get their books on these stores' shelves.

8. AIRPORT STORES

All major airports have at least one bookstore, which is constantly surrounded by a captive audience of interested—and sometimes weary—travelers looking for something to do to help pass time. What better way to while away the hours than by reading a good book—especially yours?

SELLING TO AIRPORT STORES

There are advantages and disadvantages to selling your book in this market segment. It is important to educate yourself about both so you can be better prepared to reap the benefits of the advantages, and do your best to avoid the disadvantages.

Advantages

The concept of having a "trapped" market may be helpful to your sales. Unless travelers' flights are inordinately delayed, they have minimal time to search for a book, purchase it, and get to their gate. Therefore, books can be an impulse item purchased without due consideration given to price. This fact leads to less discounting, particularly when combined with the fact that people who can afford to fly typically have more discretionary funds. Also, business travelers can often expense book purchases if the book is business-related, so they will not overly concern themselves with the price. The fact that your book is not discounted may not directly benefit you; however, it may be a benefit to airport store buyers if your book is relatively high-priced, because it may inspire them to choose it over others. Another advantage of selling your book through airport stores is that your book receives significant visibility since so many people go in and out of these stores every day. This exposure may serendipitously lead to foreign sales through exposure to international travelers.

Disadvantages

Perhaps the biggest disadvantage of selling books in airport stores is the "pay to play" philosophy, where publishers pay the stores for preferred positions; thus, unless you are willing to pay, your book may end up hidden in the back of the store. Another disadvantage is that bookstores in small airports have significant space constraints, and therefore limit the titles they stock to only the top fiction and non-fiction titles, as well as the popular classics. Moreover, the books are returnable and distribution partner discounts apply, so you automatically lose their 55 percent fee.

One other potential disadvantage of selling books in airport stores is that most stores are after security checkpoints. This means that when people purchase a book they have to carry it with them on the plane, so heavy or large books are usually not big sellers. Similarly, if you are conducting an in-store event, only those people in your concourse are able to attend.

BOOK SELECTION CRITERIA

Airport stores are different from most other retail outlets because their customers have to get on a plane and travel after they purchase a book, rather than simply get in their cars and go home. Therefore, there are certain criteria that either help or hinder book sales in this market.

Books That Sell Well

A variety of different books tend to sell well in airport stores. For example, titles for children, especially children's activity books, usually produce good sales. Harder-thinking titles also sell well among business travelers who spend a good amount of time in airports. Titles on management, investment, economics, business biography, personal finance, and health work well in airport stores, as well. Additionally, popular fiction always sells in this environment, particularly among female travelers and young people who purchase "chic lit." Somewhat surprisingly, history and science books are among the perennial best-selling titles in airport stores.

A title does not have to be a bestseller to find its way into these stores, even in large airports. These shops will also carry books by local and regional authors, as well as books pertaining to their specific locations. For example, books on major sports teams do well in their hometowns, and books about destination points generally sell well depending on the geographic region. In other words, books about Hawaii will sell better in an airport in California than they will in an airport in New York. Similarly, airport stores in the Northwest will sell more books about China and Japan than they will about France.

Experience has proven, however, that most people would rather not carry travel books with them on planes, so they often wait until they reach their destination airport and then purchase them there. For this reason, travel guides sell well at hubs and major airports in New York, Chicago, Dallas, San Francisco, and Los Angeles. Finally, buyers for airport stores consider the local population base when deciding which books to purchase. For example, Spanish titles do best in stores in Dallas and Miami.

Books That Do Not Sell Well

As a general rule, hardcover books do not sell as well as softcover books in airport stores, because people look for items that are easily portable. For this same reason, coffee table books, large books on photography, and souvenir-type books also do not sell well; therefore, they are infrequently carried in these stores. Self-help and genre fiction are generally not big sellers, either. Furthermore, gift-focused books do not sell well, because as previously stated, most stores are post-security and people do not want to have to deal with carrying them; most people ship gifts before they travel, or have already packed them in their luggage.

Some airport stores will carry a limited supply of audio books, but they are not carried in a big way because they have a tendency to "disappear." There is not a lot of security in airport stores, and people tend to walk off with audio books without paying for them. Similarly, DVDs and music items may not be carried because of lease restrictions—if there is another store nearby that sells those items, the bookstore is often not permitted to carry them.

PRICES, PAYMENT, AND SALES

All books sold in airport stores must have three things printed on their back covers: the price, an International Standard Book Number (ISBN) and bar code, and a European Article Number (EAN) and bar code. However, some exceptions to this rule are made for non-book items.

○ You can purchase ISBNs at www.bowker.com

○ For a list of EAN suppliers, go to
   www.isbn.org/standards/home/isbn/us/barcode.asp

Books in airport stores have a wide price range and are usually priced anywhere from seven dollars for mass market books, up to fifty dollars for others.

Those in the seventeen to twenty dollar range seem to sell best. People in airport stores usually expect to pay more for books than they usually would, so discounts off list prices are limited. However, this philosophy can backfire if people browse through these stores looking for books to buy later at discounted prices.

You can generally expect buyers to pay 50 percent of the amount due to you within ninety days. The remaining 50 percent is withheld as a reserve against returns, but will usually be paid to you within 180 days. Once your book takes off, you can usually negotiate different terms.

The length of time a book stays in airport stores depends on how well it sells. According to a book buyer at Hudson Booksellers, a company that operates bookstores in airports throughout North America, "It [a book] stays on the shelf until it stops selling. Some titles have sold for twelve months or more. But if no, or low sales occur in one month, it is returned." Furthermore, sales for different titles vary at different times of the year, so that is also something you should keep in mind. Summertime is the peak travel period, so as you might expect, it is also the peak bookselling period. Therefore, if your book is about where to take summer vacations, how to travel safely with kids, or any other related topic, then you should contact buyers in January when they are making their summer buying decisions. Sales also increase during the end of the year holiday season, so if your book is about dieting, taxes, how to pack gifts for travel, or something along those lines, then contact the buyers while they are making the winter buying decisions in June.

SUBMITTING YOUR BOOK

You can increase the chances of your book being accepted by airport bookstores by using a distribution partner. Most distributors and wholesalers can sell your books to airport stores. When you submit your materials to these buyers, send them a complete package. Include a copy of your book, your terms, a summary marketing plan, and when available, a sales history. See the inset on page 260 for tips on how to create these items. Also include reviews, awards, testimonials, and newspaper articles if any exist. *Chapter Six. Promoting to Non-Trade Buyers* (page 259) discusses how you can acquire these. Be sure to list the number of books per carton and how many units were published. Also include information about who, if anyone, is providing sales and marketing services on your behalf. Furthermore, since most books are displayed cover out, the front cover design is critical to the title's success.

An article by the author or about the book that has appeared in an airline's magazine would also seem to be an important factor to include with your submission. However, if that particular airline does not serve the airport in which the store you are trying to sell to is located, the article may not carry much influence with the buyer. For example, one author paid for an advertisement on "in air" television on Jet Blue Airlines, and it only had an impact on the sales of stores at airports served by Jet Blue.

Your submission package should demonstrate what the author has done, is doing, and will do to support store sales. However, keep in mind that airport stores do not want *too much* traffic. Fifty to sixty people in one of these stores at one time form a "mob." Browsers may feel uncomfortable and leave without buying anything. At the same time, security may be compromised and customers may be tempted to walk off with an item without paying. Therefore, do not promise a *major* crowd as a result of your in-store events or promotions. Suggested wholesalers and distributors to airport stores include:

❑ Alliance Entertainment, LLC; 4250 Coral Ridge Dr., Coral Springs, FL 33065
  Tel: 800-329-7664; Website: www.aent.com

❑ Atlas Books; 30 Amberwood Pkwy., Ashland, OH 44805
  Tel: 419-281-1802, 800-266-5564; Website: www.atlasbooksdistribution.com

❑ Baker & Taylor; 1120 Rte. 22 E., Bridgewater, NJ 08807
  Tel: 800-775-1800; Website: www.btol.com

❑ Big River Distribution; 8214 Exchange Way, St. Louis, MO 63144
  Tel: 314-918-9800; Website: www.bigriverdist.com

❑ Bookazine; 75 Hook Rd., Bayonne, NJ 07002
  Tel: 201-339-7777, 800-221-8112; Website: www.bookazine.com

❑ Greenleaf Book Group; P.O. Box 91869, Austin, TX 78709
  Tel: 800-932-5420; Website: www.greenleafbookgroup.com

❑ Ingram Book Co.; 1 Ingram Blvd., LaVergne, TN 37086
  Tel: 800-937-8000; Website: www.ingrambook.com

❑ News Group; (See website for regional addresses)
  Tel: 866-466-7231; Website: www2.thenewsgroup.com/US

❑ Partners Publishers Group; 2325 Jarco Dr., Holt, MI 48842
  Tel: 517-694-3205; Website: www.partnerspublishersgroup.com

❑ Southern Book Service; 5154 N.W. 165th St., Miami Lakes, FL 33014
  Tel: 305-624-4545; Website: www.southernbook.com

❑ Sunbelt Publishing; 1256 Fayette St., El Cajon, CA 92020
  Tel: 619-258-4911, 800-626-6579; Website: www.sunbeltpub.com

❑ The Distributors; 702 S. Michigan, South Bend, IN 46601
  Tel: 574-232-8500; Website: www.thedistributors.com

Overall, no matter which distribution partner you choose to work with, your submission package should demonstrate that your book has the potential to sell well in airport stores because it meets some or all of the criteria described previously. Prove that you have studied the market and are submitting your book because it will help the store chain in some way. Show that your promotion will help increase sales, and therefore, inventory turns. And state that your in-store signings will attract people who would not otherwise shop there, thereby helping to build store traffic. All of these factors will improve the chain's profitability, which is why they should choose your book over those submitted by competitors.

MAJOR AIRPORT BOOKSTORE CHAINS

There are several major airport bookstore chains. However, a good way to break into this market is to find and sell to local bookstores at your nearby airport first. Many major airports have local bookstores that will pick up regional titles. For example, The New England Travelmart at Bradley airport in Connecticut showcases the cookbook, *The Best of the Best of New England* in front of thousands of travelers every day.

The following list contains the major airport bookstore chains. It is important to note that most airports also contain national chains such as CNN Newsstand, CNBC News, and Fox News. You should contact your distribution partner if you are interested in sales to those stores.

■ *Borders Airport Stores.* Borders uses the same buyers to purchase books for its airport stores as it does for all of its other stores. The buyers will review your material to determine if there is a market for your title. If they decide that it has potential, you will be asked to complete a vendor questionnaire.

❏ Borders Airport Stores; New Vendor Acquisitions, Borders Group, Inc., 100 Phoenix Dr., Ann Arbor, MI 48108
Tel: 800-770-7811; Website: www.bordersstores.com

If you would like your book considered for sales through Borders airport stores, send two copies of your completed book along with the product submission form. Borders will only consider submissions that include this form.

○ You can find the product submission form at
http://media.bordersstores.com/pdf/product_submission_sheet.pdf

■ *Discovery Channel Airport Stores.* Discovery Channel airport stores currently operate in more than 160 countries and territories. They feature innovative products for kids, leading edge technology and gadgets, health and wellness products, and content that resonates strongly with frequent travelers. The assortment is anchored by children's products sold under the Discovery Kids, Ready Set Learn!, and Discovery Grow Toys brands. Adult-oriented merchandise is offered as well, including consumer electronics, health and wellness products, and cycling gear.

❏ Discovery Channel Airport Stores; P.O. Box 869011, Plano, TX 75086
Tel: 800-627-9399; Website: www.discoverychannelstore.com

■ *HMSHost.* HMSHost, formerly known as Host Marriott Services, operates 2,500 facilities at 105 airports worldwide and 106 travel plazas in the United States and Canada. HMSHost has revenues of more than $2 billion and is a wholly owned subsidiary of Autogrill S.p.A.

❏ HMSHost; Book Buyer, 6600 Rockledge Dr., Bethesda, MD 20817
Tel: 866-467-4671; Website: www.hmshost.com

■ *Hudson Booksellers.* Hudson Booksellers operates sixty-six full-service bookstores in airports throughout North America. The stores feature an extensive selection of magazines, newspapers, and books. Hudson's bookstores often stand-alone, or are situated as part of a Hudson News and Euro Café. Hudson boasts thousands of titles tailored to each location, celebrity book signings, expert staff recommendations, sponsorship of community literacy programs, and tote bags, bookmarks, and other purchase incentives.

❏ Hudson Booksellers; Sr. Book Buyer, 1521 Johnson Ferry Rd., Ste. 250,
Marietta, GA 30062
Tel: 201-939-5050, 800-326-7711; Website: www.hudsongroupusa.com

In addition to a broad representation of bestsellers and new releases, Hudson Booksellers also carries hardcover, paperback, trade, and children's books. Their genres include strong fiction titles, as well as books in top nonfiction categories such as travel, business, reference, and biography.

○ For a list of Hudson Bookseller's category buyers and contacts, go to
www.hudsongroupusa.com/Contact.html.

■ *Paradies Shops.* Paradies Shops operates over 450 stores in over 70 airports and hotels across the United States and Canada. These stores serve over a half-billion customers each year, and they include original brands unique to each airport, as well as national brands.

❏ Paradies Shops; 5950 Fulton Industrial Blvd., Atlanta, GA 30336
Tel: 404-344-7905; Website: www.theparadiesshops.com

Airport bookstores reach an identifiable target market. If you have content of interest to their customers, then your book has a shot at being accepted. However, as is true for all retail stores, remember that it is your promotion that moves the books off the shelves instead of being returned to you. Produce a quality book, follow each store's submission guidelines, and promote, promote, promote. Then watch your sales take off.

9. SUPERMARKETS AND DRUG STORES

There are tens of thousands of supermarkets and drug stores of all sizes around the country. Many of these stores sell books, booklets, and videos. Some of the larger supermarket chain stores even have an actual bookstore in them, rather than just a book section. In the past, most book sales through these outlets were mass market paperbacks, but today's superstores carry a wide variety of books, cards, and magazines.

BOOK SELECTION CRITERIA

Certain types of books sell better than others in supermarkets and drug stores. Since these outlets cater to a specific customer base made up primarily of women, books directed toward them tend to sell best. However, it is possible to sell content that is relevant to all family members—especially children—if you properly support it with promotion.

Furthermore, "This is one area in which fiction outsells non-fiction," said John Styron, a sales manager for one of the distribution partners that services this market. Other titles that sell well in supermarkets and drug stores are those written by local and regional authors, as well as those about local and regional topics. And softcover books almost always outsell hardcover titles—particularly in supermarkets.

SELLING TO SUPERMARKETS AND DRUG STORES

Randy Yarbrough, a distribution partner buyer, believes that independent publishers have a good shot at sales in this market segment. "We sell their titles all the time," he said. On the other hand, Steve Linville, a sales manager at the News Group, another distribution partner that services this market, holds an opposing view; he said, "There is not a lot of shelf space dedicated to the category. It can be frustrating for a small publisher to break into the market given the returns, discounts, and dating required."

Randy and Steve do, however, agree that supermarkets discount the list price up to 25 percent, so your pricing must allow for that to occur profitably. The list price on most books sold in drug stores is less than twenty dollars, and the list price on most books sold in supermarkets is less than ten dollars. However, the price can go up to twenty dollars or more for hardcover books sold in supermarkets. Randy and Steve also agree that fiction books, children's titles, cookbooks, travel books, and regional titles do well in supermarkets, while health-related topics sell best in drugstores—particularly in the form of booklets.

Authors often conduct book signings at the supermarkets and drug stores in which their books are being sold. "One of our authors recently sold 500 copies of her book during a book signing at a Ralph's supermarket in California," said

Randy. Setting up these types of events is easy to arrange; all you need to do is call your local stores and ask. You can find a good example of this in the inset entitled, "Personal Story: 'Hand Selling'" on page 54.

Finally, the following three associations can help you learn more about this market. Their websites provide a wealth of information, and it is a good idea to read as much of it as you can in order to familiarize yourself with the industry. If possible, it is also a good idea to attend their local chapter meetings to network and perhaps meet the buyers you eventually intend to approach.

❑ National Association of Chain Drug Stores; 413 N. Lee St., P.O. Box 1417-D49, Alexandria, VA 22313
Tel: 703-549-3001; Website: www.nacds.org

❑ National Grocers Association; 1005 N. Glebe Rd., Ste. 250, Arlington, VA 22201
Tel: 703-516-0700; Website: www.nationalgrocers.org

❑ National Supermarkets Association; 30-50 Whitestone Expy, Ste. 301, Flushing, NY 11354
Tel: 718-747-2860; Website: www.nsany.org

SUBMITTING YOUR BOOK

Below, you will find the contact information for the major distribution partners involved in the supermarket and drug store markets. When you submit your book to these middlemen, include a high-quality, one-page piece of sales literature that describes how and why your book will sell well through these retailers. Your submission package should also contain a summary of your marketing plan listing your proposed promotional activity, as well as the top ten reasons why people who shop at these stores will buy your book. Furthermore, be sure to include the price, author, case quantities, and a photo of any floor displays you could provide. See the inset on page 260 to learn how to create professional sales-promotional materials, and the appendices beginning on page 325 for examples.

❑ Hudson News Co.; Sr. Book Buyer, 1521 Johnson Ferry Rd., Ste. 250, Marietta, GA 30062
Tel: 201-939-5050, 800-326-7711; Website: www.hudsongroupusa.com

❑ The News Group; (See Website for Regional Addresses)
Tel: 866-466-7231; Website: www2.thenewsgroup.com/US

It is interesting to note that these distribution partners do not always wait for publishers to contact them. If their sales people notice your title in a local news story, in a publication like *Publishers Weekly,* or at a trade show, they may contact you about it first.

Personal Story: "Hand Selling"

Hill Kemp, the publisher at Guardian Angel Publishing, discovered a creative way to sell both fiction and nonfiction books in supermarkets, which he calls "hand selling." Hill's saga began when his proposal to sell his books in supermarkets through traditional distribution channels was turned down by a national buyer.

What he did next was extraordinary. He stood outside these stores over a period of time and simply observed. He watched customers as they entered and left the stores—the number, rate, and type of people—then created a demographic profile of the typical customer and a forecast the number of books that might be sold.

Armed with that information, Hill contacted the regional buyer and negotiated a program where his authors would conduct book signings at the supermarket and donate one dollar of every sale to a local library in the supermarket's name. Nineteen authors participated in this program. The result was net sales of $35,000 in one year. The program worked so well that the store manager offered to have Hill's authors conduct these events on a regular basis. Hill agreed, and instead of going through a distribution channel where he would have lost 65 to 70 percent, he negotiated a program directly with the store in which he would only have to give them 35 percent—making each sale 30 to 35 percent more profitable for Hill than it would have been otherwise, with no returns.

Do not be mistaken, though; Hill works hard to earn this money. The participating authors bring their own displays, samples, and books to sell. They also set up their own tables—usually just inside the front door so they can greet customers as they walk by. Hill said, "We had a river of people flowing right by us. There's something magical about putting a book with a reader."

While conducting these events, Hill recognized the need for a ten-second sales pitch, or "stopper," that was easily adaptable for the various customers that entered the stores. He got people to stop at his author's tables by saying things like, "Hello ma'am. May I tell you about my novel? It's a good one." He worked out several ingenious variations of this approach, and carefully chose which one to use based on the demeanor of the prospective customer. Hill also trained his authors to strategically meet and greet people as they entered. For example, he taught them to approach customers who made eye contact. "Of course they had to be rejection tolerant," Hill said of his authors, "because most people walked right by." But still, the tactics were once sufficient to outsell a display of John Grisham novels less than fifteen feet away.

The point of Hill's story is that you do not have to be a large publisher in order to sell books in this market. However, in order to be successful you do have to follow some common sense rules: Be polite to people and get their attention in a positive, fun way before you try to sell them something.

PERSONAL STORY: SMALL TOWN SALES

Do not think your sales are restricted if you do not live in, or near a large city. Nolan Lewis is an author that lives in a very small town that has a population of less than 1,000. Thus, his chances of making large sales to his local supermarket are limited, but nevertheless he has sold books there. According to Nolan, "My local grocer has sold over a hundred copies of one of my books."

The point of Nolan's story is that no matter where you live, it is possible to sell books through your local supermarkets and drug stores. Begin by contacting stores in your area, and then expand little by little. Get experience, testimonials, and some revenue coming in before you embark on a national campaign.

PERSONAL STORY: VENDOR SALES

Peggy Butler, also known as Peg Gregory, author of *Starfish,* has a motivating story about selling to drug stores. As she put it:

> I became a Walgreens vendor a few years ago, and that enables me to sell books on an ongoing basis to any Walgreens in the country. As I travel, I stop at Walgreens stores to pitch my book. The individual store managers do not have to pay for them at the time, because I invoice the corporate office at a 50 percent discount. Therefore, they are more likely to purchase a few books. I know I need only walk into any Walgreens to make a sale. Payment is delayed a couple months, but I know it will come. For a writer who does not have a distributor and has the time to travel, this is an ideal way to get your books into a store frequented by a large segment of the population. After your initial contact with the Walgreens' store managers, they might allow you to mail future shipments with the invoice enclosed, but you have to make that initial face-to-face contact. Therefore, I do not recommend mailing a copy of your book to the store managers.

The point of Peggy's story is that you can succeed in this market even if a distribution partner or a buyer at a national chain turns you down. Direct sales techniques work. Start locally, expand regionally, and then go back to the distribution partners and buyers armed with proof that your book can sell in their environment. This time around, chances are your outcome will be different.

MAJOR SUPERMARKET AND DRUG STORE CHAINS

The competition in this market is stiff due to the limited shelf-space granted to books. Buyers for these stores look for products that will give them the most profit per square foot. Therefore, if you can demonstrate that your promotional activities will help bring new customers into their stores, you will get their attention. You can submit your book and marketing package directly to the major chains, but they will usually direct you to their distribution partners. Some of the major supermarket and drug store chains include the following:

■ *Albertson's, Inc.* Albertson's is a large supermarket chain. In order to sell to Albertson's, you need to go through its parent company, which is Supervalu, Inc. Supervalu also supports other chains such as Jewel-Osco drug stores and Supervalu Pharmacies.

❑ Supervalu; 11840 Valley View Rd., Eden Prairie, MN 55344
   Tel: 952-828-4000; Website: www.supervalu.com

■ *CVS Corporation.* CVS sells prescription drugs, health and beauty products, greeting cards, books, photo processing, cosmetics, convenience foods, private label and seasonal items, and also has an online pharmacy.

❑ CVS Corporation; 1 CVS Dr., Woonsocket, RI 02895
   Tel: 401-765-1500, 800-666-0500; Website: www.cvs.com

■ *Giant Food Stores.* Giant Food Stores is a food, health and nutrition, general merchandise, and ready-made consumables retailer.

❑ Giant Food Stores; 300 E. Baltimore Ave., Lansdowne, PA 19050
   Tel: 717-240-1566; Website: www.giantpa.com

■ *Great Atlantic and Pacific Tea Company, Inc.* Great Atlantic and Pacific Tea Company operates 447 stores in the United States under 6 retail banners. These include conventional supermarkets, food and drug combination stores, discount food stores, and several in-store health clinics.

❑ Great Atlantic and Pacific Tea Company; 2 Paragon Dr., Montvale, NJ 07645
   Tel: 201-573-9700, 800-927-7368; Website: www.aptea.com

■ *Kroger Co.* Kroger operates under nearly two dozen banners and is one of the nation's largest grocery retailers. In addition to having school programs through which you could potentially sell your book, it also has affinity programs with Budget car rentals, FTD Florists, and other businesses to offer their customers added benefits. Perhaps you could convince them to conduct an affinity program with you.

   To submit a new product to Kroger, prepare a brief, one-page letter of introduction that gives background information about your company. Include brochures and/or color photographs of your cover, as well as two business cards.

Do not send samples of your book, but do send a description of it including size, colors, cost estimates, and marketing plans. Tell them if your product is on the shelves of other retailers, and if so, what the sales results have been. Finally, describe your production capabilities, shipping point, and what quantities you can provide.

❑ Kroger Co.; Book Buyer, 1014 Vine St., Cincinnati, OH 45202
    Tel: 866-221-4141; Website: www.kroger.com

■ *Marsh Supermarkets, Inc.* Marsh Supermarkets is a grocery and convenience store chain. They are also into food services and provide upscale catering, vending, concession, and business cafeteria management services.

❑ Marsh Supermarkets, Inc.; 9800 Crosspoint Blvd., Indianapolis, IN 46256
    Tel: 317-594-2100, 800-382-8798; Website: www.marsh.net

■ *Meijer, Inc.* Meijer stores offer full grocery departments, as well as over forty other departments including fashion, automotive, home decor, health and beauty care, pharmacy, electronics, and pets.

❑ Meijer, Inc.; 2929 Walker Ave. N.W., Grand Rapids, MI 49544
    Tel: 616-453-6711, 800-543-3704; Website: www.meijer.com

Meijer offers corporate business-to-business programs, such as their Mass Marketing Program which lets you deliver targeted advertising at point-of-purchase (POP) using a wide array of media tools, including context-specific promotions and messaging. Thus, if you have a title with content related to any of their departments, you may be able to partner with them to provide POP material. Meijer is also open to talking with people about using books as premiums.

○ Call 800-487-9460 to learn more

■ *Pathmark Stores, Inc.* Pathmark operates 140 supermarkets in New York, New Jersey, and Philadelphia. The stores are located in both urban and suburban marketplaces. Pathmark is committed to opening stores within the inner-cities of its trading area.

❑ Pathmark Stores, Inc.; 200 Milik St., Carteret, NJ 07008
    Tel: 732-499-3000; Website: www.pathmark.com

■ *Rite Aid Corporation.* Rite Aid is a drug store chain that operates more than 5,000 stores in 31 states and the District of Columbia.

❑ Rite Aid Corporation; 30 Hunter Ln., Camp Hill, PA 17011
    Tel: 717-761-2633, 800-748-3243; Website: www.riteaid.com

■ *Safeway, Inc.* There are 1,775 Safeway stores across the United States and Canada. These include 312 Vons stores in Southern California and Nevada, 112 Randalls and Tom Thumb stores in Texas, 37 Genuardi's store in the Philadelphia area, and 17 Carrs stores in Alaska.

❑ Safeway, Inc.; Book Buyer, 5918 Stoneridge Mall Rd., Pleasanton, CA 94588
  Tel: 925-520-8000, 877-723-3929; Website: www.safeway.com

Safeway has an online handbook that introduces potential suppliers to its business philosophy and practices. The handbook guides you through the initial steps of creating a business relationship with Safeway.

○ You can find the handbook at
  www.safeway.com/suppliers/usa/hbook/hbook.asp

■ *Shaw's Supermarkets.* Shaw's is a regional supermarket chain in New England with stores in Maine, Massachusetts, New Hampshire, Rhode Island, Connecticut, and Vermont.

❑ Shaw's; P.O. Box 600, East Bridgewater, MA 02333
  Tel: 508-313-4000; Website: www.shaws.com

■ *Stop and Shop, Inc.* Stop and Shop is a multibillion dollar corporation and is the largest food retailer in New England with a chain of more than 360 stores.

❑ Stop and Shop, Inc.; 1385 Hancock St., Quincy, MA 02169
  Tel: 617-770-8743; Website: www.stopandshop.com

■ *Walgreens Co.* Walgreens is a drug store chain with over 6,000 stores, clinics, and pharmacies in the United States.

❑ Walgreens Co.; 200 Wilmot Rd., Deerfield, IL 60015
  Tel: 847-940-2500; Website: www.walgreens.com

Supermarkets and drug stores represent good sales opportunities for independent publishers with books on a wide variety of subjects. They are flexible sales outlets because you can sell to them directly, or through established distribution partners—whichever you chose. Whether you have a fiction or a nonfiction title, you should consider selling to this market because it has the potential to be a profitable source of revenue.

10. CABLE TELEVISION SHOPPING NETWORKS

Cable television shopping networks reach millions of people every day with information about a wide variety of products, including books. Since most shopping networks broadcast twenty-four hours a day, almost every day of the year, they can be a profitable outlet through which to sell your books.

BOOK SELECTION CRITERIA

Products sold on cable television shopping networks must feature certain characteristics in order to be suitable for sale through these outlets. The following is a list of criteria that cable television shopping network buyers look for when selecting products. As you read through the list, make sure your book meets each of the conditions before contacting buyers so you do not waste your time or theirs.

■ *Demonstrates well in eight minutes of airtime.* Each product is only allotted a short amount of time—approximately eight minutes—on the air, so it must have unique and demonstrable benefits that can be quickly and easily communicated. During your airtime, you should not plan to talk about your book; rather, you should plan to discuss what the information in your book will do for the people in the audience. For example, Anya Clowers wrote a book called *Jet with Kids* that helps people safely and successfully fly with children. If she went on a shopping network to sell her book, she could talk about the products her book describes, such as children's seats, safe clothes, and games kids can play to keep busy.

■ *Solves a common problem or makes life easier.* This criterion gets back to the need for which you created your book in the first place. The people in the audience need to feel like they will be better off after having purchased and read your book.

■ *Appeals to a large audience.* Your book must address the needs of a target audience, but in order to sell successfully in this market, that audience must be of a sufficient size to generate large volumes of sales. Titles that only appeal to a small group of people will not make it past these buyers' first round of decision making.

■ *Has unique features and benefits.* You increase your chances of having your book selected if its content is different from, and better than, everything else on the market. This factor will also help you sell more books to most other markets, as well.

■ *Relates to a topical or timely subject.* If your product is associated with a current event, it is more likely to be selected by cable television shopping network buyers than one that is not.

■ *Has a selling price of twenty dollars or more.* If your product sells for less than twenty dollars, you might consider bundling several titles or products together to build the price of the package. In addition, shopping network buyers do not like to promote books that people in the audience can easily buy elsewhere. Therefore, creating a group of products that can be purchased as a set only through the network will give you an added benefit, and you will have a better shot at getting your product on the air.

Typically, the programming on shopping networks is thematic, so part of the buyers' product selection criteria is based upon how well it will fit within existing programs. Thus, it can be to your advantage to pair your book with another product being sold on a preexisting show. For example, Barney McKee, the publisher at Quail Ridge Press, said his authors sell thousands of cookbooks on QVC by coupling them with cookware products. One such cookbook included helpful hints on matching recipes with kitchen tools. According to Barney, the team of QVC's *Cook's Essentials* chefs and the cooks from the *Best of the Best* team, told people to "Pull out your *Cook's Essentials* pots and pans and enjoy this cookbook while you mix and match your way to memorable meals." By pairing this book with pots and pans, Barney was able to get it on the air, which led to numerous sales.

The following list contains examples of product categories for which QVC, one of the major cable television shopping networks, looks:

• Apparel & Accessories	• Health & Fitness	• Kitchen Gadgets
• Beauty	• Hobby & Craft	• Kitchen Electrics
• Bed & Bath	• Home Décor	• Patio & Garden
• Consumer Electronics	• Home Improvement	• Personal Care
• Cookbooks	• Home Textiles	• Pets
• Food	• Household Cleaners	• Storage
• Handbags/Luggage	• Jewelry	• Toys

The viewing audience for any individual show on these networks is idiosyncratic to the topic of the show. For instance, the show, *Home Cookin'* on QVC is for people who enjoy cooking wholesome, satisfying, homemade meals. It displays recipes, useful cooking tools, gourmet foods, and cookbooks. On the other hand, QVC's *Acer Computer Workshop* show clearly interests a very different audience than *Home Cookin'*. Learn about the different shows on each of these networks, and perhaps you can find a way to add your product as an item on an existing show, rather than creating your own show. Knowing your target market and explicitly defining it to the buyers at these networks will give you the best chance of getting your book selected.

SELLING TO CABLE TELEVISION SHOPPING NETWORKS

You should pitch your books to cable television shopping network buyers from the perspective of what is important to their viewers. For example, exclusive product launches and unique products that are being offered for the first time are always of interest to them. Your proposal should have two parts. First, demonstrate that it meets as many of the decision-making criteria listed on the previous page as possible. Second, state that you are a proficient promoter, that you are media trained (if that is the case), and that you have on-camera experience (if true). Finally, show them why your product or bundle of products offers a more profitable alternative than any other choice.

The following list answers many of the questions that publishers frequently ask about selling books to shopping networks:

■ *May I submit a product idea?* The item you submit for a product evaluation should actually exist, or at the very least, be a working prototype. If you send a galley copy of your book, the cover should be the final design and in full color. As a general practice, shopping networks will not assist you with designing or producing your product.

■ *Will I have to pay any fees?* There is no fee for a product evaluation, so you do not need to worry about sending a check with your submission. Also, it is important to note that these networks do not sell airtime. The only way your product will appear on-air is if the buyers select it.

■ *Is there a minimum quantity of product that they will buy?* A minimum purchase order for QVC is typically $30,000 to $35,000 per item at wholesale cost. The entire purchase order quantity must be received in the network's warehouse before it can be available to sell on-air.

■ *Do shopping networks sell cause-related merchandise?* At times, these networks will sell cause-related merchandise if a donation is made to a specific, known, and approved charity. As with any product they sell, the cause-related product must have general appeal and salability.

■ *Should I send a product sample with the initial application?* Unless otherwise specified, do not send unsolicited product samples. Furthermore, do not send any materials that cannot be replaced, since the networks will not return product samples that were not requested.

■ *What is the submission process?* Each network has its own forms and submission guidelines, so go to each of their websites and follow the directions you will find there. Most of the networks will send you a confirmation email shortly after you send your product submission. Then, approximately four to six weeks from the time your application is received, the appropriate buyer should contact you via email to inform you of their level of interest in your book. Sometime during that period you may receive an email requesting a sample or images of your book. If you are submitting multiple books, your reply should also include a price sheet with discount information.

Before submitting your book, call the network or go to its website—the contact information for the major networks is listed on pages 63 and 64—and follow its specific guidelines. You will discover that the submission process for these networks is much the same as it is in other market segments described in this book. Send the buyers a copy of your book, as well as your ideas for making it more interesting to their audiences. Then, continue to follow up until you learn of their decision.

SELLING BOOKS ON PBS

The Public Broadcasting Service, or PBS, is a private, nonprofit corporation that has 356 noncommercial member stations serving all 50 states. These affiliates oversee program acquisition and provide program distribution and promotion. Therefore, they are the place to begin the sometimes arduous process of selling books on PBS.

○ Learn more about PBS at www.pbs.org

The PBS affiliates do not sell books as do the cable television shopping networks. Rather, they broadcast shows that people produce, and it is through these shows that products are sold. Fortunately, PBS affiliates are like newspapers and broadcast media in the sense that they turn shows over regularly and always need fresh, pertinent content.

The general sequence of events is to first sell your show concept to your local PBS affiliate, and then to contact a program producer to pitch your idea. PBS does not produce its own programs, but distributes those produced by PBS stations, independent producers, and other sources. PBS reviews every proposal submitted, but they will only agree to work with experienced producers who are capable of managing all aspects of a project's development and production. It is also important to note that the PBS schedule is determined six to twelve months in advance, so keep this in mind when submitting programs that are timely in nature.

○ Get an idea of the types of shows aired on the PBS stations at
   www.pbs.org/search/search_programsaz.html

○ Contact information is listed for each PBS program alphabetically by title
   at www.pbs.org/search/search_contacts.html

Once you get a commitment from PBS and a program producer to proceed, you need to create a pilot show. Producing a pilot can be expensive, but even so, it is necessary to get an experienced company to do it for you—do not try to produce a pilot on your home video camera. PBS expects to see a professional, broadcast-ready production. If an affiliate agrees to air your pilot, you are officially introduced into the PBS system. The affiliates then sell their shows to other affiliates at a national, annual Development Conference, at which attendees look for new show ideas, network, and share thoughts for fundraising.

After carefully reviewing the PBS proposal guidelines, prepare your submission materials for mailing. Your materials must be accompanied by a signed proposal release form and an informational summary sheet.

○ See the PBS guidelines at
www.pbs.org/producers/proposal.html#guidelines

○ Call 703-739-5306 to request a proposal release form

When your submission package is complete, mail or fax it to the following address:

❑ Vice President, Program Scheduling & Editorial Management, PBS Headquarters, 2100 Crystal Dr., Arlington, VA 22202
Fax: 703-739-5295

All children's programming submissions should be directed to:

❑ Senior Director, Children's Programming, PBS Headquarters, 2100 Crystal Dr., Arlington, VA 22202
Fax: 703-739-7506

Proposals and tapes receive initial review by the PBS Program Development staff, which typically takes four to six weeks so do not expect a reply before then. If you have the inclination, abilities, and resources, putting together a show for PBS through which you can sell your books could prove to be a lucrative venture.

MAJOR CALBLE TELEVISION SHOPPING NETWORKS

There are three major cable television shopping networks. They are the Home Shopping Network, ShopNBC, and QVC. The following list includes details about each, as well as their contact information:

■ *Home Shopping Network.* HSN is a direct-to-consumer retailer that sells books and other products on television, online, in catalogs, and in brick-and-mortar stores. HSN reaches 90 million homes, mails 400 million catalogs annually, and operates several e-commerce sites.

❑ Home Shopping Network; New Business Development, 1 HSN Dr., St. Petersburg, FL 33729
Tel: 727-872-1000; Website: www.hsn.com

If you have a product you would like to sell on HSN, you are required to complete a submission form online. The form will ask you to provide a description of the product and your target customer, a photo or brochure that can be uploaded, the quantity of books you have available, and your suggested selling price.

○ You can find the submission form at
www.hsn.com/corp/vendor/article.aspx?aid=3382

■ *ShopNBC*. ShopNBC is a multi-media retailer that sells products through its television shopping network, the Internet, and direct mail. It broadcasts live, every day of the year, into approximately 60 million households.

❑ ShopNBC; New Vendor Department, 6740 Shady Oak Rd., Eden Prairie, MN 55344
Tel: 800-676-5523; Website: www.shopnbc.com

If you are interested in becoming a ShopNBC vendor, you first need to fill out an application form. Your submission package should include this form, as well as a brochure or photo (do not send actual samples) of your product. Upon receiving your application, ShopNBC will review your submission and will notify you if they are interested in pursuing a vendor relationship with you.

○ You can find the application form at
www.shopnbc.com/vendor/vendorinfo.aspx

■ *QVC*. QVC is one of the largest multimedia retailers in the world, broadcasts live 24 hours a day, 364 days a year, and reaches more than 166 million cable and satellite homes worldwide. It presents more than 1,000 products every week to its customers, and almost one-third of these products are new to QVC customers.

❑ QVC; 1200 Wilson Dr., Mail Code: 128, West Chester, PA 19380
Tel: 484-701-8282; Website: www.qvc.com

The first step in QVC's product review process is to complete the product submission form. Always include this form with your submissions.

○ You can find this form at
www.qvcproductsearch.com/product_submission_guidelines.htm

Another option is to attend one of the product searches that QVC hosts throughout the year where vendors and entrepreneurs are able to present items to buyers for evaluation. In any one year, approximately seven national product searches are conducted with almost 5,000 products evaluated.

○ Go to www.qvc.com for an updated list of the dates and locations of future product searches.

If you want to reach millions of people at one time and your content is important to a large niche, then home shopping networks may be the outlet for you. However, buyers in this market segment are very selective and adhere to strict buying criteria. If your content can meet their viewers' needs and your author has the personality that can sell books during live television performances, though, then you should pursue sales in this market.

11. DISPLAY MARKETING COMPANIES

The work of display marketing companies is normally hidden within the general retail market. These companies use book fairs and book displays to supply books and gift items to corporations, schools, hospitals, home parties, and early learning centers throughout the United States and Canada. They usually employ independent sales representatives who go to these different locations and set up displays. In some cases they sell books to consumers on the spot, and in others they take orders and send the books later. I have classified display marketing companies as retail, rather than non-retail outlets in this book, because although display marketing involves a great many ways of selling books, a large portion involves selling directly to consumers at book fairs.

DISPLAY MARKETING TACTICS

Display marketing companies sell books to customers in a variety of different ways and through a variety of different outlets. Their selling venues and techniques are included in the following list:

■ *Book Fairs.* Display marketing companies host book fairs for schools, businesses, and hospitals. At these fairs they set up displays to show people different books, as well as conduct on the spot sales and take orders. These companies typically give a percentage of their profits to the organizations that host the fairs. For example, if a school library contacts a display marketing company to put on a book fair, that school library will usually receive a portion of the proceeds.

■ *Drop-off Sales.* Individual sales representatives that work for display marketing companies go into schools, businesses, and hospitals and drop off a copy of one or more books. They leave the book(s) with someone that works at that venue, and put him or her in charge of letting other people in the school, office, or hospital know that the book is available for them to look through and order at a significantly reduced price. The designated contact person keeps track of orders and collects money, which the sales representatives then pick up at the end of a set period of time—usually around one week. The contact person typically receives a free copy of the book or a different incentive for their help.

■ *Home Parties.* When invited, individual sales representatives go to people's homes and sell books. Many times at these home parties books are sold in addition to other related products. For example, someone might host a cookware party at their home and invite a chef to come do cooking demonstrations with the cookware that is for sale. The party's host may also choose to invite a display marketing sales representative to bring one or more cookbooks that contain some of the chef's recipes to offer for sale to guests, as well.

■ *Infomercials.* This selling technique is rarely used by display marketing companies, but occasionally they will put together infomercials and sell copies of your book to customers that way.

The goal of display marketing companies is the same no matter which venue they are selling to or which sales technique they are using—they want to show people books and convince them to buy as many as possible at their discounted prices.

SELLING TO DISPLAY MARKETING COMPANIES

Display marketing companies buy large, non-returnable quantities of books and gift items directly from publishers and manufacturers at deep discounts—usually between 80 and 85 percent. They then sell them to consumers at discounts of up to 50 percent through display marketing events at different locations. Many of these companies often donate a percentage of their proceeds in books or cash to the sponsoring organization or to a designated charity.

Buyers in this market look for high-valued items at low prices. The consistent characteristic between all of the books that sell well through these outlets is that they "pop"—the second consumers see them, they feel like they have to buy. Figure 2.1 describes the categories of books for which some of the major display marketing companies, look.

Figure 2.1. Book Categories for which Display Marketing Companies Look

Adult Books	Description
Cookbooks	Cookbooks in a variety of formats. Includes cooking, baking, seasonal, regional, and special diet.
Non-proprietary Stationery	Stock stationery product: photo albums, greeting cards, note cards, stationery sets, scrapbooks, journals, calendars, and organizers.
General Interest	Reference and coffee table books following public interest including craft, history, health, fitness, gardening, wine and bartending, and home improvement.
Adult Bestsellers	Inspirational titles (without religious content), gift books, self-help, humor, short fiction, trivia, adult fiction and non-fiction best sellers, and young adult and teen chapter titles.
African American	African-American books and stationery across all categories. Includes all African-American children's books.
Religious	Inspirational books (with religious content), devotionals, bibles, bible covers, and religious stationery. Includes all religious children's product, excluding music.

Children's Books	Description
Children's Bestsellers	Classic 32-page, hardcover, jacketed picture books. CBS books may include a CD or DVD component or a plush.
Children's Storybooks	Treasuries or compilations of children's picture books, favorite stories, nursery rhymes, or key licenses; sets of two or more CBS titles. Includes children's chapter books, 8" x 8" readers, and young adult fiction.
Early Learning	Early concept books across a variety of formats with a built-in educational or interactive component, for ages 0-4.
Children's Educational	High-value, high quality educational books in a variety of formats and subjects often targeting teachers for classroom use.
Children's Activity	Sticker books, word searches, puzzle books, coloring, humor, and prompted journals.
Gift Items	**Description**
Gift	All non-book products (excluding Bath & Beauty). Includes electronics, home décor, novelty items, accessories, and seasonal product.
Children's Gift	Toys, electronics, activity sets, and gift sets including art, craft, hobbies, and general entertainment. Includes school supplies and posters.
Media	CD sets in a variety of genres and educational CD ROMs; VHS and DVD sets in a variety of genres including humor, war, westerns, fitness, and children's.

Display marketing companies have the ability to sell a wide variety of content to a wide variety of people in specific market segments. And this is all done on a non-returnable basis. Utilize these companies to reach targeted buyers that would otherwise be economically difficult for you to contact. Additionally, if your book is tied in with an association to promote its cause, you may be able to coordinate with one of these companies to donate to that association, as well.

SUBMITTING YOUR BOOK

When you submit your materials to display marketing companies, do not simply send them a copy of your book. You also need to include a detailed marketing summary that describes your content, including basic information about your book, why it is important to the company's target markets, and how you intend to promote it to prospective buyers. Your marketing summary should provide buyers with the following information:

■ Why you think the company is the best distribution partner for your title, how your title fits into the company's existing product lines, and, if applicable, any previous titles of yours that were sold through their company

■ The author's biographical information and credentials

■ The definition of your target market

■ A description of competitive titles and your title's competitive advantages

■ Product information, including the publication date, the size, whether or not there are photographs, the ISBN number, whether it is part of a series, the number of copies you had printed, the page count, the case quantity, and all other relevant information

■ Any relevant testimonials and awards

■ The list price, as well as examples of competitive titles' prices

■ Your promotional budget

■ Your overall promotion strategy, including any press kits, print coverage, broadcast media events, planned tours, advertising, availability for author book signings and events, etc.

Chapter Six. Promoting to Non-Trade Buyers (page 259) and the appendices (page 325) discuss obtaining and creating the above-mentioned materials. The more information you provide the buyers, the greater chance you have that they will thoroughly consider your title. Be sure that all of your information is detailed, accurate, and organized in the most coherent way possible.

MAJOR DISPLAY MARKETING COMPANIES

There are several display marketing companies throughout the United States and Canada. Several of them are included in the following list:

■ *A+ Book Fairs.* A+ Book Fairs sets up unique book fairs specifically for schools. Its book selection includes accelerated readers, popular series, award winners, and more. The company has two locations—one in Arizona and one in Utah.

❑ A+ Book Fairs; 419 E. Juanita Ave., Ste. 104, Mesa, AZ 85204
  Tel: 888-966-2665, 480-632-0440; Website: www.aplusbookfairs.com

❑ A+ Book Fairs; 100 N. 700 W., North Salt Lake, UT 84054
  Tel: 888-966-2665, 801-599-6944; Website: www.aplusbookfairs.com

■ *Adventure Land Book Fairs.* Adventure Land provides two types of book fairs for elementary and middle schools—book fairs in rolling display cases, and table top book fairs. They have hardcover and paperback selections, offer profits to sponsoring organizations, and provide all of the necessary supplies.

❑ Adventure Land Book Fairs; 4550 S. Wayside, Ste. 100, Houston, TX 77087
Tel: 713-644-1177; Website: www.adventurelandbookfairs.com

■ *A.G. City Wholesale Ltd.* A.G. City is a Canadian wholesaler affiliated with Reader's World (see bottom of page). It purchases children's literature, how-to titles, cookbooks, inspirational books, gardening titles, dictionaries, and books on wellness and motivation. Sometimes, it will buy in quantities of 50,000 or more.

❑ A.G. City Wholesale Ltd.; 760 Technology Dr., Petersborough, Ontario, Canada K9J 6X7
Tel: 705-741-1385; Website: www.agcity.com

■ *Allbook, Inc.* Allbook provides book fairs to over 100 schools in New York, New Jersey, and Connecticut. Allbook arranges author visits upon request, and it also has a year-round, online book fair service to help school's fundraise.

❑ Allbook, Inc.; 50 Division Ave., Bldg. 1N, Ste. 2, Millington, NJ 07946
Tel: 908-542-0366; Website: www.allbookinc.com

■ *Imagine Nation Books Ltd./Books Are Fun.* Imagine Nation Books Ltd./Books Are Fun is the largest display marketing company in the world. In December 2008, Imagine Nation Books acquired Books Are Fun, and the two companies are now operating as one. Through its combined efforts, the newly merged company offers hundreds of titles every season. It serves over 70,000 schools, 12,000 corporations, and 20,000 early learning centers, as well as many hospitals, universities, government offices, and non-profit organizations in the United States and Canada. It does so through four primary programs: school displays, corporate book fairs, school fairs, and daycare and business displays. Additionally, Imagine Nation Books Ltd./Books Are Fun has a unique Christian Book Fair program that operates either as a take home catalog, or as a full service book fair at Christian schools.

❑ Imagine Nation Books Ltd./Books Are Fun; 4601 Nautilus Court South, Boulder, CO 80301
Tel: 303-516-3400, 888-293-8114; Website: www.imaginenationbooks.com

Submit books to:

❑ Tim McCormick, Senior Buyer, Imagine Nation, 3628 W. Chicago St., Chandler, AZ 85226
Tel: 480-838-4309; Fax: 480-820-1011

■ *Reader's World Wholesale.* Reader's World is the United States' affiliate of Canada's A.G. City Wholesale—both companies are under the same ownership. Reader's World is the nation's largest distributor of books to independent marketers.

❑ Reader's World Wholesale; 1201 Jacobson Ave., P.O. Box 129, Ashland, OH 44805
Tel: 419-281-5952; Website: www.readersworldwholesale.com

BOOK CATEGORIES

Every book falls into one or more categories, and it is important to choose the right one(s) for your title. The Book Industry Study Group has created a Book Industry Systems Advisory Committee (BISAC) Subject Heading List to standardize category information. BISAC subjects categorize books based on their topical content. These subjects range from art, to computers, to gardening, and more. Each subject has a different nine-character code, which helps determine where a book should be shelved at brick-and-mortar stores, and how it can be searched for online. A list of all of the BISAC subject headings and their codes can be found on the website listed below. You can assign your book more than one category, but you should use the most precise categories available and list them in the order of importance.

❏ Book Industry Study Group; 370 Lexington Ave., Ste. 900; New York, NY 10017

   Tel: 646-336-7141; Website: www.bisg.org/bisac/subjectcodes/index.html

■ *Smart Start Book Fairs.* Smart Start purchases educational books, teacher aids, and adult coffee table books. It sets up book fairs in churches, schools, and organizations, and also promotes them at community events and festivals.

❏ Smart Start Book Fairs; 1416 Dunn Cove Dr., Apopka, FL 32703

   Tel: 407-257-3827; Website: http://book-fairs.net

Large-quantity sales of non-returnable books are every publisher's dream. The process of getting your book accepted by display marketing companies may be arduous, but the rewards can be enormous. These companies will initially buy in small quantities to test each title before displaying them on a national basis, but they will eventually place large orders if your title works. Contact them as appropriate to your title and be persistent in your follow up. This channel could become a big contributor to your revenue stream.

12. MUSEUMS, ZOOS, AQUARIUMS, AND PARKS

Every year, millions of people visit thousands of museums, zoos, aquariums, and parks—most of which have gift shops that sell books. You can sell a lot of books through these outlets if your book has the ability to help the gift shop operators educate and entertain their guests. Furthermore, since books are usually sold to these outlets on a non-returnable basis with discounts averaging around 55 percent, you can not only sell a lot of books through them, you can sell them profitably.

Many of these locations'stores promote education, so their book departments are very important to their overall mission. Book buyers for these stores work with the store managers to extend the experience of their guests. Profits are secondary to fulfilling the mission of the venue, which again is to educate guests and make their experience as pleasurable and informative as possible. To be successful in this market, you must carry the same mindset.

BOOK SELECTION CRITERIA

As just stated, the principal mission of these venues is education, so book buyers look for quality of production and content. The information in new titles is expected to be precise and may be subjected to a formal review process. Your submission to buying authorities should include a statement that facts and dates have been checked for accuracy.

In general, guests at these stores prefer hardcover books. According to the book buyer for Event Network, Inc., a third party retailer that sells to stores in this segment, this is because "People are generally looking for a book that their children will be able to enjoy and keep as a memento of their visit to the venue, and many educators will purchase books for their classrooms." She continued, "Content is vital, as are the title of the book and its cover design. The cover design is particularly important for children's books. We place heavy emphasis on those criteria because price in this segment is not a critical issue. Although some institutions may be more price sensitive than others, on the whole we try to promote hardcover books whenever possible." Thus, books that have the best opportunity in this segment are hardcover and full of quality, factually accurate content.

SELLING TO MUSEUMS, ZOOS, AQUARIUMS, AND PARKS

Buyers for stores in this market segment usually seek discounts of 40 to 60 percent, averaging around 55 percent. If your book sells well, it will be reordered regularly. Furthermore, many buyers in this segment buy books on a non-returnable basis, and are therefore very careful about the titles they select so they do not end up with dead inventory. For this reason, publishers must be particularly cognizant of the types of books they submit. It is very important to thoroughly research each institution before contacting it, and to only submit appropriate titles.

TIP

Stores in museums can only sell books directly related to their theme or they are subject to the Unrelated Business Income Tax (UBIT). Thus, the more targeted your titles are to the topic of the museum, the more likely they are to be purchased.

Event Network's buyer looks to the public to find titles to purchase. "If a title is popular, it rises to the top. I also look at the *New York Times* best-seller list and search the media and Internet websites for trends. Event Network also subscribes to Bowker's Books in Print for title and publisher information online. Magazines and mail order catalogs are also a rich source of product information."

TIP Bowker's Books in Print has information about millions of titles and is an is an essential bibliographic tool for libraries, booksellers, and publishers. You can find Bowker's online at www.booksinprint.com/bip/

Event Network's book buyer actively seeks out titles on her own, but she still expects publishers to send her titles to evaluate each season, too. For example, Random House downloads a PowerPoint presentation of selected titles by genre every season. Even with such submissions, though, she still does not get enough good, salable information on titles sent to her. "My challenge is to educate all publishers to bring to my attention books that are important for our business, have shown a good sales history, or if the author or book is up for a major award." Furthermore, like many other non-trade buyers, she walks the floor of BookExpo America, one of the United States' largest trade shows, searching for new titles, trends, and ideas. Therefore, networking and actively selling and promoting your book are extremely important in this marketplace.

SUBMITTING YOUR BOOK

There are two ways to reach buyers in this market segment. The first is to contact them directly. If you choose to sell directly to these stores, approach them as you would any other business. Find out the buyers' names, which are usually available on their companies' websites, and make appointments to meet with them.

The second way to reach buyers in this segment is through third party retailers that acquire books and other products for the gift shops. In essence, they buy for the venues instead of selling to them. Eastern National and Event Network, Inc. are two of the major third party retailers. Eastern National serves the national park system, while Event Network operates gift shops at zoos, museums, aquariums, science centers, and botanical gardens.

■ *Eastern National.* Eastern National currently operates over 245 bookstores at more than 150 national parks and other public trusts in 30 states from Maine to the Caribbean. It is the primary operator of federal historic sites and National Park shops in the United States, and it provides quality educational products and services to visitors of these places. Eastern National is an educational institution that functions as a part of the educational arm of the National Park Service. It is a nonprofit organization, and net proceeds from its bookstores' sales are donated to the National Park Service, which may present an opportunity for you to align your book with its cause.

In addition, Eastern National is an independent publisher and produces educational products for the National Park Service. Its publications are different from those developed by traditional publishers, because Eastern National collaborates directly with the parks to produce educational material to fit specific needs within the park. If your title does not meet its needs, you might consider offering your services to write a new book.

❑ Eastern National; Purchasing Manager, 470 Maryland Dr., Ste. 1, Ft. Washington, PA 19034

  Tel: 215-283-6900 ext. 129; Website: www.easternnational.org

Eastern National has a bookstore on its website, as well as access to all of the stores it represents. Many of the represented stores also have websites through which they market books, and you may find a greater opportunity for your titles through one of them.

○ A list of these stores may be found at
  www.easternnational.org/EasternNationalBookstoreslogo.pdf

■ *Event Network, Inc.* Event Network acts as an institution's retail partner, creating and maintaining each store with which it works. It delivers a compelling assortment of merchandise by evaluating and purchasing new products for the gift shops it operates. Event Network is not a distributor; rather, it works with its partners to extend its guests' experiences.

Event Network's stores vary from single-subject venues, such as the Abraham Lincoln Presidential Library and Museum, to multi-subject venues, such as science centers, zoos, and aquariums. When you contact Event Network's book buyer, be sure to point out the venue for which your book is most suitable, as well as the reasons why it would be a good fit for that particular venue. This is because the products Event Network purchases for, say, the Seattle Aquarium are different than those chosen for the Pacific Aviation Museum, which are also different than those acquired for the Natural History Museum of Los Angeles. Again, Event Network operates gift shops at zoos, museums, aquariums, science centers, and botanical gardens.

❑ Event Network; Purchasing Department, 1010 Turqoise St., Ste. 325, San Diego, CA 92109

  Tel: 858-488-7507; Website: www.eventnetwork.com

According to Event Network's buyer, your submission package should include a copy of the book and a sell sheet describing the data needed to make a decision. This includes the author's name, as well as his or her credentials as an expert source of the book's content. It also includes all of the data surrounding your book such as its list price, page count, ISBN number, and more. See page 327 for an example of what a sell sheet for this book might look like.

Additionally, your submission package should include a cover letter that has a brief description of why your book is relevant. How is it different from, and better than what the institution already has on its shelves? Why should one of those books be replaced with yours? See page 326 for an example of a generic cover letter for this book. By providing as much relevant information as possible, you are helping to expedite the decision process.

Finally, let the book buyer know if the author is willing to conduct—and is good at performing—on-premise events. Do not force your authors into making appearances, though. The most successful events occur with authors who are naturally people oriented, flexible, and good with children. However, even if the author is good, it does not guarantee a booming event. There are many factors that influence the success of an event: a noted author, a best-selling title, the day of the week, the scheduled time of day or evening, and even the weather. The most successful author events have been in conjunction with institutional lecture series. For example, the Abraham Lincoln Presidential Library and Museum, the Mystic Seaport Museum, and the Museum of Science in Boston all have regular lecture series in which books are brought in for the author to sign prior to, or after the lecture. Because the guests have purchased tickets to hear the speaker at the lecture, there is a captured audience for the author signing. *40. Sell Books through Speaking Engagements* (page 279) and *41. Conduct Author Events* (page 284) go into much more detail about this topic.

Content and quality are two of the most important factors for all books sold in non-trade markets, and they are particularly critical determinants of potential sales in this segment. If you have a quality book filled with important content, and your information is properly documented and meets the selection criteria, you may enjoy repetitive sales and regular income in this marketplace.

MUSEUMS

Depending on the topic of your book, museums and historical sites can be profitable sales outlets. Museums want to inform, entertain, and educate their visitors, and if you have a book that will enhance their ability to do that you may make a good sale. The American Association of Museums (AAM) estimates that there are 17,500 museums in the United States. But which types of museums receive the most visitors? Figure 2.2 on the next page, shows the median annual attendance for different types of museums, as reported by the AAM Museum Financial Information Survey.

Since there are several different types of museums, creativity is key in determining where to place your book. For example, the Association of Children's Museums found that more than 30 million people visit children's museums annually. However, even though that is a potentially huge market for children's titles, you should not stop there—remember that parents also often take their children to art museums, natural history museums, botanical gardens, state history museums, battlefields, and United States history museums. Be creative and explore all options to maximize your sales potential.

Figure 2.2. Median Annual Attendance for Different Types of Museums

Museum Type	People per Museum per Year
Arboretum/Botanic Garden	106,235
Art Museum	59,822
Children's/Youth Museum	78,500
General Museum	43,500
Historic House/Site	16,000
History Museum	10,750
Natural History/Anthropology	62,803
Nature Center	52,850
Science/Technology Museum	244,589
Specialized Museum	20,000
Zoo	440,502

There are numerous organizations and associations that provide resources that will help you find lists of museums through which you could potentially sell your book. I have divided them into general listings, regional listings, and specialty listings.

General Listings

There are several organizations and associations that encompass a broad range of museums nationwide. These organizations provide lists of, and information about all different types of museums in all different areas of the country. They include the following:

■ *The American Association of Museums.* AAM is the only organization that represents the entire scope of museums, as well as the professionals and non-paid staff who work for, and with them. AAM represents every type of museum including art, history, science, military and maritime, and youth museums, as well as aquariums, zoos, botanical gardens, arboretums, historic sites, and science and technology centers.

❏ American Association of Museums; 1575 Eye St. NW, Ste. 400, Washington, DC 20005
Tel: 202-289-1818; Website: www.aam-us.org/index.cfm

■ *The International Council of Museums.* ICOM's website lists print and online directories of museums. It also includes publications that are available for sale, as well as those that are part of ICOM's collection in its Information Center.

❏ ICOM; Maison de l'UNESCO, 1, rue Miollis, 75732 Paris Cedex 15, France

   Tel: +33-0-1-47-34-05-00; Website: http://icom.museum/museum_directories.html

■ *The Museum Store Association.* Founded in 1955, MSA is a nonprofit, international association organized to advance the success of cultural commerce and the professionals engaged in it. By encouraging high standards of professional competence and conduct, MSA helps retail professionals at cultural institutions better serve the public. MSA serves approximately 1,650 institutional members— all of whom either already have a retail store, or are in the process of creating a retail operation. Its members' stores range in net sales from less than $5,000 to more than $17 million. Because museum stores sell items—including books—that provide visitors with souvenirs and educational materials directly related to their museum experience, your book on a relevant subject could be ideal for sales through their shops.

❏ Museum Store Association; 4100 E. Mississippi Ave., Ste. 800, Denver, CO 80246

   Tel: 303-504-9223; Website: www.museumdistrict.com

T
I
P

The Official Museum Directory is another resource you can use to find museums. It covers institutions of every size and type in all fifty states, and provides verified data that reflects the latest professional affiliations, permanent and traveling exhibits, and contact information for museums, historic sites, planetariums, technology centers, and zoos. Go to www.officialmuseumdir.com to learn more about this resource and to find ordering information.

Regional Listings

In addition to the general listings, there are also a number of regional museum associations. These groups cover all types of museums, as well; however, they only provide information about those in their geographic area. They are a great resource if your book is region-specific, or if you want to find museums close to you. They include the following:

■ *American Association for State and Local History.* The mission of this association is to "preserve and interpret state and local history in order to make the past more meaningful to all Americans." It performs this service through several different methods, including an awards ceremony and a bookstore that contains both technical service books, as well as books that explore the various aspects of state and local history.

❑ American Association for State and Local History; 1717 Church St., Nashville, TN 37203
   Tel: 615-320-3203; Website: www.aaslh.org/hhouses.htm

■ *Association of Midwest Museums.* The Association of Midwest Museums provides resources to museums and cultural institutions, as well as services to museum professionals in eight states in the Midwest—Illinois, Indiana, Iowa, Michigan, Minnesota, Missouri, Ohio, and Wisconsin.

❑ Association of Midwest Museums; P.O. Box 11940, St. Louis, MO 63112
   Tel: 314-746-4557; Website: www.midwestmuseums.org

■ *Canadian Museums Association.* This is an organization that seeks to advance the Canadian museum sector and represent Canadian museum professionals.

❑ Canadian Museums Association; 280 Metcalfe St., Ste. 400, Ottawa, Ontario, Canada K2P 1R7
   Tel: 613-567-0099; Website: www.museums.ca

■ *Mid-Atlantic Association of Museums.* The Mid-Atlantic Association of Museums represents the interests of museums in Delaware, the District of Columbia, Maryland, New Jersey, New York, and Pennsylvania. It is a nonprofit membership organization with the mission to enhance the image of its member museums.

❑ Mid-Atlantic Association of Museums; 2300 N St., NW, Ste. 710, Washington, DC, 20037
   Tel: 202-452-8040; Website: www.midatlanticmuseums.org

■ *Mountain-Plains Museum Association.* The Mountain-Plains Museum Association is a regional organization that serves it members by facilitating communication among them. For example, if your book is selected by one member museum, the association will help spread the word about it to its other member organizations, as well.

❑ Mountain-Plains Museum Association; 7110 W. David Dr., Littleton, CO 80128
   Tel: 303-979-9358; Website: www.mpma.net

■ *New England Museum Assocation.* This association's member museums are all located in New England. One way in which it assists its members is by negotiating discounts on products, such as books, for them. You should contact this association to negotiate a selling price for your book, and it will then communicate that information to all its members for you.

❑ New England Museum Association; 22 Mill St., Ste. 409, Arlington, MA 02476
   Tel: 781-641-0013; Website: www.nemanet.org

■ *Southeastern Museums Conference.* SEMC is a nonprofit organization that serves its member museums in twelve states throughout the Southeastern United States, Puerto Rico, and the Virgin Islands. It offers professional development for it members and communicates with them through its quarterly newsletter. In addition to selling it your book, you may also be able to contribute articles for publication in its newsletter if your topic is of interest to the members.

❑ Southeastern Museums Conference; P.O. Box 9003, Atlanta, GA 31106
   Tel: 404-378-3153; Website: www.semcdirect.net

■ *Western Museums Association.* The Western Museums Association serves a diverse group of museums in the Western United States. Its mission is to enrich the lives of individuals who do museum work. If you have content that will help it fulfill its mission, you may find sales opportunities through the association itself, and/or through its members.

❑ Western Museums Association; P.O. Box 8367, Emeryville, CA 94662
   Tel: 510-665-0700; Website: www.westmuse.org

Specialty Listings

Finally, there are a number of museum associations that target specific types of museums and groups of people. These can be very helpful resources depending on the topic of your book. They include the following:

■ *American Public Gardens Association.* APGA is North America's premier association for public gardens. It has 500 member institutions located in all 50 states, the District of Columbia, Canada, and 7 other countries. Contact APGA if you have content of interest to people who love nature—both flora and fauna.

❑ American Public Gardens Association; 100 W. 10th St., Ste. 614, Wilmington, DE 19801
   Tel: 302-655-7100; Website: www.publicgardens.org

■ *Association of African American Museums.* AAAM is a nonprofit member organization established to support museums with a focus on Africans and African Americans. If your book contains content on how to protect, preserve, and interpret African and African American art, history, and culture, it could sell well through this association's member stores.

❑ Association of African American Museums; P.O. Box 427, Wilberforce, OH 45384
   Tel: 937-376-4944 ext. 123
   Website: www.blackmuseums.org/memberlinks/institutional.htm

■ *Association of Children's Museums.* The Association of Children's Museums is an international professional organization that represents and advocates for its member institutions. Membership ranges from children's museums, to large collections-based institutions dedicated to serving young visitors through a variety of interactive exhibits, to groups that are in the planning phases of opening a children's museum.

❏ Association of Children's Museums; 1300 L St. NW, #975, Washington, DC 20005
   Tel: 202-898-1080; Website: www.childrensmuseums.org

■ *Association of Railway Museums.* ARM was established to encourage and support railway museums. It provides many member services, including communication among them with new product ideas. If your content is railway-oriented and of possible interest to railway preservationists and historians, you should start your sales pitch with this association.

❏ Association of Railway Museums; 1016 Rosser St., Conyers, GA 30012
   Tel: 770-278-0088; Website: www.railwaymuseums.org

■ *Association of Science-Technology Centers.* ASTC is an organization of science centers and museums whose purpose is to encourage informal science learning. ASTC has more than 540 members in forty countries. These include science and technology centers, science museums, nature centers, aquariums, planetariums, zoos, botanical gardens, space theaters, natural history museums, and children's museums.

❏ ASTC; 1025 Vermont Ave., NW, Ste. 500, Washington, DC 20005
   Tel: 202-783-7200; Website: www.astc.org/sciencecenters/find_scicenter.htm

■ *Association of Zoos and Aquariums.* AZA is a nonprofit organization of zoos and aquariums. If your book is focused on animal care, wildlife conservation, education, or science, it has a good chance of selling to one or more of AZA's 200 members. There is more information about this particular association in the Zoos and Aquariums section beginning on the next page.

❏ Association of Zoos and Aquariums; 8403 Colesville Rd., Ste. 710, Silver Spring, MD 20910
   Tel: 301-562-0777; Website: www.aza.org

■ *Council of American Jewish Museums.* This council is committed to strengthening its eighty member institutions through training museum staff and volunteers. It also educates members on products related to all aspects of Jewish art and history museums, historic sites, historical and archival societies, Holocaust centers, synagogue museums, children's museums, and Jewish Community Center and university galleries.

❏ Council of American Jewish Museums; Executive Director, Center for Judaic Studies, University of Denver, 2000 E. Asbury Ave., Ste. 157, Denver, CO 80208
   Tel: 303-871-3015; Website: http://www2.jewishculture.org/?pid=cajm

■ *Council of American Maritime Museums.* CAMM is an organization with more than eighty member museums in the United States, Mexico, Bermuda, Australia, and Canada. It is dedicated to preserving North America's maritime history. If your book is about historical sites, vessels, and research, it should be applicable to its members' stores. Go to the "Meet Our Members" page on its website to access its members—your prospective buyers.

❑ Council of American Maritime Museums

Website: www.councilofamericanmaritimemuseums.org

■ *Fire Museum Network.* The Fire Museum Network promotes the interests of museums dedicated to collecting, preserving, and interpreting the products, history, and traditions of the fire service. Its website provides a list of links to all its member museums, so you can contact each directly.

❑ Fire Museum Network
   Website: www.firemuseumnetwork.org/directory/index.html

These associations can help your sales efforts in several ways. First, they can disseminate your information to their members, which gives your title instant credibility. Second, many of their websites have links to their members, which will save you time when contacting them. And finally, in addition to submitting your book to one or more of these associations for review, you might also consider writing an article for their newsletters if they have one.

ZOOS AND AQUARIUMS

The Association of Zoos and Aquariums (AZA) is the single most important association to know about when selling books in this market segment. AZA was founded in 1924 and is a nonprofit organization dedicated to the advancement of accredited zoos and aquariums in the areas of animal care, wildlife conservation, education, and science. There are hundreds of zoos and aquariums; however, AZA accredits only those institutions that have achieved exact standards for animal care, education, wildlife conservation, and science. With its more than 200 accredited members, AZA is building North America's largest wildlife conservation movement.

❑ Association of Zoos and Aquariums; 8403 Colesville Rd., Ste. 710, Silver Spring, MD 20910
   Tel: 301-562-0777; Website: www.aza.org

Included on AZA's website you will find many important pieces of information that will help you focus your marketing. The website provides the names, addresses, and telephone numbers of all of AZA's various members.

○ For a complete list of AZA accredited zoos and aquariums in the United States, go to www.aza.org/Accreditation/AccreditList/

In addition to selling your book to the actual zoos and aquariums, AZA also provides two other opportunities for selling your books on zoo-related topics. The first is to sell it to any of the nineteen AZA certified wild life sanctuaries, including the Colorado Wolf and Wildlife Center, Gorilla Haven, the International Exotic Feline Sanctuary, the Kangaroo Conservation Center, and more.

○ For a complete list of AZA certified wild life sanctuaries, go to
www.aza.org/Accreditation/CertList/

The second additional book selling opportunity is to sell your book to any of AZA's more than 250 commercial members—companies that have products and services related to zoo and aquarium animals. Among these are animal food suppliers and non-zoo gift shops such as Adventure Planet, Animaland, Polar Graphics, The Wildlife Trading Company, and others.

○ For a complete list of AZA's commercial members, go to
www.aza.org/FindCommercialMember/index.cfm

Bookstores in zoos and aquariums provide a unique outlet for you to reach people interested in your content. Use these associations as you would any other association—to give you added credibility, reach their members, or help them advance their cause; all while selling more of your books at the same time.

NATIONAL PARKS

Just as the Association of Zoos and Aquariums is the major association in that market segment, the National Recreation and Park Association (NRPA) is the most important association in this market segment. NRPA acts to advance parks, recreation, and environmental conservation efforts that enhance the quality of life for all people. For forty years, NRPA has advocated the importance of local park systems and the preservation of great community places.

❏ National Recreation and Park Association; 22377 Belmont Ridge Rd., Ashburn, VA 20148
Tel: 703-858-0784; Website: www.nrpa.org

NRPA's website has a wealth of information. In addition to having its own online bookstore that has titles ranging from targeted publications to scholarly texts, NRPA's website also allows you to search for bookstores at different national parks, and then provides you with contact information for each of them.

○ For a complete list of bookstores at national parks, go to
http://data2.itc.nps.gov/hafe/bookshop/index.cfm

Do not make the mistake of thinking that you must have a "green" book to sell to parks. NRPA encompasses ten individual branches and sections—subgroups that represent everything from aquatics, to military recreation, to natural resources, to therapeutic recreation. These branches and sections represent a broader range of sales opportunities for a variety of topics.

○ For a complete list of NRPA's branches and subsections and detailed information about each, go to www.nrpa.org/content/default.aspx?documentId=495

Furthermore, there are additional marketing opportunities through NRPA for the interested publisher, which include:

■ *Exhibit and Sponsorship Opportunities.* These are available at the annual NRPA Congress and Exposition, as well as at a number of regional events that cater to park and recreation professionals.

○ For more information go to www.nrpa.org/content/default.aspx?documentId=1619

■ *Advertising in "Parks & Recreation" magazine.* This is the official publication of NRPA. It is read by more than 19,000 park and recreation professionals, citizen advocates, and affiliates.

○ For more information go to www.nrpa.org/content/default.aspx?documentId=2780

■ *Mailing Lists.* NRPA's membership lists, as well as various other lists that are maintained at NRPA headquarters are available for rental in label format, on disk, and via email.

○ For more information go to www.nrpa.org/content/default.aspx?documentId=895

People go to museums, zoos, aquariums, and parks because they are interested in certain topics and want to learn more about them. During their visits, many of these people stop in the gift shops looking for additional information, which your book could provide. Proprietors of these shops look upon books favorably as a special service to their guests and as a source of incremental revenue.

In addition to having this built in, captivated audience, there are other benefits to marketing in these selective environments. First, your promotional dollars are more efficient because your target market essentially comes to you. Second, your book may be on a shelf with no competitive titles, and no price comparison.

Remember that the buying process may be different for each niche in this market segment. If you are ever in doubt about the proper procedures, contact the relevant associations or visit local stores to ask them how they buy books before you submit your materials. By learning about the industry's operating procedures and expectations, you can reach your potential buyers most expeditiously, and turn this into a lucrative market for your book.

13. GIFT SHOPS

People are constantly exposed to gift items—including books—through a wide range of shopping venues. Gift products are sold through national retail chains like Hallmark, Pottery Barn, and Spencer's Gifts, as well as through local card and gift stores, regional chains, and hotel and hospital gift shops. Even though the smaller gift shops are losing market share to the larger, national chains, the gift shop market as a whole offers an excellent opportunity to sell your books.

BOOK SELECTION CRITERIA

Buyers in the gift shop market look for specific criteria when selecting books. Jay Quickel, the Retail Marketing and Merchandising Manager at Hallmark, said that in gift shops, "Hardcover is the preferred binding and the price should be less than twenty dollars. Books priced between ten and fifteen dollars sell particularly well." On the other hand, titles that generally do not sell well in gift shops are coffee table books, fiction titles, and scholarly, text-driven materials.

The most important decision criterion in this marketplace is how well your title fits with a particular store's image and customer base. The types of books that sell well vary according to the image of each chain. For example, Hallmark generally deals in sentiment, so books that sell well in its stores are motivational, inspirational, humorous, and about family and relationships. Jay said, "The book is an extension of a greeting card. We are in the social expression business, and your book should complement the creative voice we are trying to capture. Any product we select must fit with the product development theme in our stores and enrich the lives of our customers. Our typical customer is female, forty-five plus years of age with older children at home, or with kids out of the home. Grandmothers are part of our demographic, too."

At the other end of the spectrum is Spencer's Gifts—a place for eighteen to twenty-five year old people to go for novelty gifts. With over 600 mall locations throughout the United States and Canada, Spencer's has a variety of unique gifts displayed in a nightclub atmosphere. Your book should fit with the store's variety of funny present ideas and gag gifts that range from G-rated to adult.

Other stores portray different images. For example, the personality of Urban Outfitters is hip products for men and women. Conversely, the Yankee Candle Company offers distinctive products that it markets as affordable luxuries and consumable gifts. These differences in image point to a strategy that will help you target your content to the appropriate retailer. Visit a variety of different stores and get a feel for what they are all about. Then use your research to guide your submissions. The more aligned your title is with the image of a store, the better chance of success you will have.

SELLING TO GIFT SHOPS

As a whole, the gift market is highly decentralized and there are many small shops that place small orders. This increases your administrative burden because it requires you to ship and bill for several small shops. However, this also represents an opportunity because you can readily reach decision makers. A good strategy when entering this market is to call local gift shop owners and buyers first. You can also go to nearby hospital gift stores and talk with the volunteers there. Most are very willing to spend time with you and describe their buying practices.

Furthermore, always do your research before contacting buyers. "Help me as a buyer," Jay said. "Come prepared. Add value to my process. Give me data and industry analysis that I can't find on my own. Help improve the productivity of my staff and you will get a lot of attention from me." Furthermore, if possible, it would be to your benefit to attend industry trade shows and gift marts for trends and analysis. You can also learn a lot about the gift market by reading the trade magazines *Giftware News and Gifts & Decorative Accessories.*

❏ Giftware News; 20 W. Kinzie, 12th Fl., Chicago, IL 60610
Tel: 312-849-2220; Website: www.giftwarenews.com

❏ Gifts & Decorative Accessories; 360 Park Ave. South, New York, NY 10010
Tel: 646-746-6400; Website: www.giftsanddec.com

Gift shop sales are seasonal in nature, so if your title is appropriate for one of the major holiday periods you stand a better chance of acceptance. "In addition to the obvious fourth-quarter holidays, sales spike around Easter, Valentine's Day, Mother's Day, Father's Day, and the June graduation period. Halloween is not a big holiday for us," said Jay. Buyers at key accounts like Hallmark and Restoration Hardware will begin looking at seasonal titles six months before the holiday, whereas, purchasing agents at local stores will often buy your seasonal books all the way up to one month before the event.

Ultimately, your best resource in this market is the stores themselves. Go to as many gift shops in your area as you can. Look around to see what types of products they sell and when they sell them. Talk to the store owners while you are there and ask them about their buying techniques. The more you learn about the unique nuances of this market, the more successful you will be.

SUBMITTING YOUR BOOK

The goal of your submission package is to make it easy for gift shop buyers to do business with you. The marketing plan you submit with your book should describe how your content fits in with the industry trends. It should also describe your visits to stores and suggest how your book could be displayed on their shelves or counters. Furthermore, you should customize your proposed promotional activities by demonstrating how your planned media exposure aligns with the store's seasonal peaks and customer demographics. You will learn more about promoting your book in *Chapter Six. Promote to Non-Trade Buyers* (page 259).

There are several different ways to contact buyers and get your book into gift shops. The following list details each of them. You should explore all of the different options and see which work best for you.

■ *Direct marketing.* You can market directly to buyers in this market segment through personal visits, phone calls, and mailings. The timing of your direct marketing campaign is almost as important as the content of your book. First locate your target companies, and then implement your marketing campaign well before you want your book on the shelves. If you have multiple titles that could work in gift shops, you should consider creating a high-quality catalog and include it in your mailings and personal visits. Be prepared to leave sample books with potential buyers. Stores will typically pay you within 120 days, but you can try to negotiate more favorable terms. See *Chapter Five. Start Selling* (page 233) for more information about the direct sales process.

■ *Sales-representative groups.* There are several independent sales-representative groups that market books to the gift trade throughout North America. While some are national organizations, most of them work regionally and cover a territory comprised of several states. Sales representatives usually seek a 15 to 20 percent commission on all books sold in their territory. You can find sales representative groups through the following organizations' websites:

○ Andrews McMeel Publishing: www.andrewsmcmeel.com/find_rep.html

○ Gift Shops of America Vendor/Representative Directory: www.giftshopsofamerica.com

○ Manufacturers Representative Profile: www.mrpusa.com

○ Manufacturers Representatives Wanted: www.manufacturers-representatives.com

○ Rep Hunter: www.rephunter.net

■ *Trade shows.* Trade shows are a great way to exhibit books and make contact with buyers. You can either display your book yourself, or you can have your sales representative group do it for you. Even if you choose the latter option, you should still attend the shows, as well, because they are great networking opportunities. *42. Attend Trade Shows* (page 288) goes into more detail about trade shows in general. The major gift-focused trade shows are both national and regional in scope, and include the following: National Stationery Show, Boston Gift Show, California Gift Show, New York International Gift Fair, Dallas International Gift & Home Accessories Market, Gourmet Products Show, San Francisco International Gift Fair, Mid-America Seattle Gift Show, Toronto International Gift Fair, and the Washington Gift Show.

○ For a more comprehensive list of gift shows and more information about those listed above, go to www.greatrep.com/trade_shows.asp

■ *Distributors and Wholesalers.* There are distribution partners that specifically service the gift trade, such as Sourcebooks and Workman. Andrews McMeel is another, and it specializes in best sellers, humor collections, general non-fiction trade, gift books, and calendars. Discounts to retailers will be about 50 percent, so distributors look for 70 percent or more, and some have minimum order sizes. For example, Sourcebooks' minimum order from retailers is $100, but others require up to $600 or more.

❑ Andrews McMeel Publishing, LLC; 100 Front St., Riverside, NJ 08075
Tel: 800-851-8923; Website: www.andrewsmcmeel.com

❑ Sourcebooks, Inc.; 1935 Brookdale Rd., Ste. 139, Naperville, IL 60563
Tel: 630-961-3900; Website: www.sourcebooks.com

❑ Workman Publishing Company; 225 Varick St., New York, NY 10014
Tel: 212-254-5900; Website: www.workman.com

As you can see, there are several ways to get your book into gift shops. You can choose to do the selling yourself, or you can enlist the help of professionals. Choose what works best for you based on your resources and skill set.

MAJOR GIFT SHOP CHAINS

There are numerous stores that sell a wide variety of gifts, novelties, and gift-related products—including books. The following list contains the names and contact information for several major gift shop chains that sell a diverse selection of products. Not all of them will be relevant to your title, and this list is by no means comprehensive. The gift shops provided are simply intended to get you thinking about the possibilities. Many more gift shops can be found by conducting an online search using your favorite search engine. Be sure to find out the name of the appropriate buyer for your title before sending your submission package to any of these stores.

❑ 1-800-Flowers.com, Inc.; 1 Old Country Rd., Carle Place, NY 11514
Tel: 516-237-6000, 800-356-7474; Website: www.1800flowers.com

❑ Aramark Sports and Entertainment Services, Inc.; Aramark Tower, 1101 Market St., Philadelphia, PA 19107
Tel: 215-238-3000, 800-999-8989; Website: www.ps.aramark.com

❑ Bed Bath and Beyond; 650 Liberty Ave., Union, NJ 07083
Tel: 908-688-0888, 800-462-3966; Website: www.bedbathandbeyond.com

❑ Franklin Covey Co.; 2200 W. Parkway Blvd., Salt Lake City, UT 84119
Tel: 801-975-1776, 800-819-1812; Website: www.franklincovey.com

❑ Hallmark Cards, Inc.; 2501 McGee St., Kansas City, MO 64108
  Tel: 816-274-5111, 800-425-5627; Website: www.hallmark.com

❑ IKEA North America; 1000 IKEA Dr., Elizabeth, NJ 07202
  Tel: 908-352-3270; Website: www.ikea-usa.com

❑ Pier 1 Imports, Inc.; 100 Pier 1 Pl., Fort Worth, TX 76102
  Tel: 817-252-8000, 800-245-4595; Website: www.pier1.com

❑ Pottery Barn, Inc.; 3250 Van Ness Ave., San Francisco, CA 94109
  Tel: 415-421-7900, 888-779-5176; Website: www.potterybarn.com

❑ Spencer's Gifts; 6826 Black Horse Pke., Egg Harbor Township, NJ 08234
  Tel: 609-645-3300; Website: www.spencergifts.com

❑ Successories, Inc.; 2520 Diehl Rd., Aurora, IL 60504
  Tel: 630-820-7200, 800-535-2773; Website: www.successories.com

❑ Yankee Candle Company, Inc.; 16 Yankee Candle Way, South Deerfield, MA 01373
  Tel: 413-665-8306; 800-243-1776; Website: www.yankeecandle.com

OTHER GIFT SHOP OUTLETS

In addition to the more traditional gift shops just listed, there are also other sales outlets in this marketplace. They are included in the following list:

■ *Cooperative catalogs.* Cooperative gift catalogs are a great way for small publishers to contact gift shops and consumers. They bring together descriptions of books and other products from a variety of different retailers and display them in one place. The best-case scenario is that placement in one of these catalogs will result in several sales. But even in the worst-case scenario, your book will still receive broad exposure to the market.

Gift Creations Concepts (GCC) produces a cooperative catalog for independent gift retailers. Participating retailers enjoy many benefits including special terms, opportunities, and advance notice about new and exclusive merchandise, networking, and educational seminars. Furthermore, you can negotiate with GCC to produce items exclusively for retailers participating in its advertising programs.

❍ For more information about GCC, go to www.gcccatalog.com

Similarly, the company Ideation creates an exclusive, full-color gift catalog that showcases top-selling merchandise in a convenient buying guide. The guide is mailed to gift-shop customers who can select products from the catalog and visit participating stores to make their purchases.

❍ For more information about Ideation, go to www.ideationgifts.com

■ *Online stores.* There are several online gift shops in which you can sell your book. One such online store is Parade of Gifts. It represents a group of independent retailers located throughout the United States, and its selection includes women's gifts, men's gifts, home accessories, inspirational and bereavement gifts, children's toys, seasonal décor, and novelties.

○ For more information about Parade of Gifts, go to www.paradeofgifts.com

To find other sales opportunities online, simply conduct a search for online gift shops on your favorite search engine. To save time, you might consider purchasing Copernic—a search engine that explores and brings you results from several of the major search engines at once.

○ Go to www.copernic.com for more information, or to purchase the program

■ *Hospital gift shops.* Gift shops in hospitals present a niche opportunity for applicable books. People in hospitals often look for ways to pass the time, and books are a great way to do so. You can reach hospital gift shops directly, through Imagine Nation/Books Are Fun (page 69), through Lori's Hospital Gift Shops, or through Linda Williams of Advantage Program. Lori's is a hospital gift shop management company that pays the hospital rent while assuming all of the store's staffing, purchasing, inventory, and accounting responsibilities. Linda Williams, on the other hand, performs a consulting function that helps managers of hospital gift shops run more effective businesses and choose products to sell in their shops.

❏ Lori's Hospital Gift Shops; New Product Review, 2125 Chenault Dr., Ste. 100, Carrollton, TX 75006
   Tel: 972-759-5000 ext. 1823
   Website: www.lorishospitalgiftshops.com/default1.htm

❏ Linda Williams, Advantage Program; 1 Hilldale Dr., Endicott, NY 13760
   Tel: 607-725-7386; Website: www.advantageprogram.com

■ *Hotel Gift Shops.* Business people and vacationers generally frequent hotel gift shops for impulse items, souvenirs, and items—including books—to help them stay entertained while away from home. You can contact hotels directly, which is probably the most effective way to get into their stores, or you can use the list of representative groups on page 85 to find representatives selling to these shops.

There are a wide variety of gift shops that sell a wide variety of books. And there are several ways to get your book into gift shop buyers' hands. Use the information provided in this section paired with your own research to create a gift shop sales strategy that works for you.

14. SPECIALTY STORES

Specialty stores target niche markets, which are made up of identifiable groups of people with a common interest. Marketing to these niches entails identifying groups of people interested in your topic, finding out where they gather or seek information on that topic, and making your book available in those locations. The range of people's interests is infinitely broad, and the places they can explore their interests are numerous. Thus, there are many opportunities to market your title based upon its topic. Depending on your title, you could sell your book in home-improvement centers, pet shops, auto-supply stores, camera shops, toy stores, garden-supply stores, or computer stores. Your opportunities are limited only by your creativity.

BOOK SELECTION CRITERIA

There are numerous specialty stores that cater to all different interests, so the types of books that sell well at one, might not do as well at another. However, one point in common among all of the various specialty stores is that softcover books sell better than hardcover books—with the possible exception of inspirational titles. Furthermore, a French flap often helps sales, especially on inspirational books.

> **TIP**
> French flaps are softcover books with extended covers that are folded inwards. They create the look of a dust jacket, provide additional space for biographies, and give readers the ability to use the flap as a bookmark.

Another similarity between most specialty stores is the price at which books sell best. Steve Meyerhoff is a book buyer for Home Design Alternatives (HDA), a distribution partner that works with specialty stores. He said, "The price varies by account, but twenty dollars and below is a good 'sweet spot,' although some books sell better at fifteen dollars and below. But what I really look for is *value.*" Buyers also look for high-quality products, because they want to make sure the books they select can withstand rough handling in the stores and still look good. When Steve looks at a book, he compares its value to a consumer to its price. If those two variables are balanced, there is a better chance of the book being accepted.

In order to be sold in a specialty store, your book must have an EAN barcode and a thirteen-digit ISBN.

○ You can purchase ISBNs at www.bowker.com

○ For a list of EAN suppliers, go to
   www.isbn.org/standards/home/isbn/us/barcode.asp

However, it is less certain whether or not the price should be printed on the book. Steve said, "It can be good, and for the most part I want the price on the book. However, this can cause a problem because the retailer cannot change it." You will probably find it most advantageous to have the price on the cover. Consumers want to know the price of products before they go to the checkout counter, and retailers can always add a discount if they want to run a special deal.

In most cases, your book will be displayed with the cover facing out, so your cover design is a critical factor. For this reason, the business buyer at Select Media, another distribution partner that works with specialty stores, prefers publishers to send a finished book whenever possible, not a Book Layout and Design (BLAD) or a galley if it can be avoided. If that is not possible, send a full-color cover with sample chapters and a sell sheet. To see an example sell sheet for this book, turn to page 327.

It is important to note that buyers in this market segment are not motivated by marketing summaries, testimonials, or willingness to conduct in-store author events. "Unless you are a national or local celebrity or authority, in-store events, signings, or classes do not sell books," said Steve. In actuality, the information that is important to specialty store buyers is the title's sales history in dollars and units. If you can prove that the book has sold well in a competitive retail environment, it means more than your endorsements. For this reason, buyers often look to Nielson BookScan to see what books are selling in key categories.

T
I
P
Nielson BookScan is the central clearinghouse for the United States book industry. It collects weekly point-of-sale information from a variety of retailers, and then makes its comprehensive reports available to retailers, publishers, and the media.

Reviews can also impact buyers' decisions, either positively or negatively. Although they read publishing industry reviews, such as those in *Publishers Weekly*, specialty store buyers are more likely to give credence to reviews and articles in specialty retail magazines like *Gourmet News* or *Home Center News*, depending on the type of store they work for. Furthermore, an article about a specific topic, like slow cooking in *Gourmet News*, might influence a buyer's decision. Steve said, "Then I know it's an important category and I will look for books on that subject." For more information about reviews and other promotional tactics, see *Chapter Six. Promoting to Non-Trade Buyers* (page 259).

CROSS-MERCHANDISING

Specialty stores create a unique opportunity for cross-merchandising, which is sometimes called the related-item approach. This technique involves promoting your book by pairing it with a related book or product. The purpose of this is to get customers to buy both items—often at a lower price than if they bought the same two items separately. Amazon.com's Buy X, Get Y advertising program is an example of cross-promoting with books. It allows you to increase the visibility of your book by pairing it with top-selling books or products, and offers shoppers added value for purchasing both items simultaneously.

○ You can learn more about Amazon.com's Buy X, Get Y program at www.booksurge.com/category/1233214081/1/Buy-X-Get-Y-on-Amazon.com.htm

Both Home Design Alternatives and Select Media look for titles that can be cross-merchandised to help sell other products throughout their stores. Therefore, when you submit your book, show the buyers that you understand this concept and give them examples of how they can use your book in cross-promotions. For example, your cookbook might be the perfect match for a promotional program with Omaha Steaks or George Foreman Grills. Or, your children's book might pair well with games or plush toys.

In addition to working well in brick-and-mortar stores, cross-merchandising also works well through online-shopping websites, like Amazon.com. Search the Internet for companies with products that might accompany your book, and then exchange links. If you can find a product with which your book can be cross-merchandised, you will have a better chance of getting your title selected in this market.

BENEFITS OF SELLING TO SPECIALTY STORES

Several benefits accompany specialty store sales. For example, large bookstores have thousands of competitive books surrounding yours on their shelves, yearning for the browser's attention. At specialty stores, however, there is much less competition, so the chance that shoppers will select your title significantly increases. In addition:

■ When people go to a specialty store, they want specific information and they are willing to pay for it, so you do not have to offer as deep of discounts as you do at bookstores.

■ You can be specific in the ways in which you contact people and the benefits you present, so your promotional dollars are more efficient and there is less wasted circulation.

■ It may be easier to sell to specialty stores than to larger retailers, because proprietors of small businesses look upon books favorably—both as a special service to their customers, and as a source of incremental revenue.

■ Most specialty stores purchase books directly from publishers, so you may not have to offer distribution discounts.

■ Individual specialty store orders will typically be smaller than those from your larger customers, but you will find that the buying period is shorter, that the process is less formal, and that you can impact buyers through mass communications.

If you are persistent and diligent in your attempts to sell to various specialty stores, and you do your research before contacting buyers, then you will most likely get your book in somewhere. As this list of benefits proves, your time and effort will pay off in profit.

KNOW WHAT THE STORES ARE SELLING

As you now know, there are thousands of specialty stores that cater to all different niches. However, even stores that compete in the same general markets often seek different arrays of books. For example, Michaels, an arts and crafts store, looks for traditional crafting titles on topics such as knitting, crocheting, scrap booking, and arranging faux floral, as well as bridal titles, cooking titles, and children's books—especially activity, coloring, and educational books. On the other hand, one of Michaels' competitors, Aaron Brothers, looks for a slightly different array of titles, and seeks out books on subjects like art, painting, and crafting, as well as those about photos and framing.

Similarly, stores known for home improvement products are not all alike in their need for books. Lowe's seeks titles on home improvement, décor, gardening, bird watching, and cooking, while Sherwin Williams looks specifically for home improvement and décor titles that are related to painting, and Menards looks for all types of books: home improvement, gardening, health and fitness, business, sports, cooking, bestsellers, children's, pets, and bird watching. Thus, when you visit specialty stores with which you think your book may be a good fit, get a sense for the image they are trying to project and the books they are already selling (if any). If your title does not fit their image or existing product line, perhaps you are better off directing your efforts elsewhere.

SELLING TO SPECIALTY STORES

When you contact specialty stores, sell your book to their buyers in terms that are important to them. This is done by describing how your book will increase their profit per square foot, as well as how your media promotion will stimulate traffic through their stores. Using this approach will help you prove that you know what their customers want, and that your titles will help increase their overall sales. The following list includes additional tips that will help you sell to specialty stores:

■ Make it easy for specialty store buyers to use your books after they buy them by providing free, countertop displays with the purchase of a minimum quantity. Be sure to include instructions for reordering your books to refill the displays. There are several companies that manufacture point-of-purchase display materials, including City Diecutting, George Patton Associates, and Merchandising Systems.

❑ City Diecutting, Inc., One Cory Rd., Morristown, NJ 07960
   Tel: 973-270-0370; Website: www.bookdisplays.com

❑ George Patton Associates, Inc., 55 Broadcommon Rd., Bristol, RI 02809
   Tel: 800-572-2194; Website: www.displays2go.com/counter_displays.htm

❑ Merchandising Systems, Inc., 2951 Whipple Rd., Union City, CA 94587
   Tel: 510-477-9100; Website: www.wireline.net/index.aspx

■ Give retailers cross-merchandising ideas. For example, if your book is about forgiveness, you could suggest that they place it near a flower or candy display.

■ When selling to larger specialty stores, contact their individual department buyers, rather than their general store item buyers. This is because the cookware buyer, for example, may be amenable to purchasing your cookbook, while general store buyers may not see its value.

■ Research each niche to learn its idiosyncrasies, discounts, terms, and distribution methods. You can find this information by going to nearby stores that are appropriate to your title and speaking to the managers. Ask them for insight on how to sell to the industry and follow up with the leads you are given.

■ Read magazines and attend trade shows to learn about the industry and to network with the exhibitors and attendees. You can find trade shows and magazines devoted to almost any topic on which books are published. For example, if your title is on a topic associated with music, you might attend the American Music Therapy Association Conference, the Music Industries Association of Canada Annual Conference and Trade Show, and subscribe to *DJ Times* magazine.

○ Find lists of trade shows at www.biztradeshows.com/usa/usa-tradeshows.mp?industry=printing

○ Find lists of magazines at
   http://en.wikipedia.org/wiki/List_of_United_States_magazines

■ Be willing to customize your products—form and content—for an industry or customer. Some stores may want your book in a special size to fit their shelves or existing display racks; others may prefer casebound or softcover books. In short, sell people books specialty-store buyers want to buy.

■ Sell benefits, not books. Prove to buyers that your book can help them improve their profits or provide some other advantage that is important to them.

If applicable, demonstrate that you have successfully sold your book through other, similar outlets.

In this marketplace, discounts through wholesalers and distributors are between 55 and 65 percent off list price, and books are fully returnable. Specialty-store buyers will occasionally buy on a non-returnable basis, but that is rare. According to Steve, before you contact specialty-store buyers, "You should walk the floor. Know where your book will be in the store. With what products could it be cross-merchandised? Think about how your book will sell in the consumer environment." That way, when you go to the buyer you can suggest placement in the store and offer ideas about similar or complementary products with which your book could be paired.

Furthermore, this research by walking around is also important because it shows you what the stores are buying. Steve said, "You may think that buyers want books, but what they really want is a way to meet their customers' needs. In this context you could provide your information as a CD, DVD, or audio book, too. People want products and information that can help them complete some specific project. We want to give them that information in the form in which they want it." Therefore, take note of different stores' existing product lines and adapt your content to fit in with them if possible.

Finally, if specialty stores do not want to buy what you are selling, then sell them what they want to buy. Large chains sometimes commission authors or publishers to provide them with custom content. Therefore, if your publishing company specializes in a particular genre, you should contact buyers in stores serving that niche and ask what content they would like to have but currently do not. Then offer to fill that void with a customized book.

SUBMITTING YOUR BOOK

Different stores have different buying procedures, and if you do not follow each store's specific guidelines when submitting your book, it may not get considered. Some stores post their submission guidelines online, but if you cannot find them there you can always call or visit local stores and ask the managers what to submit and to whom. Find out if you must use a distribution partner, and if so, which ones are preferred. Also find out what the traditional sales percentages are and educate yourself about the industry operating procedures and expectations. Finally, ask about the major industry trade shows, magazines, and associations.

The following list provides information about three of the major distribution partners that work with specialty stores:

■ *Home Design Alternatives.* HDA is a large distributor of books and magazines to the home improvement, craft, home décor, discount, kid's, and cooking specialty retail channels. It customizes its programs to fit the needs of all its retail partners using books, magazines, cross merchandising, and promotional displays. Some of the stores HDA sells to are Michaels, Lowe's, Menards, Sherwin Williams, Bed, Bath & Beyond, Macy's, and Sears.

❑ Home Design Alternatives, 944 Anglum Rd., St. Louis, MO 63042
   Tel: 314-770-2222; Website: www.hdainc.com

■ *Select Media.* Select Media creates and manages customized publications programs for specialty retailers. It focuses on the needs of each store's customers in order to maximize its retailers' sales. Select Media distributes books to arts and crafts, discount, home improvement and décor, online, natural and organic foods, office supply, consumer electronics, sporting goods, and video and entertainment retailers. Some of the stores Select Media sells to include Office Max, Office Depot, Staples, Home Depot, Hobby Lobby, and AC Moore.

❑ Select Media; Attn: Book Buyer for (your topic), 1685 Boggs Rd., Ste. 400,
   Duluth, GA 30096
   Tel: 678-380-9880, 888-236-9457; Website: www.selectmediaservices.com

■ *Source Interlink.* Source Interlink markets entertainment products including magazines, books, and related items. It operates 110,000 retail storefronts for more than 1,000 retail chains, including most every household name in specialty retail. Source Interlink manages more than 2 million square feet of distribution and fulfillment facilities, and another 1.1 million square feet of manufacturing space for their in-store display operations. It delivers magazines, DVDs, CDs, and books either next day or second day to retailers, as well as directly to consumers through third party carriers.

❑ Source Interlink Companies; 27500 Riverview Center Blvd., Bonita Springs, FL
   34134
   Tel: 239-949-4450; Website: www.sourceinterlink.com

Once you have decided which (if any) distribution partners you are going to contact, you need to determine when you should contact them. Timing is everything. Steve, as well as most other buyers, is "looking for the right book at the right time, for the right price and place." Each company is different, but all require advance planning. A general rule is to submit your book at least three months in advance—four or five months if possible. Although you should always double check your timing with the company to which you plan on sending your submission.

RETAIL SOURCING

Retail sourcing companies are outside businesses that act as buyers for large retail chains. Since buying is the only thing they do, their services extend beyond those of wholesalers and distributors. They handle every aspect of getting products into stores, including selecting new products, negotiating prices, finding manufacturers, packaging products, and more, which saves retailers money. Essentially, retail sourcing companies streamline the distribution system of getting products out to customers and look for the deepest possible discounts when doing so in order to provide the best price for their retailers.

Some retail operations, such as Petco, require that sellers work through their retail sourcing company, Siennax. There is no cost to set up a network with Siennax, but if it does accept your book, you will have to pay an annual charge based on sales—at a minimum of $300.

❑ Siennax Sourcing Services; 171 Saxony Rd., Encinitas, CA 92024
   Tel: 858-385-8900, 800-717-4565; Website: www.siennax.com

Conversely, other companies like PetSmart, do not work through the same sourcing process. PetSmart actually requires sellers to have an account with Baker and Taylor, its exclusive media vendor (see page 183). Because of these variances, when you decide which large specialty chains you want to target, you should call them to find out if they have a distribution or sourcing partner with which you will be required to work.

MATCHING YOUR TOPIC TO SPECIALTY STORES

Be creative when you are deciding through which specialty stores you want to try to sell your books. To help you with this, you should look at your product not as a book, but as an accessory to a particular industry. For example, if you have a title on how to dress for success, you might consider selling it through office-supply stores like Staples, as well as through stores that sell clothing to business executives, such as Burberry or Brooks Brothers. Furthermore, do not limit yourself to brick-and-mortar stores. There are online retail outlets that you should be sure to explore, as well.

Again, in the specialty store segment your creativity is the only thing that will stifle you. Figure 2.3 provides several examples that should stimulate your creative side and get you thinking about more places in which you can sell books.

Figure 2.3. Potential Sales Outlets Based on Category

If Your Title Is About	Consider Selling it Here
Pets	Pet stores, veterinarians, aquariums, kennels, pet supply companies, doggie bakeries, gift shops, book clubs, catalogs
Cooking, Diet	Gourmet shops, dieticians, nutritionists, department stores, supermarkets, cookware stores, home stores, food stores, health food stores, companies that sell ingredients for your recipes, food stands, campgrounds, book clubs, catalogs, fish markets

If Your Title Is About	Consider Selling it Here
Health, Fashion, Beauty	Drug stores, doctors' offices, airport stores, barber shops, beauty salons, clothing stores, college stores, book clubs, catalogs, fitness centers, gyms, plus-size stores, health food stores
Child Care, Children's Topics	Toy stores, daycare centers, nannies, au pairs, children's hospitals, children's museums, zoos, parks, Christmas shops, book clubs, catalogs, companies that produce children's items (apparel, vitamins, toys), maternity shops, juvenile furniture stores, juvenile clothing stores, school-supply stores, educational stores, novelty stores, libraries, video stores
Travel, Regional Titles, Recreation	RV dealerships, travel agents, airport stores, cruise ships, luggage stores, camera shops, gas stations, book clubs, marinas, catalogs, libraries, hotel gift shops, tourist shops, chambers of commerce, automobile dealerships
Religious, Family Life, Inspirational, or Spiritual Topics	Meditation centers, retreats, churches, book clubs, catalogs, church libraries, hospital gift shops, prison libraries, religious stores
Sports, Recreation, Games	Sporting-goods stores, country clubs, pro shops, Little League, stadiums, tennis club, gun shops, book clubs, catalogs, fitness centers, gyms, department stores, hobby shops, toy stores
Fiction	Supermarkets, discount stores, companies for use as gifts, book clubs, catalogs, hotel gift shops, cruise ships, florists

The specialty store marketplace provides a wonderful opportunity to innovate. Based upon your ability to match your content to your customers' needs, you could potentially sell your books through a variety of stores in a variety of locations. This market opens a vast array of new outlets and new sources of increased revenue.

CREATING YOUR OWN MAILING LISTS

You should now have an idea about the types of specialty stores through which you could potentially sell your title. The next step is to figure out how to reach those outlets. The North American Industry Classification System (NAICS) is a system used to classify business establishments—including specialty stores—into groups based upon the activity in which they are primarily engaged. The NAICS replaced the Standard Industrial Classification (SIC) system in 1997, and it uses a six-digit coding system—unlike the old four-digit SIC codes—to classify all economic activity into categories.

❏ NAICS Association, 129 Lakeshore Dr., Rockaway, NJ 07866
  Tel: 973-625-5626;
  Website: www.naics.com

Every business, organization, and association has a NAICS code specific to its category. For example, every sporting goods store has the same NAICS code, every health organization has the same NAICS code, every craft store has the same NAICS code, and so on.

○ You can search for NAICS codes by keyword at www.naics.com/search.htm

○ You can also download a list of NAICS codes at
  www.census.gov/epcd/naics02/naico602.txt

You could spend hundreds of dollars each year purchasing several different mailing lists from several different companies. Or, you could choose to purchase the NAICS Association's database of over 14 million United States businesses that allows you to create custom mailing lists for every business category. NAICS sells business directories with online or CD-ROM access to company profiles on over 14 million United States businesses.

○ To learn more about and purchase the NAICS business marketing software,
  go to www.naics.com/Service-CustomLists.html

Once you have the NAICS code(s) that relates to your topic, enter it into the NAICS software and you will instantly have a list of the names, addresses, phone numbers, fax numbers, websites, and email addresses of every United States business in that category. Therefore, instead of paying several different companies for access to their niche mailing lists, you can use this software to create as many customized mailing lists as you want.

Be aware that there are some problems with this software, though. First, the names of businesses are sometimes abbreviated oddly, so it might take you some time to figure out their real names. Second, since it takes time to gather information, some of the software's contact information may be out of date. Finally, businesses are sometimes categorized incorrectly, and are therefore given the wrong NAICS code. Because of this, it is a good idea to go through the information the software pulls out for you and make sure each listing provides the material for which you were looking.

Specialty stores cater to specific groups of people. The people who frequent the stores with which your book pairs well are pre-qualified potential buyers. But you have to make it happen. Since many of these stores do not sell books as primary items, you have to begin the sales process by convincing them to take on yours. Be creative, be thorough, and be persistent, and you will most likely find success in this market.

15. BOOK CLUBS

In the 1950s and 60s, the major book clubs in the United States had tremendous sales and comprised a huge part of the non-trade book market. As time went on, however, the cost of mailing increased and online bookstores began to erode book clubs' sales. Because of these factors, many of the old, established book clubs shrank in size or disappeared altogether. Even so, book clubs are still around and can be a viable marketplace for publishers.

There is a book club for almost every conceivable interest, including clubs for children, entrepreneurs, minorities, sports fans, and many more. All clubs are attuned to the interests of their members, and accordingly, their buyers have narrowly focused needs. Furthermore, even though discounts in this market may approach 80 percent, there is an opportunity to make large, non-returnable sales. You can also make up for the deep discount with all of the inexpensive advertising your book will receive by potentially passing through many hands with one sale.

BENEFITS OF BOOK CLUB SALES

Look at book clubs as you look at distribution partners—they both help you reach specific markets more economically than you could yourself. Book clubs do this by selling your books to their members on a non-returnable basis, and then providing you a percentage of the sale. The advantages of book club sales are numerous and are described in the following list:

■ Acceptance by a book club adds credibility to your title and gives you an opportunity to send out a new press release. You should also include the fact that your title is a book club selection on all of your marketing materials. This may enhance your chances of getting on a television show or having a story written about you, which will in turn lead to increased sales.

■ Books are sold to book clubs on a non-returnable basis, so you will not have to worry about costly returns.

■ When book clubs send sales-promotional literature that includes your book to their members, they are essentially providing inexpensive advertising for you, and also facilitating word-of-mouth communication about your book.

■ Book clubs represent a practical means of reaching your target markets. Since there are separate book clubs for almost every interest, the mass market has already been broken down for you.

■ Book club sales typically enhance bookstore sales.

■ In some cases, a book club may help cover your printing costs. If the book club purchases your book while you are preparing for your initial print run, you can print a larger quantity (including the books for your inventory), thereby significantly lowering your unit production costs. If instead they buy copies from your stock, they will generally pay production costs, plus a royalty of 10 to 15 percent.

The following example should help put these benefits into a real life perspective. The Vegetarian Resource Group publishes the *Lowfat Jewish Vegetarian Cookbook*. VRG offered this title through a Jewish book club. "We gave a good discount, so it was a good moneymaker for the groups, and it was a way for us to distribute the information to a niche audience and beyond. Though there was a low profit margin, it enabled us to print a larger quantity of the book." As a result of this book club sale, Debra Wasserman, the author of the *Lowfat Jewish Vegetarian Cookbook,* ended up doing cooking demonstrations on both Good Morning America and CNN, and also appeared on the Discovery Channel.

While general book clubs have experienced a decline in sales, niche book club sales have remained stable. If you have quality content that meets the specific needs of a club's members, you can potentially make a solid sale, and also experience all of the other previously described benefits.

SELLING TO BOOK CLUBS

Book club sales will vary depending on the procedures of each club. The term-length for most book club contracts is two to three years, during which time the book club has the right to distribute your book to its members as it sees fit. Generally, the major book club licenses require exclusive book club rights, meaning you cannot sell your book to any other book club. However, many of the niche clubs do not require exclusivity.

The majority of large book clubs print their own books, because printers now have the ability to print shorter runs. These clubs' runs are typically 3,000 to 5,000 books. One thing you should try to do is either get the club to buy into your run, or attach a certain number of books to theirs. That way, your unit cost will decrease because you will be printing a larger number of books. Smaller clubs will generally buy anywhere from 300 to 700 books from your existing inventory and make repeat orders if necessary.

When you contact book clubs they will usually tell you their standard terms, which will give you an idea about what price they are seeking. Do not offer them a price first. One author learned this the hard way by offering a book club an 80 percent discount, only to find out later that it only needed 65 percent. Once a book club makes you an offer, you should then see if you can make the deal work. The price needs to cover the discount to the book club—which can be as much as 80 percent—your production costs, your profit, and the author's royalty. Finally, you should request to get the money upfront, although it is sometimes difficult to do.

The royalties you can typically expect for book club sales are approximately 4 to 8 percent of the club's list price (which may be 70 percent off your book's list price), depending on whether your book is softcover or hardcover. However, the royalty percentage may be even less if your book is used as a premium. A typical advance against royalties offered by book clubs is minimal. In other words, you generally will only be paid a small amount of your royalty upfront, and will receive the rest later.

When selling to book clubs it is unlikely that you will make a lot of money on each book sold, and most niche clubs do not have a large enough member base to make up that money in volume. Therefore, it is important to work out a deal with the club that allows you to make at least some money on each sale; then simply use the club as one part of your revenue mix as you experience all of the other benefits that come with having your book selected by it, including the free advertising and prestige.

SUBMITTING YOUR BOOK

When submitting your book to various book clubs for consideration, it is best to contact their buyers six months before its publication date. But wait until you have compiled an edited and relatively complete manuscript with a finished cover design. If your book is already in print, book club buyers will usually still be open to evaluating it if its content meets their members' requirements.

Each club has its own submission guidelines, so call before you send your materials to find out what they are. You should also review clubs' websites and look for examples of the copy they use to describe competitive books. This way you will be able to provide the buyers with a sample of the selling copy you think would be most effective in presenting your book favorably.

Finally, the same advice for crafting your cover letter applies here as it does to other non-trade markets: focus on benefits. Book club buyers are not as concerned with selling your books as they are with making their members happy. You may have the greatest book ever published, but what the clubs want to know is why and how it will benefit their particular members.

FINDING EXISTING BOOK CLUBS

The Internet is changing the world of book clubs, and now, somewhere around 90 percent of them are extensions of magazines, organizations, or associations. This is because many of the smaller, independent clubs can no longer financially sustain themselves, but the magazines, organizations, and associations have the ability to promote the book clubs through their magazines and websites.

In 2000, two of the largest independent book clubs—Book of the Month Club and Doubleday—merged together. The result was a company called Bookspan, which was jointly owned by Time Warner and Bertelsmann until Bertelsmann took complete control in 2007. Then in 2008, Bertelsmann sold sister companies

Bookspan and Direct Brands, Inc. to Najafi Companies, a private investment firm. Together, Direct Brands, Inc. and Bookspan are the largest direct-to-consumer distributors of media products in the United States and Canada. Bookspan operates about forty book clubs in several categories including general interest, lifestyles, history, military, science-fiction, and more. Combined, these clubs boast over 8 million members.

❏ Bookspan/Direct Brands, Inc.; 501 Franklin Ave., Garden City, NY 11530
   Tel: 516-490-4561; Website: www.directbrands.com

Aside from Bookspan, the best way to find book clubs relevant to your book's topic is to search the Internet. You can begin by searching for magazines, organizations, or associations whose interests and target markets are the same as yours, and contacting them to see if they have a book club. Beyond that, you can also search for independent, niche book clubs. Listed below are some of the websites that provide lists of book clubs by interest area; they should give your search a good jump-start.

○ www.bookclubdirectory.com   ○ www.booksonline.com

○ www.book-clubs.com   ○ www.freebookclubs.com

Once you find the book clubs that are best for your content, submit your book as you would to any other business partner. Provide reasons why it is in their best interest to sell your book and describe how your promotional plans will help them move more books through their system. Give information on competitive titles and why your book is different from, and better than them. See the inset on page 260 for tips on creating professional sales-promotional materials for your submission package. Make it easy for buyers to say "yes" and you may hear that word more frequently.

START YOUR OWN BOOK CLUB

Another possible way to sell books in this market is to start your own book club, although doing this is only possible in extremely niche marketplaces with high levels of interest. Furthermore, you need to have enough titles to be able to sustain the club for an extended period of time—having just one or two books will not work. If you think you have the ability to start your own club, you should go to as many conventions related to your topic as you can in order to network and create mailing lists. You can then trade lists with other companies in that market to expand your own.

Wes Green's story is a great example of how setting up a new book club works. Wes started his own book club through his company, Linguality. Linguality republishes foreign language books in their original language. Wes' twist is that he includes a glossary opposite each page so the content becomes a language course. He even includes a CD containing an interview with the author in each book. Linguality groups six books together, in French or Italian, and sells them on a continuity basis. Readers subscribe to the six-book series and receive one book at a time.

Wes advertises his books in full-page ads in the *New York Times Book Review,* the *Washington Post Book Review,* the *Los Angeles Times Book Review,* the *Economist,* and the *Atlantic Monthly.* Since the people who read these publications are generally upscale, urban, educated, fifty-year olds who love to travel, they fit Wes' target market and are a great way to help him entice people to join his book club and buy his books. You may be wondering how he can afford all of that advertising; there are several reasons, and they are included in the following list:

■ By bypassing retail outlets and selling to consumers directly, Wes avoids paying a distributor's discount, which can amount to 65 percent or more.

■ Wes creates greater value for his content by writing his own sales descriptions about his books. When people believe they are getting their money's worth they may be less eager to seek out the same book at a lower price elsewhere. He also charges for shipping, which increases his profit margin, as well.

■ Wes is paid up front for the full six-book series. This tactic is called "loading up," and you can do it when you receive initial orders for the first book in a continuity series. Make buyers an offer to ship the remaining volumes for free if they pay for them up front. If you have created sufficient value in your sales literature, you may be able to get them to purchase the entire series with no price concessions. The loading up process is described in more detail in *39. Implement Effective Mail-Order Campaigns* (page 274).

■ Since Wes has an accurate forecast of demand, he prints to order instead of carrying a large inventory. By communicating prepublication with people on your subscription list, you can generate firm orders that will help you forecast what your own initial print quantity should be.

■ Wes buys his advertising "off the rate card," meaning that he gets a substantial discount and buys ad space "at much less than you would expect," he said. You can do the same thing by purchasing ad space close to a publication's release date. This is because most publications would rather sell open ad space at a lower rate than not sell the space at all.

■ Finally, Wes keeps a record of the names and addresses of the people who buy book subscriptions from him. This allows him to build and maintain a continuously updated mailing list through which he can sell subscription renewals and other related products, such as literary trips to Europe.

The money Wes makes and saves with these unique marketing techniques more than pays for his advertising space. Through Linguality, Wes has carved out a niche market and created a book club to sell to it. This innovative combination has led to a lucrative business with a bright future for expansion.

As you can see, there are many reasons why book clubs—particularly those that reach your target niches—can be a profitable addition to your marketing mix; though the major benefits may be more related to the credibility that comes with having your book selected by a book club, rather than the actual profits you will receive from the sale. A book club can be a valuable weapon in your marketing arsenal by facilitating word-of-mouth communication about your book and enhancing sales through other outlets, such as bookstores. Use book clubs as a valuable adjunct to your overall marketing strategy and you may experience a significant jump in your overall revenue.

16. CATALOG MARKETING

In the United States, there are over 14,000 printed catalogs in existence and there are thousands more online. According to the National Mail Order Association, 9,000 are consumer catalogs, and the other 5,000 are for business-to-business sales. Many of these are niche catalogs, which target groups of people potentially interested in specific topics.

○ For more information about the National Mail Order Association,
go to www.nmoa.com

Catalogs act as sales brochures for your title—helping you build awareness in your target markets. They commonly deliver an image of your book's cover, as well as its major selling points to thousands—or tens of thousands—of potential buyers. This additional exposure to people in your target markets enhances your credibility and your long-term sales. Furthermore, the recognition may spill over into increased bookstore sales, as well.

SELLING TO CATALOGS

When selling to catalogs, the first step is to become familiar with those that reach your target markets. You should be creative when doing this. For example, the World Almanac Education (WAE) catalog sells books and other items to librarians that serve students from kindergarten through high school. You might initially expect that buyers for this catalog would only seek books for children. However, Pam Matthews, one of WAE's buyers said that "The kindergarten through twelfth grade market also includes books for 'grown-ups.' If your book interests high school kids or fits in well with what they are reading in school, get in touch with me."

❍ For more information about WAE, go to www.waebooks.com

Charles Stahler of the Vegetarian Resource Group provides another example. He sold their books, *Meatless Meals for Working People* and *Vegan Meals for One or Two,* through the People for the Ethical Treatment of Animals (PETA) catalog. The catalog purchased the books since they furthered the group's aim of not eating meat.

In addition to helping you potentially expand the number of catalogs that reach your target market, being creative can also help you in another way. As it is in bookstores, the competition in catalogs is very intense, so it is difficult for your title to stand out. One way to minimize this challenge is to seek out specialty catalogs that sell products that complement your book. This way, your book becomes an accessory item. As Dan Poynter, author of *The Self-Publishing Manual,* said, "I do not sell a book about parachuting, but a parachute accessory." This strategy removes your title from the *book* category, and places it in the *specialty* category, which not only makes it stand out, but also allows you to command a higher price.

If you have never seen a particular catalog that you think might reach your target market, you should request a copy. Actually seeing the catalog will give you a better feel for how your book might sell through it. Then, when you contact the buyer you will be able to describe how your product relates to the other items offered in his or her catalog.

You should also investigate catalogs' websites before you contact buyers. You may find that you could potentially sell more books than you first thought, or perhaps you will discover that you should sell your book differently to them. For example, the WAE catalog sells sets of books from different publishers. Therefore, you may be better off presenting your book as part of a proposed set, or you may already have a set of books you can sell to them as a package. WAE also sells kits. While these are developed mostly in-house, WAE does purchase books from vendors to include in these kits. The bottom line is that you should be familiar with the websites, terminology, target customers, and product lines for each of the catalogs in your target markets before you contact the buyers.

Selling through catalogs can improve your profit if you are judicious in selecting those that reach people interested in the content of your book. By making sure your content is right for each before making your submissions, you will increase your chances of success.

PRICES, PAYMENT, AND SALES

Catalogs purchase books for inventory, not to fill orders, which allows you to save money by shipping in fewer, larger quantities. They rarely require an exclusive selling agreement, and most will pay you in thirty days. Furthermore, catalog sales are generally non-returnable, and the catalog company usually pays for shipping.

It is important to note that catalogs pride themselves on high fill rates, meaning that they fill and ship orders quickly. Maintaining this reputation requires a sense of partnership with their suppliers—including publishers. Therefore, you must meet your deadlines.

There is no standard discount among catalogs, so you have some negotiating flexibility. WAE seeks a minimum discount of 55 percent, but its buyers may try to get a discount of 60 percent or more if they believe they can sell a large quantity of your book. You should always make a counter proposal if you feel the discount offered to you is unfair.

Once a sale is completed, it is important for publishers to work closely with the catalog buyer. For Pam Matthews, "Responsiveness is the big thing." Pam has to make decisions quickly and accurately, and she needs the publisher to be responsive to her needs. "I may need samples, pricing, or information on availability, and when I do, I need it quickly," she said.

Since most catalog companies do a small-scale test first, do not expect a large order immediately after a sale is made. Note, however, that the term "small-scale" is relative, because a test may require 500 or more copies of your book. The time period in which orders will occur varies with the frequency of the catalog's publication—some publish monthly, others quarterly—as well as with the applicability of your product to the buying period and complementary products.

Finally, catalog buyers sometimes fear that small publishers will not be able to stock to their demand. For this reason, they may require you to hold inventory suf-

IT PAYS TO BE PERSISTENT

Just because a catalog originally turns down your submission does not mean that you should give up. Author Jim Leisy knows about this type of persistence. It took him two and a half years to get his book, *Common Errors in English Usage*, into the WAE catalog. He was regularly told by WAE buyers that there was no room in their catalog for his title. "You'll have to wait until we drop something else," they said. Finally, something dropped and his book was in. "Now it's a regular," Jim said.

Jim also has a similar tale to tell with the Signals catalog, which is owned by Ohio-based Universal Direct Fulfillment Corporation. Jim went to them with his calendar, *Far From the Madding Gerund*, but the buyer said, "We do not do calendars." Jim persisted, though, and finally saw a calendar in one of their catalogs. He questioned the buyer, who then told him to submit his calendar, which he did. "They picked it up and it does fine," he said. As you can see, it pays to be persistent.

ficient to meet their expected sales. Offer them proof that you can and will do so, or that you can reprint and deliver within a suitable time. You may also have to guarantee your price for the period of your contract. If you cannot meet their requirements, you may have to reconsider using catalogs as a selling tool.

SUBMITTING YOUR BOOK

The best time to submit your book to catalog buyers is when they are in the decision-making period for the issue in which you want your book to appear. For example, the decisions for a catalog of gift ideas for the fourth-quarter holiday season are made in the first quarter of the year. In other words, if you want your book featured in a winter holiday catalog, you should submit it in January, February, or March. To find out when each catalog's decision-making periods are, all you need to do is call and ask.

When you call, you should also ask how their buyers like to be contacted. Pam Matthews prefers that you initially email her to describe your book or proposal. If there is any interest on her part to continue, she will request your literature, marketing material, and a link to your website if you have one. Jim Leisy agreed that you should contact the buyers how they want to be contacted. "Call first to find out who the buyers are and then ask their preference. You will get screened before you talk to the buyer, but you will eventually be connected with the right person." Do not try to sell at this point, but do ask for their submission guidelines. Then be sure you follow their instructions.

The following list contains some tips about how to put together a submission package that should get you positive results:

■ Include a cover letter and a sell sheet with all the details about your book—from its shipping weight and size, to its major features and benefits. You should include things like how many books are in a case, how many books you have on hand, how quickly you can fill large orders, whether your book is part of a series, and all other relevant information. To see an example of a generic cover letter and sell sheet for this book, see page 326 and page 327, respectively.

■ State your book's list price and your selling terms. Include a comparison of your book's price to competitive books' prices. The optimum price for books sold through catalogs varies. A printed catalog has higher costs, and therefore must sell products in a higher price range. In these catalogs, books priced closer to twenty dollars will have a better chance of being accepted than those priced at ten dollars. On the other hand, books sold through online catalogs should be priced at the lower end of the continuum—around ten dollars.

■ Send a summary marketing plan, which should describe how your ubiquitous promotion will pre-sell your book to the recipients of the catalog. Your plan should also describe your target audience and tell buyers why your title is appropriate for their catalogs' customers. See an outline of a summary marketing plan on page 329.

■ Make your proposal stand out from the others by demonstrating how your book will actually look in buyers' catalogs. One way to do this is to tear out the page in the catalog that you think your book would be best suited and paste a copy of your book's cover, as well as promotional copy directly onto it. Send this page with your proposal.

■ Reviews are an important part of submission packages in this market. The most important reviews to include are those that have been published in journals appropriate to the buyers in your target market segments. General newspaper reviews are usually not as significant to niche catalog buyers, so they are not as important to include. For example, WAE sells to the kindergarten through high school library market, so Pam is most interested in reviews that appear in library review journals. For more information about reviews, see *35. Seek Niche Reviews* (page 259).

■ Awards can sometimes influence buyers, as well. Awards received within your particular niche market are almost always important. But if a catalog is marketed to a national audience, individual state awards are not as important as awards granted by a national competition. For more information about competing for awards, see *38. Participate in Award Competitions* (page 271).

■ Do not automatically send a sample book without permission. Buyers will request a book after they have reviewed the rest of your submission materials if they want one. If and when you finally do send a sample book, know that its cover design is particularly important in catalog sales. On a catalog page, covers are reduced in size to somewhere around one square inch. At that size, everything must still be clear and legible. Colors must have good contrast, and small or script type must be readable. Good content may be rejected because the cover is not designed for catalog sales.

Again, these are simply general suggestions for submitting your book to buyers in this market. Know that the main key to success is learning and following the submission guidelines for each catalog you contact.

FINDING CATALOGS THAT FIT YOUR TITLE

As previously stated, there are over 14,000 printed catalogs in the United States alone. Therefore, the chances that you will find one or more catalogs that suit your title are extremely high. There are several resources that will help you find information about catalogs for every different category. For example, *The*

National Directory of Catalogs published by the National Mail Order Association features detailed information on more than 12,000 consumer and business-to-business catalogs.

○ You can purchase this directory at www.nmoa.org/catalog/mailorderdir.htm

In addition to this directory, some of the best resources for discovering existing catalogs are included in the following list:

■ *CatalogLink.* CatalogLink is an online catalog directory that claims to offer the largest selection of catalogs in the world. CatalogLink.com allows you to search over 12,000 catalogs by name and category, as well as request your choice of catalogs to be sent to you for free.

❏ CatalogLink
   Tel: 831-647-6024, 866-746-7005; Website: www.cataloglink.com

■ *Catalogs.com.* Catalogs.com gives you access to more than 500 print and online catalogs—from the world's largest retail companies, to specialized companies providing unique and hard to find items. It also provides information about each catalog, as well as a direct link to the company's online catalog when available.

❏ Catalogs.com; 318 Indian Trace, Ste. 330, Ft. Lauderdale, FL 33326
   Tel: 954-659-9005; Website: www.catalogs.com

■ *Google Catalogs.* The Google Catalogs website allows you to find catalogs by category, and also has a searchable index. Additionally, this website allows you to flip through the pages of all of the catalogs it lists. This feature benefits you because when you find a catalog that reaches your target market, you can look to see if your book could potentially fit in with the other products it sells.

❏ Google Catalogs
   Website: http://catalogs.google.com

There are many benefits to selling through catalogs, one of which is the fact that you can sell large quantities of books. Catalogs also expose your name and title to thousands of people interested in your topic—people who may also spread the word about your book to their friends. This word-of-mouth advertising is a very effective way to get positive exposure for you and your book, which may in turn lead to increased sales in bookstores and other markets.

Chapter Three

Non-Trade Non-Retail Markets

Not all books are sold through retail outlets. There are non-retail outlets that buy books, as well, including corporations, associations, schools, government agencies, the armed services, and libraries. These outlets get books to end-users indirectly, and often buy them for use as textbooks, premiums, advertising specialties, motivational and inspirational tools for employees, and many more reasons. It is not necessary to choose either retail or non-retail sales outlets. In fact, you can, and should utilize both marketplaces to optimize your profits.

Most non-retail book sales are made directly; however, select non-retail outlets will also buy through distribution partners. If you choose to sell directly, or are forced to because you are selling to outlets that do not work with distribution partners, you will be required to make a lot of phone calls and personal visits, as well as network and promote—all processes described later in this book. You know your product better than anyone else, so it is up to you to negotiate prices and close deals. This hard work should pay off, though. The non-retail marketplace has the potential to significantly increase your profits.

If you do not like the direct selling process or do not feel you are skilled at it, all is not lost. As previously stated, some of these outlets work with distribution partners. Furthermore, there are premium and incentive agencies, telemarketing firms, fundraising companies, and book-marketing consultants that will represent your titles to businesses. Their fees reduce your profits, but if you view their sales as incremental revenue, you are still better off with them than without.

In this chapter, there are sections that provide detailed discussions about each segment of the non-trade non-retail market. They point out ways in which you can do all of the selling activities yourself, and also describe how and where to find distribution partners that can help you. Additionally, each section describes what criteria buyers use to make their selections and provides relevant contact information, which will significantly expedite your selling process. By the end of this chapter, you will be educated about all aspects of the non-trade non-retail market segment, and will possess all of the necessary information you need to achieve success in the world of non-trade non-retail sales.

17. BUSINESSES

Businesses, both large and small, buy books for many reasons. This creates unique and diverse sales opportunities, which you will learn about throughout this section. Overwhelmingly, non-fiction titles sell best in this marketplace, and the subjects that sell particularly well are motivational, personal growth, sales and marketing, leadership, and team building.

The business buyers with whom you will be negotiating are skilled professionals who are used to dealing with knowledgeable, competent sales people. Thus, you must always be professional when communicating with them. Additionally, you cannot simply wander into business buyers' offices and ask them how they use books, because most have probably never done so. It will be your job to teach them how books can be valuable to their businesses.

WHY BUSINESSES BUY BOOKS

All companies want to increase their sales and profits. Thus, they are always looking for ways to establish loyal relationships with their clients, customers, and employees. They do this by rewarding buyers for making purchases, enticing new customers to join or buy, providing inspirational and motivational tools for their employees, and more. Businesses like to use books for these types of programs for the following reasons:

■ Books are tasteful. "In a way, books define the taste of the giver. Their high-perceived value does not demean the sender or recipient. People like premiums that flatter their intelligence, and books do that," said Mark Resnick, a partner of FRW Company. Guy Achtzehn, president of the premium-sales representative group MSG Promotions, agreed and said, "People have been convinced since childhood that books are valuable and are to be treated with respect."

■ Books can be customized for their recipients in many ways. For example, you can alter a book's cover by printing a company's name on it, or by replacing the original with one of leather. You can also ask company presidents to write the introduction or advertise their related products and services in the back of the book. Finally, the content of books can be tailored to fit special occasions or seasons, to recognize service anniversaries, or to celebrate company landmarks.

However, before you offer to customize your book it is important to note that, "Most companies won't advance the money to pay for the production of a customized book. Be prepared to front the money yourself. Small publishers may be required to put some money in escrow to guarantee that they will fulfill the contract for the books as agreed," said Mark Resnick.

■ Books open the door for author events on company premises or at trade shows. An author appearance may draw in new and diverse clientele for the company.

■ Digital book printing allows companies to test various covers and content in order to find out which are most likely to achieve the objective of their promotion.

■ Books have varied usages and can be given to all types of people. They can be used to reward, motivate, educate, or entertain employees, salespeople, customers, or clients.

■ Books do not have the liability that various other products carry. For example, some toys may contain small parts that can potentially be swallowed by children; if a child is harmed, it can lead to negative publicity and legal problems. The majority of books, however, are harmless, which is why they are appealing sales-promotional products for businesses.

■ Companies can select books to coordinate with a season or holiday. For instance, Nestlé, Betty Crocker, or Pillsbury might purchase a Christmas cookie cookbook for use as a premium during the holiday season.

■ Additional books can be supplied quickly. If a book is customized, once the initial customization is done, printing new books can be done in a matter of weeks. If there is no customization, the publisher may already have sufficient inventory to fill immediate demand while additional books are printed.

■ Books elicit emotions in people that other products like CDs and DVDs do not. However, if shipping costs become an issue, you may want to consider offering your content in a different form.

■ Books can be used in conjunction with other products to create or extend a theme. For example, if a company wanted to promote healthy living among its employees, it could combine a book with a pedometer.

■ Books are good items to use in consumer promotions, because they can motivate consumers to buy other products. For example, they can be used in certain consumer-goods programs where people save coupons, receipts, bottle tops, or some other token to get a book as a reward.

Not all business buyers will be aware of the numerous uses and benefits that books provide. Therefore, you may want to begin the sales process by highlighting them. Then, once the buyers are sold on the business value of books in general, they will be more open to purchasing yours specifically.

HOW BUSINESSES USE BOOKS

There are two main departments within companies that buy and use books. The first is the human resources department, which is internally focused on company employees. The second is the marketing department, which is externally focused on company customers and clients. Of course, variations exist. Smaller companies may not have these formal departments defined, so you will have to dig around to find the appropriate decision maker to contact within them. There are also network marketing companies that work a little differently. The following information discusses all of these departments and variations.

Human Resources

Human resources departments, commonly referred to as HR departments, typically perform traditional administrative personnel functions, look after employee performance and relations, and are in charge of resource planning and allocation. They are internally oriented, so they are interested in books that will help motivate, inspire, educate, and recognize their companies' employees.

Using incentives—like books—to recognize and motivate employees is vital to businesses' success. Frank Katusak, chairman of the Incentive Federation, said "Of large companies—those with revenue of more than $100 million annually—more than half use merchandise incentive programs." Recently, companies using these programs spent $32.7 billion on them in one year. The most common merchandising incentives were used for non-sales employee recognition, followed by business gifts.

○ You can find out more about the Incentive Federation at www.incentivefederation.org

Because of the broad responsibilities of HR departments, several titles can be applicable for sale and use through them. For example, if a book helps employees prepare for retirement, HR department buyers may want to purchase it for their retirement planning programs. Similarly, HR department buyers may also be interested in a book that teaches employees how to improve their health, because it could help the company save money on insurance premiums.

> **TIP**
>
> The Hallmark Insights program can help you reach businesses' HR departments. It offers businesses personalized incentive and reward programs using online gift certificates, which are redeemable for books and other products that have been sold to Hallmark for its Insights program. To learn how to incorporate your book into the Hallmark Insights program, go to www.hallmarkinsights.com/corp/mp.html

In addition to employee education and recognition, another way you can approach HR departments with your title is to propose it as an addition their corporate libraries. If a company has an internal library or is interested in starting one, convince the librarians to add your title to their collections. For more information about library sales in general, see *22. Libraries* (page 175).

Marketing Departments

Marketing departments are externally focused on company customers, and are responsible for promoting, advertising, and branding their companies and products. The job of marketing departments is to increase sales and profits, as well as to set monthly, quarterly, and annual objectives. If you can demonstrate how your book's content can help them reach those goals, you will be greeted by an attentive audience. The following list contains some examples of how and why marketing professionals might use your book as an incentive to help them attain the objectives they set:

■ *Associate with a cause.* If you want to maximize the power of your book as a sales-promotional tool, connect it with a cause. A *PR Week* and Barkley cause survey revealed that nearly three quarters of consumers purchase particular brands because they support a cause in which they believe. Additionally, more than 90 percent of consumers said it is important for companies to support causes and charities. Corporate respondents said they saw positive publicity, an increase in sales and retail traffic, as well as an enhanced relationship with their target demographic as a result of cause-related marketing efforts.

○ For more information on the survey, visit www.barkleyus.com or www.prweek.com

   One cause you might consider getting involved with is organized by Reading is Fundamental (RIF). Every year, RIF provides free books and literacy resources to millions of children and families. This program is sponsored by businesses who donate books and other reading materials. For example, the Colgate-Palmolive Company has donated more than 120 new book collections, each containing 127 high-quality, hardcover children's books to RIF programs nationwide, and to United States military bases overseas. Other sponsors include Capital One Financial Corporation, Macy's, Target Corporation, MetLife Foundation, and the ARAMARK Charitable Fund. UGI Utilities, Inc. gave RIF a local twist by helping it target specific geographic areas, such as those located in UGI communities in Pennsylvania.

○ Contact one of RIF's corporate sponsors at www.rif.org to get your title involved.

■ *Branding.* Marketing professionals are always looking to establish, maintain, or improve their products' or companies' brand images and product positioning. They often use books to do that, so if they believe your book is consistent with the image they have or the one they want to create, it has a good chance of being selected. When your book is chosen for this reason, buyers are investing their companies' brand equity in it. They are essentially saying to their customers, "We believe this book has value for you, and we are putting our reputation behind it."

Terry Roberts, a book marketing consultant, feels that when buyers select a book they are thinking, "Does the cover, production, binding, editing, proofing, and content reflect the quality image we want to project?" Thus, when negotiating with buyers, demonstrate how your book's features fit the brand image their companies have established or want to create.

■ *Enhance other marketing campaigns.* Laws and do-not-call lists that limit the activities of telemarketers have increased the use of direct mail and email to accomplish the same results. Businesses conducting these direct mail campaigns want recipients to actually open their envelopes rather than simply toss them in the garbage. One way they accomplish this is by offering a "free gift inside," or an "offer for a free gift inside." Statistics have proven that this is an excellent way to increase response rates, and your book may be the perfect "gift" for one of these businesses to offer.

■ *Gift to customers.* Companies sometimes give both fiction and nonfiction titles to their customers and/or employees as gifts for holidays, unusual events, or special marketing periods to reward them and promote loyalty. Mark Resnick said, "Some cruise ship lines, among other companies in the hospitality industry, give passengers a thank-you gift upon departing the ship. People are taken aback when others, particularly businesses, say thank you, and they will tell others about it." This gifting benefits the company because it creates positive word-of-mouth advertising and goodwill, and it is also good for you because it gets your book into the hands of thousands of people who may not have seen it otherwise. Those people may, in turn, tell their friends and family about it, leading to additional sales.

Another example involves Paulette Ensign's booklet, *110 Ideas for Organizing Your Business Life.* After buying a single copy of it because it was mentioned in an article, a decision maker at a manufacturer's representative firm in the Caribbean bought 2,500 customized copies to use as its holiday greeting for that year. It was sent to the company's current and prospective clients, and Paulette received additional bulk sales from recipients of the booklet, as well.

■ *Partnership marketing.* Partnership marketing creates an alliance between companies that target similar customers. This commonly occurs between banks and publishers of financial books, such as Patty Crowe's, *Mortgages: Lose your Mortgage, Own Your Home.* In these instances, a bank will purchase several copies of a book at a discounted price and give it away to prospective borrowers. The idea is that the book will help the bank attract more borrowers. Banks win because they loan more money, authors win because they get incremental revenue, and consumers win because they get a free book containing valuable information.

One way you could offer your book as a tool for partnership marketing is by using the marketing technique of *bundling.* Bundling occurs when two or more associated products are packaged together and sold as one item. This tactic proved successful in a direct-mail campaign aimed toward parents of graduating college students. A bundle comprised of three books—*The Art of Interviewing, Help Wanted: Inquire Within,* and *Job Search 101*—was offered at a discounted price to this target segment. The campaign resulted in thousands of sales.

Book marketing consultant Terry Roberts suggests partnering with outside companies to create bundles. "Suppose Spalding wanted companies to use its basketballs as an incentive. It might be able to increase its sales of basketballs by bundling them with a book about NBA all-stars," said Terry. Talk with other sellers about combining your products in order to make them more attractive to businesses. If you succeed in doing so, the other company's sales force will be out there selling your bundle, too. You can immediately create a national sales force this way.

As you can see, there are many angles you can use to approach marketing departments with your book. Talk to the marketing professionals at your target businesses to get a feel for the goals they have set. Then, carefully select which sales strategy to use based on those goals.

Network Marketing Companies

Network marketing, which is also called multi-level marketing, is a business distribution model that utilizes direct selling. Essentially, companies that make use of this marketing scheme enlist unsalaried, independent sales people to buy their products and sell them directly to consumers. These sales people are paid by the company in commission based on the volume of products they sell.

Unlike HR departments and marketing departments, companies that utilize network marketing have a simultaneous internal and external focus. This is because their sales people are also their customers. In other words, the sales people are considered internal employees in need of training; however, those same sales people are also externally focused and look outward to increase sales. Therefore, both the information described in the HR section, as well as the information described in the marketing section apply to these types of companies.

❍ For a list of network marketing companies, go to
   http://en.wikipedia.org/wiki/List_of_network_marketing_companies

The Direct Selling Association (DSA) also provides the names of network marketing companies and suppliers. DSA is the national trade association of businesses that manufacture and distribute goods and services sold directly to consumers.

❍ Learn more about the Direct Selling Association at www.dsa.org

Regardless of whether they are focused internally, externally, or both, business managers regularly seek new ways to educate, inspire, and entice people connected to their companies. Content on leadership, motivation, self-help, selling techniques, new business topics, and much, much more could be useful to business executives. The key to making this market lucrative for you is finding the right way to approach each buyer.

SALES-PROMOTIONAL TOOLS

There are several different tools businesses use to entice and excite their customers and employees. Several of the most common are described in the following list. When contacting business buyers, be sure to tell them how they could use your book as one or more of these tools, and also how doing so will help increase their profits.

■ *Coupons.* Manufacturers may choose to offer a coupon that entitles the bearer to a discount on your book. There are several types of coupons, including dollars-off, in-pack, on-pack, and near-pack. For example, a pet food company might include an in-pack coupon in a bag of dog food for a discount on your book about dog care. Or, the manufacturer may want to offer the same coupon on-pack, so it is printed on the exterior of the package and visible to the consumer. Near-pack coupons are provided at the point of sale—perhaps as a peel-off coupon or placed in a "take-one" container—in close proximity to where the item is being sold. For example, a near-pack coupon for a book containing holiday recipes could be placed close to a display of Pfaltzgraff plates with Christmas décor.

In addition to enticing readers to buy a product, another benefit coupons provide occurs whenever customers are required to send in their contact information to the manufacturer. That allows the company to gather information to build its own database, which can eventually offset the costs of the discounts coupons offer.

> **T**
> **I**
> **P**
> A coupon or product offered in-pack is governed by strict regulations. Anything that comes in contact with food must be "food friendly," meaning that it has to be printed with special ink. Additionally, it must be odor free so it does not affect the smell or taste of the product.

■ *Incentives.* An incentive is something that encourages, motivates, or induces someone to do something. Many businesses offer incentive programs to their employees and customers. For example, a company might offer an incentive to the employee that finds the correct answer to a problem the quickest. Or, it may offer its customers a punch card that they can turn in for an incentive once it is filled.

A good example of this technique involves a small chain of children's shoe stores. The stores implemented a punch card program. Every twenty-five dollars spent was worth one punch on the card. When the card was punched four times, the child or parent was able to select two books from those available on display. The theme was "We'll take care of your children . . . from their head to their feet!" Parents loved this promotion and it benefited both the shoe stores and the books' publishers, too. Books can make great incentive rewards, and it is up to you to convince companies that yours is the best one for them to use.

Most incentive programs are not measurable, so do not try to convince professional buyers differently because they know better. What you can do to influence them, however, is tell them about the research that has been done by the Incentive Marketing Association (IMA). According to the IMA, incentive programs increase individual performance, improve team performance, and attract quality employees. They also increase sales, profits, product mix, channel share, and channel loyalty, as well as enhance employee productivity, teamwork, recognition, safety, and suggestions.

❑ Incentive Marketing Association; 1601 N. Bond St., Ste. 303, Naperville, IL 60563 Tel: 630-369-7780; Website: www.incentivemarketing.org

■ *Patronage awards.* Patronage awards are typically low-cost items that reward customers for doing something. For example, companies might give booklets away to people who purchase of a minimum quantity of some product, or as a reward for visiting their websites. One local bank used a personal finance book as a business gift to new clients who opened savings accounts. The bank purchased over 7,500 copies of the book on short discount for this promotion, which was geared towards high school and college graduates. The book featured information on loans, investing, and saving techniques, as well as information on stocks, bonds, and other investment vehicles. The bank realized that an educated customer is a long-term customer, and focusing on young clients insured years of good relationships.

If patronage awards are given as a series, they are considered part of a *continuity program.* An example of one such program occurred when a business gave its customers a cookbook in sections to be collected as a complete book over a period of time. This encouraged return visits to its website.

■ *Premiums.* Premiums are products that are given away for free with the purchase of other products. They are intended to encourage customers to buy something, thereby increasing the company's sales. For example, if the previously mentioned pet food manufacturer included your dog care book inside its dog food package—instead of just including a coupon for it—your book would be considered a premium. Or, if when a customer purchases a magazine subscription he or she is given a free copy of your book just for signing up, it would also be considered a premium.

Charles Stahler, publisher of the Vegetarian Resource Group, applies this marketing concept. He uses other publishers' remainders on vegan issues as premiums for his business, and also provides his frontlist books as premiums to other companies. According to Charles, "*Vegetarian Times* magazine bought 10,000 of our *Meatless Meals for Working People* from us for use as a premium. This enabled us to print enough so we could afford to place them in bookstores."

■ *Prizes.* A high-priced or high-valued book might be offered as a prize in a contest or sweepstakes. The basic difference between contests and sweepstakes is that contests are games of skill or intelligence, while sweepstakes' winners are determined strictly by luck. Since sweepstakes are games of chance, it is illegal to charge an entry fee. However, contests can, and usually do charge people to enter. Companies such as Extra Mile Marketing and Site Systems conduct promotional events, including contests and sweepstakes, for businesses. Contact them to see if they might be interested in offering your book as a prize.

❑ Extra Mile Marketing; 8655 E. Via de Ventura, Ste. E-130, Scottsdale, AZ 85258
  Tel: 480-443-6806; Website: www.extra-mile-marketing.com

❑ Site Systems; 5855 Green Valley Circle, Ste. 108, Culver City, CA 90230
  Tel: 310-649-0900; Website: www.sitesystems.com

■ *Samples.* A sample is a part of a product that is intended to show the quality, style, or nature of the whole. For example, to improve its image in the community, a business may give away your book to its customers or the general public as a sample of its overall goodwill. Samples can also be more literal in use. For example, Hammermill Paper Company printed over 5,000 copies of Paulette Ensign's booklet, *110 Ideas for Organizing Your Business Life,* on its own paper to serve as samples of the company's quality products and services.

■ *Self-liquidators.* When a book is sold at a price low enough to entice buyers, but high enough to cover its cost, it is being used as a self-liquidator. Many supermarkets use this tactic to allure shoppers to buy more at their stores. If customers make a minimum purchase of the store's products, they are allowed to purchase a book at a discounted price.

There are several associations that can provide you with additional information about sales-promotional tools. They are the National Association for Retail Marketing Services, the Promotion Marketing Association, the Promotional Products Association International, and the Society of Incentive Travel Executives. In addition to the information their websites provide, these associations usually host annual trade shows or conferences you might consider attending.

○ National Association for Retail Marketing Services: www.narms.com

○ Promotion Marketing Association: www.pmalink.org

❍ Promotional Products Association International: www.ppa.org

❍ Society of Incentive Travel Executives: www.site-intl.org

Publications also exist in which you can find helpful information about implementing sales-promotional programs. They include:

❍ *Brandweek:* www.brandweek.com

❍ *Incentive:* www.incentivemag.com

❍ *Occupational Health & Safety:* http://ohsonline.com/home.aspx

❍ *Promo Marketing:* http://magazine.promomarketing.com

❍ *Selling Power:* www.sellingpower.com

Selling your books as promotional tools is truly a cooperative effort between you and your customers. If you go to them with ideas and examples, they may view you as a marketing consultant, which will make you and your product instantly more valuable. They will rely on you to help them create new and productive campaigns using your book as the primary tool.

SELLING TO BUSINESSES

Business buyers are professional people trying to make rational decisions for the good of their companies. Many of them who implement sales-promotional programs tend to use lower-priced items like key chains and pencils as giveaways, because they do not want to risk a poor return on investment. For instance, hotels often provide free pens and notepads in each guestroom because they are low-cost items; however, they may have never thought about purchasing books as gifts for frequent guests or as items to sell in their gift shops, because they can be a bit more pricey.

Thus, it is your job to educate buyers that your book will add value to their businesses, and that its benefits will outweigh its costs. As Guy Achtzehn, President of the Marketing and Sales Group, said, "I know that books have value, but the buyers do not see them as 'sexy.'" Therefore, they must be informed about how books can increase their sales. That type of information will capture their attention.

Independent publishers may actually have an edge over larger publishers in this market, because companies do not like using bestsellers as premiums. If everyone already has something, it becomes less desirable as a sales-promotional tool. Therefore, a lesser known but equally applicable title may be preferred. For similar reasons, a company may ask for an exclusive on your title, because it will not want to waste its promotional dollars on a product another company is already offering.

First impressions are lasting impressions, so when you approach business buyers, present a finished copy of your book rather than a manuscript or galley. Doing so presupposes that you have carefully managed all the writing and production elements that result in a quality product. Additionally, you should arrange a well-structured, one-minute presentation. The following list will help you with your presentation preparation:

■ Develop a clearly articulated, emotionally meaningful solution statement that tells the business buyer what solutions your book can provide. In other words, define what is in it for his or her company. Learn how to create a solution statement in *25. Understand Your Competition and Differentiate Your Title* (page 207).

■ Define how your book will benefit the business. For example, Jim Leisy sold his book *Common Errors in English Usage* to corporate librarians by convincing them it could help employees improve their grammar, particularly in business communication.

■ Describe your book's competitive advantages in a way that clarifies why your title is different from, and better than competitive titles, and why that is meaningful to the buyer's business. Be able to complete the statement, "This is the only book available that . . ." Learn more about differentiating your book from its competition in *25. Understand Your Competition and Differentiate Your Title* (page 207).

■ Develop a pricing strategy that is based upon the value your book will bring to the buyer's business.

If companies will be giving your books away they will want a substantial discount. A technique commonly employed is the 50/20 rule. The company first takes a 50 percent discount, and then takes an additional 20 percent off of that figure— like taking an "extra 20 percent off" a discounted item in a clothing store. The total deduction comes out to be less than 70 percent. If you are working with a premium representative group, it may take another 10 percent off of that amount for its services. As a result, you net approximately 35 percent of the list price of your book when you sell to businesses. Figure 3.1 shows how the numbers might work out for a book with a twenty dollar list price.

Although sales in this market can be, and often are large, do not try to force a large sale to occur prematurely. Instead, proceed slowly and make sure the

Figure 3.1. Calculating Revenue

List Price:	$20.00
Initial 50% Discount	–$10.00
Subtotal:	$10.00
Subsequent 20% Discount:	–$ 2.00
Gross Revenue to You:	$ 8.00
Sales Representative's Discount:	–$ .80
Net Revenue to You:	$ 7.20

company understands that your proposal could save them money. Companies do not necessarily base their decisions solely on the price of items; therefore, you should demonstrate that your book can serve as an investment rather than a cost. In other words, prove to them that it will save them more than it costs, or help them make more than it costs, and your chances of making a sale will increase. *Chapter Five: Start Selling* (page 233) provides more sales strategies.

BE CREATIVE AND PLAN IN ADVANCE

If your first attempt at selling to businesses fails, get creative and find a different way to make it happen—this market is too lucrative to ignore. For example, Charles Stahler thought restaurants would be a good place to sell his cookbooks, but after a few sales attempts, he found that restaurants do not want to sell a book of someone else's recipes. Therefore, Charles instead created a guide to natural-food restaurants in the United States and Canada. He then contacted the restaurants listed in it and asked them if they would sell his guide, which they did.

Additionally, it may benefit you to think about where you want to sell your book while it is still in its early stages. Shel Horowitz, the author of *Principled Profits: Marketing That Puts People First,* did just that. Before his book was published, he reviewed the content and identified nine corporations he thought might be interested in buying it. He and his sales agent then sent letters and galleys to the appropriate contacts at all nine corporations. One of the nine was Southwest Airlines, which eventually purchased 1,000 copies at $5.00 each—the list price was $17.50. "The President of Southwest bought it to give to VIPs and friends of the company to demonstrate his commitment to high moral principles in business," Shel said.

Through this experience, Shel learned the importance of planning for premium sales in the writing stage. "Without padding a book with too many names," he said, "the author can mention a few company or brand names in the text and sell the book to them before publication. Such sales can cover your printing and production costs."

○ Shel Horowitz is the author of several books and may be reached at shel@frugalfun.com, or at www.grassrootsmarketingforauthors.com

Denise Richardson provides another example of the benefits of advance planning. She was able to get companies to sponsor her book, *Give Me Back My Credit,* before it was even published. She did this in two diverse ways. First, she promoted her book's message in articles and appearances on television and radio shows. After hearing Denise on the air, one company came to her asking if it could sponsor her book. "As part of their corporate commitment to accurate credit reporting, they wanted to make sure people got my message," said Denise. They did not offer her cash, but they did give her something equally as valuable—free access to their public relations firm.

Later, Denise took a more direct approach. She wrote a series of articles that she then combined to create a book. In several of her articles she reviewed specific products that are important to people trying to avoid identity theft, like paper shredders. She then contacted the companies that manufactured paper shredders, and alerted them that their products were discussed both in her article that would be appearing soon, and also later in a book. Not only did this lead to increased sales by the companies her book mentioned, but it also opened the chance to cross-merchandise her book in retail stores by placing it near the products she discussed, including paper shredders. Learn more about creative promotional ideas that you can implement for your own book in *Chapter Six. Promote to Non-Trade Buyers* (page 259).

FINDING BUSINESSES

You now know why and how businesses use books as sales-promotional tools. The next step is to find businesses that may be interested in your book specifically. There are several strategies and resources you can employ to create a list of potential business buyers, as well as hone in on those that are most relevant to your title. You will most likely find that your pool of available potential buyers is larger than you originally thought.

Patrick Snow is a keynote speaker, publishing coach, and the national best-selling author of *Create Your Own Destiny*. He sold 15,000 copies of his book to a company, which in turn gave it away to each person who registered for a seminar. Patrick suggests two ways to find companies that might want to buy your book. The first is through hotels. "Hotels host seminars almost every day. Go to hotel catering managers to learn the names of companies offering seminars there and offer your book as a premium. Of course, the hotel gets a percentage, too." The second way Patrick recommends finding companies is on television. "Watch infomercials. They are all looking for hooks to get people to order their products. If your book can tie into their product, why not use it as a premium?"

○ You can learn more about Patrick and his business at
   www.bestsellerpublishingcoaching.com

The Internet is also a great tool. Use your favorite search engine to find businesses that may be interested in buying your book. You can use the NAICS software discussed in *13. Specialty Stores* (page 97) to create a list of relevant businesses, as well. Finally, the following sources can also help you find the names and contact information for several different types of businesses:

■ *Chief Executive Officers Club.* This club is a nonprofit organization dedicated to improving the quality and profitability of CEOs' enterprises through shared experience and personal growth. Members must be CEOs of businesses that make above $2 million in annual sales; however, the average club members' companies make $20 million in annual sales. You can find links to numerous companies through this club's website.

❑ Chief Executive Officers Club, Inc.; 4 West 22nd St., 10th Fl., New York, NY 10010
  Tel: 212-925-7911; Website: www.ceoclubs.org

■ *Fortune Magazine.* Every year, Fortune comes out with a list of the 1,000 largest companies in America, as well as the 1,000 largest companies in each state. You can access these lists through links on the website listed below.

❑ Fortune Magazine

Website: http://money.cnn.com/magazines/fortune/rankings

■ *Vistage International.* Vistage International is the world's largest CEO member organization. Members meet in small groups each month to help each other get better results for their businesses. You can find several businesses through this organization.

❑ Vistage International; 11452 El Camino Real, Ste. 400, San Diego, CA 92130
  Tel: 858-523-6800; Website: www.vistage.com

It is a good idea to sit down and brainstorm all of the possible ways businesses could use your book, as well as all of the businesses that may potentially be interested in buying it. Figure 3.2 is an idea generator that will hopefully give you a starting point for creating your own list. It is by no means comprehensive; it is simply intended to jump start your brainstorming session and stimulate your

Figure 3.2. Idea Generator

Topic	Ideas for Promotional Tool	Examples of Potential Buyers
Pet Care	In-pack or on-pack coupons for pet food containers	Pet Industry Distributors and Associations; IAMS; Purina; Petco
Home Decorating	Self-liquidator for furniture retailers	Furniture, paint, or hardware stores; Sherwin Williams; Bed, Bath & Beyond; Lowes or Home Depot
Barbeque Cookbook	Premium for outdoor grill manufacturers or cross-promotion at the retail level	Manufacturers of outdoor grills; supermarkets; Lowes or Home Depot
Health and Fitness	Gift from company executives to employees; or, premium for renewing memberships at health clubs	Insurance companies; large businesses; Gold's Gyms; Curves for Women
Motivation and Inspiration	Incentive for sales people	Sales trainers; sales coaches; companies with large sales forces; multi-level marketing companies; Franklin Covey, Successories, and similar stores

mind into thinking about new places and new ways your book could be used in this market.

Once you have developed your target list of businesses, do not be intimidated by thinking you have to contact a corporate behemoth for a mega sale right away. Unless you are trained in selling, there is no reason to go after large companies until you are ready. It is a good strategy to start with small business prospects to test your persuasive techniques before setting your sights on larger sales opportunities. For example, if you have an educational, children's picture book, you might approach local and regional toy store chains before contacting the national buyer for Toys"R"Us. That way, you will gain experience asking questions, making your presentation, negotiating details, and closing sales—all the while bolstering your self-confidence. For more information about the sales process, see *Chapter Five. Start Selling* (page 233).

RELY ON OTHERS TO HELP YOU

Sales-promotional agencies and premium representative groups exist to help you reach potential buyers. Many of these companies will take on single-title authors and independent publishers, and the promotional representatives may even include your title as part of their entire line. Four of these companies are included in the following list:

■ *Incentive Manufacturers and Representatives Alliance.* IMRA is a strategic industry group of the Incentive Marketing Association. On its website you will find industry events, resources, and a list of suppliers and industry representatives. IMRA makes it easy to find sales representatives near you that can help you plan and launch an incentive program.

❏ Incentive Manufacturers and Representatives Alliance; Executive Director,
   1601 N. Bond St., Ste. 303, Naperville, IL 60563
   Tel: 630-369-7786; Website: www.imraorg.net

■ *Lifestyle Vacation Incentives.* Lifestyle Vacation Incentives is the largest leisure travel agency in the country, and is one of the nation's top sales-promotion and fulfillment companies specializing in consumer incentives.

❏ Lifestyle Vacation Incentives; 220 Congress Park Dr., Delray Beach, FL 33445
   Tel: 800-881-1900; Website: www.lifestylevacations.com

■ *Maritz, Inc.* Maritz is dedicated to improving its clients' measurable business results in sales and marketing, quality, customer satisfaction, and cost containment. It offers companies a wide range of sales and marketing services, including employee recognition programs, rewards, sales incentives, and more into which your book could be incorporated.

❏ Maritz, Inc.; 1375 North Hwy Dr., Fenton, MO 63099
   Tel: 877-462-7489, 636-827 4000; Website: www.maritz.com

■ *Premium Book Company.* Premium Book Company has a network of over 1,800 commissioned salespeople who can personally present your book to business buyers, as well as buyers in other non-retail marketplaces.

❏ Premium Book Company; 1320 Toronita St., York, PA 17402
   Tel: 800-562-4357; Website: www.premiumbookcompany.com

In addition to these types of companies, you might also consider hooking up with another publisher. Several of the large publishing houses, such as Penguin and Simon and Schuster, have marketing divisions that sell books. Whichever route you take, selling to large businesses can be lucrative in terms of large sales, but at the same time the sales process can be demanding and time consuming. Learn as much as you can about your target businesses before you begin, be professional, and always follow-up.

18. ASSOCIATIONS

There are over 135,000 nonprofit membership organizations worldwide according to Thomson Gale's *Encyclopedia of Associations.* These associations represent a significant opportunity for marketing directly to niche audiences with specific demographics. In other words, when you find an association related to your content, you can anticipate a captive audience of ready buyers.

Participating in associations can enhance your stature in an industry and provide you with opportunities to increase your book sales. Find an association with which your book is aligned and become active in its local chapter. From there, you may get a chance to exhibit and speak at its national meetings. Figure out ways to get involved that fit your personality, time, and budget, and you should see results.

CAUSE MARKETING

A good way to approach and sell to associations is through cause marketing. Cause marketing involves donating a percentage or fixed amount of each book sale to a charitable, nonprofit organization to help finance its cause. In cause marketing, you align the content of your book with the mission of a charity or association, and also promote that cause on your book's cover, your literature, and your website. Robin Bartlett of the American Heart Association lists seven guidelines you should follow in order to successfully utilize cause marketing:

■ *Make sure the cause matches the content of your book and the age level of your target audience.* Consider the title, *Ocho Loved Flowers,* by Anne Fontaine. In the book, a little girl becomes devastated when her cat Ocho falls ill. The story goes on to describe the whole process of loss—beginning with Ocho's fatal diagnosis, and following his decline through to his death. The book ends by offering parents, grief workers, and therapists creative methods to help children deal with loss and big life challenges.

The content of *Ocho Loved Flowers* lends itself well to several cause marketing opportunities with a variety of associations. First, there is the book's obvious connection to animals, specifically cats. Based on that tie, the author could get involved with state and national Veterinary Medical Associations and Humane Societies. Additionally, a quick Internet search provides about twenty more associations dedicated specifically to different breeds of cats. Examples include the Abyssinian Cat Association and the Russian Blue Breeders Association, as well as larger, national organizations like the American Association of Feline Practitioners and the American Cat Fanciers Association.

Second, the content of *Ocho Loved Flowers* can also be interpreted symbolically, and might be appropriate for the National Association for Home Care and Hospice, Bereaved Parents of the USA, the Association of Children's Hospices, or Children's Hospice International. Similarly, groups such as Positive Parenting or Mommy Tips might also be interested. You should go through this same analysis with your own title to come up with a list of associations that could potentially be interested in buying it.

■ *Do not come across as self-serving.* Decision makers at most associations receive requests from authors asking them to buy their books regularly. Associations want to work with people who believe in their cause, though, not with authors who are just trying to make a buck. Therefore, look at sales in this market as a long-term process. Align yourself personally with a cause and become a member of related associations. Devoting your time and energy to their efforts before you ask them for something in return will help prove that you believe in what they are doing. "Allow more time than you think you will need. Sales to associations can take more than a year to accomplish," said Robin.

Yelba Quinn of the American Society for Training and Development (ASTD) agreed. "The key to selling to or through an association is to really know it. Join it. Get involved. You have to know and understand the association before you can expect to do business with it. If you are in a relationship with an organization they do not see you as a threat," she said.

■ *Prepare for rejection.* Even if you personally join an association, "Do not assume that just because you are a member that your book will get accepted. The American Heart Association does not need you. If they want a book, they will do it themselves," said Robin. If you run into associations like this that are only interested in using their own materials, do not be discouraged. Instead, work with their systems.

For example, if you are an expert on a topic in which associations are interested, you can offer your services to write a book for them. However, Yelba said,

"You really have to be aligned with the mission of the organization to be considered." Similarly, another option is to sell your book's rights to the association, which will then publish it themselves.

Your rejection rate will decrease if your book is current and better than its competitors. Demonstrate that your book contains fresh research, not "me too" content. "You have to do your homework," said Robin. Know your content, your competition, and the mission of the association—which you can usually find on its website—before you attempt a sale, and you will have a better chance of success.

■ *Proceed cautiously.* Associations may take your idea and run with it on their own. "While this rarely happens, it could," said Robin. Protect yourself before revealing your book's content to associations. "Have a strong Non-Disclosure Agreement (NDA) in place before you tell them what your idea is." The inset below shows what should be included in a very basic NDA.

■ *Start locally.* Begin by contacting local and state associations to build your—and your book's—resume and reputation, and then move on to national groups. For example, going back to *Ocho Loved Flowers*, the author might implement this strategy by first dealing with her nearby Washington State Veterinary Medical Association before trying to tackle the American Veterinary Medical Association.

Carl Sams, the author and photographer of *Lost in the Woods*, started his sales in this market by contributing one dollar of every book sold to his local Michigan Library Association. He then moved up to an arrangement with the American

---

NONDISCLOSURE AGREEMENT:
(*INSERT THE TITLE OF YOUR BOOK*)

This agreement is between *(Disclosing Party)* and *(Receiving Party)* and is effective as from *(Date)*.

Terms of the Agreement:

The receiving party will treat confidential information with the same degree of care and safe guard that it takes with its own confidential information.

The receiving party agrees not to disclose confidential information to a third party regarding the content and images of *(Book Title)*.

The receiving party shall not make or permit to be made copies or other reproductions of confidential information, written material, images or ideas from *(Book Title)*.

The receiving party shall not make any commercial use of confidential information of *(Book Title)*.

Library Association. "If you prove that your concept works at the local level, you will find a more willing ear when you go to larger groups," said Robin.

■ *Understand the marketing relationship.* Yelba Quinn of the American Society for Training and Development said, "Understand that the ASTD exists to provide benefits to its members. We provide content and serve as a professional resource. Think globally—not just about getting your books in our store. Think strategically, too. Become a partner to the organization and become a speaker there, for example. Use its resources to your advantage. We want to be the leader in our field. If you can help us do that we'll work with you."

There are two major points to take away from Yelba's comments. The first is to work as a partner with an association, not as a vendor. Become a member and get to know its mission. Offer to customize your content to its needs to prove that you are flexible and have its best interests in mind. This leads into Yelba's second point. In this marketplace, it is not as much about selling books as it is about helping associations reach their goals. Show how your content can do that and you will be well on your way to making initial sales, which will most likely lead to several reorders over the years.

■ *Know what you can and cannot do.* Robin cautions you to know if and when you may use an association's logo in your marketing. "Just because you are donating money, you do not automatically get to use their logo. Make sure you negotiate the use of their logo in your marketing material or you won't have any muscle." Furthermore, Robin suggests that you donate a fixed amount of money upfront, rather than a percentage of the sale or a portion of the proceeds, because the latter sends the negative message that you are most concerned with getting your money.

Using your book to help an association promote its cause can be beneficial in many ways—not the least of which is achieving a high degree of self-satisfaction. Become a member, be patient, and prove your dedication to build the foundation for a long-term business relationship.

HOW ASSOCIATIONS USE BOOKS

There are thousands of industry associations, charitable non-profit associations, and non-profit trade associations around the world, and they all use books in a variety of different ways. The following list contains several ways that associations might utilize you and your book:

■ *Bookstore Addition.* Many associations have bookstores on their websites, so they might buy your book to sell through them. Different associations will make different purchasing arrangements. For example, the American Society for Training and Development's (ASTD) online bookstore sells from inventory and replenishes its stock as necessary. Others, such as the Child Welfare League of America's bookstore, purchase books for special occasions and have publishers drop-ship them to events. As far as discounts, Yelba said "The ASTD bookstore buys at 40 to 50 percent off list price and on a non-returnable basis. Our customers are willing to pay up to seventy dollars for the professional books they need, but other associations look for lower-priced books—somewhere in the low-twenties."

One technique that can help you show your sincerity about placing your book in an association's online bookstore is to demonstrate how your title would look on its website. Figure 3.3 illustrates this concept with Bob Prosen's book, *Kiss Theory Good Bye*. Bob realized that his book would make an excellent addition to the Association of Management Consulting Firms' online bookstore. He then researched the bookstore's website and noted how the books were displayed there. Next, Bob created a similar looking page for his book, as shown in Figure 3.3, that demonstrated how it could look on the association's website. He sent this comparison as part of his submission package.

Nierenberg and Calero's Book, *The New Art of Negotiating*

Introducing a book by Nierenberg, founder of The Negotiation Institute, and Calero, negotiation expert:

The New Art of Negotiating
by Gerard I. Nierenberg and Henry H. Calero

Click here to order *The New Art of Negotiating*

Click here to view Nierenberg and Calero's website

Robert Prosen's New Book, *Kiss Theory Goodbye*

The only business book that provides...

- Step-by-step instructions on "how" to execute
- Specific actions readers should take to improve performance
- Tools and templates that promote immediate implementation
- Content-rich information for all size companies & industries
- A proven process that can be replicated to deliver measurable results
- Help valuable to any decision maker from CEO to the frontline supervisor.

"...attacks core problems head-on." Garrett Boone, Chairman, The Container Store

"Tons of wisdom! A must-read for any executive . . ." John Signorino, CEO, Chicken of the Sea

"A practical, insightful way to get results." Peter Atabef, President and CEO, Perot Systems

Figure 3.3. Creating Similar Website Copy

■ *Fundraising Item.* Associations sometimes use books as fundraising items by selling them to raise money for a cause, event, or project. Sarah Keeney of the Savas Beatie publishing company offers this example of an association using books as fundraisers:

> Because our general and military history titles appeal to such a niche audience, we are always looking for ways we can sell books outside of the book trade. Over the years we have developed a good relationship with Civil War Preservation Trust (CWPT), the largest nonprofit organization devoted to the preservation of our nation's endangered Civil War battlefields. They frequently focus on obtaining donations for battlefields that are in particular need of being saved by offering a premium to those who make a donation. We stay in constant communication with CWPT so we know what battlefield they will be raising money for next. If we have a book on our backlist or coming down the pipeline that details that particular battle, we let them know they can offer a copy of the book as a premium to whoever makes a donation.
>
> We have done this successfully with a number of our titles such as *Champion Hill: Decisive Battle for Vicksburg* and *Chicago's Battery Boys: The Chicago Mercantile Battery in the Civil War's Western Theater.* CWPT tells us how many copies they are interested in buying and we work out a discount based on that number. We have even timed a premium to coincide with when we were planning to release a paperback version of a title. We latch their order onto our print run which brings our printing cost down. We try to provide the organization with something special to entice their members to want to donate and receive a copy of our books. Oftentimes we have the author sign bookplates, which they include with every book. This is a great way that we can work with an organization we support, help spread the word about our books to our target audience, and sell copies we wouldn't have in the book trade.

There are professional fundraising groups that can help you promote and sell your book to associations for use as a fundraising item. A good place to start is at Do-It-Yourself Fundraising Ideas where you can get free fundraising information.

❍ Do-It-Yourself Fundraising Ideas: www.fundraising-ideas.org/DIY

Once you have ideas for what you can do, browse some of the professional fundraising websites listed below to help you implement your campaign:

❍ Association of Fundraising Professionals: www.afpnet.org

❍ Fundraising Web: www.fundraisingweb.org

❍ Fundrasing.com: www.fundraising.com

❍ USA Fundraising: www.usafundraising.com

■ *Sales-Promotional Tool.* Dominion Fertility, a fertility clinic in the Virginia/ Washington, DC area, provides an example of how groups and associations can use books as sales-promotional tools. The clinic publishes *100 Questions and Answers about Infertility* and uses it to promote its services. Dominion also provides an electronic version of the book for free on its website. This generates business for Dominion through positive word-of-mouth communication.

■ *Spokesperson.* You may find an association willing to have you be its spokesperson. If you are chosen, you receive an automatic, implied third-party endorsement. Thus, your credibility in the industry is enhanced, leading to further sales and opportunities. Associations may also ask you to speak at their conferences, which provide a great way to sell more books, too. For more information about conducting speaking events, see *40. Sell Books through Speaking Engagements* (page 279).

Get to know each association you work with and find out what their needs are. Once you have a good understanding of how they are trying to reach their goals, you will know how to approach them with your book.

SELLING TO ASSOCIATIONS

The primary buying criterion in this market is price—particularly for the charitable organizations. While there is little preference for softcover over hardcover books, softcover may be preferred because of its lower price. Furthermore, your book must have an ISBN and high production quality. In general, the same characteristics that would make a book sell well in the retail sector are also essential for sales to associations.

○ You can purchase ISBNs at www.bowker.com

Before you send your submission package, be sure to call or look at the association's website to find out the name of the person to whom you should send it. Yelba said "When submitting a title to me start with an email to see if I am interested. If so, I will ask you to send a sell sheet. Then if I'm still interested, I will want to see the book. But do not send the book first." See page 327 for an example of what a sell sheet for this book might look like.

In addition to individual submissions, associations also look to other sources for books. Yelba said, "We know which titles are on the bestseller lists and we will buy those. We also look to the newsweeklies to learn what subjects may interest our members. Then we search for books on those topics. Small publishers are welcome to submit books to me, but their chances may be better if they have lots of exposure, press, and awards."

Keep in mind that you have to help the association sell your book. One way you can support the association and yourself is by speaking at association events and referring people to buy your book through them. The more promotion you do, the more people will begin to recognize your name and your book's title. As you become more familiar with associations and their members, they will be more likely to call you and work with you to sell your book.

WORKING ASSOCIATIONS' WEBSITES

Do not go to associations' websites with the preconceived notion that you will simply submit your title to one online bookstore after another. While this may sometimes be your only option, many associations' websites contain an abundance of information and opportunities for you. The following list contains components that many associations' websites have, as well as information about how you can use each to your advantage:

■ *Articles.* Read available articles to learn what others are saying about the association and your book's topic. Who else in the industry is trying to develop a theory similar to yours? How is yours different and better? Furthermore, if there are subjects that are not being covered by the current array of articles, submit yours to the association to post. This will lead to increased exposure and contribute to your reputation as the industry authority, increasing your chances of having the association select your book later.

■ *Awards.* Some associations sponsor award competitions, such as the Independent Book Publishers Association's Ben Franklin Awards. Even if you do not win the top prize, from then on your sales-promotional literature can proclaim the fact that you were nominated for an award. For more information about awards, see *38. Participate in Award Competitions* (page 271).

■ *Calendar of Events.* Many associations' websites post a calendar of upcoming events with descriptions of opportunities for industry experts. You may discover an association is looking for an exhibitor at an industry trade show, a speaker for one of its conferences, or a teacher for a seminar class. The exposure you will get by doing these things will enhance your reputation and make you more credible.

■ *Contact Us.* Most associations' websites have a "Contact Us" or "About Us" page that typically includes personal contact information for staff members, committee chairs, and the members of the association's Board of Directors. Use these lists to contact people and network your way into the association's good graces. Find the contact information for people involved in new business development, the online bookstore, and maintaining and acquiring membership.

Additionally, many associations provide a membership roster, making it easy to reach individual members. Be sure to ask the association for permission before contacting its members directly to avoid the appearance of spam and circumvent future ill will. Then, any time you contact members, include a notice that the association's Board of Directors approved your correspondence. This disclaimer will enhance your image and improve your response rate.

You may also find a list of regional offices or chapters on some associations' websites. Email the top person at each and offer your services to speak at their events. An offer to be a last-minute substitute speaker may make you a welcome addition to their list of presenters. Start by establishing a good relationship with the officers of local chapters, and then use those connections to network your way to the national board.

■ *Frequently Asked Questions.* FAQs tell you the subjects that are important to associations and their members. If you are an expert on one or more of those topics, be sure to let the associations know when you contact them regarding your book.

■ *Links.* Often overlooked goldmines are the links to other resources that many websites provide. These connections will take you to related organizations that may offer additional chances to sell your book. You can spend hours just following the links and developing potential opportunities at each destination.

■ *Message Boards, Chat Rooms, and Discussion Groups.* These resources allow you to post comments and participate in online discussions, which you should do whenever possible. These forums increase your exposure and provide subtle advertising opportunities with people in your target market.

■ *Newsletters.* If the association has a newsletter—as most do—offer to write an article for it, permit them to use an excerpt from your book, or offer your book as a subject for a review. As an author, you already have some credibility as an industry specialist and expert on the topic. The association may publish your excerpt or article in exchange for a mention in their regular emails to members.

■ *Special Reports.* Many associations publish special reports and news about the industry. Read these to keep current on relevant events. This knowledge will serve you well during your media performances, too.

As you can see, it takes time and work to get involved with associations. But the rewards can be significant. Not only will you increase your name recognition and credibility in the industry, but you can sell a lot of books, as well.

FINDING ASSOCIATIONS

There are many sources that provide the names of associations, including printed directories and online lists. There is always the option of performing a search for associations related to your topic on your favorite online search engine. While that approach will yield you a large array of relevant results, it may be time consuming if you are looking for a broad range of associations. If that is the case, try using one of the resources described in the following list:

■ *AssociationExecs.com*. This website provides a comprehensive online directory of associations. It has a unique feature that allows you decipher the association name from its acronym. To access this tool, go to the Acronym Index on the website and type in the acronym or name of the association you would like to identify.

❑ AssociationExecs.com
   Website: www.associationexecs.com

■ *Directory of Associations*. Published by Concept Marketing Group, the *Directory of Associations* is a comprehensive source of information on associations and professional societies. It provides detailed information on business and trade associations, non-profit organizations, and other charitable and community associations throughout the United States. Its over 37,000 associations can be searched using multiple criteria.

❑ Directory of Associations; Concept Marketing Group, Inc., 8655 E. Via de
   Ventura, Ste. G-200, Scottsdale, AZ 85258
   Tel: 800-575-5369; Website: www.marketingsource.com/associations

■ *Encyclopedia of Associations*. The *Encyclopedia of Associations* is a comprehensive source of detailed information on 135,000 non-profit membership organizations worldwide. Its database provides addresses and descriptions of professional societies, trade associations, labor unions, cultural and religious organizations, fan clubs, and other groups of all types.

❑ *Encyclopedia of Associations*
   Website: www.galegroup.com

■ *National Trade and Professional Associations of the United States*. The NTPA directory is a reference guide to over 7,000 national trade associations, professional societies, technical organizations, and labor unions, as well as to the more than 20,000 executives who run them.

❑ *National Trade and Professional Associations of the United States*
   Website: www.columbiabooks.com

■ *Weddles Association Directory*. The *Weddles Association Directory* lists several thousand associations from around the world by their primary professional or occupational focus, and also by their industry of interest. Since the associations are listed by category, it is easy to find exactly what you are looking for, and each listing provides a link to the website the association operates.

❑ Weddles Association Directory; 2052 Shippan Ave., Stamford, CT 06902
   Tel: 203-964-1888; Website: www.weddles.com/associations/index.cfm

Take the time to research and find associations that closely align with your book's content. Then, be patient and get involved with their causes before you attempt sales. If you bide your time and handle this marketplace correctly, you will be rewarded with large, consistent sales.

19. THE ACADEMIC MARKET

The academic market is an opportune market segment for publishers, because it uses books as a foundation for its existence. It includes, but is not limited to schools, foundations, research organizations, professional associations, libraries, students, and individual educators. This marketplace impacts people of all ages, from preschoolers to professionals. Regardless of grade, age, major, and choice of home, public, or private education, people's need for books is ubiquitous.

The academic market can be divided into three general subsegments: kindergarten through twelfth grade (K–12), colleges and universities, and professional institutions and organizations. Additionally, there is a religious side to all three subsegments, because religious institutions and organizations tend to utilize different educational materials. Homeschools and government schools have unique book-buying nuances, as well. Since the book selection criteria and selling techniques are different for each subsegment, it is important to educate yourself before you begin selling in this marketplace.

KINDERGARTEN THROUGH TWELFTH GRADE

The K–12 market includes elementary, middle, and high schools, and therefore encompasses a broad range of ages, interests, reading levels, and curriculums.

Textbook versus Trade Book Selection

In elementary, middle, and high school classrooms, teachers are required to follow a district mandated curriculum, as well as provide their students with extra-curricular reading materials. Therefore, there are two main categories of books that can be sold to the K–12 market: textbooks and trade books.

Textbooks

Textbooks are educational, fact-based books that teach students about a particular area of study. Every state has defined standards that they require the textbooks used in their schools to meet, and most require each to be approved before they are used. Some states' education department websites provide explanations of the textbook requirements for each grade level. The United States Department of Education makes it easy to find state departments of education, state contacts and organizations, state department of education press releases, and other state information.

○ To find this information use the map at
  www.ed.gov/about/contacts/state/index.html?src=ln

Be aware that some school districts create more specific standards based on their own curriculum guidelines. Therefore, it is a good idea to double check the state department information by going to your target schools' websites. Many will display course outlines, perhaps including the textbooks currently being used.

○ To find the contact information for any public school in any state, go to http://nces.ed.gov/ccd/schoolsearch/

Textbooks can be ordered by individual teachers, by a local or regional curriculum committee, or by a statewide textbook adoption committee. The main criteria used for selecting textbooks are included in the following list:

■ *Author and Book Credentials.* Textbook buyers want to know that the author is an expert on the subject matter, and that the book is high-quality and informative. Therefore, include the qualifications of the author, as well as endorsements for the book in your submission packages. This information can also be included in the textbook itself. To learn how to obtain endorsements, see *37. Get Endorsements* (page 267).

■ *Binding and Cover.* The binding and cover of textbooks should be suitable for their specific use. Some textbooks are used repeatedly and are subject to harsh use, so in those cases teachers may prefer hardcover, casebound books. However, textbooks can also be softcover, like almost all supplementary materials are. Finally, you might want to consider a spiral binding so that books can lay flat on students' desks.

■ *Teachers Aids.* A teacher's guide that supplements a textbook is indispensable. Additional materials such as sample test questions, exercises, assignments, and answer keys are also helpful. You might consider including interactive websites, power points, and smart-board exercises, as well.

■ *Quality of Production and Content.* Your book must have superior production characteristics. In most cases, this means a hardcover, heavy duty binding, and good paper quality. Additionally, the content must be current and verified according to printer's specifications.

As alluded to above, supplementary materials are also included in the textbook category and are important to successful textbook sales. Supplementary materials include items like workbooks, manuals, maps, manipulatives, and other items intended for classroom use. These items are held to less strict standards by states and school districts, but they still must be high-quality and factually accurate. Furthermore, supplements should also be accompanied by an instructor's manual.

Trade Books

Trade books are designed to sell to the general public, and can be either fiction or non-fiction. In K–12 classrooms, trade titles are selected on an individual basis by teachers themselves, or by school librarians. Note that there are libraries that cater to all three academic market segments—K–12, colleges and universities, and professional institutions and organizations. See *22. Libraries* (page 175) for more information about the library market in general. Regardless of whether teachers or librarians select the books, though, the ones that are chosen are almost always titles that have established themselves and have become well-known in the trade market first. However, do not be completely discouraged if this is not the case with your book. There is some room in this market segment for lesser-known trade book sales to individual teachers.

As you might surmise, no title is appropriate for all ages, especially in the diverse K–12 market segment. The three main criteria educators use to determine the appropriate trade books to buy for their classrooms are their students' interest level in the topic, the reading level of the book as compared to their students' abilities, and how well the book ties in with their required curriculum.

Tests exist to determine the reading level of books according to the vocabulary, the number of syllables in words, and the length of the sentences. Meta-Matrics Incorporated's Lexile Framework for Reading is an approach to reading measurement that matches students to appropriately challenging reading materials. The Lexile Framework measures both reader ability and text difficulty. Publishers can send in their books and get Lexile measurements for them to determine their reading levels. Knowing this piece of information will give you a competitive advantage in this market.

❏ MetaMatrics, Inc.; 1000 Park Forty Plaza Dr., Ste. 120, Durham, NC 27713
Tel: 919-547-3400, 888-539-4537; Website: www.lexile.com

Selling to the K–12 Market

Teachers, school board members, and members of state departments of education are the decision makers in this market segment. An excellent way to reach these people is through direct mail or email, using flyers, letters, or brochures to educate them about your book and its competitive advantages. The best time to conduct your direct mail campaign is when they are deciding which books to use during the next school year. Experience shows that this occurs in late summer and early spring.

In the K–12 market, textbooks are most often bought and sold at a fixed sales price; although, some publishers choose to offer a quantity discount. Book buyers in the academic market are often reluctant to purchase from publishers with single titles. Thus, if you do not have a product line, consider bundling with other authors and publishers who have complementary products. Then create a catalog describing your entire line. Buyers in all academic market segments place great significance on catalogs, so invest enough money to create one of high quality.

One way to network and sell to academic buyers in all three market segments is to attend educational conferences, which are held regularly throughout the year.

Perform an online search to find those appropriate to your topic and titles. Then, well in advance of the conference, contact the planners and ask to be considered as a speaker. If they choose you, hand out catalogs and flyers about your titles after your presentation, but avoid using your speaking time for selling—save that for later. You might also ask the planners if you can write an article for their conference program, which will further the perception of your expertise and potentially lead to more sales.

Finally, serendipity also plays a part in marketing books to schools. Brenda Lee, who self-published *Lunch at the Zoo*, a children's book about nutrition, provides a good example of this. According to Brenda:

> The main theme of my book concerned a little boy who learned to choose fruits, vegetables, and meats, instead of junk food and sweets. Little did I know that the [then] president's wife—yes, First Lady Laura Bush—was about to start a major initiative to stop childhood obesity. The second week my book came off the press, I got an order for 1,700 books from the state department of education. I have sold thousands of copies now to school districts that are using the book to teach nutrition to our youngsters. I've even had orders from overseas. I am in the process of converting my book to digital so other countries can purchase without the added expense and hassle of shipping. This little book with the big message has been financially rewarding to me and has proven very useful to schools and other special interest groups in the education of our children.

You must have a current, accurate, quality product, regardless of whether it is a textbook or a trade book. You then need to make phone calls and network with potential buyers persistently in order to get results. While this advice will help you succeed in any market, it is particularly relevant here because of the diverse needs of the students and teachers.

Finding K–12 Contact Information

As previously stated, direct mail is the best way to reach decision makers in the K–12 marketplace. In order to conduct direct mail campaigns, though, you first need a mailing list of recipients. An excellent resource for putting together educational mailing lists is Quality Education Data (QED), a research and database company focused exclusively on education. QED is a wholly owned subsidiary of Scholastic Inc., the global children's publishing and media company.

❑ Quality Education Data; 1625 Broadway, Ste. 250, Denver, CO 80202
   Tel: 800-525-5811; Website: www.qeddata.com

Another excellent resource for educational mailing lists is Market Data Retrieval (MDR), a D&B Company. MDR boasts the most complete, current, and accurate databases available in the industry. It can provide you with direct mail lists, email contacts and deployment, sales contact and lead solutions, and market research and analysis.

❑ Market Data Retrieval; 6 Armstrong Rd., Shelton, CT 06484
   Tel: 800-333-8802; Website: www.schooldata.com

As you will find in *39. Implement Effective Mail-Order Campaigns* (page 274), successful direct-mail marketing begins with a quality list of prospective buyers. Even the best submission package will be a waste of money if it is sent to the wrong list. Invest in the most comprehensive, cleanest list you can find and you will be much more likely to get a good return on your investment.

HOMESCHOOLS

Homeschooling serves as a good example of a non-traditional academic setting. It is one of the four K–12 educational options that parents can choose for their children, along with public schools, private schools, and distance education. Fox News reports that there are over two million homeschooled students in the United States, and the homeschooling trend is expanding as parents are looking more closely at the quality of education their children are receiving, as well as at the environment in which it is being administered.

Rick Fisher, author of the two-book series, *Mastering Essential Math Skills*, attacked the homeschool market as a true non-trade marketer. He looked at it not as one, homogenous market, but as a market comprised of manageable segments, each with diverse buying needs. The following list includes several of these smaller, homeschool market segments. The examples provided are by no means comprehensive, and you can find many more similar homeschool sales outlets by performing a search on your favorite search engine.

■ *Book Fairs and Conventions.* Homeschooling book fairs and conventions present excellent opportunities to sell books, and they occur annually across the country. For example, the Homeschool Fair occurs each Memorial Day in Ontario, California, and as its name implies, the Southern California Catholic Home Educators Annual Conference and Curriculum Fair occurs each year, as well.

○ Homeschool Fair: www.homeschoolfair.com

○ Southern California Catholic Home Educators: www.scchehomepage.com

Speaking and exhibiting at homeschooling conventions is also a great way to get industry exposure and make sales. Rick sought exhibit opportunities at shows such as the Midwest Homeschool Convention, which is a three-day event devoted to the display, discussion, and sale of educational materials and curriculum, and the Tidewater Education Expo in Virginia, which focuses primarily on the homeschool community.

○ For a state-by-state list of homeschool conventions, go to
www.thehomeschoolmom.com/states/conventions.php

■ *Categorical Associations.* There are several associations that cater to specific demographic groups within the overall homeschooling market. For example, there is a Jewish Home Educator's Network and a National African-American Homeschoolers Alliance. Homeschooling is growing among African-American families in America. The population of homeschooled African-American children is estimated to be between 84,000 and 120,000.

○ Jewish Home Educator's Network: www.snj.com/jhen

○ National African-American Homeschoolers Alliance: www.naaha.com

■ *Online Directories.* There are online directories that serve as homeschooling resource guides. They offer newsletters, support groups, message boards, tips-of-the-week, products, and online courses. Use these directories to bring exposure to you and your book, which will bring you one step closer to another sale.

○ Homeschool.com: www.homeschool.com

■ *Publications.* The media also serves this market segment. For example, Rick contacted the *Home Education Magazine,* the *LINK Homeschool Newspaper,* and *Homeschooling Today* when he was selling his books. Additionally, the *Old Schoolhouse Magazine* provides many ways to reach homeschooling families. It has a store, a print magazine with a circulation of 40,000, and three websites, including homeschoolblogger.com, which boasts 10 million page views.

○ *Home Education Magazine:* www.homeedmag.com

○ *LINK Homeschool Newspaper:* www.homeschoolnewslink.com

○ *Homeschooling Today:* www.homeschooltoday.com

○ *Old Schoolhouse Magazine:* www.thehomeschoolmagazine.com

■ *State, National, and International Associations.* There are many sales opportunities at state-level homeschool associations. Most states have a parent-educators association, or a homeschool association, network, or organization. Examples include:

○ Florida Parent Educators Association: www.fpea.com

○ Smoky Mountain Home Education Association: www.smhea.org

○ California Homeschool Network: www.californiahomeschool.net

○ Washington Homeschool Organization: www.washhomeschool.org

Additionally, there are national homeschooling organizations such as the American Homeschool Association (AHA), the Association for Experiential Education, and the Home School Legal Defense Association. Rick was able to utilize AHA's free email newsletter and discussion list to spread the word about his books to homeschoolers, media contacts, and education officials. He also used AHA's list of support groups and organizations as a resource for setting up personal presentations.

○ American Homeschool Association: www.americanhomeschoolassociation.org

○ Association for Experiential Education: www.aee.org

○ Home School Legal Defense Association: www.hslda.org

Finally, there are also international homeschooling associations. The following are a sampling of such organizations around the world:

○ Alternative Education Resource Organization: www.educationrevolution.org

○ Alternative Learning Organization: www.alternative-learning.org

○ Education Otherwise: www.education-otherwise.org

○ Home Education Advisory Service: www.heas.org.uk

○ HomeLearning Canada: www.homelearningcanada.ca

If you look diligently and strategically you may find a great source of revenue in non-traditional segments of the academic market, like homeschools. Remember to break the mass market down into manageable sub-groups and keep looking for new places in which you can sell your books.

COLLEGES AND UNIVERSITIES

There are thousands of colleges and universities in the United States and throughout the world. There are two-year and four-year institutions, private schools, public schools, technical schools, and even online schools. All of these institutions utilize books.

Textbook vs. Trade Book Selection

Similar to the K–12 market segment, colleges and universities buy two types of books: textbooks and trade books. However, this market is much more accepting of textbooks than it is of trade books.

Textbooks

At the college and university level, textbooks are needed for all of the wide variety of courses taught by the school. Although ultimately students are the ones who purchase textbooks, they do not choose them. Textbooks for large, core courses are typically selected by a senior course supervisor, or by a department chairperson or committee. On the other hand, textbooks for elective courses are generally hand-picked by the individual teachers or professors who teach them. College bookstores then order textbooks for courses based on the lists given to them by instructors and committee and department heads. Therefore, be sure you figure out who makes the selection decisions at your target schools so you can concentrate your selling efforts on them.

Trade Books

It is extremely difficult, if not impossible, to sell trade books to colleges and universities. Most all trade books read by college students in classrooms are classics or high-profile titles that have clearly established themselves in trade houses. This fact also holds true to books sold in college and university bookstores that are intended for pleasure, not classroom use. Campus bookstores want to carry items that will sell, so they generally dedicate the little shelf space they have to bestsellers and bestselling authors.

Selling to Colleges and Universities

The standard textbook discount for the college and university market segment, as well as for the professional market segment, is 20 percent, and books are sold on a returnable basis. However, some publishers have negotiated non-returnable sales by offering a discount of 40 to 45 percent. It might be a good idea to conduct a test run of your title on a local, state, or regional level before you attempt national sales, so you have an idea of how schools will respond to it before you put significant resources into nationwide marketing.

Your marketing should be directed toward individual instructors and committee and department heads, since they usually select the textbooks that will be used. It would be cost-prohibitive to send a review copy of your book to all of these people, so you should first send an initial package of information to those who might be interested in using your book as a text. This package should contain an informative letter, a copy of the table of contents, a detailed description of the content, a sell sheet, and a reply card that they can send back if they would like to request an examination copy. If printing costs become prohibitive, you could instead send a single sheet that directs people to your website and provide the same information there. Learn tips for creating professional materials for your submission package in the inset on page 260, and see an example sell sheet for this book on page 327.

The reply card included in your information package can also be used to help you obtain important marketing information. On the card, ask respondents for

> **TIP**
>
> Even by sending examination copies of your book only to people who request them, it can still get expensive. Therefore, you may want to set a thirty, sixty, or ninety day trial deadline by which people who receive an examination copy must choose to adopt, keep and buy, or return the book in a resalable condition.

their full contact information, which you can use to update your mailing list. Also ask them when they make their buying decisions, what textbook(s) they are currently using, and the course for which the title is being considered. This information will let you know the best time to contact them, give you comparative sales information, and perhaps open a market you had not previously considered.

Opportunities abound in the academic marketplace for the creative marketer at the college and university level. For example, if you have a line of career-related titles you could sell them directly to the career development offices located at most colleges. Career counselors are always looking for credible speakers to help their students find employment, so if you offer your speaking services you might have more luck making a sale. Additionally, if your book is related to a university in some way, you could sell it to the alumni association or the campus chapter of the American Marketing Association as a fundraiser.

○ Visit AMA's website at www.marketingpower.com

Finally, Ingram Digital Group (IDG) provides publishers with an opportunity to sell directly to students. IDG is an e-content distributor that enables students to purchase their textbooks and download them straight to their personal computers. Its VitalSource Bookshelf software has built-in active learning features that help students search and study more effectively.

○ For more information about Ingram Digital Group, go to www.ingramdigital.com

○ For more information about VitalSource Bookshelf software, visit www.vitalsource.com

Finding College and University Contact Information

The two companies that are listed on pages 140 and 141 in the K–12 market section, QED and MDR, also provide contact information and mailing lists for the college and university marketplace. Even though this market segment is particularly suited to direct mail, personal visits, and telephone calls, you can also reach it indirectly through school-supply stores, educational distributors, trade shows, book fairs, and more. The following are a sampling of the outlets through which you can indirectly reach colleges and universities:

Conferences:

○ Find lists of state college conferences at www.allconferences.com/Regional/State_College/

Educational Distribution Partners:

❑ Follet College Stores Co.; 400 W. Grand Ave., Elmhurst, IL 60126 Tel: 630-279-2330; Website: www.follett.com

❏ J.R. Holcomb Educational Materials; 3205 Harvard Ave., Cleveland, OH 44105
  Tel: 216-341-3000; Website: www.holcombs.com

❏ Nebraska Book Company, Inc.; 4700 S. 19th St., Lincoln, NE 68501
  Tel: 402-421-7300; Website: www.nebook.com

School Supply Stores:

❏ ABC School Supply, Inc.; 3312 N. Berkeley Lake Rd., Duluth, GA 30096
  Tel: 800-669-4222; Website: www.abcschoolsupply.com

❏ University Book Store; 711 State St., Madison, WI 53703
  Tel: 608-257-3784; Website: www.univbkstr.com

Trade Shows:

○ Collegiate Marketing Expo: www.camex.org

PROFESSIONAL INSTITUTIONS AND ORGANIZATIONS

Professional institutions and organizations represent the needs of individuals who are skilled in a particular field. The professional market ranges from scholarly areas, such as physics, to skilled trades, such as plumbing.

Professional, Scholarly, and Reference Book Selection

Professional institutions and organizations all select books a little bit differently, depending on how they use them. Some of them recommend books to readers through reviews, some purchase books for their members, and some buy books and sell them through their own bookstores. There are three types of books that can be sold to the professional academic market. They include professional books, scholarly books, and reference books.

Professional Books

Professional books are geared toward people who work in specific professions. They are most often intended to improve job performance or provide specialized knowledge in a particular field. Technical and scientific books, medical books, legal books, and business books are included in this category.

Scholarly Books

Scholarly books are designed to examine a very narrow topic on an academic level. There are scholarly books for almost every profession, occupation, field, and vocation. They contain advanced content that requires readers to have background knowledge of the topic. Most scholarly books contain numerous references and footnotes.

Reference Books

Directories, encyclopedias, handbooks, guides, readers, and dictionaries are all considered reference books. These types of books provide detailed facts and information, and are almost always used as resources, rather than read cover to cover.

Selling to Professional Institutions and Organizations

Professional, scholarly, and reference books are generally priced higher than most other books. They are often available in specialized bookstores and libraries, and may be purchased by individuals or companies.

Reviews will help your sales tremendously in this market. Send review copies to pertinent publications, including professional journals and specialty magazines that market to the profession your book targets. Learn more about obtaining reviews in *35. Seek Niche Reviews* (page 259). You should also research individual organizations to find out the name of the buyer and the submission guidelines, so you can make direct contact.

Finding Professional Institution and Organization Contact Information

Since there are so many professional institutions and organizations that target all different skill sets, the best way to find the ones that are related to your title is by performing a search on your favorite search engine. However, there are also directories and encyclopedias of associations available for purchase that can help you. They offer categorical lists of associations, non-profit member organizations, professional societies, and more. Descriptive and contact information is provided for each entry. These resources are a great way to find groups of people already segmented into various professions, and even if the actual association does not end up purchasing your book, its members might. See *18. Associations* (page 136) for more information about these resources.

Additionally, the *Ulrich's Periodicals Directory* is an excellent resource for finding professional publications. It is a unique, current, comprehensive, and continuously updated directory and database that provides information about popular and academic magazines, scientific journals, newspapers, and other serial publications. Ulrich's scope is international, but it emphasizes English-language publications. The directory's online version includes over 300,000 active and current periodicals.

❏ Ulrich's Periodicals Directory; Serials Solutions, 501 N. 34th St. #400, Seattle, WA 98103
 Tel: 206-545-9056, 866-737-4257; Website: www.ulrichsweb.com

GOVERNMENT SCHOOLS

Like homeschools, government schools represent a non-traditional segment of the academic marketplace. The education system operated by the United States Department of Defense serves the children of men and women in the armed services who are stationed in the United States, Europe, and the Pacific. Until 1994, this system was organized into two separate but parallel systems: the Department of Defense Dependents Schools overseas, and the Department of Defense Domestic Dependent Elementary and Secondary Schools in the United States. In 1994, the two systems merged together under one organization—the Department of Defense Education Activity (DoDEA).

❑ DoDEA; 4040 N. Fairfax Dr., Webb Bldg., Arlington, VA 22203
   Tel: 703-588-3104; Website: www.dodea.edu

DoDEA operates 199 schools in 14 districts. These districts are located in 14 foreign countries, 7 states, Guam, and Puerto Rico. All schools within DoDEA are fully accredited by United States accreditation agencies. Approximately 8,700 teachers serve DoDEA's 88,000 students.

○ A current list of DoDEA schools may be obtained by writing the Department of Defense Dependent Schools, Hoffman I, Rm. 152, 2461 Eisenhower Ave., Alexandria, VA 22331.

Children of military members and of most command-sponsored civilians may attend Department of Defense Dependents Schools at no cost. Students are assigned to schools based on grade level. The mission of DoDEA is to provide an environment in which students can realize their learning potential in all areas of growth and development.

DoDEA schools have active Parent Teacher Associations that are affiliated with the National Parent Teacher Association, and locally elected School Advisory Committees participate in governing DoDEA schools. In grades one through six, DoDEA begins to focus on individualized instruction. Basic skills in language arts, science, mathematics, and social studies form the heart of the academic program. DoDEA's middle schools focus on the continued social and academic growth and development of seventh and eighth grade students, and offer an exploratory program that may include home economics, technology education, keyboarding, drama, art, music, foreign language, physical education, and computer skills. High school programs accommodate specific interests and needs of individuals and groups of students, and are based upon the knowledge, skills, and attitudes of the students.

Additionally, DoDEA provides a variety of educational programs to meet specific needs of students. Its Child Find program seeks out students who have special educational needs and offers them and disabled students ages three through twenty-one a full range of learning programs. Sure Start, a comprehensive approach to early childhood education for at risk children, is another program that is available through DoDEA. Therefore, if your book is related to children with special needs, these programs may be interested in purchasing it.

The Defense Education Supplies Procurement Office (DESPO) located in Richmond, Virginia is the office that handles educational curriculum requirements for all DoDEA schools worldwide. It oversees textbook, educational software, and supplemental material selection, so your government school sales will most likely be made through this office.

○ To learn more about DoDEA procurement, go to www.dodea.edu/offices/procurement/procurementSpecialist.cfm

One message that persists throughout this book is that you cannot simply look at a market segment as one, homogeneous entity. This axiom is particularly relevant in the academic marketplace because it is so broad. The need for quality content is universal, but the type and form of content is dependent on many things and varies greatly. If you think your book might be right for the academic market, take the time to investigate how, when, where why, and to whom you could sell it so you do not waste valuable resources. Selling to the academic market can be time consuming. But if you are patient and give it time to evolve—updating your content as necessary—you could experience lucrative sales.

20. GOVERNMENT AGENCIES

How would you like to sell to a customer who needs what you are selling, has virtually unlimited funds, is required to return your calls, must pay you within thirty days or will owe you interest, and buys books on a non-returnable basis? Believe it or not, there is such as customer, and it is your own government. There are local, state, and federal government agencies focused on every aspect of people's lives. Oftentimes, these agencies seek written information to help them educate and serve their constituents. Depending on your content, your book could fill their needs.

ADVANTAGES AND DISADVANTAGES OF SELLING TO GOVERNMENT AGENCIES

Even though the government offers many opportunities to sell your book, there are some caveats of which you must be aware. There are both positive and negative aspects to selling in this massive, potentially lucrative marketplace.

Advantages

In addition to being a customer that needs and can pay for what you have to sell, there are other reasons you should consider selling to the government, as well. They are included in the following list:

■ Government agencies can, and often do buy books in large quantities. Large quantity purchases typically result in less frequent orders, which will both reduce your costs and optimize your profitability.

■ Government agencies can buy, license, or acquire your book, and they can also contract you to write new material. This opens many channels of negotiation. You can sell to them in the form they want to buy, in the way that is most lucrative to you.

■ The government is the largest printer and mailer in the world. This means that you can write material on a work-for-hire basis and have the government agency pay for the printing. Then, if it licenses your material you can get significant distribution at no cost by having it do the mailing.

■ The personnel shortage that exists within many government agencies is actually a benefit to publishers, because it requires the agencies to outsource a lot of their work. In other words, they are forced to pay publishers to create materials because they do not have the manpower to do so themselves.

■ Government agencies often pay by credit card, eliminating the purchase-order process, which is more detailed.

As you can see, sales to government agencies offer many advantages. You can negotiate on more favorable terms and reduce your costs, all the while maximizing your sales, revenue, and profitably.

Disadvantages

Even with all of its advantages, there is still a downside to selling to government agencies. Several of the disadvantages are included in the following list:

■ There are a lot of required forms to fill out, making it a laborious process, and payment is delayed until they are all properly completed. If you keep your order totals under $3,000, though, you are classified as an open market vendor, for which there is not as much paperwork. An open market vendor is one not under a specific contract to work with the government, so there are fewer forms to complete and less reporting to do. This reduces the time and frustration it sometimes takes to complete larger sales.

■ If you get a government contract you become open to government audits, according to Mark Amtower, a government sales consultant. Therefore, you must keep accurate records of your contracts, expenses, and sales.

■ Government agencies expect "most-favored-nation" pricing, which means the discounts you offer them must be better than your standard commercial discounts. Publishers typically have standard discount structures, typically based on the quantities ordered. Some government agencies expect to get your best discounts even if the quantity levels are not reached.

■ Unexpected packages that arrive in government agencies' offices are irradiated, which can damage books. Therefore, if you send a sample copy, make sure the recipient has requested it—do not send books blind.

The better you know the system and its advantages and disadvantages, the better you will be able to avoid the quagmire of forms and procedures in which you can get caught. Once you have gained and understanding of how things work, the path is clear for large-volume sales.

CONTRACT WORK

Government agencies regularly seek people to write documents, books, and pamphlets specifically for them. The federal government can actually become your publisher by contracting with you for a project and subsequently buying your work. In fact, the average author stands a better chance of getting published by writing for the government, than they do through traditional royalty publishing.

According to Mark Amtower, "In most cases, agencies prefer existing content but they will opt for a sole-source contract if more specific content is needed." A sole-source contract is one in which there is no competitive bidding. Under these circumstances, you could sell your book to an agency on an unlimited use license, which means there are no restrictions on how, where, or how many times the product can be used. Be sure to explicitly maintain ownership of the rights to sell your content in other ways, though, such as film, foreign, and electronic rights, because the government assumes intellectual property is theirs unless it is otherwise specifically stated in the contract.

The contracting process is complicated and there are countless situations, processes, and variations that can arise. Conducting research before attempting sales is always important, but it is particularly necessary in this marketplace. The following websites will help you learn about, and begin contracting with the government:

○ Register as a contractor at www.business.gov/guides/contracting/register.html

○ Find federal contracting opportunities and learn how to locate and bid on them at www.business.gov/guides/contracting/register.html

○ Learn the rules, regulations, and standards that govern the federal procurement process at www.business.gov/guides/contracting/far.html

If your existing content is not directly appropriate to the needs of the government buyers, try to establish a contract with them to customize your material, thereby creating a win-win situation. You make a sale, and they get exactly what they want.

SELLING TO GOVERNMENT AGENCIES

The United States federal government is the largest buyer of goods and services in the world. It spends roughly $30 to $40 million each working hour, and signs more than 56,000 contracts each day. The collective value of these contracts is worth hundreds of billions of dollars, and that amount does not even include the money spent for state and local contracts. Approximately 90 percent of government purchases are for $25,000 or less, and it must direct 23 percent of all its purchasing dollars toward purchases reserved for small businesses. Therefore, small publishers are actually in a superior position to get government work because the government is required to buy from them.

You should market to government buyers the same way you would market to any commercial buyer. Get to know them. Find out their needs and buying criteria. Government buyers prefer to buy locally, so make appointments to meet with buyers at your city or state's government office whenever possible. You will learn much more about the direct sales process in *Chapter Five. Start Selling* (page 233).

There is little seasonality in the purchasing process in this marketplace since it operates almost continuously. However, there is a period coined "fiscal year frenzy," which occurs in September at the end of each fiscal year. At this time, agencies are eager to spend their remaining budget dollars, because if they do not, they will lose them in the following year's budget. Therefore, you might want to begin contacting buyers in July, which is when they are planning out how to spend their remaining funds, and encourage them to spend their remaining funds on your products or services.

Local, state, and federal governments make purchases in a number of different ways. One is through a blanket purchase agreement, which is negotiated with each vendor individually. A blanket purchase order is a long-term commitment to a publisher for products or services, against which short-term releases are generated on a predetermined basis to satisfy requirements. For example, the purchase order may be for 10,000 books to be shipped quarterly in quantities of 2,500. The commitment remains to buy the total quantity, but the agency may not want the products delivered all at once.

Generally, government agencies prefer to use credit cards when procuring products and services up to $2,500. Larger purchases, on the other hand, require more paperwork so have to be handled a little differently. The General Services Administration (GSA) within the federal government has already issued more than 250,000 SmartPay cards to federal employees to use for making these smaller purchases. If your company accepts Visa or MasterCard, it will also accept GSA SmartPay cards, and the transactions can be processed through your existing merchant account. If you do not currently accept Visa or Mastercard, set-up a merchant account with one of the providers.

HELPFUL RESOURCES

As previously mentioned, selling to government agencies can be confusing. Luckily, there are extensive resources available to help you. One such resource is Fedmarket.com, which offers a plethora of products and services to help customers win federal business. It is the most comprehensive government-contracting resource in the industry, and its website includes weekly newsletters on GSA schedules, proposal writing, and federal sales.

❑ Fedmarket.com; 3 Bethesda Metro Center, Ste. M010, Bethesda, MD 20814
Tel: 301-652-9504, 866-519-4482; Website: www.fedmarket.com

However, Fedmarket.com's products can be fairly pricey. You can find much of the same information for free on one or both of Mark Amtower's websites:

❍ www.governmentexpress.com

❍ www.governmentmarketingbestpractices.com

The Office of Small Business Development Centers (SBDC) is another helpful resource for selling in this marketplace. It provides management assistance to current and prospective small business owners. SBDCs offer assistance to individuals and small businesses by providing information about buying from government agencies in centrally located, easily accessible branch locations. The small-business assistance program is a cooperative effort of the private sector, the educational community, and federal, state, and local governments, and is an integral component of SBDC's network of training and counseling services. Use your local SBDC to learn how to work your way through the labyrinth of government forms and procedures.

❍ To find an SBDC near you go to
www.sba.gov/aboutsba/sbaprograms/sbdc/sbdclocator/SBDC_LOCATOR.html

Additionally, the United States Small Business Administration (SBA) provides a step-by-step guide for selling to the federal government. It includes tips on bidding, marketing, and competing for government contracts, as well as links to free online courses.

❑ United States Small Business Administration; 409 3rd St., SW, Washington, DC 20416
Tel: 800-827-5722; Website: www.sba.gov

The SBA published a report entitled, "Doing Business with the Federal Government." This report describes the SBA's Prime Contracts Program, which is dedicated to increasing small businesses' share of government contracts. It also describes SBA's Subcontracting Assistance Program, which promotes maximum use of small businesses by the nation's largest prime contractors.

❍ This report can be downloaded at www.sba.gov/opc

The SBA also has a Procurement Marketing and Access Network, commonly called PRO-Net, which is an online procurement shop. PRO-Net's website has a search engine for contracting officers, as well as links to other important information and procurement opportunities. PRO-Net was designed to simplify the federal contracting process by creating a database of small businesses that want to do business with the government. There is no fee to sign your business up for this service, and doing so can help you work more smoothly and profitably with the federal government.

○ PRO-Net: www.pronet.sba.gov

Finally, all small businesses seeking federal, state, and private contracts can fill out and update their own profiles on SBA's website. This will simultaneously enter your business in the PRO-Net database, leading government buyers to contact you.

○ SBA's small business forms can be found at
   www.sba.gov/tools/Forms/index.html

LOCAL AND STATE GOVERNMENT SALES

Your local library can supply a wealth of information about how your local government works. Talk with the research librarian to learn about the structure of your local government and its agencies. Ask how the agencies purchase books, what books they purchase, and what paperwork is required to sell to them.

> **TIP**
>
> Get used to completing a lot of paperwork if you intend to sell to government agencies at any level.

You should attempt sales to your local government first, before moving up to state and regional agencies. Official City Sites can help you get started. It is an online resource for local, city, and state information. On its website you will find contact information and procedures to follow when dealing with government agencies in each different state.

○ Visit Official City Sites' website at www.officialcitysites.org

Additionally, speak with procurement specialists or contracting officers about local, city, and state government buying procedures at Procurement Technical Assistance Centers (PTAC) to help you get started selling to the government (See page 157 for more information about PTACs). Ask them questions about application procedures, technical requirements, and marketing suggestions. If possible, you should also attend procurement programs, which are opportunities for business people to meet directly with government officials and to learn from other companies that are already involved in federal contracting.

○ All details, locations, and contact information for the PTAC nearest you may be found at www.aptac-us.org

FEDERAL GOVERNMENT SALES

Selling successfully to the United States federal government can be intimidating, but you can make it less daunting by doing your homework before you begin selling. Registration is required to compete for federal government procurement and contracts. Before you register as a contractor and begin bidding on proposals, though, read about the programs and services that are available to help small businesses successfully compete for federal contracts in the "Small Business Guide to Federal Contracting."

○ This guide can be found at
www.business.gov/guides/contracting/small_biz.html

Once you are familiar with those programs, follow these three steps to register your business for sales to the federal government:

1. Obtain a Data Universal Numbering System (DUNS) number, which is a unique nine-digit identification number assigned to businesses. The process to request a DUNS number is free, and only takes about five to ten minutes.

○ To register for a DUNS number, call 866-705-5711, or go to
www.dnb.com/US/duns_update

During registration you will be asked to provide the following information:

- The legal name of your business

- Your company's structure—corporation, LLC, DBA, sole proprietorship—or other way in which it is commonly recognized

- Contact person's name

- Physical address, city, state, and zip code of your business

- Mailing address (if different)

- Telephone number

- NAICS code, which classifies the type of products or services your business offers

○ Find your NAICS Code at www.census.gov/epcd/www/naics.html

- Number of employees

- Headquarters name and address, and whether your location is a subsidiary or division of a larger entity

2. Register with the government's Central Contractor Registration database. For help, use the Central Contractor Registration Handbook.

○ The Registration database can be found at www.ccr.gov

○ The Handbook can be found at www.ccr.gov/doc/CCR_Handbook.pdf

3. Complete an Online Representations and Certifications Application.

○ The application is located at https://orca.bpn.gov

It is important to find the federal government agency that correctly correlates with your title. One way to find the department that is responsible for publishing books dealing with your content is to look at the official online bookstore for United States Government publications for purchase from the United States Government Printing Office. The online bookstore allows you to browse by topic, and then gives you a list of the agencies who publish books on it. For example, say you have a book on the American Revolution. By clicking on that topic, you learn that the Interior Department, the Commerce Department, the National Park Service, and the Department of Defense all publish related information. Once you discover which agencies are relevant to your title, you can contact the public affairs office within each without wasting valuable time on extraneous agencies.

○ The United States Government's online bookstore is located at
   http://bookstore.gpo.gov

Additionally, the following individual agencies' websites will provide you with helpful selling information specific to their own departments:

○ Department of Defense:
   www.acq.osd.mil/osbp/doing_business/DoD_Contracting_Guide.htm

○ Department of Health and Human Services:
   www.os.dhhs.gov/grants/index.shtml#contract

○ Department of Housing and Urban Development:
   www.hud.gov/offices/cpo/index.cfm

○ Department of Interior: www.doi.gov/osdbu

○ Department of Justice: www.usdoj.gov/jmd/pe/

○ Department of State: www.statebuy.state.gov/

○ Department of Transportation: www.dot.gov/ost/m60/

○ Department of Treasury:
   www.ustreas.gov/offices/management/dcfo/procurement/

○ Department of Veterans Affairs: www1.va.gov/oamm

Finally, the following list contains several more resources that will help facilitate your sales to the federal government:

■ FedBizOpps.gov is the website to go to for federal government procurement opportunities over $25,000. Government buyers are able to publicize their business opportunities by posting information on this website. Publishers seeking federal markets for their products and services can search, monitor, and retrieve opportunities solicited by the entire federal contracting community.

○ FedBizOpps.gov: www.fedbizopps.gov

■ Briefly mentioned before, Procurement Technical Assistance Centers (PTACs) are another great resource available to people who want to learn how to sell to the federal government. According to Mark Amtower, there are ninety-three of them located throughout the United States. PTACs are local resources available at no, or nominal costs, and they can provide businesses with assistance in marketing products and services to federal, state, and local governments. Although their main focus is providing technical assistance on selling to the military since they are run by the Department of Defense, PTACs cover sales to all government agencies through counseling, training, and procurement programs. They provide a wide range of assistance covering every phase of government contracting—from initial registrations through contract completion.

❑ Association of Procurement Technical Assistance Centers; P.O. Box 1607, 405 N 3rd St., Orange, TX 77631
Tel: 409-886-0125; Website: www.aptac-us.org

■ The federal government's Business Partner Network is the single source of vendor data for the federal government. This network creates and maintains a database of all potential suppliers to federal government agencies. Create a profile for your company by clicking on the Central Contractor Registration (CCR) link on the website's homepage. This will give you regular access to federal contracting opportunities, especially those for small businesses. It will also allow you to populate the Small Business Administration's (SBA) Supplemental Pages—known as DSBS—where your business information and capabilities statements can be viewed by contracting officers, large prime contractors, and the general public.

○ Business Partner Network: www.bpn.gov

■ The General Services Administration (GSA) is the federal government's chief acquisitions agency. It spends billions of dollars annually on products and services offered to all federal agencies. GSA's website is an excellent place to find answers to questions you may have about selling to the federal government. It has sample acquisition letters and contracts, a list of upcoming events and new vendor training sessions, downloadable reference manuals, acquisition requirements and policies, FAQs, and the names and contact information for the people you will need to work with when selling to the government.

○ General Services Administration: www.gsa.gov

○ GSA forms library: www.gsa.gov/Portal/gsa/ep/formslibrary.do

■ Acquisition Central is a website for the federal acquisition community and the government's business partners. From this website you can access shared systems and tools to help you conduct business efficiently. Acquisition Central gives prospective government vendors a place to learn about the acquisitions policies, manuals, and reports for most departments of the federal government. Through this website you can learn about regulations, systems, resources, opportunities, and training. You will also find federal agency procurement forecasts, a list of upcoming department conferences, contract award schedules, and PDF downloads for beginners.

○ Acquisition Central: www.acquisition.gov

■ Google has a separate engine for searching government websites. This makes it easy to quickly find the information you need exclusively for dealing with the federal government. The number and type of hits you get are much smaller, making your search much faster.

○ Google's government search engine: www.Google.com/ig/usgov

■ You can learn up-to-the-minute advice about selling to the government on Mark Amtower's "Off Center" radio show, which airs every Friday at two in the afternoon.

○ You can listen to the show online at www.federalnewsradio.com, or if you are in Washington, DC you can find it on station 1050 AM.

■ The Federal Acquisition Jumpstation allows you to quickly access information about selling to all of the departments of the executive branch, and also provides procurement assistance.

○ Federal Acquisition Jumpstation: http://nais.nasa.gov/fedproc/home.html

■ FedWorld.gov is a gateway to government information. It is a comprehensive central access point for searching, locating, ordering, and acquiring government and business information. On this website you can locate direct links to federal and state legislators who can help you get started selling governments. Additionally, the website provides an A to Z index of United States government departments and agencies, as well as hundreds of links to official government information and services.

○ FedWorld.gov: www.fedworld.gov

■ USA.gov is an easy-to-search, free-access website designed to give you a centralized place to find information from local, state, and federal government agency websites.

○ USA.gov: www.usa.gov

Embarking into this marketplace for the first time can, at times, be tedious, confusing, and overwhelming. But if you persist, you will be rewarded for your hard work. Government agencies have both the need for written materials and the resources to buy them. If you take the time to properly jump through the necessary hoops, you will be greeted by abundant opportunities.

21. MILITARY MARKETPLACE

The military marketplace is made up of over two million active duty personnel and dependents, almost one million civilians working for the Department of Defense, and nearly two million retired service people. Selling to this group becomes an easier task if you break it down into smaller, more manageable segments. The segments within this marketplace range from military exchange services, to military media outlets, to non-military sales channels, and more—all of which are described in this section.

THE OVERSEAS MILITARY MARKET

The overseas military market includes the military personnel and their dependents who are living at the military bases and posts located in foreign countries.

> The Army operates on *posts* or *installations*, while the other branches of the military operate on *bases*.
>
> **T I P**

The opportunity to sell books to this market segment has declined over the past few years, primarily due to the numerous troop deployments in the Middle East. The expenses to support the military efforts in that part of the world have resulted in troop redeployments from bases in Europe and the Pacific, to bases in Iraq and Afghanistan. This has also resulted in the relocation of families from these overseas bases back to the United States. According to Jerry Wigen of Jagco and Associates (page 163), a representative group that specializes in overseas military bookstores, "The number of military bookstores overseas has declined from approximately three hundred to about fifty-five over the past fifteen years." However, sales of books through the remaining stores continue to total about $20 million annually, which is still a substantial market for publishers.

Overseas stores carry a broad range of products because they do not have much retail competition. The types of books that sell best are bestsellers, cookbooks, and children's books. Other books that sell well are host-country language books and travel books about the host region. Additionally, juvenile and foreign language audio products and book and CD combinations tend to be popular. Furthermore, due to the high number of single military personnel, sexually-oriented material also sells well, but Jerry added, "The Department of Defense (DoD) monitors material of this nature closely, and it all must comply with DoD standards."

Content, durability, and price are all important criteria in book selection, because the patrons of these stores are on limited incomes and they move around a lot. Children's books in particular must be priced low, while other categories, such as cookbooks, have a little more price flexibility. In most cases, softcover books are preferred, since they are usually less expensive than their casebound counterparts. Additionally, overseas military personnel seek out books that will give them a break from the pressures of their duties, particularly in areas of conflict. Therefore, fiction tends to sell well, but non-fiction books on heavy topics—business, religion, finance, etc.—are generally not top sellers.

THE DOMESTIC MILITARY MARKET

The domestic military market includes sales to military personnel, their dependants, and retired military personnel who are living in the United States. This is a transient market and people move regularly during their time in the service. Thus, although they seek information on a broad range of topics, they particularly look for books that help them deal with the pressures of their lifestyles.

The base and post exchanges in the United States have to compete with local retail stores, so they carry a smaller selection of books. This selection is limited to bestsellers, mass market paperbacks, magazines, and some special buys to support in-store promotions. Softcover books are the majority, and hardcover books are rare. The content of the books carried by domestic exchanges is across the board. For example, books on helping children cope with moving, finding work in a new city, dealing with domestic violence, personal finance, and more have all found success. Books that typically do not sell well are on general topics such as art and photography. Coffee-table books are not big sellers, either.

EXCHANGE SERVICES

The largest buyers of all types of books in both the overseas and domestic military markets are the exchange services, of which there are four—Army and Air Force, Coast Guard, Marine Corps, and Navy. Exchanges are discount retail stores run by the military services that provide quality goods and services at low prices to active duty military, their families, retirees, and reservists. They are located on military bases and installations in the United States and overseas. Exchanges operate under commercial business and accounting practices, and carry a broad range of branded and house-brand hard goods, soft goods, and consumables. Most exchanges have a book-selling section, or in some cases, an elaborate bookstore. More detailed information about each of the different exchange services is included in the following list:

■ *Army and Air Force Exchange Service.* The Army and Air Force Exchange Service (AAFES) is a military organization that controls over 12,000 exchange facilities worldwide, including main exchanges, military clothing sales stores, movie theaters, vending centers, personal services, concessions, and package-beverage stores. AAFES has a two-fold mission. First, it works to provide quality merchandise and services to soldiers, airmen, and their families wherever they are stationed around the world. Second, it generates reasonable earnings to support Army and Air Force Morale, Welfare, and Recreation (MWR) programs. AAFES buys goods and supplies from more than 32,000 businesses—approximately 90 percent of which are small businesses. You can download the entire AAFES Suppliers Handbook by clicking on the "Doing Business with AAFES" link on its website. The handbook contains a complete list of the base and post exchanges.

❑ Army and Air Force Exchange Service; 3911 S. Walton Walker Blvd., Dallas, TX 75236
Tel: 214-312-2011; Website: www.aafes.com

AAFES procures all book and magazine assortments from local and national distribution partners serving the areas in which the exchanges are located. With few exceptions for honor-and-decency compliance, these distributors make all purchasing decisions regarding titles that are appropriate for each store. AAFES distributors base their decisions on a number of factors, including store demographics, customer demand, and the business terms they negotiate with publishers. AAFES also requires that all books and magazines purchased be provided on a "guaranteed sales basis"—in other words, they must be returnable. If you are interested in selling books and publications to exchanges, these distributors should be contacted directly.

❍ A detailed list of distributors and their points of contact may be found at www.aafes.com/pa/selling/books.html

> **T I P**
>
> AAFES is a staunch supporter of minority-owned and operated businesses, and is committed to diversity through buying and contracting with diverse suppliers. For more information about AAFES' commitment to diversity, you can email the Supplier Diversity Manager at SupplierDiversity@aafes.com

■ *Coast Guard Exchange Service.* The Coast Guard Exchange Service (CGES) provides quality merchandise and services of necessity and convenience to Coast Guard men and women at competitive prices. Because CGES provides services to its customers in remote locations, some units operate with little or no profit as a benefit to military service members and their families. On the CGES website you will find an updated, complete list of Coast Guard exchanges, including address-es and phone numbers.

❑ Coast Guard Exchange System Headquarters; 870 Greenbrier Cir., Tower II, Ste. 502, Chesapeake, VA 23320
Tel: 804-734-8253; Website: www.cg-exchange.com

■ *Marine Corps Exchange Service.* The Marine Corps Exchange Service (MCES) provides a full line of retail products to active duty marines, sailors, soldiers, and airmen, as well as to their family members, retirees, and other authorized patrons. Historically, these exchanges were decentralized buying operations, and each exchange had a buying staff that focused on their respective installation's patrons. Recently, however, they have begun the process of centralizing buying functions while still maintaining input for local needs.

The MCES' merchandising policy is to respond to customer demand when selecting items and brands. Accordingly, the stock assortment is comprised of well-known brands and private label items that offer a demonstrated value. Each buyer reviews merchandise lines and determines if a product or service should be carried based on price, terms, and customer demand.

The MCES purchases retail merchandise, supplies, and equipment from manu-facturers and suppliers through negotiation. While most purchases are still made at the exchange level, some purchase requirements are consolidated at Exchange Headquarters for negotiation of a system-wide contract. Manufacturers and sup-pliers wishing to sell to a Marine Corps exchange should contact the exchange by mail or telephone for an appointment.

❑ Marine Corps Exchange Service; MWR Support Activity, 3044 Catlin Ave., Quantico, VA 22134
Tel: 703-784-6331; Website: www.usmc-mccs.org/buspartners/index.cfm

■ *Navy Exchange Service.* The Navy Exchange Service (NES) employs over 16,000 dedicated associates in over 100 locations worldwide. With the exception of the Ship Stores Program discussed later in this section, the Navy Exchange Service is a federal, non-appropriated fund activity. Non-Appropriated Fund Activities (also known as Morale, Welfare, and Recreation activities) help subsidize purchases by service personnel.

By clicking on the "Store Finder" link on the NES website, you will gain access to a full list of Navy exchanges, including their services, hours of operation, and contact information. Additionally, all of the forms required for doing business with the NES can be found by clicking on the "Contractor/Vendor/EDI" link that is also found on the NES website.

❑ Navy Exchange Service Command; 3280 Virginia Beach Blvd., Virginia Beach, VA 23452
Tel: 757-631-3906; Website: www.navy-nex.com

The NES currently purchases the majority of its books from local distribution partners that also provide in-store services to all exchange locations. Listed below are the distribution partners with which the NES is currently doing business, so you may contact them directly:

❑ Harrisburg News; Military Book Buyer, 980 Briarsdale Rd., Harrisburg, PA 17109
Tel: 717-561-8377, 800-676-6397; Website: www.harrisburgnewsco.com

❑ Hudson News Group; Military Book Buyer, One Meadowlands Plaza, Ste. 902, East Rutherford, NJ 07073
Tel: 201-867-3600 ext. 1018; Website: www.hudsongroup.com

❑ PMG International; Military Book Buyer, 1011 N Frio St., San Antonio, TX 78207
Tel: 404-363-6669 ext. 20; Website: www.pmg-intl.com

❑ Source Interlink/Chas Levy; 1200 N North Branch St., Chicago, IL 60622
Tel: 312-440-4400; Website: www.chaslevy.com, www.sourceinterlink.com

Exchanges have the potential to be great sales outlets for your books. The wide variety of products sold through them creates many opportunities for cross merchandising. Therefore, suggest pairing your book with an existing product to increase your chances of making a sale.

SUBMITTING YOUR BOOK

In addition to direct sellers, military exchanges rely on distribution partners to purchase products for their bookstores. Publishers who wish to supply their books to military bases either in the United States or overseas can obtain a list of relevant distributors by contacting the AAFES.

○ To obtain this list, contact Lisa Lamers, Contracting Officer for books and magazines at lamersl@aafes.com

You can choose to sell your books yourself, use distribution partners, or use representative groups that sell directly to the exchanges. However, since the market is very tight right now, know that smaller publishers stand a much better chance of getting books into the exchanges by going through a distribution partner or representative group, such as Jagco and Associates, rather than going it alone.

❑ Jagco and Associates, Inc.; 598 Indian Trail Rd. South #227, Indian Trail, NC 28079
Tel: 704-684-0399

Representatives work on a commission basis and usually receive 10 percent of net sales. Distribution partners who handle books for the overseas exchanges generally want a 55 percent discount off the retail price, 120-day payment terms, paid freight, and return privileges on all products that are purchased. When submitting your books to these middlemen, it is not necessary to include a marketing plan. The book itself is the buyers' major concern.

SELLING ABOARD SHIPS

In addition to selling to overseas and domestic military exchanges, there are also opportunities to sell your books aboard ships. There are approximately 180 Ship Stores on United States Navy commissioned ships. The mission of the Ship Store program is to provide quality goods at discounted prices. As you can imagine, space aboard ships is very limited; thus, only the most necessary items in each category are held in stock. Ship Stores carry basic necessities such as soap and shampoo, as well as a limited selection of semi-luxury items such as watches, books, and consumer electronic items. However, the crewmembers may place orders for almost any items—including books—that are available through the Navy Exchange Service Command (NEXCOM). Your inquiries and correspondence should be directed to the following address:

❑ Ship Stores Program, NEXCOM, 3280 Virginia Beach Blvd., Virginia Beach, VA 23452
   Tel: 757-502-7473/7474, 800-628-3924; Website: www.navy-nex.com

Crewmembers are made aware of available items via the Ships Store Electronic Catalog (SSEC). The Ship's Supply Officer or an appointed Ships Store Sales Officer decides which titles will be listed in the SSEC. The SSEC contains descriptions of the products, ordering information, company and contact names, and prices. To have your title added to the SSEC, you must present it to the Ships Store Program for review and determination of quality, value, and applicability for the seagoing retail stores.

Along with a copy of your book, you need to submit a letter stating that you are the publisher and own all the rights to your book. In addition, include your published price list, minimum order requirements, terms, and delivery schedules. Given the tight economic conditions of people in the military, the lower your book is priced, the more likely it is to be accepted and purchased. A good pricing strategy is to ask what the Ship Store's typical terms are first, so you do not leave any money on the table. Each book must also have either a Universal Product Code (UPC) or a Bar Code. See page 40 for instructions on how to obtain a UPC.

Suppliers are required to participate in the Ships Store Electronic Commerce/Electronic Data Interchange (EC/EDI) programs. These are the same programs that are used by Costco, Wal-Mart, and other major retailers, so it's a good idea to be familiar with them in general. If you are not EC/EDI compliant, the

Ships Store Program will provide you with the necessary information you will need to become compliant. Meanwhile, your book may be added to the SSEC as a probationary item, or identified as an authorized item but available to ships by special purchase order only.

Most likely, shipboard sales will not yield significant quantities or revenue for you. However, if you have the right book at the right price, you can provide a much-needed service for these service personnel.

ADDITIONAL SALES OPPORTUNITIES ON BASES AND POSTS

In addition to the exchange stores, military bases and posts provide various other sales opportunities, as well. These include sales through their health care facilities, family support groups, employee assistance programs, spouse clubs, family centers, and more. You should research each individual base and post to find out the specific programs they offer. The website listed below will provide you with the necessary contact information:

○ www.militarytimes.com/military-installations-guide

The following list contains some examples of the places and programs available on military bases and posts that could potentially turn into solid sales outlets for your books:

■ The Defense Commissary Agency (DeCA) operates a worldwide chain of commissaries providing groceries to military personnel, retirees, and their families. If you have a book that can be cross-merchandised with grocery products, contact these buyers and give them your ideas.

❏ Defense Commissary Agency; 38th St. and East Ave., Bldg. 11200, Ft. Lee, VA 23801
  Tel: 757-483-8515; Website: www.commissaries.com

■ The National Guard Family Program exists to establish and facilitate ongoing communication, involvement, support, and recognition between National Guard families and the National Guard.

It does this through education, outreach services, and partnerships. Contact this program to see if your book can help them meet National Guard families' needs.

❏ National Guard Family Program; 1411 Jefferson Davis Hwy., Arlington, VA 22202
  Tel: 703-607-5414; Website: www.guardfamily.org

■ The Defense Department Child Development Program is the largest employer-sponsored childcare program in the country, serving children from newborn to age twelve. It includes child development centers, family childcare, and school-age childcare programs. If you have a children's book, you may want to start here.

○ Defense Department Child Development Program:
www.allmilitary.com/spouseandfamily/daycare/CDS.html

■ The Employee Assistance Program helps Coast Guard service members and their families with problems. The centers serve not only active-duty members and their families, but also reservists on active duty, Defense Department civilians, and military retirees. Your book may be a good tool for use through this program.

○ Employee Assistance Program:
www.uscg.mil/WORKLIFE/employee_assistance.asp

■ Life skills educational programs help military families with parenting, stress management, and other life skills. If you have related content, be sure to inquire about sales through these programs.

○ Life skills educational programs: www.milspouse.org/Educ/

■ Relocation assistance helps families plan moves and manage the challenges of adapting into a new community. Your book could help them with their mission.

○ Relocation assistance: www.milspouse.org/Relocate/

■ Special-needs family member assistance programs offer information and support to family members who have special requirements for medical, educational, or mental health services. If your book is on a related subject, they may be interested.

○ Special-needs family member assistance programs:
www.milspouse.org/Benefits/SpChild/

■ Spouse clubs are found at most military installations. They help spouses get acquainted with new communities, make friends, and find support. If your book can help them do this, there is a good chance you will make a sale.

○ Spouse Clubs: www.milspouse.org

Finally, most bases and posts have a library. Refer to *22. Libraries* (page 175) for information about selling both to libraries in general, and about selling specifically to military libraries. Department of Defense Dependant Schools are also relevant to this discussion, and *19. The Academic Market* (page 137) will provide you with all the information you will need to sell to them.

The military actively seeks to support and help the family members of its service personnel. It offers a wide variety of assistance programs and needs collateral and supplemental materials to assist them. If the program related to your content does not currently offer books as a resource, convince it to start with yours.

HELPFUL SALES RESOURCES

Selling to the military can be a complicated process, so do not hesitate to rely on available resources to assist you. The following websites are gateways into their respective departments, and will help you find all of the necessary information to first educate yourself about the sales process, and then to actually get started selling:

○ Air Force: www.selltoairforce.org

○ Army Corps of Engineers: www.usace.army.mil/business.html

○ Army Security Assistance Command:
   www.usasac.army.mil/Business/mainbiz.htm

○ Department of Defense: www.defenselink.mil/other_info/business.html

○ Department of Veterans Affairs: www1.va.gov/oamm/

○ Navy: www.donhq.navy.mil/OSBP/

Additionally, there are resources dedicated specifically to small businesses. The Office of Small Business Programs provides DoD information, publications, and programs to help small, disadvantaged, or minority-owned businesses compete for DoD contracts.

❑ Office of Small Business Programs; Crystal Gateway North, Ste. 406 West
   Tower, 201 12th St. South, Arlington, VA 22202
   Tel: 703-604-0157; Website: www.acq.osd.mil/osbp

The Office of Small Business Programs' website also includes *The Guide to DOD Contracting Opportunities*, which tells you how to obtain a Data Universal Number System (DUNS) Number, how to register with Central Contractor Registration, tips to identify your target market within DoD, ideas to familiarize yourself with DoD contracting procedures, and other assistance. You can access this guide at the following website:

○ www.acq.osd.mil/osbp/doing_business/DoD_Contracting_Guide.htm

Finally, the Defense Logistics Agency also provides valuable information for small businesses wanting to sell to the military.

○ There are many DLA locations around the United States and contact
   information for each may be found at www.dla.mil/facts.aspx

MILITARY ASSOCIATIONS

Military associations represent the interests of active, reserve, veteran, and retired military members and their families. The associations provide services to their members, inform them and the general public about issues of concern, and also help bring together military communities with similar interests or backgrounds.

Apply the same principles when contacting military associations as you would when contacting other associations. Instructions for doing so may be found in *18. Associations* (page 127). The following list includes some of the armed services associations, information about what they do, and how to get in touch with them:

■ *American Logistics Association.* The American Logistics Association (ALA) is a non-profit trade association dedicated to promoting, protecting, and enhancing the quality of life for active duty, retired, and reserve military personnel and their families. ALA's members are manufacturers, manufacturer's representatives, brokers, distributors, publishers, and service providers who sell or provide products and services to the military resale systems. The term "military resale systems" is used to include all military exchanges, commissaries, Department of State stores, and Veterans' Canteens (now partnered with AAFES).

ALA also sells to the Morale, Welfare, and Recreation (MWR) services industries. MWR provides free and discounted recreation facilities and supplies to military personnel and their families. MWR programs include fitness centers, pools, marinas, bowling centers, golf courses, restaurants, conference centers, and special events. Perhaps your book could be used in conjunction with one of these programs.

The ALA produces two publications. The first is "Executive Briefing," which is a weekly electronic newsletter that keeps ALA members up to speed on the latest business and legislative developments, as well as important association and industry activities. Read this newsletter to learn more about selling to the government and for potential promotional opportunities. The second publication is "The Worldwide Directory," which is ALA's member directory. It lists ALA members and serves as a reference guide to the military resale industry. The annual directory is distributed to all association members and its military trading partners, making it a good vehicle for print advertising to give your company added exposure.

Additionally, the ALA holds meetings and expositions. The first is the MWR Exposition, which is a biennial tradeshow. It is the single largest gathering of MWR professionals, and it brings together the many components of the MWR industry. The event features products and services that are sold to military and government agencies for use in community support activities on military installations throughout the world. If your company manufactures, distributes, sells, or represents products or services—or wants to—you should consider exhibiting at the next MWR Expo. Each branch of the Armed Forces has an MWR unit. Contact them to see if your content applies and if they will allow you to exhibit.

Secondly, ALA's All Services Exchange Roundtable is an annual educational event. It provides the opportunity for ALA members to meet with military representatives from regional and local military resale operations. Attend these events to network your way in to ALA. You can find the upcoming event schedule on ALA's website.

And finally, the Government Relations Forum is an annual event that enables people to meet and talk with the individuals in Congress that have a direct connection to the military resale and MWR activities of the United States Armed Forces. The most effective way to get into ALA is through networking—the more people you know, the more likely it is that you can get your book into the system.

❑ American Logistics Association; 1133 Fifteenth St., Ste. 640, Washington, DC 20005
Tel: 202-466-2520; Website: www.ala-national.org

■ *Gold Star Wives of America.* The wives of servicemen go through a lot. Congress charted Gold Star Wives of America (GSW) in 1980 to provide these women with information on benefits and programs for which they might be entitled. If you have relevant content, go to the GSW website and find the local chapters.

❑ Gold Star Wives of America; 5510 Columbia Pike, Ste. 205, Arlington, VA 22204
Tel: 888-479-9788; Website: www.goldstarwives.org

■ *National Military Family Association.* The National Military Family Association (NMFA) serves the families of the uniformed services through education, information, and advocacy, and is dedicated to identifying and resolving issues affecting them. Convince them to use your book to help them reach their goals.

❑ National Military Family Association; 6000 Stevenson Ave., Ste. 304, Alexandria, VA 22304
Tel: 703-823-6632; Website: www.nmfa.org

■ *Retired Officers Association.* The Retired Officers Association (ROA) aims to benefit members of the uniformed services and their families and survivors through efforts to preserve earned entitlements, and to maintain a strong national defense. Membership is open to active duty, retired, National Guard, reserve, former commissioned officers, and warrant officers of the Army, Navy, Air Force, Marine Corps, Coast Guard, Public Health Service, and National Oceanic and Atmospheric Administration. If your book can help ROA, get in touch.

❑ The Retired Officers Association; 201 N. Washington St., Alexandria, VA 22314
Tel: 800-245-8762; Website: www.troa.org

■ *Veterans of Foreign Wars.* The Veterans of Foreign Wars (VFW) provides programs and services that strengthen camaraderie among members, perpetuate the memory and history of fallen soldiers, foster patriotism, defend the Constitution, and promote service to our communities and our country.

❑ Veterans of Foreign Wars; 406 West 34th St., Kansas City, MO 64111
Tel: 816-756-3390; Website: www.vfw.org

Military associations are not much different from associations in general, in that their mission is to serve their members in some way. Find out what each association's particular mission is and try to relate your content to it. Attend their local chapter meetings, sell your books through their online stores, and work with them as you would work with any non-military association.

○ A website with a list of most military associations may be found at www.military.com/benefits/resources/military-and-veteran-associations

SELLING THROUGH MILITARY MEDIA

It is difficult to promote the sale of your titles to the military segment through advertising in general print media, because magazines and newspapers have only light penetration into military households. The reason for this is that the military personnel are transient. Local news is not particularly important to them, and if it is, they generally only subscribe to their hometown newspapers.

Therefore, the best way to reach this market is through military publications. The following list contains information about several of these publications, as well as their contact information. Contact them to ask for current rate cards, which will tell you the cost of advertising at different frequencies and sizes, and give you the closing date for each issue.

■ *Armed Forces Journal.* The *Armed Forces Journal* is published by the Army Times Publishing Company, the world's largest publisher of professional military and defense periodicals. It has publications serving all branches of the United States military, and it addresses the needs of the consumer and business-to-business communities served by its publications.

❑ Armed Forces Journal; 6883 Commercial Dr., Springfield, VA 22159
   Tel: 703-750-9000; Website: www.afji.com

■ *Family Magazine.* This is a magazine written exclusively for military commissary and exchange shoppers. It includes coupons, promotions, and articles written specifically for military shoppers.

❑ Family Magazine; 370 Old Country Rd., Ste. C20, Garden City, NY 11530
   Tel: 516-746-2000; Website: www.familymedia.com

■ *Military Living.* This publication contains the largest amount of military travel information for all uniformed services members—active and retired—and their family members.

❑ Military Living; P.O. Box 2347, Falls Church, VA 22042
   Tel: 703-237-0203; Website: www.militaryliving.com

■ *Military Markets Magazines.* There are *Times* magazines for each of the military branches. Every week, the *Army Times, Navy Times, Air Force Times,* and *Marine Corps Times* deliver news and analysis about military careers, pay, and benefits.

Each paper has community information and active lifestyle features of interest to military personnel and their families.

❑ Army Times Publishing Company; 6883 Commercial Dr., Springfield, VA 22159
  Websites: www.armytimes.com, www.navytimes.com, www.airforcetimes.com, www.marinecorpstimes.com

■ *Salute Magazine.* This magazine targets active duty military personnel.

❑ Salute Magazine; 370 Old Country Rd., Ste. C20, Garden City, NY 11530
  Tel: 516-746-2000; Website: www.familymedia.com

■ *Stars and Stripes. Stars and Stripes* is a newspaper for service members, government civilians, and their families in Europe, the Middle East, Africa, and the Pacific. It offers national and international news, sports, and opinion columns.

❑ Stars and Stripes; 529 14th St. NW, Ste. 350, Washington, DC 20045
  Tel: 202-761-0900; Website: www.estripes.com/index.asp

In addition to daily pages, *Stars and Stripes* offers the following specials at various times throughout the week:

- Sunday Magazine: A feature magazine that includes stories on military life and history, as well as guest columns by readers.
- Timeout: Feature articles on sports, often focusing on upcoming major events.
- Stripes Travel: Articles on travel worldwide.
- Accent: News and information on lifestyles, including recipes and decorating tips.
- Your Money: Highlights business news.
- Mini Pages: Educational information exclusively for children.

Use these resources as you would use general print media. Read previous editions to learn more about how they operate. Then, contact them to see if they will review your book. You might also offer to write articles and try to barter your articles for advertising space.

NON-MILITARY SALES OUTLETS

In addition to the opportunities previously discussed, there are also sales opportunities to groups and organizations associated with the military, but not actually part of the government. These outlets may be less onerous to contact, and they can still yield you positive results.

Clubs and Organizations

There are many groups, clubs, and organizations that are military-related, but not actually part of it. These include the American Red Cross, the American Retirees

Association, the American Overseas Schools Historical Society, the Armed Services YMCA of the U.S.A., the National Military Family Association, the Toys for Tots Foundation, and more.

○ For an exhaustive list of these organizations go to
   www.military.com/benefits/resources/military-and-veteran-associations#sf

The opportunities are virtually limitless if you have a little creativity and the time to search all the possible links leading to sales. Do not leave any stone unturned and you may run across a goldmine of opportunities to sell your books.

Chat Rooms and Forums

Just as in the general population, military personnel are more likely to purchase from you if they are familiar with your name, your title, or your publishing company. If you actively participate in targeted forums and discussion groups, you can create name recognition, and consequently, more sales. The following two online communities will give you a place to start making a name for yourself in this marketplace:

■ Military City hosts an online forum that allows people to talk with others in the military community, post a message on a bulletin board, and respond to others' messages.

○ www.militarycity.com/forums

■ Military Brats Online is an online community linking the children of the United States military with their heritage and each other. "Military Brats" can read about reunion and school announcements, connect with friends and family, and access other online resources.

○ www.militarybrats.com

It is not considered appropriate to use these forums for commercial purposes. Instead, regularly respond to inquiries or statements made by others, which will establish your credibility as an expert. After awhile, begin subtly posting information about your topic, inviting questions to which you can respond. Include your book's title in your response signature, if nowhere else in your posting. The bottom line is that the more people see your name, the more likely they are to buy your book, and online communities provide great exposure.

Museums

There are numerous military museums on many different topics. The following list includes a few examples, and many more can easily be found through a quick online search on your favorite search engine.

■ The National Museum of the United States Air Force has an enormous display of military aircraft. The gift shop is equally large, with books on many aspects of military aircraft and flight in general.

❑ National Museum of the United States Air Force; 1100 Spaatz St., Wright-Patterson AFB, OH 45433
Tel: 937-255-3286; Website: www.nationalmuseum.af.mil

■ Fort Huachuca Historical Museum endeavors to bring to the military community and general public a heightened awareness of, and an increased appreciation for, the colorful history of the Southwest—especially the prominent part played by the United States Army.

❑ Fort Huachuca Historical Museum; Museum Director, U.S. Army Garrison, ATTN: ATZS-TDO-M, Fort Huachuca, Arizona 85613
Tel: 520-533-5736; Website: http://huachuca-www.army.mil/HISTORY/museum.htm

■ General Sweeney's Museum of Civil War History highlights the war in the Trans-Mississippi theatre. Use the contact information below to obtain information about selling books in its gift shop.

❑ General Sweeney's Museum of Civil War History; Tom Sweeny, 5228 South State Hwy. ZZ, Republic, MO 65738
Tel: 417-732-1224; Website: www.civilwarmuseum.com

As previously stated, this is by no means a comprehensive list. Search for museums that are related to your book and you may get lucky. For more information on selling to museums in general, see *12. Museums, Zoos, Aquariums, and Parks* (page 71).

Websites

Websites can provide a plethora of information if you know which ones to look at and how to use them. Additionally, most have links to other, outside resources where you can find even more potential opportunities. *43. Use the Internet to Your Advantage* (page 297) will guide you through using the Internet in more detail. The following list includes several military websites to help you begin your search:

■ Military.com is the largest military and veteran membership organization. It was started in 1999 to revolutionize the way Americans with military affinity stay connected and informed. With free membership, it connects service members, military families, and veterans to all the benefits of service. Perhaps your books on career and job-search topics can enhance military.com's career and education services. Or, your books about military trivia, gear and surplus, and equipment can help improve its key-product offering.

○ www.military.com

■ Militaryfamily.com supplies United States military bases—stateside and overseas—with tools to help them manage the challenges and hardships of military life. Its on-site bookstore has a selection of titles for service personnel and their families.

○ www.militaryfamily.com

■ Militaryonesource.com offers education and support for service personnel and their families. If your book is about managing workgroup problems, dealing with coworkers, non-traditional work arrangements, time management at work, work stress, or management skills, it might fit into the Spouse Training, Education and Career center. If your book is about adoption, children's mental health, childcare, or parenting skills, it could augment the product offering in the Children and Youth center. Content on topics as diverse as elder care, legal matters, relocation, transition to civilian life, and addiction and recovery may also be needed. Additionally, militaryonesource.com offers podcasts, webinars, discussion groups, and moderated chat rooms. You could participate in these to increase your exposure in this segment, which will help you sell more books.

○ www.militaryonesource.com

■ Militaryfamilybooks.com offers a wide selection of books for grownups, books for kids, and books on deployment and reunion, general interest, grief, and military life. It also offers multimedia selections. To submit your book, create a package including a review copy and cover letter. Learn more about creating professional materials in the inset on page 260.

❑ Militaryfamilybooks.com; 8362 Tamarack Vlg., Ste. 119-106, Woodbury, MN 55125
  Website: www.militaryfamilybooks.com

■ The Supply Sergeant at www.militaryclothing.com sells books, videos, and DVDs on military topics.

❑ Militaryclothing.com; Book Buyer, 845 Brenkman Dr., Pekin, IL 61554
  Tel: 800-336-5225; Website: www.militaryclothing.com

■ Militaryspot.com has a section for selling military-related books. You could also increase your exposure in this segment with a page on "My Military Space," where you can create a customized profile, upload your pictures, blog, make friends, and much more on this online social networking community created just for the military.

○ www.militaryspot.com

■ Onmilitarymatters.com sells new and used military books, both fiction and nonfiction. It also has a military magazine, board games, military art, and many other categories in which you could sell your content.

❑ On Military Matters; 31 West Broad St., Hopewell, NJ 08525
   Tel: 609-466-2329; Website: www.onmilitarymatters.com

■ The Military Book Club features military history books on a wide range of topics including World War One and Two books, American Civil War books, Vietnam War books, Special Operations selections, and more.

○ www.militarybookclub.com; www.militarybookclub.co.uk

In most cases, selling to the military market is the same as selling to any other market segment. There may be a little more paperwork involved, but if you subdivide the segments into their various components, find out what the people in each need, and then promote to them on a regular basis you can sell a lot of books. If you exploit all of the various means of reaching this market—exchanges, spousal programs, media, associations, museums, discussion groups, chapter meetings, etc.—you will keep busy for a long time.

22. LIBRARIES

The library marketplace is made up of almost 120,000 locations and is divided into many segments. In addition to the more than 16,500 public libraries and their branches, there are academic libraries, religious libraries, hospital libraries, prison libraries, military libraries, niche libraries, and more. This translates into an excellent opportunity for book sales, and typically, libraries do not return books unless they are defective or the orders for them were processed incorrectly.

Marketing to libraries has changed dramatically over the past several years. The number of titles available, the move toward electronic ordering, the increasing market segmentation, the more demanding base of patrons, and the increasingly value-added distribution system have all created a more sophisticated book-marketing opportunity. These changes can work in your favor if you have an understanding of how to work under the evolving conditions.

THE LIBRARY ACQUISITION PROCESS

Librarians have an obligation to meet the educational, informational, and recreational reading needs of the people who visit their institutions—their patrons. These needs can vary dramatically depending on the geographic location and type of the library, but in most cases, the library director, acquisitions librarian, or acquisitions committee—whoever is in charge of purchasing books at a particular library—is presented with the dual responsibility of satisfying these local needs, while also administering to broader needs. This is done by manipulating the library's collection in two categories.

The first category involves establishing and maintaining a credible core collection of materials. Librarians must anticipate the information needs of their patrons through their compilation of general non-fiction titles, such as reference books and books of national importance. Current events drive this assortment, as do reviews of new titles.

The second category involves building and continuously updating a patron-driven collection. Typically, librarians make purchases depending upon the nature of the communities they serve. This might include large-print editions for the visually handicapped or Spanish translations for a nearby Hispanic population. This category has a tendency toward fiction, and local authors sometimes have an advantage. It is important to note, however, that smaller publishers' fiction titles can be very difficult to get into libraries, because they have to compete against the major publishing houses and nationally known authors.

The acquisitions process in libraries can vary depending on the size and type of a particular library. Most small libraries are run by a director or acquisitions librarian who handles sales. Mid-sized libraries, on the other hand, are typically run by a director, or by several acquisitions librarians each in charge of a different category of books. And finally, large library systems have committees that select an array of books from which their branches can choose.

Regardless of who or how many people are in charge of acquisitions at any given library, though, the same criteria are used by all of them during the selection process. Librarians generally choose books that fill a community need, are in demand by their patrons, and have received good reviews from credible sources.

MARKETING YOUR BOOK TO LIBRARIES

Due to diminishing budgets and the ever-increasing number of titles from which to choose, the purchasing emphasis in the library marketplace has shifted from "what to buy," to "what is the most practical content for our patrons." To improve the chances of getting your book selected by the appropriate librarians, your promotional literature must stress the competitive advantages of your content and specifically describe your target reader.

As a general rule of thumb, electronic submissions are preferred. Mass mailings are less effective than they once were, most likely because more and more librarians are concerned about the impact of the increased use of paper on the environment. Additionally, a professional presentation of your materials will also enhance your credibility. A black and white image will not have the same impact as a full-color rendition of the cover of your book, a sample table of contents, and a cover letter that both describes how your book will benefit the library's patrons and how it fits with the library's preexisting collection. Furthermore, make it simple for librarians to order your books by providing an easy-to-use order form, perhaps available on your website.

You can purchase library mailing lists, but these lists are expensive and several libraries' addresses may have already changed by the time you get the list in your hands. Furthermore, you should carefully consider the profits you anticipate deriving from your use of the mailing lists before you buy them, making sure that they will outweigh the costs of the actual lists. Perhaps a more effective and cost efficient way of obtaining the same exposure is by getting good reviews from reputable sources; that, along with other helpful tips you should keep in mind when marketing your book to librarians, is discussed in more detail in the following list:

■ *Demonstrate the credibility of the author.* A nationally known author has a credibility factor that gives him or her an advantage in the library selection process. Yet all is not lost for lesser-known authors. Develop literature especially for libraries that includes a description of the author's credentials. If the author has qualifications that make him or her particularly suited to writing the book, be sure they are mentioned.

■ *Produce a quality product.* The quality of your book may be its most important selling feature. If it is not properly designed and produced, it does not matter how well you communicate its benefits to librarians. A quality book has all the proper registration information, including a Library of Congress Catalog Number (LCCN), also called a Preassigned Control Number (PCN), as well as an International Standard Book Number (ISBN).

○ A free LCCN is easily obtained online at http://pcn.loc.gov

○ An ISBN may be obtained at www.bowker.com

You will also need to apply for, and obtain Cataloging in Publication (CIP) data. CIP data is a bibliographic record prepared by the Library of Congress that pre-assigns cataloging information for a book that has not yet been published. When the book is released, the publisher should include the CIP data on the copyright page, thereby facilitating book processing for libraries. Make sure the information you submit to the Library of Congress is complete and accurate. If they incorrectly catalog your title, it will be misfiled in every library across the country.

○ You can apply for CIP data at http://cip.loc.gov/cip

In addition to this required information, librarians seek quality in the way books are put together. Due to the regular and sometimes rigorous handling to which library books are subjected, most librarians prefer more durable hardcover books over softcover books. Brodart, a distribution partner that services libraries, actually has a bindery that rebinds books as hardcover. Editions with special library bindings or acid-free paper are also appreciated. Children's books must be especially durable to withstand the (friendly) abuse to which they are subjected. Furthermore, librarians do not like fill-in-the-blank books because the first patrons to use them may fill in the blanks, thus ruining the book for everyone else who checks it out after that person.

Quality is also sought in the content of books. A non-fiction text must be well written and accurately documented. Historical fiction must be accurate in its detail, too, and fiction must be written in an entertaining fashion. Reviews quickly point out any shortcomings in quality writing. Finally, librarians also appreciate books that have a glossary, bibliography, and index.

■ *Get positive reviews.* The most economic, effective, and important way for publishers to market their books to librarians is to get good reviews. A well-written book with content relevant to consumers is the first step to getting these reviews, which are essential to having your book selected by librarians. The most valuable reviews are those that are done by the major library review magazines:

○ *Booklist:* www.booklistonline.com

○ *Kirkus:* www.kirkusreviews.com

○ *Library Journal:* www.libraryjournal.com

○ *Publishers Weekly:* www.publishersweekly.com

All four of these major magazines require you to send them a bound galley—except for *Publishers Weekly,* which requires two—at least three months in advance of the publication date. They also require a cover letter that contains information about the book, the author, and specific details like the number of pages, whether it is hardcover or softcover, and other similar, relevant information. These requirements are non-negotiable, and you should consult each publication's website for its exact submission guidelines before sending your package.

In addition to those four publications, reviews in smaller, specialty magazines can also have an impact on librarians, depending on the type of book, publication, and library involved. For example, a review in the *School Library Journal* would be effective if sent to librarians in the academic market, and a review in the *Medical Law Review* would be important to hospital librarians. It is a good idea to perform a quick, online search for more of these smaller review publications relevant to the genre of your book and the libraries you are targeting, because you cannot always count on getting reviewed by the major publications. Furthermore, the submission requirements for specialty magazines are often less strict, and do not always require you to send them an advance copy.

○ For a list of niche reviewers, go to www.bookcentralstation.com

Book Central Station is the only place where you can find book-publishing suppliers based on ratings and referrals posted by previous clients. At Book Central Station you can scan a list of reviewers, look at reviews of their work, and make an informed decision to choose the ones to whom you will submit your book. After, you can post your own experiences with them, too. There is an annual subscription fee for this website, but you can try it out for two weeks at no charge. For more information about reviews, in general, see *35. Seek Niche Reviews* (page 259).

> Your library promotional materials should always include a quotation from a review by either a major magazine or a well-known person. Librarians typically respond better to quality, credible reviews than they do to advertisements, which is a bonus for you, too, because reviews are generally cheaper to obtain.
>
> **T I P**

■ *Network and Promote.* Acquisitions librarians must be aware of your title before they can order it. Therefore, promotion to the library market is as critical as it is to other market segments. Author appearances on the air and interviews in print media stimulate patron interest, and since librarians pay particular attention to their patrons, the word-of-mouth advertising your appearances will stimulate will benefit you greatly.

Trade shows are an excellent place to introduce your book to librarians, as well. There are national, regional, and local shows at which you can exhibit your books and network with interested librarians.

○ Dates and locations for library trade shows can be found by clicking on the "Conferences and Events" link at www.ala.org

It is also a good idea to utilize library associations. The two major library associations in the United States are the Independent Book Publishers Association (IBPA) and the American Library Association (ALA).

❏ American Library Association; 50 E. Huron, Chicago, IL 60611
   Tel: 800-545-2433; Website: www.ala.org

❏ Independent Book Publishers Association; 627 Aviation Way, Manhattan Beach, CA 90266
   Tel: 310-372-2732; Website: www.pma-online.org

IBPA offers cooperative mailing programs to libraries. Cooperative mailings are packages comprised of flyers from several different publishers that alert librarians to new titles. These mailings also help smaller publishers reach librarians easily and economically. Additionally, IBPA conducts individual mailings dedicated to titles on fiction, poetry, business, children, health, travel, and multicultural topics, among others. It sends its mailings to public, academic, and corporate libraries, and even has a color catalog that it sends to newspaper, magazine, and media book reviewers, which features the front cover of books and ordering information. If you are marketing through a distribution partner, be sure to include its ordering information on your literature.

○ For more information about including your title in one of IBPA's cooperative mailing programs, go to www.pma-online.org/programs/programs.aspx

○ If you would like a more complete list of library associations, go to
   www.acqweb.org/assn.html

■ *Give librarians advance notice of titles.* The composition of each library's collected
works changes over time, and librarians have to keep up with the constant collection turns. They must have a sufficient number of desired books on hand to satisfy their patrons' transforming needs. In order to do that, librarians need
information as quickly and efficiently as possible, and they rely on advance notice
or automatic ordering processes to get it.

Some distribution partners, including Baker and Taylor, help librarians build
and maintain their collections through several notification and promotion programs that publishers can buy into. Before you decide to pay to have your book
included in any such program, however, you should carefully consider whether
you think the number of books the promotion will help you sell will cover or
exceed the cost of the promotion itself. The following list includes several notification and promotion programs offered by Baker and Taylor:

• The First Look program features automatic monthly notification of forthcoming
  titles for free. If you are already a Baker and Taylor client, be sure to notify them
  of your upcoming titles so they can be included in this list.

○ First Look Basic: www.btol.com/pdfs/FirstLook_Basic.pdf

• First Look Plus is a paid subscription program that offers lists for university
  press, scientific, technical, medical, computer, Spanish adult, and children's
  titles, as well as United Kingdom adult titles and music and videos.

○ First Look Plus: www.btol.com/pdfs/FirstLook_Plus.pdf

• First Look Custom is also a paid program that delivers fully customized selection lists for both print and non-print materials based upon libraries selection
  criteria.

○ First Look Custom: www.btol.com/pdfs/FirstLook_Custom.pdf

• Finally, Baker and Taylor offers a specialized program called Automatically
  Yours, which delivers the latest titles from popular authors to the library automatically.

○ Automatically Yours: www.btol.com/promo_details.cfm?id=32 Automatically
   Yours

The bottom line is to promote your books early and make it easy for librarians to order from you. Work on their timelines, not yours.

■ *Target the appropriate buyer.* Individual libraries may have different buyers for
different types of books. For example, one person could be responsible for purchasing children's titles, and another for purchasing reference books. Find out

who the decision maker is for your book's subject matter, and contact that person directly with the reasons why your title meets his or her needs better than competitive titles. Directing your submission to the appropriate buyer will better insure that your submission receives full and fair consideration.

As an example of buyer-appropriate marketing within libraries, Baker and Taylor has a Children and Teen Services program. Through this program, Baker and Taylor provides libraries with a free, monthly, comprehensive guide to juvenile selections featuring titles appropriate for all interest levels—from toddlers through young adults.

○ Baker and Taylor's Children and Teen Services Program: www.btol.com/promo_details.cfm?id=398

Other library distribution partners offer similar services, as well. Quality Books provides libraries with small press books that are not widely available through other distributors. Its Small Press Select is a free service that facilitates collection development for librarians.

○ Quality Books' Small Press Select: www.quality-books.com/smallpress_select.htm

■ *Use timing to your advantage.* Librarians want their libraries to appear up to date to their patrons, so they quickly seek titles related to current events. In fact, there are sometimes situations where timing is the overriding selection criterion. Maintain complete and accurate records of your potential library buyers. When a news story breaks that is relevant to your content, contact librarians to explain why they should purchase your book now.

■ *Recognize your competition.* Similar to the bookstore situation, in the library marketplace your book has to compete with hundreds of thousands of new titles every year for limited space on bookshelves. However, the competition for shelf space in libraries may actually be more severe than it is in bookstores, because in libraries, it has to compete not only with other books, but also with other readily available sources of information and entertainment. Reference materials are increasingly available in electronic form, which make them easier to retrieve. And many librarians supply their collections in many formats, including electronic books, audio books, DVDs, and video programs.

Because of this competition, your title has to stand out. One way to accomplish this is to offer it in a combined media package. For instance, you could bundle your book with a related DVD. Or, you could even turn your content into a DVD with text, sound, and full-motion video. Expand your thinking and you may broaden your sales opportunities in the library marketplace.

Library buyers are not too different from other buyers. They want information that is pertinent to their patrons and available when it is current. Show them that your content meets these criteria, and you will be well on your way to increasing your sales to this segment.

LIBRARY DISTRIBUTION PARTNERS

Library distribution partners offer many services to all types of libraries. Thus, if you decide to market directly to librarians, they might expect the same capabilities from you. In most cases, individual publishers will not be able to provide them, so it behooves you to use a distribution partner in this market. Some of the services they provide to libraries are included in the following list:

■ *Opening-Day Collection Service.* Some distribution partners will recommend an opening-day book list for elementary, middle, and high schools based on discussions with library media specialists and national review sources.

■ *Automated Cataloging and Processing.* Most distribution partners complete the details of cataloging and processing. A range of processing options provides shelf-ready books or loose components for new material processing at the library. Your distribution partner knows what the librarians want and the forms in which they want it. Let them do that for you.

■ *Machine-Readable Cataloging.* Machine-Readable Cataloging (MARC) provides the mechanism by which computers exchange, use, and interpret bibliographic information, and its data elements make up the foundation of most library catalogs used today. Some distribution partners provide MARC records for books shipped in a variety of formats compatible with the library's management software.

■ *Online Services.* Online ordering is fairly common these days, and distribution partners' distribution systems typically allow librarians to search online for title information, and also check status and availability.

■ *Electronic Data Services.* An order should be easy to enter with as little information as an ISBN and the quantity. Distribution partners' databases are normally updated to reflect the most recent changes in book status and availability, which makes quick and easy ordering possible.

■ *Collection Development.* Distribution partners can assist schools with core-collection development and curriculum support because they have access to award and best-seller lists and review sources. Once a library provides selection criteria, the distribution partner can provide a customized selection list based on its requirements.

■ *Title Suggestions for New Schools.* Opening a new school library is a time-consuming process that involves a number of complex tasks. Distribution partners can help librarians get through every step of the process by suggesting a complete selection of titles.

In addition to helping librarians establish and maintain their libraries, distribution partners can also help you sell your book. Furthermore, distribution partners give you a third-party credibility factor that is important to librarians in their selection process. Your distribution partner will be of more help to you if you establish a regular and consistent communication channel with it. Let the person in charge of your account know about your upcoming titles, changes to old titles (pricing, binding, etc.), and details about your promotional plans. Furthermore, you should look into advertising in its magazines or newsletters if it offers such an opportunity.

There are three different types of distribution partners that service the library marketplace. The first type is the marketplace giant. Baker and Taylor is the only distribution partner that currently fits this description. In addition to selling books to libraries, Baker and Taylor also offers the advance notice programs listed on page 180, and essentially dominates the library marketplace.

■ *Baker and Taylor.* Baker and Taylor is a leading full-line distributor of books, videos, and music products to libraries and retailers. It maintains one of the largest combined in-stock book, video, and music inventories in the United States, and provides its customers with value-added services, proprietary data products, customized management, and outsourcing.

❑ Baker and Taylor; Director, Publisher Relations, P.O. Box 6885, Bridgewater, NJ 08807
   Tel: 908-541-7460; Website: www.btol.com

The second type of distribution partner actually goes out and sells to libraries, rather than simply waiting for library orders to come in. There are two distribution partners that fit this type: Quality Books and Unique Books. These distribution partners sell on a consignment basis—meaning that you get paid when your books actually sell—and they have sales people who know the library market, what the librarians are looking for, and when they want it. You can take advantage of these relationships and at the same time, create instant national coverage for your titles.

■ *Quality Books, Inc.* Quality Books is a distribution partner of small-press books, special-interest videos, audiotapes, CDs, CD-ROMs, and DVDs on subject matters ranging from ethnic and environmental issues, to health, fitness, and business.

❑ Quality Books, Inc.; Manager, Publisher Relations Dept., 1003 W. Pines Rd., Oregon, IL 61061
   Tel: 800-323-4241; Website: www.quality-books.com

■ *Unique Books.* Unique Books is a library distribution partner of books, videos, and audio books published by small and independent presses. It carries more than 12,000 titles from over 1,600 publishers, and specializes in popular reading adult and juvenile non-fiction. Titles are chosen for the timeliness of their content, as well as their accessibility. Only about one out of every five titles that publishers submit to Unique Books is chosen to offer to libraries.

❑ Unique Books; 5010 Kemper Ave., St. Louis, MO 63139
   Tel: 314-776-6695; 800-533-5446; Website: www.uniquebooksinc.com

Finally, the third type of distribution partner performs valuable services for publishers, but waits for libraries to place orders rather than actively selling to them. The distribution partners that fit this type are Book Distribution Partners, Brodart Books, EBSCO Book Services, Emery-Pratt Company, Matthews Medical Book Company, and Rittenhouse Book Distributors.

■ *Book Distribution Partners, Inc.* BWI is a Follett Corporation Company and a full-service book and audiovisual vendor with special emphasis on children's and young adult materials. It serves only public libraries.

❑ Book Distribution Partners, Inc.; 1847 Mercer Rd., Lexington, KY 40511
   Tel: 859-231-9789, 800-888-4478; Website: www.bwibooks.com/index.php

■ *Brodart Books.* Brodart supplies English- and Spanish-language titles, as well as audio and video products to public and school libraries. It offers state-of-the-art online tools, bibliographic services, and consulting exclusively to libraries. There is more detailed information about Brodart and Spanish-language titles later in this section.

❑ Brodart Books; 500 Arch St., Williamsport, PA 17705
   Tel: 800-233-8467; Website: www.brodart.com

■ *Coutts.* Coutts Information Services is actually made up of two businesses—the United Kingdom based Business and Medical Book Company and John Coutts Library Services. In 2006, these became part of Ingram Industries. Coutts is one of the leading distribution partners in the library market.

❑ Coutts; 1823 Maryland Ave., P.O. Box 1000, Niagara Falls, NY 14302
   Tel: 800-263-1686; Website: www.couttsinfo.com

■ *EBSCO Book Services.* EBSCO serves corporate libraries with web-based ordering for millions of book titles from all disciplines. Invoicing and reporting options help organizations manage and track book purchases. Payment options include monthly consolidated invoicing, purchase orders, and corporate purchasing cards.

❑ EBSCO Book Services, Division Headquarters, 5724 Hwy. 280 E., Birmingham, AL 35242
   Tel: 205-980-5623; Website: www.ebscobooks.com

■ *Emery-Pratt Company.* Emery-Pratt is a book distribution partner that serves academic, public, and hospital libraries.

❏ Emery-Pratt Company; 1966 W. Main St., Owosso, MI 48867
   Tel: 517-723-5291, 800-248-3887; Website: www.emery-pratt.com

■ *Ingram Book Company.* Ingram is a leading distribution partner in the library market, especially public libraries, K–12 libraries, and academic libraries.

❏ Ingram Book Company; Ingram Library Services, Inc., 1 Ingram Blvd.,
   LaVergne, TN 37086
   Tel: 800-937-5300; Website: www.ingrambook.com

■ *Matthews Medical Book Company.* Matthews is made up of three affiliated companies: Matthews Medical and Scientific Books, Matthews Book Company, and McCoy Health Science Supply. It can help you get your medical information into libraries.

❏ Matthews Medical Book Company; 11559 Rock Island Ct., Maryland Heights,
   MO 63043
   Tel: 314-432-1400, 800-633-2665; Website: www.mattmccoy.com

■ *Rittenhouse Book Distributors.* Rittenhouse Book Distributors, Inc. distributes to health sciences, scientific, and technical fields. It offers collection development tools, inventory solutions, and marketing support.

❏ Rittenhouse Book Distributors; 511 Feheley Dr., King of Prussia, PA 19406
   Tel: 800-345-6425; Website: www.rittenhouse.com

Regardless of the type of content you have to offer, you can find a distribution partner that specializes in providing it to the library market. Find one with experience in your genre. Then work with it to provide the best materials and services to its library customers.

SELLING SPANISH-LANGUAGE BOOKS TO LIBRARIES

Public libraries are in need of credible, high-quality, Spanish and bilingual titles in most genres. Brodart is a library distribution partner that has provided Spanish-language materials to the school and public library markets for over forty years. Nerissa Moran, the Manager of Spanish Purchasing and Collections at Brodart, feels that, "As a general rule, whatever titles sell in English could be translated and sold to the Hispanic market. And in general, there is greater demand for Spanish-language books, audio books, and DVDs than there is supply."

Because of this need for Spanish-language materials, you have a good chance of getting your books into the library marketplace if you have them translated. The author does not necessarily have to speak Spanish in order to promote to librarians either, because most speak English. Nerissa said that "Unless there is something majorly wrong with it, we will put it in our title file." The "major" problems that could keep your book from getting onto Brodart's Spanish list are poor translation and poor copyediting.

The text should be translated into Universal Spanish, which is Spanish that is appropriate for all Spanish-speaking people, including Mexicans, Puerto Ricans, and people from Spain. However, it should also reflect cultural differences—the undertones known only to someone with that cultural experience. This can best be accomplished by hiring a translator who understands the vernacular—not an English-speaking person who has studied Spanish.

○ For examples of good translations, go to www.csusm.edu/csb/english/lists/caldecot.htm where you will find Caldecott Medal winners translated into Spanish

According to Nerissa, "Perhaps the biggest failing for a publisher is not having a good copy editor. This is particularly evident in children's books. A publisher will be well advised to get a native speaker to do the translation. He or she will know that words are taught to children with the article in place. Then children get to know the gender and the meaning of the word at the same time."

In addition to strictly Spanish-language materials, there is also a high demand for bilingual children's books. Nerissa has found that, "In many households, the parents are mono-lingual and the children are bilingual. Bilingual books make reading them a shared experience." Of course, in some books it is not possible to make a literal translation. Dr. Seuss is an example where making it bilingual would not help, because there are so many words that are made up that they would make no sense to a Spanish-speaking person; the rhyming would also be lost.

Submission packages sent to distribution partners that distribute Spanish-language and bilingual materials to libraries should contain the same information that is included traditional library submission packages. You should send your book with a summary of your marketing plan. Most distribution partners and librarians are bilingual, and they expect your sell sheets to be in English. You should also send copies of reviews, particularly those appearing in *Criticas*, published by Reed Business Information, or other magazines directed to the Hispanic market.

○ Learn more about *Criticas* at www.criticasmagazine.com

Finally, you should let them know if you plan to exhibit at any major book fairs that specifically cater to the Hispanic market. The following three are just a sampling of the array that exists:

○ Guadalajara Book Fair: www.fil.com.mx/ingles/i_index.asp

○ Miami Book Fair International: www.miamibookfair.com

○ Reforma National Conference: www.reforma.org

The following list contains three distribution partners that distribute Spanish-language materials to libraries:

■ *Brodart Books.* Brodart supplies English- and Spanish-language titles, and audio and video products to public and school libraries. It offers state-of-the-art online tools, bibliographic services, and consulting exclusively to libraries.

❑ Brodart Books; 500 Arch St., Williamsport, PA 17705
   Tel: 800-233-8467; Website: www.books.brodart.com

■ *Lectorum Publications, Inc.* Lectorum has a selection of Spanish-language books for adults and children, offering more than 25,000 titles.

❑ Lectorum Publications, Inc.; 205 Chubb Ave., Lyndhurst, NJ 07071
   Tel: 800-853-3291; Website: www.lectorum.com

■ *Spanish Book Distributor, Inc.* SBD serves public and school libraries. It sells libraries, schools, and booksellers books from a wide variety of topics including business, childrens, cooking, fiction, parenting, romance, self-help, and many more. It provides many services and has a blog on its site.

❑ Spanish Book Distributor, Inc.; 6706 Sawmill Rd., Dallas, TX 75252
   Tel: 800-609-2113; Website: www.sbdbooks.com

If your book is applicable to Hispanics, seriously consider having it translated. Then, immerse yourself in selling to this marketplace. There are several helpful distribution partners and you can have a wonderful time attending the festive book fairs.

K–12 SCHOOL LIBRARIES

The critical factor determining the selection of textbooks for K–12 school libraries is the credibility of the title in relation to the school's curriculum. And just as the composition of patrons varies from public library to public library, the curriculum varies dramatically from state to state. Titles that work for the public libraries may not work for school libraries, so the process of marketing to them is different. For more information about the K–12 market in general, see *19. The Academic Market* (page 137). Schools may purchase books independently, or their school system may have a centralized purchasing system. Since you have to research the proper procedures for each school system, it makes it even more beneficial to market to school libraries through wholesale distribution partners.

In addition to Baker and Taylor and Brodart books—both discussed previously on pages 183 and 184 respectively—the following two distribution partners cater specifically to the K–12 marketplace:

■ *Follett Library Resources.* Follett Library Resources is the largest supplier of books, eBooks, and audiovisual materials to K–12 schools.

❑ Follett Library Resources; 1340 Ridgeview Dr., McHenry, IL 60050
   Tel: 815-759-1700, 888-511-5114; Website: www.flr.follett.com

■ *Mackin Library Media Services.* Mackin Library Media Services offers many services for school librarians, classroom teachers, and curriculum directors. It has more than 2 million titles from 18,000 publishers. Services include opening day collections and free collection mapping that analyzes how an existing collection can be updated.

❑ Mackin Library Media Services; 14300 W. Burnsville Pkwy., Burnsville, MN 55306
  Tel: 952-895-9540; Website: www.mackin.com

As you can see, there are several choices, so do not rush into a commitment. You will have the most success if you do your due diligence and pick the distribution partner with which you feel the most comfortable.

COLLEGE AND UNIVERSITY LIBRARIES

While curriculum is a major consideration in the book selection process in college and university libraries, entertainment and research are also criteria. These libraries seek a collection that is relevant to their patrons—college students and teachers. This may include materials that supplement textbooks and classroom discussions, but it may also include reference books, general non-fiction, and top-selling fiction books. Titles must be current and related to the students' needs. Additionally, titles pertaining to research may also be applicable to teachers who need the information and data for their publishing requirements. For more detailed information about the college and university market in general, see *19. The Academic Market* (page 143).

An added dimension in this marketplace is the field of distance education. Students who take online courses must also purchase textbooks and titles related to the courses offered. Since most publishers think of libraries as brick-and-mortar buildings, they often overlook those in this other dimension—the Internet. One such online opportunity is the Internet Public Library. This is a public service organization on which you can place a link to your website.

○ Internet Public Library: www.ipl.org

○ A directory of distance learning locations may be found at
  http://dir.yahoo.com/Education/Distance_Learning/

As previously discussed, good reviews can significantly increase the chances of librarians selecting your books. There are several academic specialty publications that do book reviews targeted toward the college and university marketplace. Two of the most prominent are *Choice,* which is published by the American Library Association, and the *Chronicle of Higher Learning.*

○ *Choice:* www.acrl.org/ala/mgrps/divs/acrl/publications/choice/index.cfm

○ *Chronicle of Higher Learning:* www.chronicle.com

The following distribution partners service the college and university library market:

■ *Blackwell North America, Inc.* Blackwell provides services to librarians all over the world. These include standing orders, cataloging, and eBooks, as well as opening day retrospective collections.

❑ Blackwell North America, Inc.; 6024 SW Jean Rd., Bldg. G, Lake Oswego, OR 97035
  Tel: 503-684-1140, 800-547-6426; Website: www.blackwell.com

■ *Follett Educational Services.* Follett Educational Services sells a variety of products and services to educational institutions. It sells used textbooks, workbooks, and teacher's editions through online and printed catalogs. It also sells paperback novels and reference books.

❑ Follett Educational Services; 1433 International Pkwy., Woodridge, IL 60517
  Tel: 800-621-4272; Website: www.fes.follett.com

■ *NACSCORP.* NACSCORP is a national distribution partner that services college stores and campus resellers. It offers over 160,000 text and trade book titles from more than 300 publishers. NACSCORP is an industry service offered by the National Association of College Stores (NACS), the professional trade association representing more than 3,000 collegiate retailers, and about 1,000 associate members who supply books and other products to college stores.

❑ NACSCORP; 528 East Lorain St., Oberlin, OH 44074
  Tel: 440-775-7777; Website: www.nacscorp.com

■ *YBP Library Services.* YBP Library Services is a Baker and Taylor Company, and it provides books and supporting collection management and technical services to academic, research, and special libraries around the world.

❑ YBP Library Services; 999 Maple St., Contcoocook, NH 03229
  Tel: 603-746-3102, 800-258-3774; Website: www.ybp.com

Academic libraries cater to the needs of their patrons in an educational environment. If you can demonstrate that your content is applicable to the needs of this market segment, you are likely to connect with a distribution partner that can help you reach the appropriate acquisition librarians.

PROFESSIONAL LIBRARIES

There are several types of professional libraries. Two of the most common are health and medical libraries, and law libraries. Health and medical libraries are designed to assist physicians, health professionals, students, patients, consumers, and medical researchers in finding health and scientific information to learn more about health care. Medical libraries are typically found in hospitals, medical schools, private practices, and medical or health associations.

○ For a list of Medical and Health Sciences Libraries, go to
   www.lib.uiowa.edu/hardin/hslibs.html

The Medical Library Association (MLA) can also connect you with these libraries. It is a nonprofit, educational organization of more than 1,100 institutions and 3,600 individual members in the health sciences information field. It is committed to educating health information professionals, supporting health information research, promoting access to the world's health sciences information, and working to ensure that the best health information is available. MLA has an online bookstore that also contains videotapes and DVDs of continuing education teleconferences. Its conferences and chapters offer many opportunities for publishers with relevant titles.

❑ Medical Library Association; 65 E. Wacker Pl., Ste. 1900, Chicago, IL 60601
   Tel: 312-419-9094; Website: www.mlanet.org

T
I
P
October is National Medical Librarian's Month, intended to raise awareness of the important role of the health information professional. If possible, relate and time your promotional efforts to this period. This could help prove that you are a knowledgeable, aware, and serious participant in this segment.

Law libraries are designed to assist law students, attorneys, judges, and their law clerks in finding the legal resources necessary to implement their profession. Law schools and courthouses have law libraries, and some of the larger law firms maintain private libraries for their own attorneys. Furthermore, some states require by law that all counties maintain a public law library for the benefit of the general public. The American Association of Law Libraries is a good source for finding information about law libraries.

❑ American Association of Law Libraries; 53 W. Jackson, Ste. 940, Chicago, IL
   60604
   Tel: 312-939-4764; Website: www.aallnet.org

HOSPITAL LIBRARIES

Hospital libraries offer many services to a diverse clientele. Depending on the size of the hospital, the library could carry medical reference materials for professionals, patients, and visitors. It might also include general fiction to help patients and visitors while away their time. In most cases, they are private libraries, meaning that they serve only the employees and staff of the institution. Patients and visitors may sometimes use these libraries, but cannot check out materials, search databases, or utilize library services. However, some libraries offer many services to patients and visitors—some for free, and some for a fee.

The following list includes several resources that can provide you with lists of hospital libraries and help you sell to them:

■ *Hardin Library for the Health Sciences.* Hardin Library for the Health Sciences at the University of Iowa maintains and updates a list of national and international health science libraries by state and country.

❏ Hardin Library for the Health Sciences; 600 Newton Rd., Iowa City, IA 52242
  Tel: 319-335-9151; Website: www.lib.uiowa.edu/hardin/hslibs.html

■ *J.A. Majors Company.* J.A. Majors is one of the oldest and largest medical book distribution companies in the country. It is a significant factor in the distribution of books to hospitals, as well as to corporate libraries. J.A. Majors was acquired by Baker and Taylor in 2004. Therefore, if you are already listed with Baker and Taylor, you have ready access to Majors.

❏ J.A. Majors Company; 530 E. Corporate Dr., Ste. 600, Lewisville, TX 75057
  Tel: 972-353-1100, 800-633-1851; Website: www.majors.com

■ *National Network of Libraries of Medicine.* The National Network of Libraries of Medicine serves to advance the progress of medicine and improve the public health by bettering the public's access to information that will enable them to make informed decisions about their health. Most hospital libraries are part of this network, but there may also be an Area Health Education Center in your geographic area that serves rural and unaffiliated healthcare professionals, so you should look into that, as well. The network's actions are coordinated by the National Library of Medicine and are carried out through a nationwide network of health science libraries and information centers. There are eight regional offices under contract to the National Library of Medicine.

❏ National Library of Medicine; 8600 Rockville Pike, Bldg. 38, Rm. B1-E03,
  Bethesda, MD 20894
  Tel: 800-338-7657; Website: http://nnlm.gov

Think of hospital libraries not only as a collection of medical journals, but also as a source of information and entertainment. Patients and visitors seek medical information written in lay terms, and they also seek solace, diversion, and in some cases, simply a way to pass the time. Your book may be just what the doctor ordered.

PRISON LIBRARIES

In the United States, there are over 900 libraries in correctional facilities operated by state and federal government authorities, as well as hundreds more library service arrangements in local jails and detention centers. Most provide access to reading materials for recreational, educational, and informational purposes, and many have well-established libraries that function much like regular public libraries.

Since incarcerated people have a high demand for information, learning materials, and self-improvement resources, prison libraries serve an important role. Prisoners generally have the same reading interests and information needs as other individuals, but they do not have physical access to libraries in the outside community. Demographic data show that they are further disadvantaged by a disproportionate level of illiteracy, lack of educational attainment, and insufficient vocational skills. However, these facts demonstrate an opportunity for publishers to sell materials that can help inmates.

Professional librarians work in both adult and juvenile institutions, and their patrons range in age from school children to older adults. The fastest growing inmate group is the elderly, and a large number of inmates—between 50 and 60 percent--have not completed high school. These facts demonstrate the diverse needs of incarcerated people.

Inmates who want to use their time constructively are likely to become avid library users, and when the time comes to prepare for their release, the prison library can provide them with a wealth of job and career related materials, as well as community information. Additionally, there are approximately 200,000 Hispanic inmates in the United States so there is also a need for Spanish-language materials in this marketplace. Prison libraries' primary needs are for the following types of materials:

■ Popular and recreational reading materials for independent use, and for book discussions, film showings, cultural programs, etc.

■ Independent learning materials, including information on careers and vocational skills, reference services, and assistance with correspondence courses

■ Formal education support, including information about educational opportunities, as well as materials and services supporting adult basic education, English for non-native speakers, vocational education, and post-secondary education courses

■ Legal information ranging from research tools, to case materials, to forms, and more

■ Resources to support substance abuse treatment and anger control programs

■ Information on the outside community, including reentry information, contact information, social service agency referrals, and other related resources

■ School curriculum support including materials that supplement textbooks and enhance classroom activities and study for juvenile facilities

Because of limited civilian staffs in prisons, the librarian may be the only professional employed, with inmates acting as support staff. The librarian, therefore, manages the entire library operation. During book selection, he or she concentrates on materials and services that will have the greatest impact on the largest number of patrons. Other factors taken into consideration are the demographics of the inmate population and the range and nature of other activities and services available, such as treatment and education programs, social services, and inmate employment opportunities.

The Federal Bureau of Prisons Library offers a wide variety of traditional and automated information services. Its website provides a wealth of resources covering the fields of corrections, criminology, sociology, psychology, and business. You should also use its website to update yourself on current trends. Become knowledgeable about the needs of this market segment and you can make a desirable and critical contribution to this section of society.

❑ Federal Bureau of Prisons Library; 500 First St., NW, 7th Fl., Washington, DC 20534
  Tel: 202-307-3029; Website: http://bop.library.net

Finally, there are programs specifically designed to acquire book donations for prisoners. These programs only accept donated books so you will not make a profit, but they are a great way to get rid of remainders and increase your company's image in the community. One such program is "Books through Bars." Founded in the late 1980s, it was established to address the need for educational resources and programming made available to prisoners. The program facilitates prisoner education and promotes successful community reintegration.

❑ Books through Bars; 4722 Baltimore Ave., Philadelphia, PA 19143
  Tel: 215-727-8170; Website: www.booksthroughbars.org

Another such program is the Women's Prison Book Project. Since 1994, it has provided women in prison with free reading material covering a wide range of topics from law and education to fiction, politics, history, and women's health. of the more than two million people confined in United States prisons and jails, over 150,000 are women. More than half of all women in prison are women of color, and two-thirds have at least one child under eighteen. Additionally, most of these mothers had primary custody of their children before going to prison. These facts mean that women in prison have specific needs for information on families, children, women's self-help, women's health, and legal aid. There are also many lesbian, bisexual, and transgendered prisoners who often have trouble obtaining information that is relevant to their lives, so if your book is applicable, this program will most likely be interested.

◯ Women's Prison Book Project: www.wpbp.org

Other, similar programs are included in the following list:

○ Amherst Prison Book Project: http://prisonbooks.org

○ Books to Prisoners: www.bookstoprisoners.net

○ Boston Prison Book Program: www.prisonbookprogram.org

○ Chicago Books to Women in Prison: http://chicagobwp.org

○ Ohio Books to Prisoners: www.freewebs.com/books4prisoners

MILITARY LIBRARIES

Most of the libraries operated by the federal government are under the direction of the Department of Defense. Unfortunately, there is no central way for a publisher to sell to all of them simultaneously. This is because librarians in each branch of the armed forces have their own process for acquiring titles, and most have separate budgets for title acquisitions. However, there are some central locations that will at least provide you with a place to start, and they are included in the following list:

■ The National Library of Medicine's (NLM) online services provide information about library programs, services, links to specialized web servers, and multimedia features.

○ National Library of Medicine: http://locatorplus.gov

■ The Joint Forces Staff College located in Norfolk, Virginia, is affiliated with the National Defense University Library—formerly the Armed Forces Staff College.

○ Joint Forces Staff College: www.jfsc.ndu.edu/library/default.asp

■ The Pentagon Library in Washington, DC contains reference sources of military interest, especially bibliographies, briefing guides, and quick lists on current topics including military conflicts, military statistics, and legislative histories.

○ Pentagon Library: www.hqda.army.mil/library

■ The National Defense University Library in Washington, DC is an electronic library that serves the academic, research, distance learning, and professional information requirements of National Defense University staff, faculty, students, and alumni through a program incorporating both print and digital information resources.

○ National Defense University Library: www.ndu.edu/Library

■ Defense Link provides a listing of all libraries at the Service Academies, as well as post and base libraries stateside and overseas.

○ For a listing of Service Academy and post and base libraries, go to
   www.defenselink.mil/other_info/libraries.html

■ The Military Librarians Division brings together those interested in the improvement of military library service. It is a forum for the exchange of ideas and information on military librarianship; it conceives and carries out projects that assist members in improving services to their constituencies; it works to promote the professional advancement of its members and to enhance understanding of the importance of libraries to a successful national defense.

❑ Military Librarians Division; Suzanne Ryder, Naval Research Lab Research Library, Code 5225, 4555 Overlook Ave., Washington, DC 20375
Tel: 202-767-2269; Website: www.sla.org/division/dmil

■ The Department of Defense has its own library system. Through it you can find links to academic libraries, medical libraries, and post and base libraries—stateside and overseas—for all the military branches.

○ Department of Defense library system: www.dod.mil/other_info/libraries.html

Military libraries serve a large patron base. They have books and other materials for the service personnel, but their collections also reflect the needs of the families of the service people. This concept opens this segment to a wide variety of fiction and non-fiction work—possibly yours? Learn more about the military marketplace in general in *21. Military Marketplace* (page 159).

NICHE LIBRARIES

There are innumerable libraries devoted to amassing collections for specific niche markets. For example, say you have a children's book that you want to get into libraries. While most grade schools have libraries devoted to their students and public libraries have children's sections, there are other ways of reaching this market, as well. One such way is through the Books for Kids Foundation, which creates and furnishes libraries within existing children's centers. It enables children who may not have access to a public library to discover the world of books. Books for Kids purchases and donates library bound books to create an actual lending program that familiarizes children with standard library practices. Each library is created with an age-appropriate collection that includes a core group of standard titles. Books are selected to reflect the backgrounds and life experiences of the children in each different community.

❑ Books for Kids Foundation, 225 W. 35th St., 3rd Fl., New York, NY 10001
Tel: 212-252-9168; Website: www.booksforkidsfoundation.org

As another example, think of the need for books for those who are visually impaired. Some large libraries have sections with content in Braille, and most have a selection of audio and large-print books. There are even some libraries specifically dedicated to the visually disabled. You might also consider selling or donating copies of your book to this segment through Bookshare—a free service for all

United States students with qualifying disabilities. Bookshare has a searchable online library of more than 42,000 books and resources.

❏ Bookshare; Publisher Liaison, 480 S. California Ave., Palo Alto, CA 94306
Tel: 650-644-3412; Website: www.bookshare.org

There are many more niches that all have a need for books. The previous two examples are simply intended to give you a glimpse into this segment. Perform an online search for libraries related to your book specifically, and you should find several new sales opportunities.

In the more traditional sense, a library is simply a collection of books. But today's libraries are increasingly being redefined as places where patrons can get access to a wide variety of information in many different formats. In addition to books, libraries are now also repositories for audiotapes, audio books, CDs, cassettes, videotapes, and DVDs. Thus, if your book is rejected, inquire about its acceptance possibilities if the format is changed.

Since the library market is so diverse in its patrons, needs, and the content required to meet those needs, your book may be applicable to a variety of different types of libraries. Therefore, you have to be creative in selling it. Your children's books could be sold to public, school, military, and children's libraries, as well as Book For Kids. Your content about finding a job could be sold to public, school, prison, and military libraries. Similarly, there are distribution partners that can help you reach each library acquisition department. Know how your book can be used, and then search the array of potential distribution partners to create a team that can successfully penetrate this book-marketing goldmine.

Chapter Four

Do Your Homework Before You Start Selling

You now know about all of the various segments in both the non-trade retail and non-trade non-retail marketplaces, but that does not mean you should immediately start contacting buyers and attempting sales. A little preparation will take you a long way. You might get only one chance to sell to a major buyer and you could ruin your chances if you are unprepared. Avoid the "On Your Mark. Go. Get Set." syndrome by first "getting set" and planning what you are going to do before you do it. Take time to establish a foundation upon which you can build a formidable marketing juggernaut, and your time and effort will pay off in the form of solid sales.

You cannot effectively market your book to every person in every market, so a good place to start the non-trade sales process is to define the marketplaces in which you wish to compete. When in the ring, boxers sense where they are in relation to the ropes and their adversary. This innate understanding helps them use the corners and boundaries strategically. As you develop this sixth sense about the non-trade marketplace, you, too, will instinctively make better decisions about the segments in which your book will have the most success.

Developing this intuition occurs with experience, but you can accelerate the process by getting the information you need, and then managing and manipulating it into a profitable marketing strategy. It sounds simple—and it is. But is it not necessarily easy. The sections in this chapter will walk you through the steps you should follow in your sales preparation process. This chapter begins by teaching you how to define your target buyers, and how to organize those target buyers into groups. You will then learn how to describe your competition in each segment. After that, you will discover how to conduct simple market research, perform basic test marketing, and find lists of people to contact. Finally, you will learn how to qualify your prospective buyers and rank them in prioritized clusters.

A new title does not have to deliver earth-shattering content to be successful in non-trade markets, but it must meet an existing need and be sufficiently different from the other titles addressing the same topic in the same niche. Therefore, do your research and find out where your book might fit within the existing market. This preparation process is dynamic, and for many reasons makes the marketing process more efficient. When you are finished with this chapter, you will have a good grasp on the people and markets on which you should focus your attention.

23. DEFINE YOUR TARGET BUYERS

As you have seen, the number of non-trade marketplaces is large, and the number of people within each of those marketplaces is even larger. You can find an endless number of people who buy books. However, not all of those people are necessarily prospective buyers for your book in particular.

To provide an analogy, suppose you are looking for a job in accounting. You might explore your local newspaper or search online to find lists of companies currently hiring. It would be a waste of time, effort, and money to send a resume to every company listed, though. So what do you do? You eliminate the companies that are looking for people in specialties not related to yours. You are then left with a list of "buyers" looking for what you are "selling"—accounting skills. The lesson to take from this analogy and apply to selling books is to eliminate people who will not be interested in your book by creating a profile of people who will.

CREATING YOUR BUYER PROFILE

When you begin brainstorming about the types of people who might be interested in your book, think about why you wrote it in the first place. Who were you trying to inform or entertain? How did you want people to feel after reading it? Who did you hope received your information and message? Use these types of questions to help you and always be open to new ideas. Do not let yourself get stuck in your earlier conceptions and do not get too specific. Your buyer profile can, and should contain everything from potentially interested people's occupations, to their possessions, to their attributes—anything that connects them to your book in some way.

Author Denise Richardson wrote *Give Me Back My Credit* to help people restore their good credit record after identity theft or inaccurate credit reporting. Her initial profile of potential buyers included credit card holders, baby boomers, and people with home, car, and other major loans. However, during this buyer profile brainstorming process she stumbled across three new groups of people that she had not previously considered: college students, teenagers, and the military. According to Denise,

College students are the number-one target of identity thieves because the students have loan debt and easy access to credit cards. Teens are the number-two target because they are so green in their understanding of credit, and they use their social-security numbers when seeking a job. When I noticed an increase in daily hits from all branches of the military in my web stats, I realized that the military would be an important market segment, too. While troops are off defending our country, their families often find themselves forced to fight off illegal debt collection practices and fraud. The troops and their families actively seek ways to prevent these dishonest acts.

As Denise's story shows, you should not assume you already know who all of your potential buyers are. Always be on the lookout for new groups who could benefit from your book. Jim Leisy learned this lesson, too. He published the title, *Common Errors in English Usage.* He first defined his target audience as "thinking people" and sought a literary audience, which led him to the *Bas Bleu* catalog, teachers, students, and women's book clubs. However, a little more strategic thinking allowed him to expand on his first instincts, and drove him to nostalgic baby boomers who long for the days when people cared about proper grammar, and to grandparents buying books for their grandchildren.

This first step of defining the types people with which you should be working is critical. Always remember that selling involves *people,* not market segments. Ask yourself the following question: *How often do people think about themselves and their problems?* Then ask yourself: *How often do people think about my book?* You will probably agree that people think more about how they can solve their problems, learn something, improve themselves, or be entertained, than they do about your book. However, if you can show them how they can help themselves in some way by reading your book, you are likely to capture their attention.

ELABORATE ON YOUR LIST

After you have your basic buyer profile, take some time to expand upon your initial thoughts and hone in on specific details. Too many authors, when asked who their target buyers are, simply reply, "Everyone who likes (their topic)." This answer will not help you increase your sales and profits, though. Just think how much time it would take and how much it would cost you to reach "everyone" frequently enough to make an impact—assuming you could find a way to do so.

Consider Gloria Boileau's title, *Stop the Fear! Finding Peace in a Chaotic World,* a book about ways to resolve fear. The premise of Gloria's book is that at some level, everyone is afraid of something. But how can you tell "everyone" the ways in which your book will help them? One way is to divide them into categories. Using this technique, Gloria might separate "everyone" into people who are afraid of flying, dying, being in a relationship, and other types of fears. Categorizing people not only makes marketing more manageable, but it also specifies exactly who you are trying to reach, and allows you to direct a more personal message to them.

So which people in *your* target market segments should you focus on? To help you figure this out, let us continue with the title, *Stop The Fear!*. Say Gloria had "typical moms" as one group of potential buyers on her original buyer profile. Moms are often fearful for the safety, health, and future of their children, so this makes sense. However, not all moms feel this way. Therefore, Gloria needs to get more specific and define the "typical moms" who may be interested in her book in terms of age, education, life style, geography, and more. She could do this by seeking answers to the following questions, which would help her create a composite of the specific moms to whom she should market:

■ What is her average level of education?

■ About how old is she?

■ How much money does she make?

■ To what ethnic or religious groups does she belong?

■ In what leisure activities does she participate or watch?

■ What magazines and newspapers does she read?

■ In what current events or issues is she most interested?

■ Is there a particular life event she is facing, like divorce, career balance, or childbirth?

■ What makes her happy? Unhappy?

■ What are her problems or ponderous issues?

■ What organizations or associations does she join?

■ To what radio and television shows does she listen and watch?

■ Are there geographic concentrations of women like her?

■ How can you reach her?

As you can see, the answers to these questions would significantly narrow Gloria's original "typical moms" instinct, and allow her to conserve resources by focusing only on those with a potential interest in her book. The same analysis should be done for every group listed in your own buyer profile. Think about your book from *their* perspectives. Get to know them and how you can help them meet their needs. Once you develop that understanding, you will have a better idea about where and to whom you should sell your books.

24. SEGMENT THE MASS MARKET

Now that you have created your buyer profile, the next question to ask yourself is, "What marketplaces reach those people?" In other words, "Where do my prospective buyers congregate, work, and shop?" The answers will help you break down the mass market and determine where you will likely have the most success selling your books. This process is called *market segmentation* and it is relatively easy to accomplish.

For example, if the people who might be interested in your book travel, sell it to travel agents, rental car companies, airport stores, or cruise ships. If they attend church, place your book in church libraries, retreat centers, or mobile bookstores that visit churches. If they cook, contact health-food stores, appliance stores, and restaurants; and if they golf, sell your book through sporting-goods stores, golf magazines, or in golf pro-shops. The process of market segmentation will help you promote and sell your book where interested, prospective buyers congregate, and may save you from wasting time, effort, and money—all valuable commodities to independent publishers.

MARKET SEGMENTATION

The essence of non-trade marketing is this concept of market segmentation—the act of breaking the mass market down into smaller segments that are relevant to your particular title. The total non-trade market is actually made up of hundreds of mini-markets, each of different size and with varying degrees of suitability to your title. These mini-markets are identifiable subgroups within the total population. They are comprised of a limited number of people that exhibit a common need for the content of your book, and they are not mutually exclusive—continuing with the previous examples, your target reader may be a church-going chef who is an avid golfer and loves to travel.

Markets can be segmented in a variety of ways; there is demographic segmentation, geographic segmentation, psychographic segmentation, transactional segmentation, profit-potential segmentation, marketing segmentation, and assembly segmentation. All of which you will learn about in this section.

Demographic Segmentation

Perhaps the most popular means of segmenting a market is by quantifiable, demographic characteristics. People who are of similar ages, genders, educational levels, and income brackets tend to exhibit similar buying habits. You may find your sales efforts more successful if you define each category of your typical buyers by these objective criteria. As an example, if you find that readers of your book are over fifty-five years of age, you might design the page layout with a larger type size and greater leading.

Consider the market for selling job-search books to unemployed people. Not everyone in that total market has the same career needs, skills, or aspirations. There are both college students seeking their first positions, and middle-aged people with families and greater financial obligations. Women, minorities, blue-collar workers, and Hispanics all have different needs, require different information, and may look for job-search assistance in diverse places. A title describing the basic functions of how to get a job could, and should be marketed differently to each segment.

The first thing you should do is to simply compile a demographically segmented list for each group of buyers you listed in your buyer profile. It is not necessary to be too specific. For instance, all you need to do is state whether people who need your book are in high-, medium-, or low-income brackets; whether they are male or female; whether they are children, students, adults, or the elderly; and on and on until you have exhausted demographic classifications. This list, along with the following lists you will create for each of the different segmentation categories that follow, will give you valuable information that will help you target your marketing and sales.

Seasonal Segmentation

Another way to segment your prospective buyers is by the time of year during which they typically make purchases. Some buyers, like colleges serving the employment needs of their graduating seniors, represent an annual source of recurring revenue regardless of the economic conditions that might impact your sales to the general public. However, other buyers require better timed pitches that coincide with specific celebratory periods. For example, September is Read-A-New Book Month and June is National Fresh Fruit and Vegetable Month. If you have related titles, you could increase your marketing efforts to participating groups at these times and possibly see increased sales

To provide another example, the book *Sugar Shock!* by Connie Bennett, M.S.J., C.H.H.C., describes how eating sweets and refined carbohydrates could adversely affect people's physical and emotional well being. See a case history of *Sugar Shock!* in *47. Case Histories* (page 317). Using seasonal segmentation, Connie may be able to sell her book to parents around Halloween, to dentists' offices in February during National Children's Dental Health Month, to fitness centers throughout May during National Physical Fitness and Sports Month, or healthcare professional and people with diabetes in November during National Diabetes Month. Use the ideas in Figure 4.1 on the next page to stimulate your thinking about promotions that could possibly work for your book during appropriate marketing periods.

The lesson to take away from all of this is to try to match your promotion to a period that is likely to attract the attention of your prospective buyers. This should help better situate you as "one of them" instead of an outsider just trying to make a sale.

Figure 4.1
Possible Promotions in different Marketing Periods

Marketing Period	Date	Non-Trade Sales Ideas
Diet Month	January	Sell your healthy eating books through Whole Foods, wellness groups, gyms, and fitness programs.
Solo Diners Eat Out Week	First Week of February	Promote books about relationships among restaurants, or "cooking for one" books among singles groups and groups like Parents Without Partners.
Employee Appreciation Day	March 7	Sell your books about productivity, health and fitness, or self-help to companies that want to motivate or recognize their employees, or to Globoforce, a company that helps businesses motivate employees by recognizing their achievements. ○ www.globoforce.com
National Employee Benefits Day	April 2	Contact the International Foundation of Employee Benefit Plans to use your related book as a premium. www.ifebp.org
Senior Citizen's Day	May 1	Books on retirement planning, grandparenting, or care-giving might sell through the Boomer Café. ○ www.boomercafe.com
Zoo and Aquarium Month	June	Contact Event Network to get your books into zoos and aquariums (See 12. *Museums, Zoos, Aquariums, and Parks* (page 71)) and conduct in-store events to support your sales.
National Avoid Boredom Week	Third Week of July	Promote your books on humor, fun things to do, travel, sports, national parks, cruises, recreation, and hobbies.
Romance Awareness Month	August	Your romance novel might be the perfect premium for 1-800-FLOWERS, Godiva Chocolates, or romantic nights out at restaurants.
National Dog Week	Fourth Week of September	Work with Petco or PetSmart for a special promotion on your book about dogs; perhaps you could entice the American Society for the Prevention of Cruelty Animals or the American Kennel Club to do the same.
Universal Children's Day	October 1	Sell your children's books to daycare centers, military exchanges, toy retailers, children's hospitals, and schools to celebrate children's special day.
National Alzheimer's Disease Month	November	Enter into a co-promotion with the Alzheimer's Association, the National Council of Senior Citizens, or the American Geriatrics Society.
Safe Toys and Gifts Month	December	Create promotions with toy manufacturers, toy retailers, and schools.

Geographic Segmentation

Geographic segmentation is the process of organizing people in terms of where they are now, or where they want to be (vacations, retirement). Doing so will help you pinpoint your promotion, making it more effective an efficient. The book *Skiing in Colorado* demonstrates this concept.

Your marketing instincts might immediately suggest selling *Skiing in Colorado* through Colorado ski resorts. But do not stop there. Expand your thinking and consider not only the book's geographic setting; also think of where people would seek such information. Skiers come to Colorado from all over the world and you might reach them in ski shops, airport stores, sporting-goods stores, or travel agents around the country. Thus, sell your book both where it is directly and indirectly relevant in order to maximize your opportunities.

Psychographic Segmentation

Psychographic segmentation groups people according to their lifestyles, attitudes, self-images, and aspirations. Since most publishers do not have the budget to undergo psychographic studies, let it suffice to say that not every female, thirty-year-old, college graduate making $50,000 per year and living in California thinks like every other person in those demographic and geographic segments. Be aware of the differences among people and market your books to those differences.

For example, one thirty-year-old, female, college graduate making $50,000 per year and living in California may be an avid traveler, seeking information on destinations abroad; while another may be a mother looking for information on how to be a better parent. If you made accurate assessments early in the process in your buyer profile, you should have a good idea about to whom you are selling and why they are buying, without shelling out large amounts of money for expensive research.

Transactional Segmentation

Another form of segmentation categorizes people according to their buying patterns. This is called transactional segmentation, and it facilitates reaching prospective buyers with the appropriate message at the right time. For example, people who have not purchased from you before may need to see or hear a different promotional message then those who have purchased your previous titles. Those in the first group want to know how you can help them and why your book is different from, and better than others. Those who have purchased your previous titles, on the other hand, simply want to know when and where they can buy your newest book.

Furthermore, some people buy in large quantities infrequently, and others buy in small quantities more frequently. Keep accurate records of your sales to different buyers so you can track their buying tendencies, which will help ensure that you send them the right message at the right time in the future. For example, say you want to quickly move your inventory. In this case, you could offer incentives to your large-quantity buyers for making immediate purchases. Or, say you are trying to save money on shipping expenses. If that is true, you could offer a quantity discount to people who typically buy in smaller quantities, or give them an incentive to place larger orders, since it is more economical to ship large amounts.

Profit-Potential Segmentation

Segmentation by profit potential alludes to the fact that some sales are more profitable than others. For instance, you can sell directly to buyers on a non-returnable basis, rather than through a distribution partner, and you will make more money. Assume your book is priced at fifteen dollars. You would have to sell 1,000 books to airport stores—where returns are possible—through a distribution partner taking a 60 percent discount in order to net $6,000. On the other hand, you would net the same amount by directly selling only 400 of the same title at list price.

Marketing Segmentation

Segmentation also applies to your marketing actions. Instead of submitting your book to a general publication like the *New York Times* for a potential review, you might seek reviews in more niche outlets. For example, you could try to get a review of your romance novel on the "Romance Reviews Today" website, a review of your recently published educational book in *Education Review*, or a review of your technical book on the "Computer and Technical Book Reviews" website. Similarly, instead of contacting *Publishers Weekly*, you might seek a review for your science fiction book in *The New York Review of Science Fiction* or a review of your mystery on the "Mystery Ink" website.

○ "Romance Reviews Today": www.RomRevToday.com/index.htm

○ *Education Review:* http://edrev.asu.edu/index.html

○ "Computer and Technical Book Reviews": http://victoria.tc.ca/int-grps/books/techrev/mnbk.htm

○ *The New York Review of Science Fiction:*
http://ebbs.english.vt.edu/olp/nyrsf/nyrsf.html

○ "Mystery Ink": www.mysteryinkonline.com

Assembly Segmentation

The best way to get people to buy your books is to make them available where interested people already shop or visit. Deciding where this happens is the process of assembly segmentation. For example, Dan Poynter writes books about parachuting. He uses assembly segmentation and sells his books in parachuting equipment stores, among the 34,000 members of the United States Parachute Association, and in stores located in drop zones, because those are the places his buyers assemble.

MARKET MAPPING

After you have gone through the market segmentation process and have broken down the mass market into segments relevant to your title, you should create a visual map of your target markets. To do this, first calculate the number of people in each segment as best as you can. Then estimate how many books those buyers are likely to purchase, taking into consideration things like how much they are willing to spend to acquire your book, how competitive products are priced, whether there are geographic concentrations of potential buyers, whether potential buyers purchase seasonally, and any other factors that influence purchases.

Once you have a good handle on how many books buyers in each of your target markets are likely to buy, use *market mapping* to visualize it. Draw a large circle representing the total non-trade market for your book. Then inside that circle, draw other, smaller circles—one for each of the market segments in which your book could compete. The size of each circle should depict the relative opportunity for that segment—the larger the circle the greater its potential for sales. The circles in Figure 4.2 depict a market mapping example of the non-trade sales opportunities for a children's book. The varied sizes of the segments demonstrate the potential profitability of selling books to each, allowing the publisher to visually see how he or she should prioritize marketing strategies. In the case of this children's book, the publisher will probably spend more time marketing to schools, mom's groups, children's libraries, daycare centers, and government agencies than to the other segments.

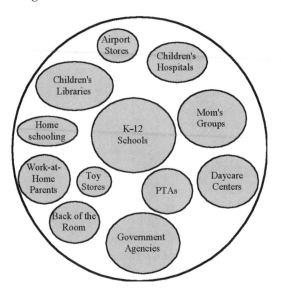

Figure 4.2.
Market Mapping Example

You may be asking, "Why go through all this?" As a general answer, it will make your marketing actions more effective, efficient, and profitable, by helping you target your promotional efforts to the needs of your highest-potential .buyers. Segmentation, if properly applied, can tailor your promotion, pricing, and distribution of your products and services to the groups most likely to purchase them.

25. UNDERSTAND YOUR COMPETITION AND DIFFERENTIATE YOUR TITLE

Marketing books is not done in a vacuum. There are competitive titles and you should know how yours is different from, and better than them. Understanding your competition and knowing how it changes by market segment is important to establishing a leadership position in your niche. It begins by learning about your competition. How do their prices compare to yours and why?

Once you understand how your title fits into the array of existing alternatives, its points of difference should be obvious. If not, you may have a "me-too" book and your strategy might have to rely on price positioning to create an advantage in the minds of your prospects. If there is something that separates your book from its competition, though, and you have the credentials to make this concept real and believable, you can create a marketing program that will help you build a profitable business without adjusting your list price.

LEARN ABOUT YOUR COMPETITION

You can easily find information about your book's competitors by doing a brief search on Amazon.com, or a quick walk-through at a local bookstore. It is not only important for you to know what your book's competition is, but also to know how your book compares to it. For example, when selling a job-search book, potential buyers will typically ask how it compares to the perennial market-leading title, *What Color is your Parachute*, by Richard Nelson Bolles. A ready and plausible answer will go far in helping you complete a sale.

There are two basic ways to compete and prosper in any market segment. You either need to have a strong differentiation strategy, or be a low-cost seller. In other

> Competition in the book industry is made up of different publishers with different costs and goals. Duplicating others' strategies may be disastrous. You will be more successful if you perform activities that are different from those of your competitors, or perform the same tasks better.

TIP

words, if your book is not different, it must have a low price. If your book has a high price, it must be different. Once you have researched your book's competition, it should be fairly easy to determine under which category yours falls. Choose which way you will position your book in the minds of your customers, and then implement your advertising, publicity, and selling strategies so they interact and consistently project this image favorably.

CONDUCT A PROBLEMS, ACTIONS, RESULTS ANALYSIS

After you have learned a little bit about your book's competitors, you should spend quality time differentiating yours from them. A good way to do this is to conduct a Problems, Actions, Results (PAR) analysis. A PAR analysis is a brief description of the *problems* relevant to your target readers, the *actions* your book recommends they take to rectify their situations, and the *results* they can expect if they follow the recommendations. For each major problem, issue, situation, or circumstance, describe how your book's content will show readers how to take some action to address or resolve it. Then, explain the results the reader can expect after taking that action. For example, let us assume you are selling a book about how to get a job. Figure 4.3 shows how the PAR analysis might unfold.

Figure 4.3. PAR Analysis

Problem	Action	Result
The reader does not know when to use a functional resume versus a chronological resume.	The book has a checklist that will help the reader decide exactly when each should be used.	The reader is more likely to use the best tool at the right time; thus, increasing his or her professional image in the minds of potential employers.
The reader does not know what questions to ask an interviewer.	The book includes a list of sample questions to ask interviewers.	The reader is more likely to make a good impression and come across as prepared and intelligent.
The reader does not know how to write a good cover letter.	The book includes a formula used by advertising copy-writers that shows readers how to write a variety of convincing cover letters.	The reader is more likely to write a persuasive cover letter that will enhance his or her chances of getting an interview.

The most important information is the results column. It contains the benefits your target audience will derive from your book. Rank the items in this column in order of importance to your target readers, and then communicate them in your publicity, advertising, sales promotion, and personal selling, as well as on your website and your book's back cover.

In the publishing industry, benefits are typically referred to as "handles" or "hooks," so the next time you are in a sales meeting and someone asks you, "What are your book's handles?" you will know what they are referring to and be prepared to respond.

T
I
P

USE YOUR PAR ANALYSIS TO DEVELOP A SOLUTION STATEMENT

Often times, you will only have a few seconds to sell your book to a prospective buyer. Additionally, the number of words you can use to describe your book is limited in your promotional materials. Therefore, it is important to come up with one sentence that quickly and effectively tells potential buyers how reading your book will benefit them. There is a formula for writing one of these *solution statements,* and it comes from your PAR analysis. The formula is as follows:

"My book helps (*your target audience*), who want (*problem they want to solve*), get (*results they want*)."

Using the example PAR analysis from Figure 4.3 on the previous page, your solution statement for the job-search book might read: "My book helps unemployed people who want practical answers to questions about finding a job learn effective job-search techniques and get the best job quickly." For another example, the solution statement that might persuade small publishers to purchase this book might read: "*How To Make Real Money Selling Books* helps independent publishers who want to increase their sales and margins get more profits and fewer returns on sales to non-trade market buyers."

Kathleen Shaputis, author, ghostwriter, and professional speaker, uses this concept regularly. According to Kathleen, "With my first book, *Grandma Online: A Grandmother's Guide to the Internet,* I made up a badge about 2.5 x 3 inches in the colors of my book cover with the words 'Ask me about Grandma Online.' I printed and decoupaged the piece and wore it everywhere. I had a strong 75 percent of people smile and say, 'Okay, what is it?' And I had my ten-second pitch ready."

Market leadership is gained and maintained by owning the position in buyers' minds as the "one and only" in your category. Use your solution statement as a means to invent and own a distinct category among the people in your target markets. Make them think, "This is the *only* book available that . . ." Keep your solution statement in mind as you create your promotional materials, and recite it when people ask you about your book.

A well-defined and well-communicated image will help attract and keep customers, improve relationships with your distribution partners, help you better utilize your resources, and contribute to your long-term growth. PAR statements will help you focus your attention where it belongs—on the needs of your prospective buyers—and help you mold your image. Define your target buyers, conduct a PAR analysis, write a solution statement for the typical buyer in each of your target segments, and you will be well on your way to selling more books, more profitably.

26. CONDUCT SIMPLE MARKET RESEARCH

Do you wear a watch, glasses, or earrings? If so, were you thinking about them before you were reminded? According to the principle of accommodation, you probably were not. This principle states that people become so comfortable with certain things that they stop paying attention to them. Only when something like your watch is missing and you check your empty wrist for the time are you reminded about how frequently you consult it.

This same principle applies to selling books. Non-trade sales opportunities are so ubiquitous that many publishers fail to see them. They become so used to seeing gift shops, toy stores, beauty salons, and museums for what they are that they do not think of them for what they could be—potential sales outlets for their books. As you become aware of these new opportunities, you can develop them into revenue. This discovery process begins by conducting basic market research that will help you find out information such as what the people in your target markets want, the form in which they want it, where they want to buy it, how many books they typically buy, and the price they may be willing to pay.

THE TYPES OF QUESTIONS TO ASK

Basic market research—as applied to books—involves asking people in your target markets two types of incisive questions. You will not have a complete sense of the market until you get both sets of answers. The first questions you should ask are those that inquire about what people would change about their existing books: Are they too vague? Do they not have enough charts or graphs? Would they be more accessible in a different form?

The second types of questions are those that probe for information about what needs people have that are not currently being filled. In an ideal world, this inquiry process may lead you to discover that your title fills an existing need, but

TIP Do not fall prey to the conclusion that a good book will overcome the need for market research. People do not care how much you know until they know how much you care about them.

the marketplace does not yet know about it. If that is the case, your new marketing strategy becomes one of improved communications. If that is not the case, then you have good feedback to help you rewrite your content so it solves your target readers' problems in ways different from, and better than existing alternatives.

Continue asking questions of your target buyers to learn the form in which they want information delivered, and the price they are willing to pay. You may find that a less expensive eBook, rather than a customized print edition, will optimize your revenue and profits. Furthermore, try to get a feel for how many books they may buy, so you can build a more accurate sales forecast. Keep asking questions until you have a good handle on the majority's opinion.

WHO TO ASK

Market research is easier and more valuable when it is conducted among people in your target market segments, rather than the general public. In other words, even if you ask the right questions, if you do not ask the right people you will not get anywhere. An example is found in the job-search market, beginning with the assumption that there are 6 million unemployed people in the United States. If you could afford the time and money to survey all of those people, you would probably find that each wants different information customized to his or her specific needs. However, it does not make sense to publish 6 million unique books, so you would end up no better off than where you started.

Thus, the first thing you should do is narrow your focus. Look for points of similarity among your potential customers, and rule out those to which your book does not specifically apply. This is similar to the concept of market segmentation, which is discussed in great detail in *24. Segment the Mass Market* (page 201). In the afore-mentioned example, once you have sorted through which of the 6 million unemployed people your book applies to, you can more manageably attempt to interview a cross-section of them for your research. Then, use the majority opinion to guide you.

Suppose your job search book is more specifically geared toward helping graduating college students find employment. You can rule out most of the mass market and direct your research questions to a sampling of career-development counselors, bookstore managers, librarians at colleges, and the students themselves. You can choose to contact them by email, mail, telephone calls, or personal visits.

When you reach them, ask them both sets of questions previously discussed: What would they change about their existing content? And, what needs do they have that are not currently being met? More specifically, you could ask the following questions: What job-seeking titles for college students are currently available? What are their strong and weak points? What title is the market leader and why?

Without this background information, you might blindly rush into this segment, erroneously thinking that the information in your book is unique and necessary. Remember that you only get one chance to make a first impression in a marketplace. Contacting the right people and asking them the right questions before you attempt any sales will help you gather the necessary information to help make your first impression a success.

WHERE YOU CAN FIND MORE INFORMATION

Arguably, the most important market research you can conduct is through direct question-and-answer sessions with your potential buyers, as previously discussed. However, there are numerous additional sources that can help you expand upon what you learned from your initial emails, mailings, telephone calls, or personal visits, as well. The following list includes resources that are simple to use, sometimes free, and have the ability to broaden your knowledge about potential buyers' whereabouts, tendencies, and habits, as well as the industry as a whole:

■ *Bookstores.* You can perform free, basic market research by walking around bookstores. Talk to employees and ask them what books are selling well in your category and why. Flip through competitive titles, specifically looking at their tables of contents, sizes, prices, cover designs, number of pages, and internal layouts. Taking this information into account and using it to make your book better should benefit your sales—especially in places where your books are displayed face out, such as in airport stores, supermarkets, catalogs, and drug stores.

■ *Data available for purchase.* If your budget allows, solicit a research company to compile statistical information for you. Data research companies can help you understand market trends, identify opportunities, and develop strategies. Many also have existing information and reports available for purchase that will assist you in your market research efforts. The following list includes a sampling of these companies:

❑ Cap Ventures, Inc.; 600 Cordwainer Dr., Norwell, MA 02061
   Tel: 781-871-9000; Website: www.capv.com

❑ ICv2 Publishing; 448 W. Washington Ave., Madison, WI 53703
   Tel: 608-284-9400; Website: www.ICv2.com

❑ Market Data Retrieval; One Forest Pkwy., P.O. Box 907, Shelton, CT 06484
   Tel: 800-333-8802; Website: www.schooldata.com

❑ Outsell, Inc.; 330 Primrose Rd., Ste. 510, Burlingame, CA 94010
   Tel: 650-342-6060; Website: www.outsellinc.com

❑ Subtext/Open Book Publishing, Inc., P.O. Box 2228, Darien, CT 06820
   Tel: 203-316-8008; Website: www.subtext.net/founders/founders.htm

■ *Distribution partners.* If you have an existing relationship with a distribution partner, ask them for information about how and why certain books sell better than others. Even if you do not use a distribution partner, you can still visit their exhibits at trade shows and talk with their representatives. These people know the ins and outs of the book business, and are therefore a great resource to utilize.

■ *Industry publications.* It is important not only to learn as much as you can about the publishing industry, but also to keep up with all of its changes. A great way to do that is to read industry publications. You should subscribe to all the major industry magazines, read books by the industry's leading experts, sign up for newsletters, and browse industry websites. The following resources are great places to begin:

Magazines:

○ *Book Business:* www.bookbusinessmag.com

○ *Publishers Weekly:* www.publishersweekly.com

○ *Publishing Executive:* www.pubexec.com

Books:

○ For a comprehensive list of books related to writing, publishing, and marketing, go to
www.bookmarketingworks.com/bookstore/bookstore.htm

Newsletters:

○ *Book Marketing Matters:* www.bookmarketingworks.com

○ *John Kremer's Book Marketing Tip of the Week:* www.bookmarket.com

○ *Publishers Lunch:* www.publishersmarketplace.com/lunch/subscribe.html

○ *Publishing Basics:* www.publishingbasics.com

○ *Publishing Poynters:* www.parapublishing.com

○ *PW Daily:* www.publishersweekly.com/enewsletter/CA6629030/2286.html

○ *Shelf Awareness:* www.shelf-awareness.com

■ *Internet.* Go to your favorite search engine and explore the Internet using your topic as a keyword. An excellent by-product of this exercise is that you may find several ideas for new places in which to sell your books. Additionally, you can join online groups and participate in discussions. Ask questions and read others' posts. Keep in mind that while the participants mean well, their postings contain opinions that may or may not be in your best interests to adopt. Evaluate what you read and apply that which seems most relevant to you.

○ For a list of discussion groups, go to http://groups.yahoo.com

■ *Online stores.* Similar to brick-and-mortar bookstores, you can also search online bookstores for information on competitive titles, such as their pricing, cover designs, book size, number of pages, and bindings. On Amazon.com you can sort books by relevance, bestselling, price, average customer review, or publication date. Margot Silk Forrest performed basic market research for her title, *A Short Course in Kindness* on Amazon.com. She searched the "kindness" category and found 336 competitive titles. She then sought the best-selling titles in that category by sorting the results in order of their sales. This quick scan allowed her to learn competitive information about the segment leaders and the price range people seemed willing to pay.

■ *Publisher associations.* Becoming a member of publishing associations can open a world of opportunities for you. They can provide you information, education, networking opportunities, and more, and they are a great resource for market research. There are three major publisher associations. They are the Association of American Publishers (AAP), the Independent Book Publishers Association (IBPA), formerly the Publishers Marketing Association, and the Small Press Association of North America (SPAN). You should join one or more of these associations and take advantage of all of their resources and opportunities.

○ AAP: www.publishers.org

○ IBPA: www.ibpa-online.org

○ SPAN: www.spannet.org

■ *Seminars.* Seminars conducted by associations and industry experts are a great source of information and can help you with your market research. They are also great networking opportunities. Most of the major associations put on a major, national seminar, as well as smaller, regional seminars. If you are not a member of a particular association, you can typically still attend its seminars, but your cost of admission will be higher. Perhaps the biggest seminar is IBPA's Publishing University.

○ IBPA Publishing University: www.thepublishinguniversity.com

○ A list of writers' workshops and conferences may be found at http://writing.shawguides.com

■ *Trade shows.* BookExpo America (BEA) is perhaps the single best source of first-hand information about the book-publishing industry in the United States. Most of the top companies in the publishing industry gather to introduce their new titles at BEA. While you are there, talk to as many people as possible and attend the seminars and other events that occur.

○ BEA: www.bookexpoamerica.com

Keeping abreast of the industry and its evolution is a never-ending chore. But you need to remain up to date so you can optimize your marketing opportunities. You either move ahead or you lose ground. Do not become complacent or you will quickly become obsolete.

ANALYZE THE INFORMATION YOU GATHERED

After you have questioned the people in your target markets and researched the industry and competitive titles, you should take some time to analyze what you have learned. For instance, what opportunities and trends do you see that others have not? Where are the holes in competitors' product lines? Back to the job-search market, there are a myriad of titles focusing on the basics of writing effective resumes, creating persuasive cover letters, and conducting successful interviews. Rather than duplicating existing titles, you might decide to publish a title about how to dress for interviews, job-search skills for women, or performance tips for the first few months at a job. These are all subsets of the umbrella category for which you may have not known there was a need before performing your market research.

Finally, remember that your competition may not be a book—it may be a state of mind or a circumstance. To continue with the job-search example, college students are typically frugal. They can get free information from their school's career-development offices and libraries, so why should they pay money to buy your book? Discovering these hidden competitors will better equip you to be more efficient in your marketing and sales efforts. In this case, it might lead you to market and sell your books to the parents of graduating students or to instructors for use as a textbook, rather than to the students themselves. Or, you might instead decide to create low-priced booklets that are more affordable for students.

Conducting market research will help you find out where people interested in your topic gather, work, reside, play, or shop. This information will help you pinpoint your promotion, distribution, and positioning, and work as efficiently as possible. As a result, you should experience more profitable sales, more quickly.

27. PERFORM BASIC TEST MARKETING

Test marketing is the process of finding out if your product offering meets the needs of, and is saleable to, prospective buyers. Its objective is to confirm the value of your existing content, format, and cover design, or to provide you with feedback on ways to improve them before going into full production. Taking the time to properly test market your book will give you an idea about how it will be received by buyers, save you money, and give you the impetus and knowledge to make successful sales.

PRINT ON DEMAND

The advent of digital printing and its ability to print on demand (POD) has made test marketing much more viable for independent publishers, because it limits their cost liability. Using POD, you can produce a small number of books to test under a variety of conditions for a variety of purposes. Most—but not all—printers now have digital printing capabilities. The following list includes a sampling of companies that use digital printing to produce books:

○ Amazon.com's BookSurge: www.booksurge.com

○ Infinity Publishing: www.infinitypublishing.com

○ Ingram's Lightning Source: www.ingrampublisherservices.com

○ Lehigh Phoenix: www.phoenixcolor.com

○ Lulu: www.lulu.com

○ Tri-Ad Litho, Inc.: www.triadlitho.com

○ For a more complete list of POD companies, digital printers, and publishers, go to www.bookcentralstation.com

WHERE AND HOW TO TEST MARKET

Where and how you should test market depends on the content of your book and the markets toward which it is geared. Several examples of how different types books can be test marketed are discussed in the following list:

■ *Book Clubs and Catalogs.* This type of test marketing is a little non-traditional, but could end up paying off because it doubles as a sales attempt. Submit your galley to book clubs and catalogs. Do not let them know that you are using them for your test marketing, though—send them your materials as a regular submission. If they pick up your book, you will know that all of the elements are okay and you will make a sale. If they do not pick it up, however, it can still be time well spent if you ask for feedback on why they did not select it.

■ *Bookstores.* If you are test marketing a trade book, you could contact local bookstores and ask to schedule a book signing. If they agree, use digital printing to create twenty to thirty copies of your book, give a small speech about it at the signing, and then see how many people buy it. As follow-up, enclose a self-addressed stamped postcard or your email address in the books people buy, asking the recipients for feedback on certain characteristics of your book and their overall impression of it. This feedback will help you in your non-trade sales, as well.

■ *Businesses.* If you have an employee training manual, for example, a good place to test market it is in businesses that may potentially buy it. Call relevant, local businesses and ask for the names of the people who make book buying decisions. Then, send them a free copy of your book and ask for advice on how you could modify it to meet their needs and make it the best one of its kind.

■ *Colleges and Universities.* If you have a college textbook, workbook, or manual, you can send it directly to schools to seek feedback. Find out the names of relevant course coordinators at local universities and send them a copy of your book. Include a cover letter asking them to let you know if there are any changes that could be made in order for your book to better meet their needs. Also include a self-addressed, stamped postcard or give them your email address and ask them to send you their opinions. If you get lucky, you will receive some responses. If you get really lucky, some of the schools might even adopt your book.

■ *Focus Groups.* An option for test marketing any type of book is to put together a focus group. Give each member of the group a copy of your book and ask them for feedback. You may want to give them a questionnaire to fill out, or you may simply want to ask them questions and conduct the session verbally. Typically, members of test groups are provided with compensation—anywhere from $50 to $100. The outcome of this type of test marketing is based on the quality of the people you use. Be careful not to let two or three people start leading the conversation, because that will skew your results.

■ *Trade Shows.* Trade shows are another great place to test market your book. You can display your book, or you can simply walk around and show it to people in the industry who can give you accurate, constructive feedback. The following two websites provide lists of trade shows around the country:

❍ www.biztradeshows.com/usa/usa-tradeshows.mp?industry=printing

❍ www.greatrep.com/trade_shows.asp

Start your test marketing locally with a group of at least five—up to fifty or so—people. If it is successful and sparks interest and sales, you can then expand your efforts regionally and nationally. Mistakes are the most expensive part of publishing. By using test marketing to reduce the number of mistakes you make, you can increase your profitability.

WHEN TO TEST MARKET

When submitting your book for test marketing, you should always aim to ultimately achieve a sale. People buy according to their schedules, not yours. Therefore, it is important to submit your book for test marketing before, or during the time of year that buyers make their decisions. You may have aggressive test marketing and sales plans, but they are meaningless if they do not reflect the buying patterns of your prospective buyers.

A good example comes from the academic market. If you send your book to schools for test marketing in September, it is too late for them to adopt it for that school year, and you will have to wait a whole year to try again. Create a realistic timeline for putting your test marketing plans into action.

WHAT TO ASK

Test marketing can be very beneficial if you ask the right types of questions. The following list includes different topics that you could, and should ask about during the test marketing process. Each book is unique, though, and you may be particularly curious about how people feel about a certain element of yours that is not listed here, so do not be afraid to think outside the box.

■ *Cover Design.* Get feedback on what image your cover projects and whether or not it grabs people's attention. You may want to come up with several different cover designs and have people vote on their favorite. The quality and appeal of the cover will play a big role in your book's success, so this may be the most important feedback you receive. As Eric Kampmann, President of Midpoint Trade Books, wrote in his book, *The Book Publishers' Handbook* (reprinted here with permission):

> Why does the book jacket matter? The obvious answer is that it is the best and cheapest advertising vehicle you will have for your book. But the obvious answer is not always the right answer. Here I am thinking about the competitive factor. Does a good book jacket help get the book into stores initially? The answer is a definitive yes. The reason is clear to those who sell everyday because we get to see the stacks and stacks of book jackets sitting on the buyer's desk ready to be accepted or rejected. The problem is that your book is in the same stack as the Random House book or the Putnam or Harper Collins books, all professionally produced. If your cover design does not measure up to the best, then the likelihood of that title ending up in the rejection heap increases dramatically. So you need to have a good designer and you often have to get them to produce more than one design concept; and you need to talk to your distributor's sales people early in the process so that mistakes are minimized.

■ *Features.* Ask people about your page layout, font, type size, and other features of your book. You may discover that people are bothered by fuzzy pictures, that there are typing errors you missed, that it would be of more use in a different form, or any number of other erred features that need to be corrected.

■ *Overall Impression.* Find out what people think about your book as a whole. You might ask them to list five words that best describe it, and then state whether they would purchase it. If responses are negative, ask what changes would need to be made to alter their opinions.

■ *Potential buyers and markets.* After seeing your book, your test subjects may have ideas for new buyers, new markets, and new reasons why your book is attractive, so be sure to ask for their suggestions.

■ *Price.* Any price is too high if people do not see the value in the product. Seeing what your book has to offer will enable people to give you more accurate feedback on the price you have chosen.

In addition to testing your book, you may also want to test your website and order-fulfillment process. Test your website under actual buying conditions. Have people navigate through it and test your shopping cart. Then give them a free galley or PDF for doing so. You can also test your order-fulfillment processes. If you choose mail-order marketing as one of your distribution methods, find out how many orders you can manually fulfill, and at what point you should utilize a fulfillment company.

BENEFITS OF TEST MARKETING

The market feedback you accrue before printing a full production run should yield many benefits. First, you may get information that will help you create more accurate and persuasive proposals and improve your negotiation positions. For example, if eight out of ten businesses to which you sent your book for test marketing ended up buying it, you could add that piece of information to your promotional materials, showing people that it is a desired commodity.

Along those same lines, test marketing also gives you the opportunity to get endorsements. Once people see the quality of your content and production, they may be more willing to endorse your book. Put the best endorsements from the most well-known sources on your promotional materials. To learn more about endorsements in general, see *37. Get Endorsements* (page 267).

Finally, test marketing may lead to sales or even sponsorship. Implement a product-placement strategy by using a brand name in your fiction or non-fiction book. Then, go to that manufacturer seeking sponsorship or a pre-publication order. If your first choice declines, change the brand name and try again with another manufacturer.

If your test marketing is successful and your book is well-received, that is great, but do not let yourself get carried away. It is never a good idea to print books on the assumption that they will become bestsellers. Initially, you should be as conservative as possible with the number of books you print, because you can always reprint quickly. Along those same lines, do not let the printer talk you into printing a larger run just to get a lower unit cost. If you cannot sell all of the books, you will end up with a huge unsold inventory and will not have saved yourself any money.

Use test marketing to discover manuscript improvements, get testimonials, evaluate cover designs and page layouts, get accurate cost information, create buzz about your book, and assess your marketing plans. Leave your ego out of the analysis, take criticism constructively, evaluate feedback objectively, make the changes you believe are warranted, and the result will be a book that is more likely to succeed.

28. FIND POTENTIAL BUYERS

At this point, you have defined potential buyers, segmented the mass market, defined your competition, differentiated your title, conducted market research, and performed test marketing. Your next step is to find the names and contact information of potential buyers to whom you could sell in each of your target markets. Your objective is to come up with as many people who might be prospective customers as you can, deferring judgment as to their relative ability to buy until later. Think quantity not quality as you begin to make your list. There are essentially two ways to find your potential buyers: You can purchase lists of them or search for them yourself.

TIP

It is important to remember that you are dealing with the *people* in prospective sales outlets. Always be sure find out the name of the correct person to contact—never use, "To whom it may concern."

PURCHASE LISTS OF POTENTIAL BUYERS

There are companies that compile and sell many different types of mailing lists, software, and directories; all of which will give you prospective buyers' names and contact information. All three of these options have benefits and drawbacks, so weigh your options and choose which is best for you.

Mailing Lists

There are many brokers that sell business and consumer mailing lists. Sources of specific lists abound, and different companies offer different types. You can purchase lists of consumers, businesses, new homeowners, physicians, students, boat owners, churches, voters, new parents, and countless other categories of people. The following are some examples of companies that sell such lists:

○ American Student List: www.studentlist.com

○ Amity Direct: www.amitydirectinc.com

○ CAS: www.cas-online.com

○ InfoUSA: www.infousa.com

○ National Mail Order Association: www.nmoa.org

○ USAData: www.usadata.com

Some mailing lists may be directed to people's titles—Occupant, Sales Manager, Parent, etc.—instead of their names. So, be sure to specify which method you prefer, and make sure the company can accommodate that preference before you make a purchase. Additionally, mailing lists are sometimes old, so ask how recently the one you are interested in has been updated. Mailing lists are quick and easy to obtain, and if they fit into your budget they are a great way to gather contact information for potential buyers. When evaluating the relative cost of a list, though, remember that you are paying for a pre-made list of names, of which only half may be useful to you, and even fewer may actually generate a sale.

When you purchase a list, it is usually for one-time use. Do not attempt to use it twice, since most are seeded with the names and addresses of people who will monitor how many letters they receive from you. If you send them multiple mailings, you can be charged for another use of the list and perhaps excluded from buying it again.

T I P

North American Industry Classification System Software

Instead of purchasing several, specific mailing lists from outside sources, you could choose to create your own. The North American Industry Classification System (NAICS) is a system for classifying business establishments into categories based on their primary business activity. The NAICS Association has software available for purchase that contains a database of over 14 million United States businesses searchable by category. This software allows you to create and customize your own mailing lists over and over again. See *14. Specialty Stores* (pages 97 to 98) for a comprehensive discussion about the NAICS.

❑ NAICS Association, 129 Lakeshore Dr., Rockaway, NJ 07866
   Tel: 973-625-5626; Website: www.naics.com

Directories and Encyclopedias of Associations

There are directories and encyclopedias of associations available for purchase. They offer categorical lists of associations, non-profit member organizations, professional societies, and more. Descriptive and contact information are provided for each entry. These resources are a great way to find groups of people already segmented into various interests, and even if the actual association does not end up purchasing your book, its members might. See *18. Associations* (page 136) for information about available lists of associations.

SEARCH FOR POTENTIAL BUYERS YOURSELF

The second technique for finding buyers is more time consuming, but it is less expensive and may lead to surprising, unsought opportunities. It involves using the Internet and/or networking to find potential buyers on your own.

Explore the Internet

Scour the Internet for the names and contact information of potential buyers. Once you find one candidate, continue searching with an open mind for other opportunities to present themselves. For instance, if your book is about Sasquatch, you might logically start by going to your favorite search engine and typing in, "Sasquatch Association." One of the top results is the Winnipeg River Sasquatch Association. This website opens doors to many different opportunities. Not only does it have a bookstore, but it also has Sasquatch FAQs, networking opportunities, reports, and links to similar websites that offer even more marketing opportunities. As you uncover related items, begin new searches using those terms. Figure 4.4 depicts how your search might progress.

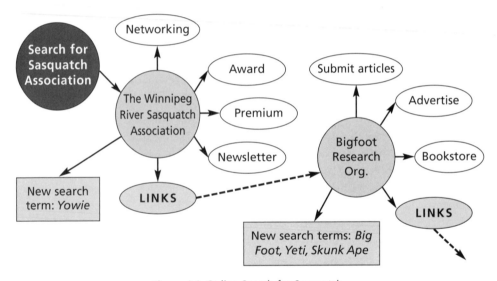

Figure 4.4. Online Search for Sasquatch

The Internet provides an almost unending source of sales opportunities for all books. Each time you find a new website, approach it with the mindset that it could lead you to other resources, people, and chances to sell more of your books. Be sure to build a database of all of the contacts you come across during your search, and before you know it, you will have a current, customized list of potential buyers.

Network

According to the six degrees of separation theory, everyone on earth can be connected to all other people through a chain of acquaintances that has no more than five intermediaries. Thus, right now you could be only five phone calls away from your next big sale. In order to make that possibility a reality, though, you need to network. Networking involves talking with people to find out who they know and how they might help you. Each contact brings you one step closer to a sale.

Constantly collect business cards, and keep a file of the people you meet through your networking. The more contacts you have and the broader their spheres of influence, the more likely you are to meet the right people and acquire the proper information when you need it. Regardless of where you network, there are several rules to which you must adhere to get the most out of every encounter:

■ *Be creative.* Frequently ask "What if..." questions, while keeping in mind that people offer information from their own perspectives. Learn to analyze and manipulate their feedback to address your particular circumstances.

■ *Be positive.* Use networking meetings to discuss opportunities, not problems. Accept help graciously, criticism constructively, and rejection in stride.

■ *Be prepared.* Before attending a trade show, make a list of the people you want to reach and their exhibit numbers. Arrange appointments beforehand and carry a large supply of business cards.

■ *Be reciprocal.* Networking is more effective if it is not one-sided. Willingly share any (non-confidential) information you have that might be helpful to others and you will be more likely to get the same in return.

■ *Be resourceful.* Look for networking opportunities everywhere—on airplanes, at parties, in elevators, online, and anywhere else you might run into to helpful people.

■ *Be respectful.* If you call people, first ask if it is a convenient time for them to talk before beginning; if you approach someone in person, do not interrupt them if they are engaged in conversation with someone else.

■ *Be thorough.* Be sure to obtain all relevant contact information from the people you meet. Keep records of all your contacts in a form that is easy for you to use. This could be on index cards, in a loose-leaf binder, or on your computer.

Remember that networking is the process of building relationships, and it takes time. If you try to force yourself on people in an attempt to get quicker results, it will almost always end up backfiring. According to Charles Stahler of the Vegetarian Resource Group, "We have 94,000 *Meatless Meals* in print and we'll end up publishing over 100,000 of these books. We owe this success almost exclusively to networking and building relationships over time." Nurture relationships by consistently showing up where your prospective buyers are. This may be at trade shows, seminars, industry events, or association meetings. As Charles says, "If you go to these events, you are more likely to be successful because your competition probably won't be there." Take the initiative to meet people and spread the word about you and your titles.

> **T**
> **I**
> **P**
> You can expand your business and become more profitable by using the knowledge, creativity, energy, and contacts of other people. Use other people's minds as a resource that you can tap as frequently as you need.

Most networking is informal and may be conducted at business or social gatherings. Other times, it is done through planned events or structured meetings. Networking conversations typically go through the following series of stages:

1. *Introduction.* The extent of this stage depends on the level of familiarity you have with the person. Create rapport quickly by mentioning a mutual acquaintance or shared interest.

2. *Summarize your intentions.* Provide a frame of reference so the individual knows the context in which to give his or her recommendations.

3. *Keep the conversation moving.* Ask pertinent questions, listen responsively, and take notes. In person, show that you are actively listening by nodding your head in agreement periodically and using facial gestures to show you understand what is being said. During telephone calls, make "listening noises" so the other person knows you are still on the line. If you are taking notes on your computer as you listen, tell the other person and make sure he or she is not aggravated by the constant clicking noises coming from your keyboard.

4. *Offer a quid pro quo by asking if you may reciprocate in some way.* Give examples of how you might reciprocate the person's help. For example, if he or she says, "I'd like to write a book someday," you could offer the name of your editor, designer, or publisher.

5. *Summarize and close.* Once you have gathered all of the information you need, summarize the main points of your conversation and list the names of the other people you wish to contact. Be sure to ask whether or not you may use the person you have been speaking with as a referral in future conversations.

6. *Send a thank-you note.* Send your networking contacts thank-you notes and let them know if their referrals were helpful.

Your networking will be most productive if you use common sense and courtesy. Conduct friendly conversations for mutually beneficial exchanges of information—do not interrogate people. Your objective is to obtain information and referrals. Network consistently and soon you will find the people who will help lead you to your goal.

WHAT IF THERE IS NO "BOOK BUYER"?

Again, throughout the networking process you are trying to find the names of people at each business, association, school, etc. who are in charge of buying books. If a company has a history of buying books, it will be easy to find the right person to contact because there is already a designated book buyer. However, at some point you will almost certainly run into a situation where you are dealing with a company that has never bought books before. When that happens, with whom do you ask to speak? How do you get past the secretary who says the company is not interested because they do not buy books?

You have a few options. First, if there are buyers who purchase other products, ask to speak to one of them. When you are connected, ask for some general information about the company's buying practices, and also who he or she thinks would be responsible for buying books. If you receive good information, that is great; follow the advice you were given and go from there.

If that does not work, however—either because there are no buyers or the buyer you spoke to could not help—call back and ask to speak with the product manager, brand manager, or marketing director. If that again proves unsuccessful, try speaking to someone from the publicity department, and finally, to the president. If all else fails, you can try to track down the advertising agency or publicity firm that works with the company and see if you can make a sale through it. If phone calls do not work, send letters. Most importantly, do not give up. Just because a company has not purchased books in the past does not mean it never will.

Successful non-trade marketing is a matter of numbers. The more research you do and people you know, the more likely it is that you will stumble across something great. Do something every day—no matter how small—to find and follow up on new opportunities. Search online, buy a directory, network with one more person, do something, and you may find the needle in the haystack that will be your next big sale.

29. QUALIFY, CLASSIFY, AND PRIORITIZE YOUR LIST OF POTENTIAL BUYERS

In the previous section, your goal was to create the largest list of potential buyers that you could, not worrying about quality. Now, however, your objective is to sift through that list and qualify, classify, and prioritize the entries. *Qualifying* is the act of going through your list and deleting those with no real interest or buying power. *Classifying* is grouping the remaining entries into categories, which will help you organize when, where, and how to contact them. And *prioritizing* involves ranking the entries according to their buying potential and the order in which you will target them.

Going through this process will allow you to get an idea of the approximate number of people who desire your book, your expected revenue, the number of books to print, and where and how to spend your marketing budget. In short, it will allow you to concentrate on selling to those who are most likely to buy.

QUALIFY POTENTIAL BUYERS

There are most likely at least a few buyers on your list of potentials that do not represent viable sales opportunities for any number of reasons. People may need the content of your book, but not have the ability to buy it. Or, they may have alternative sources of information readily available. For example, unemployed people need tips for finding jobs, but they may not be able to afford to buy a book. They also have the option of getting the same information at libraries or through state departments of labor. Take each name and/or company on your list and evaluate whether it is really a promising prospect or not. Be honest with yourself and get rid of all those that will more likely than not prove to be wastes of time.

CLASSIFY POTENTIAL BUYERS

Not all prospective buyers are equally disposed to purchase your book, and they may be at different points in their buying processes. The following list contains several classification criteria. Take each entry in your newly qualified list of potential buyers and discover how it should be classified under each criterion. Be sure to write down the classifications for all of your potential buyers so you remember where they fall within each category when it comes time to prioritize them.

■ *Your familiarity with the market.* You probably know more about some market segments than others. As you look through your list of potential buyers, make a note of whether you know a lot, some, or very little about the marketplace in which each of them belong. It is beneficial to do this because contacting those with which you are most familiar first, while learning the buying habits and purchasing nuances of others, will save you time in the long run.

■ *Their awareness of your topic.* People move through a series of stages before buying a product such as a book. First, they are unaware that it exists. Then, they hear about it but may not understand its benefit to them. Finally, after a series of exposures to your message they decide whether or not to buy it. Your potential buyers are at various points along this continuum. Decide where they fall based on their pre-existing knowledge of your topic and your book, so you will get an idea of how much time, information, and persuasion will be required to make a sale.

■ *The size of the opportunity.* Each of your sales will be for a different amount of books, depending on the needs of individual buyers. For instance, online bookstores may display your title on their websites and purchase from you as sales are made, so orders will come in for one or two books at a time until sales warrant stocking larger quantities. On the other hand, a business buying your books to use as a premium may purchase thousands of books at one time. Estimate whether each potential buyer is likely to make a large, medium, or small purchase.

■ *The immediacy of orders.* Some sales will only take a few weeks to complete, while others will take a year or longer. Going back to the previous example, you may be able to start selling your book through online bookstores the same week you contact them, but it may take over a year to close a large deal with a business. Decide how long you think it will take to complete a sale to each of your potential buyers. You should first contact those likely to purchase quickly and easily, so you will receive revenue while you are working on longer-term sales.

■ *Their buying schedule.* Buyers purchase books at different times throughout the year. For example, some retail outlets purchase seasonally based on holidays, whereas other outlets such as catalogs make purchases based on their publication dates. Whatever the case may be, find out and write down the time(s) of year during which each of your potential buyers make their decisions. That will help you determine how soon you need to begin contacting them.

■ *The means of communication.* Some people prefer to be contacted by telephone; others by email, direct mail, fax, or personal visit. Find out the preferred method of each of your potential buyers and write it down. This information will not necessarily help you prioritize and rank potential buyers, but it will allow you to organize your selling days.

> Vary the way you spend your time so you do not get burned-out on one technique, particularly if you do not like doing it. For instance, spend an hour or so each morning making telephone calls, then spend time sending and responding to emails. Next, write and send letters, and if there are trade shows or prospective customers nearby that warrant significant use of your time, visit them personally.
>
> **T I P**

Knowing who your buyers are and the order in which you should contact them can make your marketing efforts more effective and efficient. Categorizing people based on their needs and awareness will allow you to tailor your message more accurately, perhaps shortening the sales cycle. Then you can sell more books more quickly.

PRIORITIZE POTENTIAL BUYERS

Now that you have qualified and classified your potential buyers, the next step is to use that information to rank them according to the order in which you will contact them. To do that, you should create three separate lists—A, B, and C—each with a different priority level. Initially, limit these lists to ten buyers each so you do not get overwhelmed and can spend quality time with each. Then, as you become more adept at selling to them, you can increase your list quantities as your available time permits.

■ *A List.* The buyers you put on this list become your top priority. You might put them here for any number of reasons. Maybe you already know a lot about them, or they about you. Maybe they have the potential to purchase a large quantity quickly. Or, maybe their buying period is just about to end. Regardless, these are the buyers you want to get started contacting right away.

■ *B List.* The buyers you choose to put on this list are those that do not need immediate attention, but still have significant potential.

■ *C List.* The buyers that end up on this list either do not need to be contacted in the near future, or do not have much potential. These buyers may say they have no budget now, but tell you to call back in six months. Or, they may have recently purchased a similar book. Remember that these buyers may turn into top priorities in the future, but if you discover that they have no need for your title and never will, remove them from your list completely.

Take the time to go through this same process with your book. Immediately begin learning everything you can about your A-list and B-list potential buyers. But do not forget about your C-list buyers, because they could become A-list prospects at any time. Periodically remind them that your book will be around when they are ready to buy. Focus on learning about, and preparing for one buyer at a time until you have moved through each list. The next section will guide you through this process.

31. MATCH BENEFITS TO BUYERS

You are almost ready to start making sales, but before you do, there is one, final, preparatory step you need to take. During job interviews, the more you know about the company with which you are interviewing, the better you can align your benefits to its needs and be successful in landing the job. Similarly, you should learn as much as you can about each of your A-, B-, and C-list potential buyers; that way, you will be ready to communicate the precise reasons why your book will benefit them when you finally make contact.

LEARN ABOUT INDIVIDUAL BUYERS

Learn about the people on whom you will be calling. Review their websites. Go to trade shows and talk with their sales people. If they are located nearby, stop in to pick up their literature, and study it to discover the reasons why your book will help them become more profitable. The more you know about buyers, the better idea you will have of what motivates them to buy. Then, you will be able to take the benefits you will learn how to formulate in this section, and properly match them to each buyer.

TURN FEATURES INTO BENEFITS

Most products, including books, are combinations of tangible and intangible elements. People do not buy books for their tangible features. They are not solely interested in the size, number of pages, or number of photos in them. Rather, they buy books for their intangible benefits. People purchase fiction to receive a vicarious feeling of fantasy, romance, adventure, or mystery, and they purchase non-fiction to gain information, knowledge, motivation, or help. Thus, it is important to learn the differences between your book's *features, advantages,* and *benefits,* so your sales efforts and promotional materials reflect people's reasons for buying.

A *feature* is an attribute of your product. For a book, it could be its size, binding, title, or number of pages. While important, features are not what motivate people to buy books. An *advantage* takes it one step further and describes the purpose or function of a feature. Advantages are more important to buyers than features, but still do not necessarily convince them to make purchases. A *benefit*, then, is the value the reader receives in exchange for purchasing your book. The benefits are what grab readers' attentions, so it is well worth your while to turn your book's features into benefits.

One way to distinguish among these three definitions is to use the "So what?" test. To employ this test, make a statement about a feature of your book to an imaginary buyer. The imaginary buyer then responds, "So what?" Your answer will most likely be an advantage of the feature, to which the imaginary buyer again responds, "So what?" Keep going back and forth until your answer becomes a benefit and the imaginary buyer says, "Oh. Now I understand." Go through this process for every one of your book's features. Here is one example of how it might play out:

Feature: My four-color cookbook has a spiral binding. (*"So what?"*)

Advantage: It will lay flat while you are preparing the meal, making it easy to read. (*"So What?"*)

Benefit: Because the spiral binding allows the cookbook to lay flat making it easy to read, you will be more likely to prepare the meal precisely as directed; therefore, when you serve it you will feel like an accomplished chef. (*"Oh. Now I understand."*)

Similarly, the *price* of your book is a feature, whereas its *value* is a benefit. Customers attach value to books in proportion to the extent they believe the books will help them solve their problems. If your book is more expensive than its competitors, your promotional materials must translate the price into value for the consumer. One way to do this is to describe the incremental difference and what the reader receives for it.

For instance, if your $19.95 book is $5.00 more than its competition, demonstrate to potential buyers—perhaps with endorsements, guarantees, or slogans—what they will gain in exchange for paying the extra $5.00. Or, you could instead choose to appeal to their fear of making a wrong decision and demonstrate how much they will lose by not spending the additional $5.00. In either case, you will be more effective if you communicate the value your book offers your customers, rather than just its price.

> **T**
> **I**
> **P**
> Even the way you write the price makes a difference. For example, which looks like a larger figure: $5 or $5.00? If you want to make a price look smaller, do not include the numbers to the right of the decimal point. On the other hand, if you want to accentuate the difference, include the decimal point and zeroes.

TAILOR YOUR BOOK'S BENEFITS TO DIFFERENT BUYERS

Have you ever watched golfers look through the assortment of clubs in their bags before choosing just the right one for a particular situation? Think of your title's benefits as individual clubs, each to be brandished as circumstances warrant. When your buyers tell you what and why they want to buy, pull out the club that will describe what is important to them specifically. Do not use a driver when a sand wedge or putter is the better choice.

Different people have different reasons for having an interest your book, and if you do not appeal to the correct reason, you will not motivate them to buy it. Convey the proper benefits to the proper buyers, and you should sell more books. For example, when selling to buyers at retail stores, you could demonstrate that your superior promotional plan will bring more people into their stores; thereby increasing their inventory turns and profitability. However, an appeal to inventory turns and profitability would not entice librarians to purchase your book, nor would it persuade college instructors. They need to be told different benefits.

To demonstrate this concept, assume you are selling a book about child safety. Choose the letter of the benefit in the right column that corresponds to the number of the buyer in the left column; then check your answers at the bottom of the page.

1. Online Store	A. Has an extensive safety resource section
2. Toy Manufacturers Association	B. Use as a premium to sell more products
3. Parent	C. Comes with supplementary materials
4. Librarian	D. Aligns with their cause
5. School teacher	E. Includes home and neighborhood safety tests

Answers: 1B, 2D, 3E, 4A, 5C

As you can see, the same book can have several different benefits that connect with different potential buyers. It is important to choose the benefit that pulls at each individual buyer's underlying motivation for buying books. This requires knowledge of what your customers need and want. In some cases, you can aggregate benefits and present them via mass media to several, related buyers at once. In other cases, it will be necessary to personalize the benefits of your content to an individual. In all cases, however, sell the content of your book from the buyer's perspective, not from your need to sell more books.

CREATE AN ACTION GUIDE

After you have listed all of your book's various benefits and matched them with your potential buyers, condense that information into a handy action guide that you can use for a quick reference. To create this valuable guide, align a page horizontally and divide it into four columns. In the first column, list your target markets. In the second, define the decision maker for that segment. Use column three to describe the benefits your title will provide this person, and finally, list the general marketing strategies you will implement to convey the benefits in column four. Figure 4.4 demonstrates this technique as it applies to one of my other books, *It's Show Time,* which describes how to perform on television and radio shows.

Figure 4.4. Example Action Guide

Target Market	Contact Person	Benefits	General Marketing Strategy
Publishers	Director of Publicity	An author who is media trained will perform more effectively on the air, and therefore, sell more books and make the publishing company more profitable.	Communicate via direct mail, exhibit at IBPA University and relevant seminars, advertise in SPAN's Newsletter.
Writers Groups and Associations	President	Make the group more profitable by giving it away as a gift to new members who sign up and existing members who renew.	Use direct mail followed by personal telephone calls.
Libraries	Acquisitions Librarian	The information in this book is in demand by a large number of your patrons.	Participate in cooperative marketing programs and mailings through a distribution partner.

When buyers face a variety of alternatives, they want to deal with a brand they trust. Communicating the correct benefit to each of your target markets will reassure buyers that you understand what they want and have created a book that will meet their needs. Keep your action guide handy when you are convincing people to buy your book and you will sell more copies, have fewer returns, and become more profitable.

People make purchases for emotional reasons, and then try to explain their decisions rationally. If you work with them—solving their problems with your content—then you help them reach their goals according to their needs. In so doing, you will make repeat customers, not just one-time sales. People would rather be part of the problem-solving process than to simply have solutions imposed upon them. Give them the benefits of your content as applicable to them, specifically, follow the principles described in the next chapter, and you will become successful in the non-trade market.

Chapter Five

Start Selling

Selling books to both trade and non-trade markets requires personal selling, even if you use a distribution partner. For some, this is bad news. Many authors struggle to make sales because although they like to write and have a quality book, they do not like, and are often afraid of personal selling. The good news is that successful sales techniques can be learned. Consummating a sale requires little more than listening to what the buyers want, showing them how your book can meet their needs, and negotiating the terms and conditions of the sale until they are mutually agreeable.

This chapter teaches you how to start selling, whether through a distribution partner or personally. The first section tells you everything you need to know about selecting, arranging, and working with a distribution partner. The sections that follow discuss in detail how to achieve success through direct selling—even if it does not come naturally to you. You will learn several skills, including basic selling techniques, telephone etiquette, how to create a personal sales kit, and how to negotiate. After you are through reading this chapter, you will know whether or not to utilize a distribution partner, and you will also have gained knowledge that will give you confidence to pick up the phone and call your first potential buyer.

31. UTILIZING DISTRIBUTION PARTNERS

In some non-trade market segments—particularly retail—using a distribution partner is mandatory. However, in many, it is optional and the choice is left up to you. There are both positives and negatives to partnering with a distributor or wholesaler. Some of the drawbacks are that they take a percentage of your profit, there may be returns, and payment periods are sometimes drawn out to ninety days or more. On the other hand, some of the advantages are that they give you instant representation nationally, regionally, or in a particular market segment, and they also perform the functions of shipping, billing, and collecting. Thereby freeing more of your time to do what you do best—writing, publishing, and promoting.

DECIDING WHEN TO USE A DISTRIBUTION PARTNER

The quick answer to whether or not to use a distribution partner is, "It depends." If you are selling to airport stores, supermarkets, or many of the other non-trade retail segments, then you most likely should. But if you are selling to a non-trade non-retail segment, such as a corporation or association, than you probably should not. Take the following factors into consideration when choosing whether or not to use a distribution partner:

■ *Your book's topic.* Based on the topic of your book and your familiarity with its target markets, there are certain instances when it would be in your best interest to rely on a distribution partner. For instance, if your book has been translated for a non-English speaking audience and you are not familiar with the buying habits of that market segment, it would benefit you to sell through a distribution partner who is. And in most cases, fiction is better sold through a distribution partner, because the readers are often dispersed and difficult to reach.

■ *Your talents and abilities.* Self-published authors and independent publishers may not have the time, ability, or inclination to contact buyers, negotiate contracts, ship, bill, and collect for books sold. In these cases, it would be well worth their time to have a distribution partner do it for them. Be aware, however, that distribution companies often charge you extra for these services, so make sure the benefits outweigh the costs. Furthermore, you will still be responsible for promoting your book, but distribution partners will relieve the majority of your administrative burdens.

T I P   If you happen to be a person who is nervous about the sales process and want someone to do the selling for you, visit my website: www.premiumbookcompany.com

■ *The marketplace.* Several sales outlets in certain marketplaces, such as discount stores, warehouse clubs, supermarkets, and drug stores, require publishers to sell through one of their distribution partners. In those cases, the marketplace dictates your decision. Call and ask your potential buyer, or refer to the sections appropriate to your target marketplaces in Chapters Two and Three to see whether the buyers require or prefer the use of distribution partners.

Unfortunately, there is oftentimes no clear-cut answer as to whether to use a distribution partner. In any given market segment, you may or may not need one. It all depends on industry standards, as well as your particular situation. Before you begin selling in any market, take some time to see how its distribution is conducted. Then decide if you will benefit more from the services of a distribution partner, or be better off on your own.

CHOOSING WHICH DISTRIBUTION PARTNER TO USE

Sometimes when independent publishers call potential buyers directly, they are immediately told the name of the appropriate distribution partner to contact because the buyer does not deal with direct sellers. Thus, it may behoove you to team up with an established distribution company right from the start. These companies have relatively standard distribution discounts and agreements, and they can make life easier for independent publishers.

It may be necessary to partner with more than one distribution partner in order to best reach all of your target markets. For example, you might choose Anderson Merchandisers or Levy Home Entertainment for distribution to discount stores and warehouse clubs, or Choice Books, Hudson News, or the News Group for supermarkets and drug stores. In most sections in Chapters Two and Three, you can find a list of distributors and wholesalers that specialize in servicing that particular marketplace. If none are listed, you may have just as much success selling to buyers directly. You can find a complete list of all of the distribution partners mentioned in this book, along with the markets they serve and their contact information in the Resource section on page 331.

○ You can also visit my website at www.bookcentralstation.com for a list of distributors, rated and reviewed by their current and previous clients

A key to optimal profitability is to customize a non-trade distribution network that works with your marketing objectives, distribution strategies, product lines, target markets, and selling skills. Therefore, apply due diligence in your distribution selection process. The inset entitled, "A Distribution Partner Evaluation Guide," beginning on the next page, provides a list of questions to which you should find answers before committing yourself to a distribution partner. As you learn more about the offerings of different companies, compile a list of possible partners for each of your target markets in which you decided it would be beneficial to have one.

CONTACTING DISTRIBUTION PARTNERS

Once you have compiled a list of potential distribution partners for each of your target markets, call them to learn the name of the person to whom you should send your materials. The package you send them should include the following information:

A Distribution Partner Evaluation Guide

Here is a list of questions you may use to compare alternative distribution partners. Some may be more important to you than others, or be more applicable in one niche over another. Therefore, compare potential partners on the points that are most critical to you in each particular segment.

■ **Book selection**

- What categories of books do they offer?
- Will your title fit into their current line?
- Will it benefit you to be part of this selection?
- What competitive titles do they carry?

■ **Geographic coverage**

- What territories and markets do they represent well?
- Do they have regional strengths?

■ **Representatives**

- Do they use commissioned representative groups, in-house sales people, or some combination?
- How many sales representatives do they have?

■ **Support Staff**

- How knowledgeable is their support staff?
- Is there a major-account sales force?
- How many people are on the sales-support staff?
- What access will you have to them?

■ **Marketing**

- Do they have a high-quality catalog?
- How many catalogs are printed and to whom are they distributed?
- At which trade shows or conferences do they exhibit?
- Do they offer the opportunity for you to exhibit at their booths?
- Will they advertise your title, or perhaps offer cooperative advertising opportunities?

■ **Order fulfillment**

- Do they make it easy for customers to order your books?
- How do they package orders?
- How quickly are orders filled?
- Do they charge you for packaging and shipping?
- What return rate can you expect?
- Upon return, are the books inspected before adding them back into inventory?
- What happens to damaged books?

■ **Monthly statement**

- Does your monthly report itemize where the books were sold?
- What results can you expect?

■ **Miscellaneous expenses**

- Do they charge for storage?
- Do you need to purchase insurance?

■ **Accounts receivable**

- Do they require a reserve for bad debts?
- Are bad debts passed on to you?

■ **The contract**

- What discounts and terms do they offer to their customers?
- What percentage do they take out of your sales?
- What is the payment schedule?
- What is the duration of the agreement and how can it be terminated?
- Is an exclusive agreement required? If so, for which niches or geographical territories?
- What are your contractual responsibilities and what are theirs?
- Can you sell directly without conflicting with the contract?

Use these questions as a guideline, not as an exhaustive list of areas in which to make your comparisons. Add questions that better reflect your needs and circumstances, and tailor it to the various market segments for which you are seeking a distribution partner.

■ *Cover Letter.* Your cover letter represents the first impression of you and your book. It should describe your book in the context of your target market(s), discuss how it will benefit buyers, establish its validity within the marketplace, and briefly touch on the author's credentials. In short, it should grab their attention and make them view your book as an important asset that they need to have. See page 326 for an example of how a general cover letter for this book might read.

■ *Sell Sheet.* A sell sheet is a one-page document that contains all of the important information about your book. It should include the title, author, publisher, publication date, list price, page count, book size and type, category, thirteen-digit ISBN, and case quantity. Additionally, it should feature the book's cover and a description of the content. Finally, it should include information about the author that conveys his or her expertise on the subject. The sell sheet should look professional and be easy to read and understand. See page 327 for an example of how a sell sheet for this book might look.

■ *Sample of the book.* If you have a pre-existing relationship with a particular distribution partner, then you should go ahead and send them a copy of your book. However, if this will be your first time working with one, you should call before you send a copy to make sure it is worth your while. If you send a galley, send one with a completed cover, perhaps wearing a flag affirming that it is an "Advance Reading Copy," or "Unedited Proof."

■ *Awards, endorsements, and reviews.* If your book has been reviewed, or has received any awards or celebrity endorsements, include a separate document listing them. Also note if a prominent industry person wrote the foreword or introduction. As Mitch Rogatz of Triumph Books said, "Buyers do not care if the author says it is the best book on the subject. However, these same words will have impact if taken from a major review, or if uttered by a celebrity or industry notable." You will learn more about awards, endorsements, and reviews in *Chapter Six. Promoting to Non-Trade Buyers* (page 259).

■ *Top ten sales handles.* List the top ten ways your book will benefit the people who read it. Use the benefits you came up with in *30. Match Benefits to Buyers* (page 228). Again, these should be written from the distributors's standpoint, not from yours.

■ *A summary marketing plan.* It is not necessary to send your complete marketing plan. Instead, summarize the parts that would convince a distribution partner to choose your book over another. Include a fifty-word description of each of these topics: the author's credentials, your content, the target audience, competitive titles, and your competitive advantages. Then provide more detailed information on your promotion plans and budget. The marketing plan is one of the most important parts of your proposal. A weak book with a strong promotional campaign will almost always outsell a well-written book that is not heavily promoted. See page 329 for an outline of a summary marketing plan.

The package you send to potential distribution partners is a reflection of the level of professionalism you bring to the table. They are looking to partner with savvy book publishers—ones that can help them sell a lot of books. Demonstrate through your submission package that you understand what makes books sell, and that you have done your homework to make this particular title one that will do well.

WORKING WITH YOUR DISTRIBUTION PARTNER

If you work closely with your distribution partner(s) you are more likely to establish a long-term, mutually profitable relationship, and sell more books. Here are several tips for creating and maintaining a professional connection:

■ *Communicate frequently.* Meet with your distribution partner—at least your local sales representatives—and get to know the people behind the company. You can do this at trade shows, such as BookExpo America, or by visiting their offices. If you send out a regular newsletter about your title or subject matter, make sure they are on your mailing list, too.

■ *Share marketing programs.* Show your marketing plans to your distribution partners to get input and keep them updated on your promotional activities. Each month, send them a list of the personal presentations and media appearances you have scheduled, and a list of what you accomplished during the previous month. Tell them well in advance of your major media appearances so their sales people can sufficiently stock their customers' shelves. Send them samples of all of your promotional materials, including literature, advertising, and direct-mail letters. Take advantage of any cooperative marketing programs that are consistent with your strategies.

■ *Meet their deadlines.* Distributors' deadlines for catalogs and promotional materials may be months before their salespeople go out on their rounds. If you are not sure of the deadlines, ask your distribution partner.

■ *Help them control your inventory.* Some distribution partners buy your books; however, distributors that require exclusivity do not buy books from you; they take them on consignment and you still own them. Have your distributor send damaged copies to you so you may use them to send to producers of radio shows. Sometimes the cost of having them pack and send damaged books back to you can be high, though, so be sure that cost is worth the potential benefit. If you receive orders from non-trade customers not covered under your contract, have the books shipped directly from your distribution partner rather than reprinting an additional supply. Careful management can help you minimize the money you have tied up in inventory, while also minimizing the fulfillment time for major orders.

■ *Keep your perspective.* Non-exclusive distributors and wholesalers do not proactively work to sell your books; the responsibility for creating demand rests solely on your shoulders. Exclusive distributors, on the other hand, will sell and promote your title; however, you should still piggyback their efforts with your own to create an even greater demand. Do not duplicate their sales efforts, though, and make sure you are working within your contractual agreement before you contact any buyers directly.

Sculpt the best combination of distribution partners that will allow your books to be as successful as possible, and then work closely with them for a mutually profitable, long-term relationship. Communication is key. If you have new information or an upcoming promotional activity, tell them because it will help them sell more of your books. On the other hand, if you have concerns about their sales activity, you should also tell them so it does not fester into a negative relationship. Do your homework to decide whether and when to use distribution partners, and your sales efforts will likely become more effective and efficient.

32. MAKING THE INITIAL PHONE CALL

Once you have decided which markets will be most profitable to contact directly, it is time to begin calling potential buyers to schedule appointments and discuss your proposal. Some people tremble at this step and fear picking telephone. But if you are prepared, knowledgeable of the target buyer's needs and how you can meet them, and have a passion for your book, you will be able to speak eloquently and persuasively on the telephone. This section will help you get to that point.

WHAT TO EXPECT

When you call a potential buyer, one of two things will occur. A person will either answer the phone, or you will be transferred to voicemail. In either case, you must quickly get the person's attention and give a reason why he or she should listen to what you have to say. If the person answers, lead with the solution statement you created in *25. Understand Your Competition and Differentiate Your Title* (page 207), and then ask if the person has time now to learn more. If the person is running to catch a plane or attend a meeting, it will do you no good to give your pitch. Ask for a better time to talk and call back then. If they do have time to talk, begin following the script you will learn how to create later on in this section.

If no one answers and you are instead transferred into voicemail, you must leave a concise, provocative, benefit-laden message giving the person a reason to call you back. If you are calling based on a referral from a mutual acquaintance, use his or her name as a hook during your brief introduction. If you do not have a referral, you could lead by asking a quick, yet interesting question requiring a *yes* or *no* answer. Or, you could say that you have an important piece of information perhaps related to some current news topic. Your message should be no more than twenty seconds and should follow this sequence:

- Name and brief introduction

- Solution statement

- Request for a return call

- Your contact information

- Thank you and close

Be persistent and you should eventually be able to get through to the proper people. But, do not expect a callback from your first call, or even the second. Call frequently and change your message each time you are put through to voicemail. If there is no reply after a few attempts, add that person to your C list and go on to the next potential buyer on your list.

WRITE A SCRIPT

Actors and actresses use scripts to make sure their performances are precise and capable of being reproduced regularly, and professional speakers use scripts so they can deliver their presentations smoothly and completely. Similarly, you can use a script to make your telephone calls more effective and efficient. Your script should not be a detailed document you read word-for-word to potential buyers, because that would eliminate your spontaneity and charisma. Instead, it should be an outline providing consistency, security, and momentum to your calling efforts.

- *Consistency.* Telephone calls are rarely identical to one another, so your presentation should be flexible and natural. However, the sequence in which you present your information should be consistent, because it is important to get the listener's attention before you begin reciting detailed information and benefits to him or her.

- *Security.* A script ensures that you say everything you want to say, while keeping the conversation moving methodically and sequentially. If you begin to lose track of your thoughts, your script will get you back on track and keep you moving forward. It can also eliminate unwanted periods of awkward silence, because you will not have to search for the proper words to use or what to say next.

- *Momentum.* You should always keep your script in front of you, even after you have made several phone calls and are starting to get the hang of it. If you are having success, it will help you maintain your confidence and allow you to continue on a roll. Conversely, it can help you bounce back quickly from a particularly negative discussion.

Similar to the voicemail outline previously discussed, the first thing your script should offer is a hook to get the listeners involved. Begin the conversation by saying you have an idea that could help them. Make a statement or ask a question that involves them in what you have to say. Be precise and forthcoming. Immediately tell your prospects who you are and why you are calling, and give an indication of how much time the call will take.

Always project friendliness, but get down to business quickly. If you talk about the weather until the buyer says, "I'm really busy now. What's your point?" you have probably succeeded in aggravating him or her past the point where he or she will be amenable to your proposal. Finally, be persuasive. Speak from the listener's perspective. If you say that you really need this sale because your money is tight, you are not giving them a reason to listen. Think about their needs, not yours. Do they want increased profits? More satisfied customers? Better employee morale? How can your books help them reach their goals?

Here is an example of a script I could use when telling "Mr. Jones" about this book over the phone: "Is this Mr. Jones? Good morning Mr. Jones. I have a new service that Susan Williams asked me to tell you about. It could increase your sales and profits. Do you have about three minutes now to talk about it?

If *yes:* "Thank you. My name is Brian Jud. I have just written a book that teaches publishers who want increased revenue and profits exactly how to make non-returnable sales in non-trade markets. It begins by describing all of the various non-trade market segments, both retail and non-retail, in great detail. It then tells you how to decide whether to use a distribution partner, and teaches you all about how to successfully sell directly. The book finishes by walking you through all available promotion options, and by helping you set up an overall business plan and timeline. I could swing by your office on Tuesday to show it to you and tell you more about how it will help you sell your books. Does noon work for you?"

If *no:* "I understand. Briefly, I have written a new book that helps publishers who want to increase their revenue and profits get non-returnable sales in non-trade markets. May I check back with you later in the week to tell you more about it? Is Thursday good for you?"

Again, this is just an example. You may feel more comfortable putting your points into a bulleted list, or any number of other possibilities. The most important thing is to keep your important information in front of you as a security blanket, of sorts. But always remember that conversations are two sided, so listen to the person on the other end and go with the flow.

TELEPHONE TIPS AND TECHNIQUES

The telephone is an important ally. Use it to make appointments, follow-up with potential buyers, research, arrange media interviews, network, and more. However, the one thing you want to try to avoid doing on the telephone is selling. Save that for a face-to-face meeting whenever possible. If distance does not allow that, though, then go ahead and try to sell.

It is up to you to contact, follow-up, persuade, and close sales with potential buyers. The following list includes some tips and techniques that will help you improve your telephone-communication skills and your chances of selling more books, more quickly.

■ *It's normal to be apprehensive.* Most people approach telephoning anxiously, finding reasons to delay calling. Some even refer to this communication device as the "200-pound telephone." But the more calls you make, the easier they will become. You will find most people polite and sympathetic, even if they are not interested. Just sit down, start calling, and soon you will feel more comfortable doing it.

■ *Do not call your most promising contacts first.* Practice telephoning your C-list potential buyers first. That way, you can work the kinks out of your conversation skills and familiarize yourself with the questions and objections people will have without potentially jeopardizing one of your most promising A-list sales. Begin calling your A-list potential buyers only after you feel comfortable with your telephone talents.

■ *Allocate time for different types of calls every day.* Block out time each day for sales, networking, and follow-up calls. Set a target for the number and types of calls you will make, and for the results you anticipate for each. Then stick to your schedule.

■ *Set an objective for each call.* Have a definite sense of what you want to accomplish during a call before you dial. You may want to make appointments, follow-up with potential buyers, research, arrange media interviews, or network. Regardless, have an end-goal in mind before you begin.

■ *Get attention quickly.* It is very important to get buyers' complete and immediate attention, and to give them a reason to listen to what you have to say. You do not want to come across as if saying, "I was randomly dialing the telephone and got you. You don't need any books today, do you?" To avoid giving that impression, make a list of possible opening statements using different ways to get the listener's attention under a variety of conditions. The best way to begin is with a referral, such as, "Sue Jones asked me to call you because . . ." Or, start with some late-breaking news or other information important to the listener. You should also always incorporate the person's name into your conversation. Leave room at the top of your script to pencil-in the name of each person as you call him or her.

■ *Ask for permission to talk.* If your call is unexpected, potential buyers will probably be busy doing something else. If you go directly into your pitch right when they answer, they may be irritated by your interruption and lack of courtesy.

> **T**
> **I**
> **P**
> Write the correct spelling of a person's name in your records, but write it phonetically on your script because it could cause ill will if you mispronounce it.

Instead, use your solution statement to briefly get their attention and then ask, "Is this a good time to talk about this, or should I call back later?" If they request that you call back, set a specific time to do so. If they say they have a few minutes, begin following your script.

■ *Do not try to sell on the first call.* Once you have your prospective buyer's attention and permission to proceed, follow your opening statement with a comment enticing him or her to invite you to come in for a personal meeting, or to meet at an upcoming trade show or association meeting. Do not try to sell your book if you can avoid doing so. Your objective should be to arrange personal meetings with the ultimate decision makers whenever possible.

Follow general telephone etiquette and you will have little trouble talking with people. Trust your instincts and if you sense impatience or lack of interest, try a different strategy. That is another reason why it is best not to call your best prospects first. Make your mistakes where they will do the least damage. If you do all you can and the potential buyer is being unreasonable, then cross him or her off your list and move on to the next one. Do not waste your time at a dead end.

EARN THEIR TRUST

Prospective buyers have to know and trust you before discussing any concrete plans on the phone or in person. They want to know that the information you are giving them is accurate, and that you will keep up your end of the deal. Furthermore, they may be planning two years into the future and do not want competition learning of their intentions. Thus, you have to earn their confidence, and it takes an extended period of time to establish the necessary degree of trust.

Begin the sales process by selling *you*. Demonstrate your trustworthiness and confidentiality by taking the time to build relationships. One way you can earn buyers' confidence is by *assisting* them instead of *selling* to them. In other words, tell them how your book will help them be better at whatever it is they do. Prove you have done your homework by giving them accurate figures and information. Show how your title is different from, and better than its competition. Make suggestions as to how your title may be used to stimulate their sales. Follow up professionally and persistently, and do what you said you would do, when you said you would do it.

In short, people like to buy from people they trust, particularly if they are making a large purchase. They do not care how much you know until they know how much you care. If you come across as trying to sell something instead of trying to solve their problems, you will get little sympathy and few sales.

ASK AND ANSWER

Convincing people to buy your book is initially a question-and-answer process, with you asking most of the questions. Your goal is to accumulate information upon which you can later make a more formal proposal. Find out what buyers want so you can better accommodate them in your proposal and negotiations. For example, you may want to sell a 6″ x 9″ book on dieting. As you will see in the following dialogue, even though a potential buyer may like your book's content, he or she may think your book is too large for the store or too expensive for the budget. You will lose the sale if you persist in pushing your book as is. Instead, a successful dialogue might go like this:

Buyer: "That is great information, but I was looking for something smaller that I might use as a premium."

You: "If the information were available as a booklet rather than a book, would you be interested in buying it then?"

Buyer: "Yes. Sales are down this month and that would be more likely to fit my budget, while still allowing me to provide my customers with this necessary information."

By asking one simple question, you learned that cost is a factor for this buyer. You also learned that he or she is looking for a premium and likes your content, but does not want it in the form of a book. Now that you have this important information, you can shift your attention to trying to accommodate the buyer and make this sale possible. Will the sale cover the cost of converting your book into a booklet? If not, would any of your other potential buyers prefer a booklet, as well? Regardless, you can now understand how important asking questions and gathering information is to making a sale. Learn, then earn.

Finally, always remember to keep detailed, accurate records about when you contacted each potential buyer and what exactly you talked about with him or her. Immediately plan when your next contact with that person will occur, and then before it does, refer back to your notes so you know where the last conversation ended. Continue to follow up until you either receive a negative response, in which case you can add that buyer to your C list and try again in six months or so, or a positive request for more information, in which case you can use the information in the following section to prepare a proposal.

33. CREATING A PERSONAL SALES KIT

If your telephone calls are successful and get prospective buyers interested in what you have to offer, they may say, "Send me a proposal." What they are asking for is a summary of what you discussed, more information about your book, and a confirmation of your price and terms. They may be using this request as a delaying tactic so they can put off making a decision, or they may truly be interested in what you have to say. Since you will not know for sure, always send or deliver a personal sales kit, of which your proposal is a component, and then follow up.

WHAT IS A SALES KIT?

A sales kit is a tool that puts in writing everything you have already discussed with your potential buyers on the telephone. It reminds them of all the reasons they liked your idea in the first place, emphasizes the importance and benefits of your book, presents your pricing, and makes it easy for them to make a favorable decision. You want to be sure that there is nothing in your sales kit that raises a red flag. You are dealing with experienced buyers who expect to see a professional presentation.

It is a good idea to present your sales kit to buyers in person whenever possible. If you cannot, though, be sure to alert them that you are sending it in the mail so it does not get lost or end up on the bottom of a pile. You should also try to set up a time that you can call and go through your kit with them over the phone. If you use and follow the information in this section, you can meet or exceed their standards and appear as an expert. Give them more than they expect, and everything they need to make their decision.

INFORMATION TO INCLUDE IN YOUR PERSONAL SALES KIT

Your personal sales kit should visually support what you have previously discussed with buyers on the telephone. Seeing is believing, and buyers will be more apt to take you seriously if they see your information in writing. When you cannot meet with a buyer in person, be sure to send a cover letter that reminds him or her of your previous conversation(s) and introduces your sales kit.

Your personal sales kit should include an executive summary, a situation analysis, background information, your experience, a sell sheet, your proposal, the timing, compensation, a conclusion, and an order form—in that order. The following information describes each of these components in detail.

Executive Summary

The executive summary should remind your potential buyers about your book and yourself. Begin by describing the book in the context of that particular buyer's business or organization. This involves summarizing the existing market conditions and discussing the way the potential buyer is currently doing business. Define his or her business' critical points of concern, then discuss how your book will alleviate, if not remedy those problems. Show the buyer that buying your book is better than the other options he or she may be considering. This discussion should also include a brief explanation of why it is advantageous to buy now, and what the likely results of the sale will be.

Next, establish your book's validity within the marketplace—in other words, show your potential buyers that there is an existing target audience that demands this information, and describe why your book is the best resource to deliver it. Then, tie this information back into the buyers' needs. Close with information about yourself—assuming you are the author. Stress your expertise and assure the buyers that your book will help them achieve the results that they want. This puts you both on the same side of the table.

While you can create a generic executive summary to use as a model, you will have to rework it for each potential buyer to whom you send it. It is extremely important to customize the information with individual buyers' names and circumstances. Finally, keep your statements general and avoid any guarantees of positive results.

Sell Sheet

Following your cover letter should be a sell sheet—a multi-color piece of general sales literature that will make a favorable and professional impression of you and your title. Including the sell sheet right behind your executive summary will give buyers an initial, at-a-glance view of your book before the in-depth information that will follow. For an example of how a sell sheet for this book might look, see page 327.

Situation Analysis

The next document in your sales kit is a situation analysis. It should expand upon the present market conditions you mentioned in your executive summary, as well as point out and emphasize that particular buyer's major business concerns. A concern may be a history of declining test scores in the school, a new competitor entering the marketplace, or a decline in an association's membership. State how your potential buyer is currently, if ineffectively, addressing these concerns. Conclude by conveying your understanding of the situation, and describing how your book can help.

Background

Next, include a description of the events that led up to the current situation. Describe the research you did on the potential buyer's business or organization, and how the information you learned lead you to make this is proposal. Then, list the criteria the potential buyers cited as their conditions of the sale during your phone conversation(s). By reminding them of their contributions, you are giving them some equity in the outcome.

You should also define the key performance indicators that will measure the success of the sale. For example, if your book is being used as a premium by an association to increase its membership, discuss how many new memberships the book will be expected to generate, or by how much the rate of renewal for existing members will be expected to increase. Define the parameters of success so you can demonstrate accomplishment, and at some point in the future, make a case for repeat orders. However, make your book a contributing factor in the achievement of these objectives, not the sole source of success, so you have some wiggle room if the metrics are not reached. Never guarantee any specific outcome.

Your Experience

You may know your potential buyers need the content you offer, but you still need to convince them that you are the best source to provide it. Buyers want to know they are dealing with a reputable supplier. Tell them how long your publishing company has been in existence and discuss some of its notable achievements. List your company's—and the author's if it is not you—credentials. The purpose is to convince buyers that you are the most qualified person to deliver this particular information. You may even offer a brief case history describing how you helped a different organization in a similar situation.

In short, make the buyers feel that, "It's you and me against them." "Them" may be a competitor, business problem, market situation, or a frame of mind. It really does not matter as long as the buyers perceive that you are both on the same side, working as a team to solve their problems.

Your Proposal

Your proposal is the centerpiece of the sales kit and the bulk of your discussion will revolve around it. Use subheads, white space, a clear type face, graphs, and good leading to make it a functioning, working document. This is the heart of your proposition, detailing what you are offering, why the buyer should be interested, and when, how, and at what price the sale should be made. Thus, do not feel like you have to limit yourself to one page.

Everything you have presented to this point was simply a recitation of facts that have the set stage for you to make your case. You now get the chance to become the champion—the solution to the problems the buyers have declared to be unsolvable. Make your proposal in the form of a mini marketing plan, ready for immediate implementation. The sequence is important and should be divided into these three sections:

■ *Objective.* Define the goal of implementing your proposal. What is it specifically that you and the buyer expect to achieve together through the use of your book? Be clear, but not too specific in terms of setting this goal. Your goal should not be exact, because you can rarely prove how much your book contributed to the attainment of a specific metric. Instead, use general phrases such as "an improvement in attitude," "an increase in sales," or "a reduction in employee turnover." Do not bring in new information, but simply restate that to which you have already agreed during earlier conversations.

■ *Strategies.* Once you have stated the desired outcome to which you have previously agreed, discuss various ways in which your book could help make it happen. Concentrate on different plans of action, not on numbers. In other words, make the numbers arbitrary and describe possible strategies for reaching the objective. If you give specific numbers, you may be held to them as make-or-break factors in reorders. Instead, simply suggest different uses for your book that may help the buyer reach his or her objective.

■ *Tactics.* Finally, propose how the strategies will be implemented. What specifically will you do to achieve the objective? What actions do you expect the buyers to take? What specifically do you propose they do with your books? How will you assist? Use visuals wherever possible to reinforce and demonstrate what you propose to do. Lead the buyer, step-by-step, to the logical conclusion that using your book is the best solution for his or her situation.

Your proposal should outline what you want to accomplish, how you plan on accomplishing it, and the specific actions required to make it happen. Having a potential plan in place will make your buyers may feel more comfortable. They will certainly have more confidence in you as a sales-professional who is prepared to work with them as a competent marketing partner.

Timing

Your proposal may be for a one-time sale, or perhaps for something more long term. In the latter case, it might be more effective if it is not implemented all at one time. If appropriate, suggest sequential implementation, such as a regional trial leading to a national rollout as certain metrics are surpassed. Or, you might suggest using *Title A* for an initial blitz, followed by a more intense campaign featuring *Title B*.

For example, a national health insurance company was interested in promoting a healthier lifestyle among new clients. To accomplish this goal, an ongoing educational program was implemented. During each of the first three months after signing a new member, a mailing was done on behalf of the company. The first month, a booklet promoting the benefits of walking was sent to the new members. The booklet gave suggestions on how to incorporate walking into even the busiest schedules, and promoted a book on the same subject.

Then, in month two the company mailed the same new members a cookbook that showed busy people how to prepare healthy meals quickly, and how to eat when time is limited. Finally, in month three a journal was sent to each participant along with a pedometer. The result was a sale of several thousand books in each of the first two months. This helped further the insurance company's goal of having a healthier clientele so they would have to make fewer payouts.

In any case, your sales kit should offer a timeline that meets the buyers' schedules. Show an approximate, initial shipment date and the time it will take for the plan to be complete. Again, this should not present any surprises, but should be a recitation of the timeline to which you have already agreed. At this point, you and the buyer should have agreed on everything but the implementation time and the compensation.

Compensation

Price can always be an excuse for indecision if the value of your book is not properly presented. Any price you ask is too high if the buyer has no need for what you are offering. (Would you pay $1.00 for a ballpoint pen sharpener?) That is why you never want to lead with your pricing. Instead, progressively build a case portraying your book's value and buyers will feel like they are getting a bargain when they finally see your bottom line.

Some people feel that the first person to give a price loses. The assumption is that if you give a price first, it may be too low and leave money on the table. Or, it may be too high and discourage further negotiation. A position that results in having a winner and a loser is not a good way to enter a business relationship. You want a long-term association with many repeat orders.

If you are suggesting a sequential introduction—a local, to regional, to national roll out, for example—divide your total price into more manageable subtotals, the sum of which may appear less costly than simply stating the entire amount. This strategy also reduces the buyer's anxiety and makes it easier to make positive decisions, since the dollar commitment is spread over time. If you are not suggesting a sequential introduction, present the total price of what it will cost per month, or per units sold.

If you show the price of each implementation phase, also show the proposed level of goal attainment for the money invested at that time. Visuals can help you tremendously here. For example, you could create a bar graph that shows the incremental growth in sales. This serves several purposes. First, it shows the value received for each dollar spent. Second, it takes the emphasis off the *price* of your plan and places it on its *value*. For example, say you are willing to sell 10,000 copies of your book to the buyer at $40,000. But if the incremental net revenue in the sales of their products is projected at $50,000 through the use of your book, focus on the $10,000 value he or she is actually receiving.

And finally, it gives buyers an exit strategy—an option that may be used if the plan is not going as scheduled. The validity of this argument is relative to the size of the commitment you are requesting. For example, if you propose a sale of 100 books at $6.00 each, the buyer's commitment is much lower than if you propose 10,000 books at $4.00 each. The following list includes several other tips for presenting your compensation request:

■ Do not make your proposal a take-it-or-leave-it mandate or you will remove any room for negotiation. Instead, give three scenarios: worst case, best case, and most-likely case. Show pricing based on different quantities derived from your three scenarios.

■ Be aware of the impact of the words you choose. For example, instead of using the words "price" or "cost," use the words "investment" or "value" to reinforce the fact that buyers will be better off implementing your plan than rejecting it.

■ Do not show all the details of your plan; just the bottom line. If you have everything out for all to see it will invite discussion on, or resistance to, minor topics such as where the books will be stored.

■ When forecasting results, use general terms like "month one" and "month two," instead of specific time periods like "January." This eliminates an argument of when the program should begin, and of having to recalculate the numbers if you agree to begin on a different date from that which you suggested.

■ Use charts and graphs to make your points visually. For instance, you might prepare a table that shows currently forecasted sales, and also shows the incremental volume that might be achieved by implementing the campaign you are proposing.

■ Forecast when the break-even point (BEP) of the sale will likely occur. The BEP occurs when the revenue equals the total expenses. In other words, it shows you the level of sales required before making a profit. Calculate the BEP for both you and your buyers, but only refer to theirs during the negotiations. Keep your BEP confidential.

■ If you offer a discount for an immediate order or an order for a greater quantity, show the resulting savings. For example, if you only tell them that buying within ten days will reduce the total price from $99,985 to $97,365, they would have to stop and calculate the difference, which would be distracting. On the other hand, if you say it will drop the price by $2,620, the difference is immediately clear.

■ Never guarantee anything except your determination to make the project succeed. The implementation of a marketing campaign is beyond your control. If you guarantee a sales figure will be achieved and it is not, the buyer may seek to place the blame on your books. On the other hand, you control your own work efforts, so it is safe to guarantee that you will follow through.

Selling books is a sequential process between or among people. It may occur over a period of days, weeks, months or years. Begin talking in general numbers. As you proceed through negotiations, your figures will typically become more specific because you will be adding criteria important to the buyer and eliminating that which is unimportant.

Conclusion

Wrap up your sales kit with a bulleted list of all the ways in which the buyer will be better off buying your book than not. Make each benefit stand out so the buyer does not have to sift through long paragraphs of explanation. After all, this is your summary section—not the time to bring up new information.

> **TIP**
> Only send or give buyers a book if there is a potential for a bulk sale. If you send a copy of your book along with your sales kit to buyers who only have use for one copy, like librarians, they will have already obtained all they need and will have no need to make a purchase.

Order Form

Prepare an order form or sample letter of agreement so you can consummate the order immediately, if possible. Leave blank lines to fill in quantity, price, delivery date, and payment terms. Review the letter with the buyer and make any changes necessary in order to get his or her approval on each section. Then get the buyer's final signature. This is an essential part of your sales kit, because if you do not close the sale right then, you will have to make a return visit or another phone call. That will require you to go back to the beginning and summarize each component of your sales kit, which will waste valuable time.

> **TIP**
> Do not ask someone to "sign a contract." This has the connotation of a major decision and potential liability, and will increase his or her anxiety. However, if you instead as that person to "approve your letter of agreement," you are minimizing negative implications and simply asking him or her to formalize that to which you have already agreed.

Once you have finished going through the entire sales kit, the negotiation process begins. *34. Negotiating* (page 253) will give you insight into the negotiation process, so you will have the necessary knowledge and confidence to succeed in closing a sale with favorable terms.

BE READY FOR QUESTIONS

After you present your proposal, buyers may begin to have doubts. Therefore, a few days prior to your meeting or phone conversation, prepare a list of responses to common questions they may have. That way, you will be ready with answers that will assure them that they should purchase your book. Do not include this list of questions and answers in your formal sales kit or presentation, since it brings up possibilities the buyer may have not considered. Just have it prepared so you are ready with answers if necessary. The following list includes example questions and guidelines for answers. You will find that you have already done most of the work the answers require; therefore, you simply need to gather it together into one, easily accessible document, and fill in the missing pieces.

■ *What if we decide to write the material ourselves?* This is the *buy* versus *build* quandary. Your answer should discuss how a decision to write their own book would result in higher costs, time delays, and perhaps having to add a new employee to their payroll. You should also stress your expertise on the subject area, emphasizing that you are the best person to deliver this material. In short, tell them how and why it would be more economical and effective to purchase your book, rather than create their own.

■ *What if we go with a competitive title?* The analysis you conducted in *25. Understand Your Competition and Differentiate Your Title* (page 207) will prove its worth here. After asking which competitive titles are under consideration, describe how your proposal differs from, and is superior to each.

■ *What if we do not purchase a book at all?* There is an opportunity cost associated with not taking a course of action. Describe how doing nothing could extend the current negative conditions that you described in your situation analysis.

■ *What if we delay the decision and do this later?* Remind the buyer again of the current market situation and his or her major business concerns. Then discuss how a delay could cost more than what you have proposed.

Add and subtract questions for different buyers however you feel is necessary. The most important consideration when creating this answer key is projecting your professionalism and expertise while continuing to sell your book's value. After you have convinced the buyer that your book is worth buying, you will need to work out the terms of the sale so they are agreeable to both you and the buyer. The next section will help you do just that.

34. NEGOTIATING

Selling is different from negotiating. Selling involves describing and communicating the features and benefits of your book, which is the purpose of your initial phone calls and sales kit. After you present your sales kit to a buyer, you are essentially done *selling* to him or her. At that point, the two of you enter into a period of *negotiation*. When you negotiate, you listen to what the buyers are saying, or not saying, about what and why they want to buy. Then, you respond in kind, reinforcing the positive and minimizing, compensating for, or eliminating all concerns they may have.

BEGINNING THE NEGOTIATION PROCESS

Your ultimate objective is to close a deal with a buyer immediately after you go through your sales kit with him or her for the first time. However, this is unlikely to happen, particularly for a large order. There is almost always a period of negotiation before sales are finalized—a back-and-forth discussion until both parties are satisfied with the terms.

The negotiation process begins when the buyer disagrees with, or objects to one or more of your terms or conditions, so will not sign off on the sale. When that occurs, start working toward a resolution by asking questions. Find out as much as you can about the buyer's concerns—do not refer to them as objections because that could reinforce the negativity in the prospect's mind—including why he or she did not accept your initial proposal, how far apart your positions are, and if there are any possible compromises that could be made.

Some pundits recommend negotiating on one issue at a time. In other words, finishing the discussion and reaching some sort of agreement about the buyer's first concern before moving on to the second. While each issue is being discussed, both parties should treat it as the most important topic, without worrying about any other concerns at that time.

On the other hand, there are other experts who believe it is better to negotiate multiple issues simultaneously. That is, identify all the issues up front and put everything on the table at the same time. Then go back and forth, perhaps trading off one against the other. Both are good strategies, so you might consider combining them. First, get all the issues out in the open. Then, ask the buyers which are the most important so you can prioritize them and plan the order in which you will address them. Once you know all their concerns, you can eliminate them one at a time in a logical order. After you discuss each, ask if the solution you both come up with addresses the concern to their satisfaction.

TIP

During negotiations, consider the circumstances surrounding each sale. For example, a non-profit organization is probably not in the same position as a Fortune 500 corporation to buy a large number of expensive books. Thus, you would need to negotiate differently with each.

IDENTIFY YOUR BEST NEGOTIATED OUTCOME

Be prepared for your negotiations. If possible, you want to avoid having to go back to the buyer later with more, or different information. Know in advance the pricing parameters within which you must negotiate, and what the best negotiated outcome (BNO) would be. Also know what you are, and are not willing to negotiate away to get that outcome.

■ *Make a list of all the outcomes that would be acceptable to you.* There may be several end results for which you would be willing to settle. Ideally, your BNO might be one, large order of books sold on a non-returnable basis at a high price. But you might also be willing to accept a smaller quantity to be shipped on a regular basis if the customer pays the shipping charges. Create a list of all of the end-results to which you would be willing to agree.

■ *Which of these alternatives would be best for you?* Prioritize your various acceptable outcomes from most to least attractive. If you cannot successfully negotiate the first one on your list—your BNO—move on to the next one. Having this information in a ranked order prior to the negotiation will ensure you do not leave anything on the table.

■ *What are you willing to negotiate away in return for the BNO?* Some criteria will be more important to you than others. For example, you may want a certain profitability margin and are willing to sell fewer books in order to maintain it. Or, you may be willing to pay freight for especially large orders. Know in advance the tools with which you have to work, as well as the limits of your willingness and flexibility to negotiate on items like price, terms, delivery, and quantity.

Negotiating is a give-and-take process. If you concede on one point, seek a quid pro quo. Know in advance what you want, and decide what you are willing or unwilling to negotiate away in order to get your BNO.

PRINCIPLES OF NEGOTIATION

Many negotiations go awry because the two parties involved incorrectly assume that they understand each other's motivations. You will have better luck negotiating if you take time to learn about and understand the concerns and buying parameters of the other party. In other words, find out what the buyer's ultimate objective is, as well as what his or her criteria for reaching it are. The following list includes six principles of negotiation that you should find helpful during this process. For ease of description, the same example is referred to throughout.

■ *Discover your counterpart's concerns.* Sometimes buyers will tell you their hesitations outright, but other times you will have to do some probing and uncover them yourself. For example, say it is August and you are negotiating a large-quantity sale. The potential buyer works for a company that wants to use your book as a premium to increase its sales. You have agreed upon a price that is satisfactory to both of you, but the buyer is still balking at signing the agreement and will not tell you why.

You need to uncover his or her concerns in order to move forward, and you can do that by asking a series of questions. Begin by enumerating areas of agreement. For example, you could say, "We have agreed that using this book as a premium can help your company increase sales significantly above its cost. Correct? And we have agreed that the price is fair, right? Then what is it that is keeping us from agreeing to this proposal today?"

These types of questions may allow you to discover that the bottleneck is not desire or price, but rather, it is the timing of both payment and delivery. For instance, in this scenario the buyer might say, "Yes, all of that is correct. But my budget is shot for the rest of the year. I cannot spend any more money until January first, but I must have the books by November." The key is to find out what the concern is, so you can begin to try to find a way around it.

■ *Verify that accommodating the concerns will complete the sale.* Learning what the buyer's concerns are is the first step. But before moving forward, you need to make sure that if you accommodate those concerns, you will for sure get the sale. For example, in response to the buyer's answer to your questions above, you could say something like, "So you are saying that if we can delay payment for the books and the shipping charges until next year, but still get the books to you by November, you will okay the agreement today?" If he or she says yes, you have verified that under those conditions the buyer will sign an agreement, and you are one step closer to completing the sale.

■ *Work toward a solution.* After you have the buyer's hidden concerns on the table and know that accommodating them will get you the sale, you can move forward and begin to create a solution. For each concern, work with the buyer to arrange one of several solutions that will allow you to alleviate the buyer's apprehension and close the deal. In this case, in regard to the timing of the payment, you could delay billing from your printer, send an invoice today but date it the first of January, accept a check dated January 1 of next year, or come up with another mutually agreeable solution.

In regard to the timing of the delivery, you know that you can print the books and *most likely* deliver them by the buyer's promotional blitz in November, which is three months away. But "most likely" is not good enough for the buyer, so in working toward a solution you might ask him or her if the company has any discounted shipping agreements with trucking companies. If the answer is yes, suggest having the buyer pay for shipping through that trucker, with guaranteed delivery in less than three months. This way, the buyer is happy and you are also better off in several ways. You are no longer paying for shipping, you are no longer responsible for glitches in shipping, and you have made the buyer happy, opening the door for future business.

■ *Seek to maintain a status quo.* Given that you had to make a few concessions to get to this point, you might now want to add a condition or two to the sale for your "trouble." In other words, seek to maintain a status quo. For example, since you agreed to delay the buyer's payment obligation until the first of the year, you might add a price increase to cover the interest your printer will charge you for extended billing.

In regard to delivery, even if the buyer does not have an outside shipping option, you can still create a win/win situation. If you are confident you can deliver the books on or before schedule, you might offer to pay a penalty if the books are delivered late. That would probably catch the buyer off guard, and make him or her feel as if you really want to be accommodating and find a solution. Then, while the buyer is still debating your proposal, add that you want a bonus if the books are delivered early.

■ *Be creative.* If the first solution you offer is rejected, do not give up. For example, what if the buyer remains adamant that he or she must have the books delivered in three months, and claims the penalty you offered would not compensate for his or her potential loss? You could then suggest another option, and ask if he or she must have *all* the books delivered by November. You may be able to guarantee a partial shipment before then, perhaps with a bonus for a complete delivery. Use your creativity to try to meet your buyer in the middle.

■ *Continue to probe even after a deal is lost.* If after all of this you still lose the order, follow up by asking why you did not get it. Always ask for constructive feedback so you can learn from the experience. For example, in a bidding situation, you may have had the lowest price, but did not mention some needed service or feature. Ask the buyer what it would have taken for the two of you to reach an agreement. The answer might be something you can accommodate and incorporate into future negotiations.

The bottom line is that if buyers want to do business with you, the details will not prevent it from happening. And if they do not want to do business with you, they will blame the details. Assuming they do want to reach some agreement, keep talking things out until there is nothing left to discuss and you have closed the deal.

As Ralph Waldo Emerson said, "The game requires coolness, right reasoning, promptness, and patience in the players." Good sales and negotiations require that all involved parties are willing to listen to, and discuss issues in search of a win/win agreement. Sales are only good if both sides come away thinking that the final accord was fair, and that the door is open for future business. Newly equipped with the information in this chapter, you should feel like you have all of the necessary skills to accomplish just that.

Chapter Six

Promoting to Non-Trade Buyers

Promotion is the process of communicating with prospective buyers. Use it to inform them your book exists and convince them they should purchase it. Publicity, reviews, articles, testimonials, direct mail, advertising, sales promotion, media performances, trade shows, and awards are all promotional tools that can increase awareness about you and your book, and potentially lead to sales. These tactics should be implemented in concert with one another in order to persuade the largest number of people to buy your book in the shortest period of time.

Promotion is as effective in non-trade markets as it is in trade markets. However, the fundamentals are applied a little differently in non-trade promotions, because the emphasis is on publicizing to niche market segments rather than to the masses. Of course, national exposure cannot hurt your non-trade marketing, but you are more likely to have success gaining access to niche media.

In this chapter you will learn many of the ins and outs of promoting you and your book to non-trade buyers. There are numerous ways to raise awareness about your book, and this chapter will teach you about all of them. You will learn about everything from getting your book reviewed, to conducting mail-order campaigns, to hosting author events. When you are finished with this chapter, you will have the information and know-how necessary to effectively and efficiently spread the word about your book to the people in non-trade markets.

35. SEEK NICHE REVIEWS

People read magazines and newspapers to learn more about subjects of interest to them. Therefore, they can be a great way to reach your target audience. Advertisements can be cost-prohibitive and ineffective, though. A better way to reach readers is through book reviews. Reviews in these publications are free, and they deliver a more credible message than space ads because they come from objective, third-party sources. Reviews also raise awareness about your title and stimulate word-of-mouth advertising—another source of credible, free promotion.

MAJOR REVIEWS VERSUS NICHE REVIEWS

Most publishers seek reviews of their titles among the major review publications, which is not a bad idea. The major review publications include *Publishers Weekly,*

CREATE PROFESSIONAL SALES-PROMOTIONAL MATERIALS

Your submission materials, promotional items, and catalogs are sales tools used to present you, your company, and your books in the most compelling way possible. Non-trade buyers are used to seeing professionally prepared literature, so anything of lesser quality will detract from your sales efforts. The following list includes six tips that will help you create effective sell sheets, flyers, mail inserts, catalogs, bookmarks, and more:

■ *Use a professional designer.* Most people can take one look at a book or flyer and know if it was prepared by a professional designer or by a self-published author on a tight budget. Buyers know the difference, too. They want to be confident that the books they buy will add to, and not detract from, their companies' images. Trained designers know how to communicate a specific message and image using the nuances of layout, typeface, photography, illustrations, color, and white space. Rely on their knowledge and skills to create sales literature of which you can be proud, and you should sell more books.

○ To find a list of designers rated by previous clients, go to www.bookcentralstation.com

■ *Grab attention.* Some promotional materials draw in readers by caressing the words and layout with emotionally charged subtleties. Strong sales literature has a definite starting point with an easy-to-follow path that leads readers through a field of benefits to a logical and positive conclusion. Grab the reader's interest with an attention-getting opening statement, boldly state if anything is new or free, highlight your other titles and personal accomplishments, and include ordering information.

■ *Talk benefits, not features.* Non-trade buyers tend to care less about your book's attributes than they do about the benefits your book will bring them. Therefore, your sales-promotional literature must convey what your books will

ForeWord Magazine, BookPage, Kirkus Reviews, CHOICE, Midwest Book Review, Library Journal, and *School Library Journal.* Assuming your book gets a good review, you will accrue several benefits from it, including increased exposure, greater credibility, a source of endorsements, and potential sales. These publications receive countless requests for reviews, however, and the competition is stiff. Furthermore, sending review copies to all of them can get expensive.

Niche publications, on the other hand, are often overlooked as sources of reviews. There are specialty magazines that review books for people interested in

---

do for buyers. Bring them up to a boiling point with a captivating description of reasons why, and how they will be better off with your book than without it. Then ask for the order, providing details on pricing, quantities, and discounts. You will almost certainly have to create different literature for different audiences. Buyers in the retail sector may have different hot buttons than buyers in the non-retail sector. Similarly, you may have to create new literature for special occasions.

- *Form follows function.* In the words of Thoreau, "Simplify, simplify, simplify." While creativity is a good thing, do not get carried away. Your main priority is to pass along easily understood information. Additionally, it is of the upmost importance to make sure everything is grammatically correct and properly spelled on all of your materials. Finally, use the proper paper. There are so many options available that it sometimes becomes difficult to choose. If you are creating a mailing piece, you may opt for a lightweight paper to reduce your mailing costs. But if you integrate a business reply card, you will need heavier paper to meet postal-service requirements.

- *Make it easy to order.* Always provide complete contact information that the reader can use to write, email, or call to find out more information or to place an order. When possible, include an order form people can complete and return. Make sure you ask for all of the information you will need to complete the order, including the credit card's expiration date and a valid signature. Always ask for a telephone number, because there may be times when illegible handwriting makes it necessary to call the buyer for clarification. Additionally, give some assurance of quick delivery, and prominently display guarantees if any are being offered.

- *Offer a discount or an incentive to order.* If you have multiple products, organize them into associated groups to encourage larger orders. Then, offer a discount for combined or volume purchases. Or, use a premium to encourage an early decision.

subjects as diverse as stay-at-home dads, minority executives, homeschooling, skydiving, health, celebrities, fiction, and many, many others. For example, the *Journal of Communication* publishes articles and book reviews on a broad range of issues in communication theory, research, practice, and policy; and the *Astronomy and Astrophysics Annual* publishes annual reviews of scholarly research in the fields of astronomy and astrophysics. The advantages and disadvantages for the major review publications also apply to niche reviews. But an important, added advantage of niche reviews is that they are more likely to be seen, and perhaps acted upon by your target buyers.

Most authors seek reviews with the major book reviewers. You do not have to ignore them, but seek niche reviews, too. Opportunities for reviews may exist in local newspapers, industry magazines, association newsletters, and even local television and radio affiliates. Using these outlets as sources of reviews to reach your target buyers is a tactical marketing tool that can yield excellent results.

SUBMITTING YOUR BOOK FOR REVIEW

Send your book to every niche newspaper, magazine, newsletter, and website of relevance that reviews books. Even though mailing review copies can be expensive, do not be miserly about sending them. Be selective, choosing those that are related to your content and most likely to reach your buyers. But at the same time, send your material to as many potential niche reviewers as possible, because the results could generate broad exposure, awareness, and sales in your niche markets.

Even though most publications that do book reviews have a designated book-review editor, it is not always best to submit your review copies to that person. Instead, you could send it to the editor of the section that best aligns with your book's content, whether it is sports, travel, food, business, leisure, or something else. Section editors receive far fewer books than book-review editors, so your chances of them selecting your book to review are better. They might even publish a more complete article about the author to go along with the review, as well. You can usually find the names of the section editors, as well as their contact information on publications' websites.

Send reviewers a press release that details your book's content, page count, list price, and all other important information. Be sure that you include your full contact information, as well. The press release should be visually appealing and written in a way that gets reviewers excited about your title, making them want to review it as soon as possible. Learn more about creating professional sales-promotional materials in the inset on the previous two pages, and see how a press release for this book might look on page 328.

You can include a copy of your book with your submission, or you can simply tell reviewers to contact you for a copy if they are seriously considering reviewing it. Sending a finalized book is always preferred. However, if that is not possible, make sure the reviewer is okay with receiving a bound galley before you send one, and clearly print "Review Copy" on the front. If possible, time your submission with special, themed issues of publications that correlate with your title; doing so might increase the chances of having your book selected. Finally, be persistent and always follow up.

FINDING NICHE REVIEWERS

Niche publications that conduct book reviews are everywhere, but it will take some diligence to locate those relevant to your book. Jim Cox of Midwest Book Review has an extensive list of niche reviewers on his website. Additionally, Book Central Station's website offers a list of reviewers, rated by other authors. Finally, you can find many more book reviewers by searching online.

○ Midwest Book Review: www.midwestbookreview.com

○ Book Central Station: www.bookcentralstation.com

When you contact publications, follow their submission guidelines, keep good records, and follow up. Additionally, make sure everything you send them is professionally constructed. Niche marketing, in general, is a strategy that can increase your sales, and getting niche reviews is an excellent way to implement that strategy. A review by someone at a known and respected publication can be a strong influence on people debating whether or not to make a purchase.

36. RAISE AWARENESS THROUGH NICHE MEDIA

Before people will buy a product, they need to have a certain level of confidence about it. That confidence is gained through repeated exposure. Think about your own buying practices. When you are at a store, are you more likely to purchase an item that you have some familiarity with, or one you are seeing for the first time? If you are like most people, you will pick up and buy the product that you have previously seen.

Raising awareness about your title through niche media—print and broadcast—is important in both trade and non-trade outlet sales. When people walk into a bookstore they are most likely looking for a book, but yours is just one of thousands on the shelves. And when they walk into a gift shop, discount store, supermarket, or pharmacy, they are probably looking for other items—not books. Therefore, in either case it is important to do whatever you can to make your title stand out. If shoppers have previously seen or heard about your book in the media, it will be more likely to catch their attention and cause them to pick it up and buy it. The same is true for buyers in corporations, associations, and schools. If they have heard about you or your book before you contact them, you are more likely to get a favorable response.

REACH AND FREQUENCY

Your book has no perceived value to prospective buyers before they know it exists. Even after they hear about it for the first time, it may still carry little significance in their minds. As your message reaches them more and more frequently, however, they will begin to understand why your content may benefit them in some way. This is why raising awareness about your title through niche media is so important. Your media publicity will not only let prospective buyers know your book exists, but it will also help the value of your book exceed its cost in their minds.

Two forces come in to play in this process: *reach* and *frequency*. Reach is the number of people that are exposed to your message, and frequency is the number of times each person sees or hears your message. The goal is to reach as many people as you can, as frequently as possible. Most publishers do not have unlimited funds to accommodate this expansive marketing scheme, though. Therefore, a tradeoff between the two is needed, and niche media can help

Appearances in and on mass media may reach everyone who could eventually buy your book. However, only a minority of the general public may be interested in your content, and obtaining publicity in mass media outlets is difficult and expensive. So, instead of trying to reach everyone, only try to reach those people who are potential buyers. You can best do that through broadcast and print niche media outlets that appeal to specific audiences. By decreasing your reach and only targeting interested individuals through niche media, you can afford to increase your frequency; thereby getting your message to those potential buyers more often, and increasing your chances of making sales.

T I P

Print media may have an advantage over broadcast media in niche publicity. Pam Lontos, the owner of the publicity firm PR/PR, said "It has more longevity, since people tend to keep it for future reference. It may also be more believable. If people see it in print, they are more likely to think it is true."

TIMING

You can increase the impact of your reach and frequency combination by timing your media appearances and interviews to coincide with a relevant marketing period. For example, November is Child Safety and Protection Month. If your book is related to that topic, your media exposure will likely have a greater impact during that time period. Likewise, July is National Corrective Posture Month. If your book is about backpacking, gardening, exercise, or any other related topic, plan your media exposure accordingly.

For more marketing period ideas, see *24. Segment the Mass Market* (page 203). You can also use the website IdeaCalendar.com to learn about different possibilities for associating your book with a national event. The idea calendar has lists of special days, weeks, months, anniversaries, birthdays, and other events that occur every year, and it may provide different marketing ideas and opportunities for you.

⭕ www.ideacalendar.com

If there is no pre-existing marketing period that coincides with your title, create your own. Dan Gordon, co-author of *Haunted Baseball: Ghosts, Curses, Legends & Eerie Events,* did just that. According to Dan,

> We capitalize as much as possible on media events. We declared 2007 the spookiest baseball postseason ever, since seven of the eight teams in the playoffs had some sort of supernatural lore attached to them that was focused on in our book. This prompted numerous radio and television appearances and feature articles in the *New York Sun, Akron Beacon,* and *Boston Herald.* We spoke about the Cleveland Indians so-called 'Curse of Rocky Colavitio' when signing in Cleveland, which got us radio and television interviews. And after the Red Sox won the World Series, we speculated whether the ghosts of Fenway past now favored the past, citing several stories from our book.
>
> The overlap of Halloween and the baseball postseason certainly helped us garner more national and regional attention for the book. In addition to sports radio, we're continuing to be invited to paranormal-themed radio shows, including the popular radio show 'Coast to Coast' with George Noory. We also emailed baseball play-by-play broadcasters and told them of players on the teams they cover who have a firsthand ghost story. This has earned us several on-air mentions.

Both you and media outlets share a common goal. You need to spread the word about your book, and they need to fill air-time. However, they also need to attract and keep listeners and viewers. Therefore, it is up to you to convince them that discussing your book will help them do that, too. Timing your request with a relevant marketing period or current event will make your job that much easier. You might have to be as creative as Dan Gordon. But after all, you *are* creative. You wrote a book.

FINDING NICHE MEDIA

Similar to niche reviewers discussed in the previous section, niche media outlets are everywhere. A good place to start looking is Book Central Station's website. It has direct links to major and niche radio and television shows, magazines, newspapers, and electronic media. The more closely you can align your topic with the audience of a show, the more likely you are to get selected as a guest. Find the appropriate outlet for your story, and you can achieve good reach and frequency in your target segments.

○ Book Central Station: www.bookcentralstation.com

You can also conduct online searches on your topic. One suggestion is to go to your favorite search engine and type in your subject, followed by the word "media." If you find that such a search yields an overwhelming number of results, modify your search and instead of "media," use "TV," "radio," "magazines," etc. You should also search blogs, newsletters, webinars, and other online outlets as appropriate. Other sources for finding niche media outlets include the following:

❑ *All-In-One Directory;* Gebbie Press, Inc., P.O. Box 1000, New Paltz, NY 12561
   Tel: 845-255-7560; Website: www.gebbieinc.com

❑ Radio and Television News Directors Association; 1025 F St. NW, 7th Fl.,
   Washington, DC 20004
   Tel: 202-659-6510; Website: www.rtnda.org

❑ Broadcast Interview Source; 2233 Wisconsin Ave. NW, Washington, DC 20007
   Tel: 800-932-7266; Website: www.expertclick.com

However, television and radio share a common drawback: You must listen or watch at the precise time an event is broadcast. Podcasts, on the other hand, post information online where interested people can download it and listen or watch on their schedules. Podcasts are relatively easy to produce and can be created by anyone with the right equipment—computer, internet connection, and audio recorder. Once created, they simply need to be uploaded to a website where they can be found and downloaded. Podcasts can either be just sound, or they can be sound and video. A video podcast is sometimes called a vidcast. The following websites will lead you to directories of various available podcasts:

○ www.podcastdirectory.com

○ www.podcast.net

○ www.podcastingnews.com

○ www.podcastpickle.com

○ www.podscope.com

○ www.podcastcentral.com

Regardless of the type(s) of niche media you choose to pursue, though, the goal is the same. You want to extend the reach and frequency of your message to your target audience as far as possible. Doing your research to find the outlets most closely aligned with your book's topic will pay off in the long run, because the right people will hear you.

CREATE A MEDIA KIT

Contacting media outlets is a little different than contacting buyers. Instead of sending them a submission package, you need to send them a media kit. The following list includes materials that are typically found in media kits:

- A cover letter explaining why the media person should be interested, as well as what is included in the kit

- A press release for the book (See page 328 for an example)

- An about the author biography

- A professional photograph of the author

- A list of suggested interview questions the media person can ask the author

- A small excerpt from the book (optional)

- A review quote page or photocopies of reviews in their entirety

- A list of any other media appearances or interviews done by the author (if applicable)

- A list of other works by the author (if applicable)

- A media reel, which is a DVD or CD with clips from the author's previous media appearances or interviews (if applicable)

Media outlets receive countless requests for interviews and appearances through media kits, so be sure everything included is professional and complete or it will be thrown out immediately. Additionally, always follow up with a personal phone call. Media exposure can be a great way to spread the word about your book. If you follow the guidelines discussed in this section, you have a good chance of finding yourself and your book on the radio, television, or Internet sometime soon.

37. GET ENDORSEMENTS

Endorsements, also called testimonials or blurbs, are statements by people attesting to the quality of writing and the value of the content in your book. If you can get celebrities or industry experts to endorse your book, it can have a significant positive impact on prospective buyers. In marketing terms, this is called the "Halo Effect," meaning you benefit from another person's or organization's notoriety. Celebrities have attention-getting value, and if one or more of their names is connected with your book, their renown can be transferred to it. Similarly, if you have an industry expert substantiate your content, it gives you and your message more credibility, especially if you are not well known in your niche.

> **T**
> **I**
> **P**
>
> Aim high. Before you ask a celebrity or expert for an endorsement, ask him or her to write the introduction to your book. Most people will be flattered to be asked, but will probably turn you down. You might just get lucky, though.

GETTING CELEBRITY ENDORSEMENTS

Obtaining endorsements from celebrities may seem impossible, but in actuality it is not. The best way to go about contacting celebrities is through networking. If you can somehow find a mutual acquaintance to contact a celebrity on your behalf, you will have a better chance of getting his or her time and attention. See *28. Find Potential Buyers* (page 222) for more information about networking.

Another option for getting in touch with celebrities is through mailings. The key is to make it as easy as possible for them to reply to your request. Your initial query should include a cover letter that asks for their endorsement of your book. You should also include the table of contents, a galley copy, or sample chapters for their review, as well as a self-addressed, stamped envelope (SASE) for their reply. Let them know you recognize how busy they are, and send sample testimonials from which they may choose if they do not have the time to create their own. The following list includes several organizations and websites that can help you begin your search for celebrities:

■ The Screen Actors Guild represents nearly 120,000 actors in film, television, commercials, and music videos. SAG has two locations—one in California and the other in New York—and many branches. In addition to learning about industry standards and terms through SAG, you can search its branches to find the nearest one. Then, visit or call to learn how you can contact celebrities locally or nationally.

❑ Screen Actors Guild; 5757 Wilshire Blvd., Los Angeles, CA 90036
   Tel: 323-954-1600; Website: www.sag.org

❑ Screen Actors Guild; 360 Madison Avenue, 12th Fl., New York, NY 10017
   Tel: 212-944-1030; Website: www.sag.org

■ Celeb Fan Mail claims to have a database of over 15,000 reliable celebrity addresses. There is a fee to join, but once you are registered you will be given full access to the members' area, which allows you to search the database of celebrity addresses.

○ Celeb Fan Mail: www.celebfanmail.com

■ You can join Contact Any Celebrity for a fee and get access to an online database that contains the mailing addresses, phone and fax numbers, email addresses, agents, managers, publicists, and charitable causes for several celebrities.

❑ Contact Any Celebrity; 8721 Santa Monica Blvd. #431, W. Hollywood, CA 90069
Tel: 310-691-5466; Website: www.contactanycelebrity.com

■ Reel Classics, the classic movie website, provides a free list of addresses for certain celebrities that have approved the use of their contact information.

○ Reel Classics: www.reelclassics.com/Address/address-list.htm

Responses from celebrities can take time, but if you do not hear back from someone you sent a request to in two or three weeks, send a follow-up letter or email. Celebrities are busy people, and their mail is often screened by an assistant, which can delay or even prevent your request from getting to them. Therefore, try to make direct contact with them if possible. For example, many receive people following their performances, so you might try to grab their attention then. That is how I received a testimonial from Wayne Dyer. Or, if a notable person is conducting a book signing, speak to him or her there. I had my picture taken with Oprah Winfrey and Jack Canfield at two similar events. I even got them to pose for the photograph with a copy of my book in hand—an implied endorsement. Do what it takes to ethically get celebrities to endorse you or your book, and the results will follow.

GETTING INDUSTRY EXPERT ENDORSEMENTS

If you have been in an industry long enough to write about it, you probably know, or at least know of, the leading authorities on your topic. Your research might have even been based on some of their earlier writings. Many experts are willing to endorse authors like yourself, particularly if you use their theories or mention their titles or papers as a source. Find their websites and contact them directly. If you cannot find their information, try going to the website of the major associa-

Endorsements go both ways. Be sure the celebrities and experts you ask to endorse your book portray images with which you are comfortable being associated.

T
I
P

tion in your industry to find out if your target authority is a member, or perhaps on its board.

OTHER ENDORSEMENTS

If you are having trouble obtaining endorsements from celebrities or experts, it can still be useful to get them from average readers. Sometimes the sheer number of endorsements can have significant impact, regardless of who they are from. Author Bill Creed solicits testimonials creatively. "I make sure that a bookmark is in every book I sign and encourage readers to send me a testimonial. For this reason, my personal email is on the bookmark. I get many responses, and of course, I save the email addresses for future use."

When listing average endorsements in your book and sales-promotional literature, apply the marketing principle of primacy and recency. This principle states that in a list of more than three items, people are more likely to remember the first and last entries. Therefore, list your celebrity and expert endorsements in the first and last positions, and all of the others in between.

USING YOUR ENDORSEMENTS

Endorsements can be very persuasive, so you want to be sure prospective buyers are able to see them easily. You should include the best blurbs on your website and in your personal sales kit, press releases, media kits, advertising, and sales-promotional items. You could also place them on the rear cover of your book. Or, if you have an especially powerful endorsement from a top celebrity or a recognized industry expert, you should consider putting it on the front cover.

If an endorsement goes over two or three short sentences, it may be too long for people to grasp its meaning before losing interest. In those cases, extract a short phrase that characterizes the essence of the testimonial and use only that. Be sure that doing so does not misrepresent the intention of the endorser, though. According to the Federal Trade Commission,

> The endorsement message need not be phrased in the exact words of the endorser, unless the advertisement affirmatively so represents. However, the endorsement may neither be presented out of context nor reworded so as to distort in any way the endorser's opinion or experience with the product. Endorsements must always reflect the honest opinions, findings, beliefs, or experience of the endorser.

Do not rely on your name and message as the sole technique for communicating the advantages of your content. Apply the Halo Effect and use the impact of a connection to a celebrity to support your message and extend your name recognition. This is particularly important if you are not a well-known person in your niche. You may be surprised at how often and vocally television and radio hosts will refer to your book if it has a celebrity connection on the air. People are enamored with notoriety, and your association with fame can only add to your sales and positive exposure.

38. PARTICIPATE IN AWARD COMPETITIONS

Winning an award has the potential to separate your book from the pack of competitive titles quickly, since it is a statement by an objective third party that your book is worthy of recognition. Additionally, many awards are based on the content of your book rather than its design, so they become valuable sales tools in non-trade markets. You probably will not experience significant sales based on awards alone, but there are other benefits. Perhaps most importantly, awards could enhance your credibility among prospective buyers. Also, your status as an award-winning author may increase your chances of getting on the air or in print, and may give you more leverage among agents, publishers, and distribution partners that turned you down in the past. Some award competitions even compensate their winners with monetary prizes.

CHOOSE AWARD COMPETITIONS CAREFULLY

While the benefits of winning legitimate awards can be great, proceed with caution. Do adequate research about the company sponsoring the award, and make sure the value of winning will outweigh the cost of your submission. In the trade, only a handful of awards make a difference. Winning a nationally recognized award is important and will help your sales. However, winning a less recognized award does not always result in additional sales. In other words, lesser-known awards may be great for your ego but not for your wallet. On the other hand, all types of awards *may* have a positive influence on sales in non-trade markets. But still make sure you consider the marketplace and contemplate awards in light of how effective they will be in each particular market.

COMPETING FOR AWARDS

There are both major, national awards and smaller, niche awards. The major awards include the Pulitzer Prize, the National Book Awards, and the Lambda Literary Awards. The likelihood of being a competitor for one of these awards is so minute that it is probably best to place your time on others for which you have a better chance of winning. If you would like to participate anyway, visit the websites below and follow their individual guidelines.

❍ Pulitzer Prize: www.pulitzer.org

❍ National Book Awards: www.nationalbook.org/nba.html

❍ Lambda Literary Awards: www.lambdaliterary.org/awards/guidelines.html

However, it is not necessary to compete for these major awards in order to experience benefits. Instead, consider competing for more accessible, niche awards. These awards can enhance your credibility among prospective buyers and potentially generate sales. There are numerous niche awards, so you should have no trouble finding one in your category. The processes for submitting your book are as varied as the awards themselves. Visit the websites of those you choose to enter and follow their individual guidelines.

Since many of these awards will not be well known among the general public, concentrate your award-related publicity efforts to prospective buyers and customers in your target markets only. The following list includes a sampling of the diversity in award competitions, many of which offer monetary prizes:

■ *800-CEO-READ Business Book Awards.* These awards recognize the best business books of each year.

○ 800-CEO-READ Business Book Awards: http://800ceoread.com/bookawards

■ *Benjamin Franklin Awards.* The Benjamin Franklin Awards recognize excellence in independent publishing. Winners are recognized at IBPA's gala event prior to Book Expo America.

○ Benjamin Franklin Awards: www.ibpa-online.org/pubresources/benfrank.aspx

■ *Edgar Awards.* The Edgar Allan Poe Awards—popularly called the Edgars—are presented every year by the Mystery Writers of America. They honor the best in mystery fiction, non-fiction, television, film, and theatre published or produced in the past year.

○ Edgar Awards: www.mysterywriters.org/?q=AwardsPrograms

■ *Eric Hoffer Award.* The Eric Hoffer Award recognizes excellence in art, general fiction, commercial fiction, children, young adult, culture, business, reference, home, health/self-help/religion, and legacy independent books.

○ Eric Hoffer Award: www.hofferaward.com

■ *Mom's Choice Awards.* This is an annual awards competition that recognizes authors, inventors, companies, parents, and others for their efforts in creating quality family-friendly media products and services.

○ Mom's Choice Awards: www.momschoiceawards.com

■ *National Best Book Awards.* These awards were established to recognize meritorious works by writers who self-published or had their books published by a small press or independent book publisher. POD books are eligible.

○ National Best Book Awards: www.usabooknews.com

■ *National Indie Excellence Book Awards.* This competition presents an opportunity for all independent, small press, and self-publishers seeking more recognition within the publishing industry.

❍ National Indie Excellence Book Awards: www.indieexcellence.com

■ *National Jewish Book Awards.* These awards are designed to give recognition to outstanding books, to stimulate writers to further literary creativity, and to encourage the reading of worthwhile titles that reflect a rich variety of the Jewish experience.

❍ National Jewish Book Awards: www.jewishbookcouncil.org/page.php?7

■ *National Outdoor Book Awards.* This is the outdoor world's largest and most prestigious book award program.

❍ National Outdoor Book Awards: www.noba-web.org/policy.htm

■ *Scott O'Dell Historical Fiction Award.* This award honors works of historical fiction for children or young adults.

❍ Scott O'Dell Historical Fiction Award: www.scottodell.com/odellaward.html

This is by no means an exhaustive list of potential award competitions. It is meant to serve as an example of the variety of awards available. Search online for others that may give your sales a boost if you win. Then, follow their guidelines and wish for the best.

MAKE THE MOST OF YOUR AWARDS

Winners of recognized, legitimate award competitions gain added prestige in their genres, which sometimes leads to greater sales. However, no one will know about your award unless you tell them. The following list includes some tips for making the most of the awards you win:

■ Point out the awards in all of your sales-promotional literature, your email signature, your business cards, and your letterhead. Also include the award logo on your website.

■ Announce winning the award in a press release and send it to prospective buyers. If you do not win, still send a press release mentioning that you were nominated or a finalist.

■ Design and include a new sheet describing your awards in your press kits. Create a similar PDF file that you can email.

■ Make a poster that you can use at your store events and personal presentations to promote your awards.

■ Place award stickers on all your book covers to announce the fact that your book won the award. Award stickers are official symbols that proclaim the winners and runners-up of competitions. Some competitions give them to winners for free; others make them available for purchase.

■ Create and send postcards to your customers, prospective buyers, and the media that show the cover of your book prominently displaying the award sticker. This official declaration will spread the word about your accomplishment and make your claims more believable.

■ If you publish a sequel or second edition, state that it is part of an "award-winning series."

Awards can give a psychological lift to you and your potential customers. Although they may or may not be beneficial to your marketing efforts and revenue, the fact that your book was deemed more outstanding than all the other competitors can be worth much for your attitude. And if you win several awards—particularly those well-known in your niche—you may convince the media and potential buyers that yours is a worthy product to evaluate and perhaps purchase.

39. IMPLEMENT EFFECTIVE MAIL-ORDER CAMPAIGNS

Mail-order marketing is a term that refers to many different methods of selling products and services through various print and electronic means, including direct-mail letters, flyers, and catalogs, as well as emails and electronic catalogs. When you have a mailing list of known recipients, direct-mail marketing can be an effective and cost-efficient way to reach them. For information on creating mailing lists, see *28. Find Potential Buyers* (page 220).

PURPOSE OF MAIL-ORDER MARKETING

Mail-order marketing has been given a bad reputation by many due to overuse, misleading offers, and poorly designed mailing pieces. People often perceive all direct mail as "junk mail," and its Internet equivalent as "spam." However, in reality direct mail is a targeted marketing weapon that can help you sell more books, test new titles, generate sales leads, and communicate the benefits of your products. When done correctly, direct marketing is a valuable adjunct to your marketing mix. Produce a quality piece or package that, by virtue of its quality and content, will be opened, read, and acted upon when it is received. For tips on creating professional sales-promotional materials, see the inset on page 260.

When you are targeting market segments with limited, identifiable groups of potential customers, direct mail may be the most effective and efficient marketing tool you can use to reach them. It gives you control of the timing, delivery, and content of your promotion, a predetermined, fixed delivery cost, and the means to forecast and measure the return on your marketing investment. Mail-order marketing requires you to be persistent—it takes time to build a base list of people who continue to purchase from you.

Always think about the next order. Have follow-up products for which you can conduct additional mail-order campaigns to get people to make repeat purchases.

**T
I
P**

DECIDING WHETHER YOUR BOOK IS SUITED FOR DIRECT MARKETING

Not all books are suited for direct marketing. To decide whether yours is, ask yourself several questions. First, is it a real and obvious value for the price you are asking? The more apparent value your product has for your prospective buyers, the less significant its price becomes. If you are trying to deplete your inventory of over-priced books simply by offering a reduced price via direct mail, you may be disappointed. If the content was not of value at your original price, people may still be uninterested even at a lower price. Instead, think about your book from the recipients' perspectives. Is your unique selling proposition different from what competitors offer, and is that difference of value to your prospective buyers?

You should also ask yourself if the cover design creates a good first impression. Your cover will be a focal point of your mail piece. It must be able to communicate the proper message without you being there to explain it. And the type must still be legible when the cover is reduced to a smaller size.

Similarly, you need to determine if your potential customers can buy something more current and less expensive from your competitors. If so, mail-order campaigns are probably not for you. This is because people may look at what you are offering through your direct-mail piece, and then go online to find the same—or more current—information at a lower price. Your message must communicate unique value to get the recipient to buy *your* book, *now*.

You should also estimate shipping costs before you decide to implement a mail-order campaign. Will the total package's cost structure support the discount you intend to offer? Or, will the discount you offer eliminate any profit you might make? You do not always have to offer a discount. But since you are not there to personally describe all reasons why the recipient should buy your book and there is limited space on mailings, a discount may serve as the impetus to overcome people's inertia.

Mail-order marketing can sell products, including books, if it is done correctly and professionally. A high response rate for direct-mail campaigns may be only 2 to 3 percent of all recipients, but depending on the size of your mailing list, that can still be a significant number of people—not to mention the word-of-mouth advertising and buzz your mailing will generate, even among the recipients who do not respond.

CREATE A MAIL-ORDER CAMPAIGN PLAN

Direct marketing is too often implemented by simply purchasing a mailing list and sending a pre-existing brochure to the people on it. This is not the best way to go about conducting a mail order campaign, though. Instead, it is important to make sure the sales-promotional literature you send out is tailored to describe the specific benefits of your book for each particular market niche. For information on how to do this, see *31. Match Benefits to Buyers* (page 228). Do not settle for one, generic mail piece, or you will almost certainly be disappointed with the results.

Additionally, unless you first prepare a tactical plan, including a way to evaluate your relative success, you will probably end up wasting money and becoming disillusioned about the potential effectiveness of a strategic mail-order campaign. Your plan should lay out your thoughts and ideas in four key areas: the offer you are making, the format of your mail piece, the ways in which you will test your plan, and how you will evaluate your implementation.

The Offer

Every direct-mail piece should have a reason for its existence. It must give recipients some motive to spend their time perusing it. The most important part of your direct mailing is persuasively conveying your book's value. People want to get some benefit in return for their money, so you have to state those benefits clearly and persuasively. In other words, the offer made in your mail piece must answer the question they are all thinking: "What's in it for me?"

There are several basic offers you can use by themselves or in various combinations, depending on your objective. Your objective may be to pre-sell books, reduce inventory, tie-in with a national theme, invite people to visit your exhibit at BEA, or any number of others. Whatever your objective is, though, the offer should support it. The following list contains several offers from which you can choose. You can use them individually, or concurrently—the choice is up to you.

■ *Bounce-backs.* This offer succeeds on the premise that the best time to sell to people is right after you have sold to them. Consider including forms offering more of the same title, related books, or items totally different from that originally purchased with your shipments or invoices.

■ *Deluxe alternatives.* Give the customer a choice between a perfect-bound book and a more expensive, deluxe alternative, such as a leather-bound edition or an autographed copy.

■ *Discounts.* A discount is a popular lure and is particularly effective where the value of your book is well established. Three types of discounts are typically offered: Discounts for cash, for introductory orders, or for volume purchases. A cash discount might involve offering a percent off the list price, an introductory order discount might involve offering a percentage off the price of pre-publication copy orders, and a volume discount might involve a steadily increasing discount based on the number of books purchased. Providing free shipping could also be considered a discount if the customer is used to paying for freight.

■ *Free gift.* People like receiving things for free, and are more willing to accept offers if they include additional items at no extra charge. Therefore, you could give away a t-shirt, coffee mug, pencil, or key chain—all with your book's title prominently displayed—with every purchase to entice people to buy. However, even free gifts must have value to the recipients in order to be effective, so be conscientious of your selection. The most important criteria for gift selection are appropriateness, effect on repeat business, and net profit including the cost of the gift.

■ *Free information.* This is often the most effective offer, particularly when your objective is to generate leads for future business. Tell people that when they order a copy of your book, they will also receive a special report that you have written, or some other free, useful information on your topic. You can also direct people to your website for a free download of information that complements or adds to your book. For example, if your book describes how to get on television and radio shows, you might offer a free list of top television or radio shows for buying your book and visiting your website.

■ *Guarantees.* The words "satisfaction guaranteed" are at the heart of all mail-order selling. This is because people feel more confident buying an unknown product if they have some assurance that they can get their money back if they are dissatisfied with it. Sometimes a guarantee is only for exchanging one product for another of equal or lesser value. If you include a buy-back option, though, it becomes even more effective. A buy-back option tells people they can get their money back with no strings attached.

■ *Load-up.* This is a favorite of publishers of continuity series. With it, you offer a set of twelve books, for example, with one to be released each month. After the customers have received and paid for the first three books, you invite them to receive the remaining nine all in one shipment, with the understanding that payments may continue to be made monthly. This benefits buyers because they immediately get all the books they ordered, but can still pay on extended terms. And it also benefits you, because people are less likely to back out of the deal once they have the complete set in hand—invariably resulting in more sales.

■ *Optional terms.* The objective of this offer is to give the buyer the option of choosing terms at varying rates—the bigger the purchase, the better the bargain.

■ *Samples.* If you are selling booklets or other low-cost items, a sample will show people the level of information and quality they may expect when purchasing from you. Perhaps making an excerpt available on your website will accomplish the same result for your books. Only send full samples to buyers who have a need to buy your product in bulk. Otherwise, after they receive the sample they will have no need to make a purchase.

■ *Time limit.* Setting a time limit for ordering on a given offer forces action, either positive or negative. Usually, it is more effective to name a specific date rather than a time period, so recipients do not have to make any calculations. Allow enough time for deliberation, but not so much as to cause apathy.

When people are not familiar with the publisher, author, or title of a book, they may not purchase it without an added incentive to do so. Furthermore, even if the recipients know you, they may not be motivated to take immediate action. But if you offer them some incentive to act—and to act now—you will increase your chances of reaching the objective you set for a particular mail-order campaign.

The Format

The standard format for direct mail is a three-piece package consisting of a cover letter describing the offer, a brochure detailing your book, and a reply mechanism, such as a business reply card or self-addressed, stamped envelope. However, you can create many variations of this traditional package depending on your unique needs and circumstances.

Additionally, it is a good idea to include a teaser on the envelopes to get the recipients to open them. The exact copy will depend on your content and offer, but some examples include "Free Offer Inside," or "Do you want to lose ten pounds by summer?" While this can be an effective strategy, be careful not to demean your offer with unnecessary text or clip art that could distort the impression you want to make. When in doubt, remember the "KISS Principle"—Keep It Straightforward and Simple. In short, make your cover letter informative and persuasive, your flyer attractive and descriptive, your reply mechanism complete and easy to use, and your envelope enticing to open.

The Test

Before you embark on a large, nationwide mailing, test the salability of your book, the mailing list you will use, the offer you will make, and the different formats you might use on a smaller scale. Also test the timing of your mailing, as well as alternative geographic areas. Invariably, you will learn ways to fine-tune your strategy and more accurately forecast the results you can expect on the larger mailing.

In addition to conducting a small-scale test before launching a major mail-order campaign, you should also decide if this marketing tactic will be profitable for you. Typically, mail-order campaigns for low-priced titles are less likely to be profitable than those for bundled titles or more expensive books. Do not send out a large mailing where you need a high response rate to break even. If you do, the chances are high that you will lose money on it.

○ You can purchase a wizard to automatically calculate the break-even point for your direct-mail campaigns at www.bookmarketingworks.com/shopcart/default.asp?catid=4

The Evaluation

After the campaign, analyze your profitability. Be sure to allow adequate time for responses before doing so, which is typically a few months. Did you reach or exceed a 1 to 2 percent response rate—the average proven by the Direct Marketing Association? Did you exceed your break-even point? Calculate your gross margin per book sold so you can quantify your profits.

○ You can purchase a wizard to automatically calculate your gross margin per book sold at www.bookmarketingworks.com/shopcart/default.asp?catid=4

Mail-order campaigns are a marketing tool. Like any tool, they must be used properly by competent professionals in order to achieve their intended purpose. If you simply write a letter and send it to a list of prospective buyers, the likelihood of you making any money is almost non-existent. But if you get the right list, create a provocative offer, prepare a professional package, and send it at the right time, the chances of you reaching your objective are tremendously improved.

40. SELL BOOKS THROUGH SPEAKING ENGAGEMENTS

If you are a proficient public speaker, you may find success selling your books at list price prior to, or following scheduled presentations. This is called back-of-the-room selling, and it has the potential to be very profitable. Speaking engagements are typically held in auditoriums, but they can take place anywhere there is an audience. They include speaking at bookstores, libraries, or specialty shops, lecturing at colleges, universities, and high schools, conducting professional seminars, being part of a convention's programming, and other similar events.

SELLING AT YOUR PRESENTATIONS

Selling books through speaking engagements can be very lucrative, because at these engagements you have an attentive audience that is eager to learn about one or more topics in your book. You will have the most success if you incorporate your book into your presentation, alluding to topics it covers and telling audience members they should purchase it to learn more information.

There are a few different ways books are sold through speaking engagements, and they depend on the preference of the sponsoring company or organization. Some places have a preexisting relationship with an outside company—typically a bookstore—that will buy a certain number of copies of the speaker's book before the presentation, and sell them for him or her before, during, and after it. Other companies and organizations will buy and sell the books themselves. And sometimes, everything is left up to the speaker. When you call to set up and arrange the details of an engagement, be sure you ask the event planner what his or her company's preference is.

If the venue that is hosting your speaking engagement utilizes the services of an outside company to purchase and sell books, or does so itself, you should try to get the event organizer to buy your books in advance. This way, you can avoid a middleman's discount and sell on a non-returnable basis at list price. Persuade him or her to buy enough books for everybody in the audience, perhaps by offering to let the company record and redistribute your presentation—with certain limitations—without paying you a royalty. You might even encourage these advance purchases by incorporating the cost of the books in your speaking fee. There is no such thing as a typical speaking fee. Meeting managers are used to negotiating with speakers to get the best deal. Thus, it is important to be flexible and creative in your pricing structure, so you end up with a good deal, as well.

On the other hand, the company for which you are speaking may require that you handle everything, as previously mentioned. If it is left up to you, at the end of the lecture announce that your book is being sold at the back of the room, and that you are available for signatures. If possible, do not do the sales work yourself. Get someone—a friend, family member, or business partner—to collect money and distribute books for you. That way, you can focus on working the crowd while you sign.

Regardless of who is in charge of selling your books, though, always have them available for sale at the site of your presentation. The least effective way to sell your books is to make arrangements with a local, off-site bookstore and direct people there following your presentation. People will not want to make an extra trip somewhere, and will lose their desire to purchase your book days after your presentation.

T
I
P

Do not be so obsessed with trying to sell your books that you lose sight of the other benefits of speaking; not the least of which is greater name recognition, leading to increased future sales and speaking opportunities.

HOW TO GET SPEAKING ENGAGEMENTS

There are a couple different ways to arrange speaking engagements. You can hire a publicist or a speakers' bureau, or you can do it yourself. But because speakers' bureaus are not likely to take you on if you are not well-known in your field, it is a good idea to learn how to do it yourself regardless. Dick Bruso is the past president of the Colorado Chapter of the National Speakers Association. He suggests a two-step system to help you get speaking engagements. The first step is to determine what you want to say and to whom you want to say it, and the second step is to use your network to find speaking outlets.

Determine What You Want to Say and to Whom You Want to Say It

Begin by determining what the topic of your presentation will be, so you will be well prepared to make a good pitch. If possible, try to pull several different topics from your book on which you could lecture. Then, depending on your audience, you can customize your presentation pitch to the needs of each company or organization you contact.

To illustrate this process, let us use Phil Glosserman and Larry Pinci's book, *Sell the Feeling*. It describes a six-step system for getting people to do business with you. To set up speaking engagements through which to sell their book, Phil and Larry could approach many different industries, such as insurance, real estate, and pharmaceuticals. To get the best results, they would need to tailor their proposal to each. Thus, they would want to be sure to use proper industry terminology, as well as prove that their book addresses the peculiarities of each audience.

Taking this idea one step further, even within individual industries there are various organizations with unique needs. So, your presentation pitch should cater to those, as well. For example, within the real estate industry there are real estate brokers looking to educate their sales people, and there are also large companies trying to lure in more brokers. Associations represent another subdivision of the real-estate industry. Phil and Larry might contact realty associations, architectural associations, mortgage associations, home inspectors associations, and home builders associations. As you can see, their message would have to be customized further for each of these audiences. The key is to think about what each audience will want to hear. The more closely related to a company or organization's needs your presentation pitch is, the more likely they will be to ask you to speak.

Use Your Network

After you have determined which of your presentation topics matches each audience, you need to find related companies and organizations that will hire you. You can reach more meeting planners in a shorter period of time if you have a network of people talking about your speaking prowess. Ask people you know and respect to refer you to people in their networks who hire speakers. For more information about networking, see *28. Find Potential Buyers* (page 222). Similarly, if you have already conducted a speaking engagement, go to your previous and existing clients for endorsements and ask them to spread the word, too. For more information about obtaining endorsements, see *37. Get Endorsements* (page 267).

There is a wide assortment of speakers' bureaus, as well. Some are based on topic, such as the Aviation Speakers Bureau, which promotes aviation related personalities. Others are based on audience level, like the Executive Speakers Bureau, which provides professional motivational, inspirational, and leadership speakers. And still others cater to very specific audiences or nationalities, like the Hospice, Palliative, and Home Care Speakers Bureau, and the Latino Speakers Bureau. Finally, there are even speakers' bureaus that focus on unique presentation types, such as the Humorous Speakers Bureau, which represents humorists and clean comedians for corporate events, meetings, and banquets.

- Aviation Speakers Bureau: www.aviationspeakers.com
- Executive Speakers Bureau: www.executivespeakers.com
- Hospice, Palliative, and Home Care Speakers Bureau: www.nhphc.org
- Latino Speakers Bureau: www.latinospeakers.com
- Humorous Speakers Bureau: www.humorbureau.com

If you are good enough, you can get taken on by a speaker's bureau, which will then book speaking engagements on your behalf. Speakers' bureaus operate much like literary agencies in that they represent your capabilities to third parties. Both literary agents and speakers' bureaus work on a commission basis. And in both cases, they can more easily make money by representing people who have proven to be accomplished speakers with substantial followings. Research different bureaus' websites to see if you are qualified.

WHAT TO SEND

Contacting people—event planners and speakers' bureaus—about speaking engagements is different than contacting people about buying your book. Thus, you need to send them different information. When you contact people about setting up a speaking engagement, send them the following materials:

■ *Proof of your speaking ability.* This can be a video or DVD, but in either case, it should be a ten to twelve minute portrayal of your ability to speak before an audience. You will probably need a three-camera shoot in order to capture the reactions of people in the audience. Showing audience response will prove that you can communicate with well with them.

■ *A one-page tip sheet.* This sheet should contain all the pertinent information, including your biography, most-popular speaking topics, references, endorsements, contact information, website, and the top three things for which you are "known."

■ *A copy of your book.* Upon seeing your book, the meeting planner will be able to get a good sense of the quality-level of your content and professionalism. A poorly produced book says that your presentation will be poor, as well, and vice versa.

■ *Business cards.* Prepare a professional business card. It may have your photo or a photo of your book's cover on it. Regardless, a four-color business card proves that you are serious about your speaking career and about selling books. Send event planners at least two cards—one to keep, and the other(s) to pass on to additional planners who may also be interested in you.

Whether you are contacting speakers' bureaus or event planners, your submission materials should all be aimed at convincing them that you are a competent, salable candidate. Assure them that they can make money selling your services as a professional speaker.

WHAT TO DO IF YOU HATE PUBLIC SPEAKING

You can still make money from back-of-the-room sales even if you abhor public speaking by having professional speakers sell your book for you. Professional speakers earn their living making presentations to groups of people, but their speaking fees are only part of the income they receive from each engagement. The other part comes from selling their products before or after their presentations. Although many have their own books to sell, just as many do not. Contact speakers who are knowledgeable on your topic and see if they would be willing to sell your book for a percentage—usually somewhere around 40 percent—of the sale. You can locate speakers and their contact information through the National Speakers Association.

❍ National Speakers Association: www.nsaspeaker.org

There are also training operations that help people of all talent levels become better public speakers. One such company is Toastmasters International. It specializes in helping beginning speakers and has several chapters, so there is probably one near you. Toastmasters helps its members improve their presentation skills while fostering self-confidence and personal growth. On its website you can find quick answers to such questions as how to overcome fear, how to make business presentations, how to accept an award, and more.

❍ Toastmasters International: www.toastmasters.org

The National Speakers Association (NSA), on the other hand, is for more advanced speakers—those who make a business of speaking professionally. If you fall into this category, NSA offers an excellent forum to improve your skills, increase your speaking business, and network with other professional speakers. Check the NSA website for links to local chapters and attend a meeting to see if it is for you.

❍ National Speakers Association: www.nsaspeaker.org

Finally, Dale Carnegie also offers many courses, some of which are devoted to helping people become a better public speakers. For example, it has one- and two-day seminars on public speaking, making high-impact presentations, and improving communication skills. Go to its website to learn more about what is has to offer and figure out if that is what you need.

❍ Dale Carnegie: www.dalecarnegie.com

Whether you are an experienced public speaker or not, do not ignore the potential speaking engagements hold. They are a great way to promote and sell books, either through your own presentations, or by joining forces with a professional speaker. Your segmented, captive audience will be eager to listen to what you have to say, and hopefully, to make purchases.

41. CONDUCT AUTHOR EVENTS

Author events are promotional in nature, and their purpose is to generate positive publicity, which will hopefully lead to increased sales. You do not have to be an experienced media performer or professional speaker to host promotional events; nor do you have to limit yourself to simple signings. The trick is to be creative and cater to your book and your abilities.

There are a variety of different types of events that authors of all talent and experience levels can conduct, including demonstrations, workshops, readings, home parties, and many more. The idea is to create a personalized media event in which your book is the center of attention. Your main objective during the event should not be to take orders; rather, it should be to ignite positive publicity and advertising both for you and your book, and for the hosting venue.

CHOOSE THE RIGHT EVENT AND VENUE

It is important to select an event and venue that are conducive to your book, skill set, and available resources. Both demonstrations and workshops can be very effective. For example, if you have a cookbook or a guide to different cooking techniques, you might choose to go to a culinary shop and—either by demonstration or interactive class—cook a recipe or show off cooking techniques. Similarly, if you have a sewing book you could go to a craft shop and teach a lesson.

Another effective idea is to schedule a launch party, which formally introduces your book by virtue of an invitation-only party at an appropriate venue that will garner media attention. For example, if you have an artistic book, you could schedule and host a launch party at a well-known gallery and serve cocktails and appetizers.

If instead you would like to do something a little lower key, you could to do a reading at a hospital, elementary school, nursing home, or other appropriate venue. John Harnish, author of *Everything You Always Wanted to Know about Print-On-Demand Publishing but Did Not Know Who to Ask*, recounts an example of another author who did just that:

Jane M. Martin wrote *Breathe Better, Live in Wellness: Winning Your Battle over Shortness of Breath* to help improve the quality of life for people suffering with some form of chronic lung disease. Instead of doing a traditional reading at a bookstore, Jane, a certified Respiratory Therapist, conducted in-services for the patients and staff of the Martha Jefferson Wellness Center in Charlottesville, Virginia. It would have been physically challenging for some of the pulmonary patients to go into a bookstore, so Jane took her book directly to her target audiences at the patient-friendly wellness center.

Be creative in where and how you make your own presentations to get the audience involved in what you have to say. A creative event will be more memorable and perhaps stimulate word-of-mouth advertising for you. Additionally, always alert local media of your event, which will hopefully broaden its coverage and lead to more book sales.

If you prefer to stick to something more comfortable, like a traditional book signing, be sure to choose its location wisely. If you have a non-fiction niche book, holding a book signing at a related store can work out very well—often better than at a traditional bookstore. For example, Nick Russell, a self-published author, said, "I have self-published five books on RV travel, and have had good results with book signings at RV dealerships, RV supply stores, and RV campgrounds."

Similarly, Lynda S. Burch, the publisher of Guardian Angel Publishing, has her authors successfully conduct children's book signings in multiple venues including libraries, book fairs, state fairs, horse shows, 4H fairs, historical societies, violin stores, music stores, cruise ships, schools, teacher meetings, religious bookstores, Wal-Mart stores, and more. The lesson here is that for best results, you have to take your message to your audience—physically and figuratively. Conduct your events where your readers congregate and communicate your message in a memorable way. If you do that, more sales should occur.

SCHEDULING AND CONDUCTING EVENTS

After you have thought about possible events and venues, it is time to start scheduling them and making your availability known. The first step is to prepare literature about your presentation topic and format. See the inset on page 260 for tips on creating professional sales-promotional materials. Next, you should create a special page on your website announcing your availability. For more information about creating your own website, see *Use the Internet to Your Advantage* (page 297). You then need to set up events by calling potential host venues and working out all of the details with them directly. The information in the following list will help you confirm, prepare, and conduct your event after you get it scheduled:

■ *Confirm your visit.* Once you establish the date, time, and parameters for an event, send the venue a confirmation letter summarizing the agreement. Both parties should sign it and keep a copy for their records. The letter should summarize everything to which you have agreed, especially the amount and timing of payment (if any), as well as the date, time, and parameters of the event. If you agreed on payment of your expenses or any special audio/visual needs or seating arrangements, spell these out, too. This is not the time to bring up new specifics, but to make sure both parties know what to expect of each other. As necessary, get directions and a list of nearby hotels and restaurants.

■ *Generate additional publicity.* Ask the hosting venue to publicize the event with local stores and media outlets. Then, even if it does promote your event, do more yourself in order to get the maximum exposure from every event you conduct; do some research to find the contact information for local media outlets, libraries, bookstores, schools, and specialty shops, and send a letter to each that contains information about your visit and about how to order your book. Make these contacts as early as possible, because you may be able to get on a local radio or television station to advertise the event before it occurs, thus attracting even more attention and publicity.

■ *Prepare.* Tailor your event to match the audience and venue. For example, if you are doing a reading at an elementary school, you will need to find out the grade level of the class to determine how long to make your presentation, among other things. You might consider preparing a multimedia presentation to capture and hold the students' attention. If instead you are hosting a launch party, you will need to prepare invitations and perhaps call a caterer. Your preparation will depend on your event, but there will always be something that needs to be done.

■ *Make your book available.* Even though the main goal of author events is to generate publicity, you should always bring some copies of your book to try and sell. Also, bring a stack of sell sheets to give to people as they leave if they do not purchase your book. That way, they will have all of the information necessary to do so if they change their minds. It will also give them something to show their friends later, which may lead to even more sales for you. To see an example sell sheet for this book, turn to page 327.

■ *Follow up.* Send a thank-you note to everyone who helped plan and put on your event, as well as to all of the media outlets that attended. This simple gesture will leave the door open and allow you to conduct similar events that will garner just as much, or more exposure in the future.

As the saying goes, the devil is in the details. Conducting these events can be fun if all the specifics are considered and agreed upon by both parties in advance. You are responsible for making sure everything runs smoothly. In fact, you should assume the responsibility of overseeing all of the details, including publicizing the event, making sure your books arrived, and even ensuring that the room is the correct temperature. You do not want any surprises arising at the last minute, because that will reflect poorly on you.

BE CREATIVE

Have fun at these events. Keep a smile on your face. Be a little outlandish and the audience will respond positively, particularly if it is comprised of children. If you have fun, so will the people who come to see you. Do not conduct a simple, boring reading or you will lose your audience and likely, your sales.

Jehan Clements is a storyteller, musician, author, illustrator, and inventor. He does not simply read his two children's books, *Alfred the Ant* and *The Banana That Ate New York*, in schools, he performs them to groups of children everywhere. He dresses as Alfred and the infamous banana respectively, which brings his environmental stories to life. Jehan said, "While performing for the children, I demonstrate my invention to the teachers. It is my very own, do it yourself, 'storytelling flip-over picture book.'" Converting books into this format allows teachers to keep the illustrations in full view of the children while maintaining unobstructed access to the words. What you should take away from Jehan's example is to become your book. Be its characters, theme, or moral. Bring your event to life and not only will your audience will respond positively, you will have more fun.

> If you are a little squeamish about performing in front of a crowd, enlist members of the audience to do it in your place. For example, you could have volunteer audience members act out a scene from your book instead of doing something yourself.
>
> **T I P**

Kamilla Reid, author of *The Questory of Root Karbunkulus: Item One: Mist*, provides another example, and proves how creative an author can be. While watching an episode of CBS's *Amazing Race*, Reid formulated the idea of having children race in a hunt for magical items. She had a group of children at her event create their own race to find the hidden items mentioned in her book. Of course, when the parents saw the kids enjoying themselves so much, they had to buy the book. Additionally, dressed in costume, she performs dramatic readings from her text, complete with sets and special effects.

While dressing up and performing may prove effective for fiction, it does not translate as well into non-fiction. So what can you do? Be creative. For example, if your book is about safety, bring an off-duty policeman or fireman to your event. If you are speaking to a business audience, use creative audio/visual tools. One author wrote a book about golf and tried to break a Guiness World Record by stacking golf balls one on top of the other to draw a crowd. The bottom line is this—do not be just like everyone else. You have to stand out from the crowd to make your message heard and your books sold.

This may all seem like too much to do, but know that you do not have to go to these extremes. To be successful, you simply need to think of something that will entertain your audience beyond a simple reading. Think about the times you anticipated attending an event and it turned out to be boring. Did you purchase the product if it was available? Probably not. But if the event became an interactive, enjoyable, or even educational surprise, you most likely had a good time, purchased the product, and left with a fond memory of the evening. As you prove yourself to be an entertaining speaker, your reputation will expand and you should get more speaking events, which will in turn lead to more sales.

42. ATTEND TRADE SHOWS

A trade show is an event where specialized sellers display their products to a group of corresponding buyers over a period of several days. Hundreds, sometimes even thousands of people in that particular industry including the media, potential customers, suppliers, distributors, and more congregate at these expositions looking for new products, information, contacts, and ideas. There are numerous different types of trade show all across the country. There are large, national shows, and also smaller, niche shows. Thus, no matter what your book's subject is and what your available resources are, there are trade shows for you.

Exhibiting at trade shows can be expensive; however, you do not have to display at a show in order for it to be productive. If possible, it actually makes more sense to first walk the show floor to see if that venue could be a productive exhibiting opportunity for you the following year. If it is not possible to walk the floor first, go to the show's website to learn more about it before committing to exhibit. Find out if it attracts the right audience for your product line, how many people typically attend, what it costs to exhibit, where the show is, and whether it will be adequately promoted among your potential buyers. Essentially, you need to figure out if exhibiting at the show will be cost effective for you.

FINDING TRADE SHOWS TO ATTEND

Depending on the books you are selling and your target markets, there are many available trade shows from which to choose. The most well-known and high-profile trade show in the book publishing industry is the annual BookExpo America (BEA). It is the largest of all the book-related exhibitions in the United States. At BEA you can find major suppliers to help you produce, distribute, and promote your content. It is also an excellent networking event that allows you to make contacts in many different market segments.

❍ BEA: www.bookexpoamerica.com

On the other hand, you might want to exhibit at a show with a more specific audience, such as the Natural Products Expo West, the Gourmet Housewares Show, or a Wine Expo. Niche shows are excellent sources of leads, information, and possibly sales in a more targeted arena. The smaller, local and regional shows usually cost less than national shows, but the number of exhibitors is also smaller, since the cost is based on the number of people attending.

○ Natural Products Expo West: www.expowest.com

○ Gourmet Housewares Show: www.thegourmetshow.com

○ Wine Expos: www.wine-expos.com

For a more complete list of trade shows, visit your local library and look for *Trade Shows Worldwide* published by Gale Publications. It is a directory of trade shows that provides information about most of the major shows including their costs, dates, and locations. The following websites will also provide you with more comprehensive lists of various tradeshows:

○ www.bookcentralstation.com

○ www.biztradeshows.com/trade-shows-by-industry.html

○ www.greatrep.com/trade_shows.asp

PLANNING FOR A SHOW

Inexperienced exhibitors often believe it is necessary to sell enough books at each show to cover their costs of attending. However, although sales are important, you will rarely sell enough books at a show to defray all of your expenses. Receiving orders should not be your sole criterion for success, because trade shows' true benefits do not accrue until after the show is over. Your main objectives for attending any book-industry exposition should include initiating contacts and performing other activities that will give you the best long-term return on your investment. These activities include performing market research, discovering new ideas and trends for future titles, continuing your education, networking, socializing, stimulating publicity, creating national or international distribution, and uncovering opportunities for non-trade sales or foreign rights.

A lot of work goes into preparing for trade shows. After you have created a list of the shows you would like to attend, you need to prepare a budget to figure out if you have the financial resources to do so, choose your exhibit space, construct your display, and devise a theme in order to get the most out of your trade show experience. Finally, before the show, promote the fact that you will be exhibiting so more people will stop by your display.

Prepare A Budget

While exhibit space is a large part of a trade show's total cost, it is not the only expenditure to consider. You also need to take into consideration transportation and living expenses, as well as the cost of your display, sales-promotional literature, and shipping. Calculate a budget to determine the cost of each show. Figure 6.1 is an example of the expenses you are likely to incur at a major trade show, such as BookExpo America. After you have determined a budget for all of the shows you are interested in, look at your overall budget to see how many shows you can actually attend.

○ For a spreadsheet that will help you calculate your break-even point for any trade show, go to www.bookmarketingworks.com/shopcart/default.asp? catid=4

Figure 6.1. Example Trade Show Expenses

Exhibit Space (Main Floor)	$3,650 (10' x 10')
Carpeting	$ 100
2 chairs, waste baskets	$ 60
8' Table	$ 110
Display	$ 500+
Hotel, meals	$ 250 per person, per day (more in major cities)
Round-trip transportation	Varies
Car Rental/Parking	$ 75+ per day
Electricity	$ 100
Booth cleaning	$ 65
Shipping to/from the show	Depends on the type of exhibit
Giveaways	$ 150+
Literature	$ 250+
Promotion and publicity	$ 500+

The total cost of trade shows can sometimes seem overwhelming, but there are a few ways to cut back. For example, you could reduce the cost of exhibit space by sharing a booth with a non-competing company. Go to the show website and check the exhibitors list to see what companies have a large space. Then contact the exhibit or marketing managers at those companies and ask if you can sublet from them. Or, you could purchase discounted exhibit space from groups to which you belong, such as IBPA or your distribution partner. Also remember that you can still get a lot out of trade shows even if you do not exhibit at all.

Additionally, there are ways to conserve out-of-pocket expenses. Use frequent-flyer coupons for airfare, or contact the sponsoring association to see if it is offering any special rates on airfare, car rentals, or lodging. Stay with friends or relatives if you have that option, or book a room with a kitchen so you can prepare your own meals. The most important thing is to prepare an accurate budget, and before you commit to anything, make sure your estimated benefits will outweigh the costs.

COMPARING THE RELATIVE BENEFITS OF TRADE SHOWS

Compare the relative benefit of exhibiting at different shows using cost per thousand, also known as cost per mille (CPM), as your metric. CPM is the amount of money you spend per thousand hits (exposures to target buyers). For example, assume you want to reach buyers of children's books. You might consider two exhibiting options—BEA and the Bologna Children's Book Fair in Italy. On average, exhibit space at BEA costs $4,500 and there are 50,000 attendees, making the CPM $90. The Bologna Children's Book Fair, on the other hand, costs about the same as BEA but only about 5,000 people attend, making the CPM $900. Thus, at first glance, BEA looks like the better option.

However, look at it a little more closely. At BEA, only about 1,000 of the attendees are actually buyers of children's books, because the show has such a broad appeal. Therefore, your CPM is in fact $4,500. But at Bologna, the world's leading children's publishing event, all 5,000 attendees are potential buyers. So its $900 CPM—about one-fifth of BEA's—seems much more reasonable. Comparing marketing opportunities this way helps you maximize your budget dollars and optimize your opportunities.

○ Bologna Children's Book Fair: www.bolognachildrensbookfair.com

Choose Your Exhibit Space

Immediately after you decide to attend a trade show, contact the sponsoring company and request an exhibitor's kit. In many cases, this information will be on the show's website, downloadable as a PDF file. Exhibitor's kits have all the information you need regarding the specifics of the show, including its floor layout, prices, and available services.

Decide upon the location of your booth space on the show floor as early as possible. Generally, you will be asked for a first, second, and third choice for your preferred location. Most in-line spaces provide ten feet of aisle access and are usually eight or ten feet deep. There are also corner, island, and peninsula locations available for those with larger budgets. If possible, choose a space that is visible from a high-traffic zone such as an entrance, restaurant, or autographing area. Some shows, like BEA, cluster exhibitors by topic. This makes it easier for attendees to find the suppliers important to them. It also benefits exhibitors because it increases the odds that potential buyers of their products will find them.

Construct Your Display

Once you know your exhibit location and its dimensions, you can begin to figure out what you want to do for your physical display. You have several options from which to choose: you can build your own, buy a used one, or rent a portable exhibit. Building a custom display is usually the most expensive choice, because you have to pay for its design and construction. You also have to consider the need for shipping containers for the display and transportation costs. But in the end, you will have a custom exhibit, portraying your image and books strategically, which can generate increased sales in the long run. For a glimpse at all the design options from which you could choose for an exhibit, look at the design calculator at World Exhibit Brokers.

○ World Exhibit Brokers: www.webisales.com

> **T**
> **I**
> **P**
> You can occasionally find free, used displays on the World Exhibit Brokers website, too. These are available through companies that want to avoid accumulating storage fees, and to dispose of old displays in an environmentally friendly way.

You may instead choose to purchase a used display. This is a good option if you want to make a solid appearance, but do not have the budget to design and create something new. You can buy used displays through places such as Exhibitor Trader and Impact Marketing Displays.

○ Exhibitor Trader: www.exhibittrader.com

○ Impact Marketing Displays: www.used-trade-show-booths.com

Finally, there are also panel, pop-up, and tabletop exhibits you can purchase, either new or used. They come in tight packages, are generally lightweight, and may be checked as luggage on your flight or shipped in advance to your hotel. While these are less expensive to buy and ship, they do not project a "big-company" image. However, they may be just what you are looking for. Consider your budget, then choose the option that is best for you.

Devise A Theme

Attracting the attention of potential customers as they wander past your exhibit is a key to trade show success. To do that, devise a theme for your booth that is consistent with your line of books and your company image. Your theme should convey what your company, products, and services are all about. Everything you do, say, wear, and offer should support your theme, so people passing by are not confused about what you are selling.

The purpose of your themed exhibit is to make passers-by who are not necessarily looking for what you are promoting and selling stop and ask questions. It should have one focal point—one element that will attract attention. This could be your most recent release, your historical bestseller, or your most well-known author. Use both graphics and copy to encourage eye movement to your books. Your display should be distinctive, creative, and attention-getting. It should also project a first-class image and be appropriate, tasteful, clean, inviting, neat, and attractive. Photographs, signs, and other elements used in the display should be professionally prepared, because hand-printed banners or homemade posters pinned against a backdrop will make you look like an amateur.

Finally, you might also consider planning demonstrations or events that will make people stop and look. Magicians and celebrities—or celebrity impersonators—usually attract attention. Other possibilities include holding a raffle or conducting a game that awards prizes on the basis of participation. Sound and motion are typically good at stimulating awareness, as well. However be sure to check the show rules before you decide on anything, because sometimes shows place restrictions on height, noise, or distance from the aisle.

Conduct Pre-Show Promotion

Serious trade-show attendees plan their tours of the exhibit floor well in advance of arriving there. They want to know which exhibits are "must sees," and which have no bearing on their needs. Conducting pre-show publicity will help attract those who are interested in what you have to offer.

Put your booth number on all of your communications such as your literature, email signature, direct mail letters, and on your website, so people know where to find you. Additionally, prepare literature specifically for each group of attendees explaining why it is in their best interest to seek you out. You can usually purchase a list of people who have registered to attend from the show management. It is not necessary to print as many brochures as there are attendees, because in all likelihood, less than 10 percent of the attendees will visit your exhibit and most of them will not want to carry excess literature with them. Be sure to collect names and addresses so you can follow up after the show.

You will also want to prepare multiple copies of a media kit to leave in the trade show's media room. Most shows have a room devoted to helping the press find information about exhibitors, their products, and special offers. These rooms also serve as a meeting place. See *36. Raise Awareness through Niche Media* (page 267) for more information about what to include in a media kit. Finally, maximize your investments in out-of-town shows, and try to schedule local in-store events, make appointments with prospective customers and distributors, and arrange appearances and interviews with local media.

Trade show exhibiting is a strategic and potentially profitable marketing tool. You can meet many prospective buyers, network with industry colleagues, and shmooze with your customers. Receive all these benefits by planning in advance to succeed. Within your budget, promote your appearance at the event as much as possible, and you will have the most success.

DURING A SHOW

There are several rules to abide by during trade shows. Your success is only partially dependent on what you do before the show. If you do not conduct yourself professionally during the event, all your pre-show work will be for naught.

What to Bring

Set up your exhibit area as you would a small office. Bring tape, a stapler, additional pens, and paper clips. Have a good supply of literature on hand, as well as business cards. Keep a pad of paper handy to record what you promise people you will do. It is not necessary to bring a large supply of books, just a few to display. This is because people will not want to carry them around or transport them back to their offices. If they want a copy, they will most likely ask you to send them a sample after the show. Also, make sure you bring a camera to get pictures of your crowded booth and shots of you with celebrities. Finally, keep plenty of water on hand, and do not forget breath mints.

Staff Your Booth With Knowledgeable People

If your pre-show promotion was successful and your exhibit is well-designed and professional, you should draw between 1 and 10 percent of the trade show's attendees to your booth—a general figure used by most experienced trade-show managers. These visitors expect to speak with knowledgeable salespeople when they stop at your display. The quickest way to turn them away is to make them feel unwelcome.

Therefore, you need to staff your booth with knowledgeable people who know about all of your titles, as well as their authors, prices, and discounts. It is also a good idea to have them memorize a thirty-second, descriptive sound bite for each title, so they will be prepared for questions. Additionally, make sure everyone working your booth asks visitors for their business cards. It is helpful to jot a few notes on the back of each card regarding the nature of the conversation, so your memory will be jogged when you later follow up with that person.

You should try to have at least two people working at your booth at all times. That way, each person will have time to rest, talk with multiple visitors, walk the show, network, and look for new ideas at different times throughout the day. Finally, attend and network at evening social events, but do not "party hearty." You want to be sure you show up alert and energetic each morning, always greeting people with a smile.

Be Professional and Engaging

If you are in your booth talking with fellow exhibitors or reading a novel to pass the time, passers-by may not stop for fear of disturbing you. Thus, you need to appear ready to talk with the show's attendees at all times. Do not smoke, sit down, work on your laptop, talk on the telephone, or read in your booth. Keep breath mints on hand and use them regularly, and also keep snacks, water, and fruit at your booth for refreshment for both you and those who stop to talk with you.

You do not want to appear overanxious, so do not stand like a vulture at the edge of your booth space saying, "How are you today?" to every person who walks by, because chances are those people have already heard that question multiple times. In fact, do not ask any questions that could be answered with a "yes" or "no." Questions that can be answered in that manner usually begin with verbs. For example, "Are you a buyer at a bookstore?" or "Do you sell job-search books in your store?" Those types of questions give people the option of answering in one word and then walking away.

Instead, ask open-ended questions beginning with who, what, where, when, why, or how to spark a discussion. For instance, you could say, "What type of books are you looking for?" You could also look at their badge to find out where they live and use that as a non-threatening conversation starter: "I see you are from Cincinnati. I used to live there. Is XYZ restaurant still open?"

Badges are also helpful for another reason. They are usually color coded, so you can tell if a person is an exhibitor, bookstore owner, press member, visitor, or author. However, judging the relative importance of a person in the context of your objectives by the color of his or her badge may be misleading, so be careful. Many people switch or borrow badges, and you may neglect a major sales opportunity by ignoring someone with a bogus visitor's badge. It is in your best interest to be professional and courteous to everyone.

Finally, if used properly, a giveaway item may help you get people to stop at your booth and talk with you. The item does not have to be big or elaborate; ad specialties such as key chains, pencils, or pads of paper with your company name or book title usually work well. Some companies choose to make water, coffee, or candy available for free, and that also gets people's attention.

Trade shows only give you a few days to talk with a large percentage of people in your target market. However, it would take you months and many dollars to accomplish the same feat otherwise. Make the most of your time at trade shows to reach your sales, exposure, networking, researching, and customer relations objectives. Do not give in to non-selling distractions and use all your time productively.

Walk the Floor

Take time to walk the trade show floor. Walking the floor will allow you to network, make new friends, and look for new trends and ideas. Study other exhibits that catch your eye to get ideas for your display the next year, and also to see what sales-promotional items are well received by attendees. Listen to others' presentations for ideas you can incorporate into your own, and collect their literature and samples to review later.

Nanette Miner, president of BVC Publishing, was exhibiting at a salon trade show in Orlando, Florida and traffic at her booth was slow. She said, "I got bored sitting behind my booth, so I took an armful of my booklets with me and started dropping them off at other vendors' booths. Within a week of returning to my office, the publisher of *Salon Strategies* newsletter—an exhibitor at the show—called me and asked if he could purchase 750 copies of my booklet to use as an incentive for subscriptions or renewals to the newsletter."

Take plenty of business cards with you when you walk around and give them out generously. You might even hand-write a quick note on them before handing them out, so people will later be reminded of your conversation. Finally, you might consider being creative with your apparel, so as to draw positive attention to yourself as you walk the floor. Do not be so creative that you get everyone laughing at you, though. People walk the show floor with a variety of costumes to attract attention, some more successfully than others. Tasteful options include dressing as a character in your novel, as a chef if you have a cookbook, or in a jogging suit if your book is about exercise. However, make sure what you are wearing will get people to think about the title of your book, not about your costume.

Begin the Follow-Up Process

The follow-up process starts before you get back home. Each night during the trade show, review your daily performance and plan how you can improve the next day. If you have time, begin writing your thank-you notes. This is a good idea for two reasons. First, the people you are writing to will be fresher in your mind, and second, you will save yourself time when you get home.

You should also do some preparation during the show for your follow-up after the show. You might consider taking pictures of people with you at your display, and then mailing them a copy later. You could also photograph your exhibit when it is teeming with visitors and send a copy to your local newspapers, potential customers, and distribution partners. Your local paper may publish it as news about its "home-town hero," giving you increased exposure and credibility. Your potential customers may be encouraged to buy your book once they see how popular it is, and your distribution partner will be happy to be kept in the loop about your promotional activities. Finally, keep a running list of everything you need to do upon your return home in order to fulfill all the commitments you made during the show.

AFTER A SHOW

Soon after the show is over, evaluate your experience while the information is still fresh in your mind. Should you exhibit again next year, and if so, what would you change? Which booth locations seemed to get the most traffic? Which displays seemed to attract the most people? Did you see a large number of people walking around with a giveaway item from one particular company? What was your cost-per-inquiry, and does that make the show worth it to you? On what new ideas or trends should you act? What new relationships did you make and what old friendships were rekindled? If you were seeking opportunities for entering new markets or selling foreign rights, were you successful?

Participate in every trade show with a strategic plan of action to get the most out of your investment. Plan your exhibit carefully and implement your plan professionally. The contacts you can make at these events can help you increase your business now, and in the long run. You will meet new potential customers, develop more business with existing customers, and find new ideas for reaching buyers in segments you might have otherwise overlooked. Finally, always evaluate the relative success of your actions. Decide what you can do to improve at the next show, and then begin the process all over again.

43. USE THE INTERNET TO YOUR ADVANTAGE

The Internet is a ubiquitous and strategic tool that should be a part of your book-marketing arsenal. Not only is it inexpensive, but it is relatively easy to use and it can be very effective. You can promote and sell your book online by blogging, networking, and creating a website—even if you feel you are an introvert. Additionally, you can use the Internet to find the names and contact information for potential buyers, research companies and industries, conduct test marketing, and promote through podcasts and email blasts. In short, the Internet allows you to create a virtual business without ever leaving home.

BENEFITS OF THE INTERNET

There are many benefits to online marketing. The following list contains a few of the major ones:

■ *Increases sales.* You can promote and sell books through third-party online bookstores, catalogs, and book clubs. You can also sell your book at list price on your own website; even if you offer a discount, it will still be more profitable than selling through a traditional bookstore.

■ *Boosts reach and frequency.* Given a limited budget, marketers always face the dilemma of whether to reach more people less frequently, or fewer people more frequently. When presented with this choice, it is better to reach fewer, targeted people more frequently. However, the Internet allows you to achieve a high level of both reach and frequency, so you do not have to choose between the two.

■ *Cost effective.* Browsing the Internet is free, as are most online communities. Additionally, once you have your website up and running, the only recurring charge to maintain it—assuming you learn how to update it yourself—is your annual hosting fee.

■ *Allows media outlets to find you.* Producers and reporters often search online for experts on a particular topic. If your website is constructed properly or if you have asserted yourself in a blog, you could come up in their search as the expert most worthy of a story in print or on the air.

■ *Suited to all personalities.* It does not matter if you are introverted or extroverted. Any personality type can use the Internet effectively.

■ *Eliminates the necessity for bookstore stocking.* You do not have to have large amounts of inventory on consignment on bookstore shelves. With the advent of digital printing, you can have a limited inventory and replenish it as necessary.

■ *Presents networking opportunities.* Online discussion groups, blogs, and more allow you to increase your exposure and meet new people who may lead you to future sales.

As you can see, the Internet provides numerous benefits. And it is perhaps the most cost-effective promoting you can do. When used as part of your overall marketing mix, it can have a significant impact on your sales.

CREATE YOUR OWN WEBSITE

Years ago, you were considered a pioneering entrepreneur if you had a website. Today, you are not taken seriously as a book provider without one. But just having a website is not enough. It has to be professional, easy to navigate, informative, and complete. It must have current and credible information. And most importantly, it must make it easy for people to buy your books, or at least learn enough about them to entice them to call you for more details. The following list includes several basic elements productive, professional, and profitable websites should have:

■ *A strategic domain name.* The Universal Resource Locator (URL) that you choose for your website address is very important. It should be memorable, easy to say on the air, and reflect the topic of your website. You could use your book's title, your name, your company's name, or even one of your character's names as the URL. Try to create one that is available with a ".com" suffix, rather than ".net," ".info," ".biz," or others that may be available, but less functional. Go to a website such as www.register.com or www.godaddy.com to immediately determine if your choice is available, and if it is, sign up quickly so someone else does not beat you to it.

■ *Functional and pleasant components.* Employ a professional designer to create your website. Give him or her specific instructions about the tone you want to project, the colors you prefer, and the functionality you want. Then, let your designer build the website. It should be simple in appearance and easy to navigate. You might use an audio or video clip to introduce you and your products or services. Or, you might make your book's cover immediately visible and give a brief summary with bullet points that list reasons why people should buy it.

Provide links to pages with your biography and perhaps a photo, and keep reader endorsements in plain sight.

■ *Current information.* Visitors to your website will not stay long if it appears outdated or too busy. For example, if your upcoming book signings are listed but the dates are months past, viewers will think the rest of the website is equally outdated and immediately look elsewhere. Thus, continuously update your upcoming events, contact information, endorsements, and other information as necessary.

■ *An easy ordering mechanism.* One of the most important aspects of your website is providing users with an easy way to order your books and products. You might consider setting up a merchant or PayPal account so buyers can easily use the payment method of their choice. Alternatively, you could have your purchasing process linked through a retail site such as Amazon.com. Regardless, make sure you abide by your state's sales-tax-collection laws.

Getting people to your website is only the first battle. Once they are there, you need to give them plenty of reasons to stay and look around at all you have to offer. Making sure everything is current, high-quality, and accessible are all great ways to do just that.

JOIN AND PARTICIPATE IN ONLINE COMMUNITIES

The Internet offers several online communities, including blogs, discussion groups, social networking websites, and webrings. These outlets bring together groups of like-minded people looking to explore the interests and activities of others. Online communities are regularly used by millions of people. They provide their members ways to communicate and share information through a variety of means, including searching directories or profiles, sending emails or instant messages, or posting notes. By joining and participating in online communities, you can find clusters of prospective buyers, as well as boost your image within a particular marketplace. The following lists include descriptions of each of the different types of online communities, as well as several resources to get you started:

■ *Blogs.* Blogs, short for weblogs, are online, frequent publications of personal thoughts and web links. Many blogs provide commentary or news on a particular subject, while others function as more personal online diaries. Some allow readers to submit their own replies to the blogger's posts, making them more interactive. Use the websites listed below and search the Internet for blogs written by industry experts that can give you insider information about book marketing. Also look for blogs related to your book's topic and work on building relationships with the bloggers in that niche. Your networking might just lead to sales. Finally, you might also consider starting your own blog as a way to create a buzz about you, your book's topic, and your book.

○ Book-marketing blog: www.blog.bookmarketing.com

○ Directory of blogs: www.blogtoplist.com

■ *Discussion groups.* Online discussion groups provide people with a shared interest a place to meet, get to know each other, and stay informed. Users post messages that appear in chronological or question-and-answer order, which can later be viewed by the general public. Instant messaging services and chat rooms provide discussion venues as well, but are typically used for real-time, private exchanges. Like blogs, discussion groups related to your book's topic are a great way to network and promote your book.

○ Find discussion groups at www.groups.yahoo.com

■ *Social networking websites.* Social networking websites allow users to become part of a virtual community. When people join, they create a custom profile that allows them to share their lives with others without having to develop their own websites. After creating a profile, users can communicate directly with each other by adding friends, sending messages to one another, and leaving comments directly on friends' profiles. These websites provide an opportunity to keep in touch with old friends, and to meet new people, as well. Use social networking websites to connect with people who are interested in the topic of your book.

○ www.facebook.com

○ www.linkedin.com

○ www.myspace.com

○ www.squidoo.com

○ www.twitter.com

○ www.youtube.com

■ *Webrings.* A webring is a collection of websites organized around a specific theme. Users can go to the webring's main page to find a list of its associated websites; thereby eliminating the need to conduct multiple searches to find the same information. Each member website has a common navigation bar containing links to the all the related websites. By clicking "next," you can toggle through all the connected websites until you eventually reach the one at which you began—thus, the term webring. Get involved in webrings associated with your content, and your website could soon see more traffic.

○ You can find a directory of webrings at http://dir.webring.com/rw

People like to buy from those with whom they are familiar. The more people know about you, the more likely they are to feel comfortable enough with you to purchase your book. Create and increase your exposure through blogs, discussion groups, social networking, and webrings, and you could see a real increase in your sales.

MAKE YOUR BOOK AVAILABLE AS AN EBOOK

An eBook, short for electronic book, is the digital media equivalent of a traditional printed book—sometimes referred to as a pBook. EBooks are typically downloaded to, and read on personal computers or eBook readers, such as Amazon's Kindle. Some mobile phones can also be used to read eBooks.

There is no standard for packaging and selling eBooks. One eBook format is Adobe's PDF format, while open-source programmers support others. Up to this point, eBooks have yet to achieve widespread distribution. However, this may change in the near future, because eBooks offer many benefits. Some of their advantages are included in the following list:

■ A single eBook reader containing the contents of hundreds of books is easier to carry than just a few printed books.

■ Size and font can be adjusted for those who need or prefer larger text.

■ Animated images and multimedia clips may be embedded.

■ Some eBooks offer full-color displays.

■ The backlights on the reading devices allow for reading in low light or even total darkness.

■ EBooks can be converted to audio books fairly easily with text-to-speech software.

■ EBooks are easier to self-publish and can be more profitable because of the lower production and distribution costs.

■ EBooks are environmentally conscious because their production does not consume trees and other resources that are used to produce printed books.

However, as with most things, there is another side to the story. EBooks also present disadvantages, some of which are included in the following list:

■ People must either purchase an eBook reader or additional software for computers in order to use them.

■ EBook readers are more susceptible to physical damage than printed books, and they can malfunction due to faults in hardware or software.

■ Many people simply prefer the touch and feel of a printed book.

Some publishers produce eBooks at the same time their books are published in printed format, so both are available simultaneously. Other publishers print books first, then later scan and convert them into electronic form. And in some cases, only the electronic version of a book is published. Regardless of when or how eBooks are created and released, offering your content in this format increases its value, function, and potential-buyer base. In other words, it gives you the opportunity to make more profit. There are numerous companies that perform print-to-electronic conversions of books. So, if this is something you are interested in, search the Internet to find one with which you would feel comfortable working.

SELL THROUGH EMAIL MARKETING

Email marketing can be an inexpensive way to reach a wide audience quickly. But with its many benefits come a few negative side effects. For example, if an email is deemed spam, it will automatically be blocked and will never reach its intended recipients' inboxes; thereby defeating its purpose and wasting your time. In order to make sure this does not happen to your emails, you can work with a company like Constant Contacts. This company sends out emails for people and ensures they do not show up as spam. It can also help you create email campaigns, build your list of contacts, track your emails, and more. And all of its services are reasonably priced.

○ Constant Contacts: www.constantcontacts.com

Similarly, if people are not expecting your email, they may immediately delete it even if it reaches their inboxes. Thus, whenever possible, use *opt-in* lists, which are comprised of people who have requested your materials or have given you their permission to send them emails. In contrast, an *opt-out* list is one in which people are included until they ask to be removed. If you are using this type of list and people unsubscribe, respect their wishes and do not send them anything else. Doing so could create unnecessary ill-will among that person's entire network. The bottom line is this: use common sense and *netiquette*—Internet etiquette— when deciding who to send information to, and email marketing can be a productive, effective, and efficient way to spread your message and generate sales.

When writing your emails, follow a formula that has been proven to work for advertising copywriters. Begin with something that grabs attention and stimulates interest. Next, describe reasons to buy, increasing the desire for your product. And finally, close with a call to action. In emails, the attention-grabbing needs to start with the subject line. The following list includes various ways to get readers to open and read your emails with positive expectations:

■ *Present your book as important news.* Feature your book as a noteworthy item of timely interest. Announce your book's publication date or its primary benefit in the style of a news headline. People are interested in announcements and emails with headline-written subject lines tend to have high readership. Use words and phrases such as "announcing," "introducing," "presenting," "just published," "at last," "new," and "now." Of course, do not use this technique in the subject line unless you really are "announcing" something.

■ *State your book's primary benefit.* This subject-line style is a simple statement of the most important benefit your book offers this particular group. One of the most important benefits of books in competitive segments across the board is good value, so you can always rely on that if necessary. Additionally, the words "free" and "discount" are always attention getters.

■ *Appeal to some emotion.* A common approach is that of capitalizing directly upon the emotions of the readers. For example, "New Help for People Who Lost Their Retirement Savings" gives hope to people who are struggling financially. Typically, emotional subject lines have no direct-selling value. They simply make an emotional appeal to get readers to open the email.

■ *Employ a gimmick.* It is not always necessary to take the sane, sound, common-sense approach to snagging attention. There are times when a gimmick—a light-hearted opening that has no apparent relationship to the title or content of the book—can be the best option. For example, if your book is about memory or a related topic, your subject line could challenge recipients: "Can You Pass This Memory Test?" Engaging recipients with something interactive may be just enough to get them to open the email.

■ *Arrouse curiosity.* Leaving something unanswered or unknown is a great way to allure people into opening emails. You can do this by asking a question in the subject line. For example: "What Ever Happened to Sex Education?" You can also do this by making a curious statement, like "Three Inches from Life."

■ *Be direct.* This technique is most useful when you wish to get immediate action from recipients. Directive headlines begin with phrases such as "Go Now!" or "Call Today!" and are best used when addressing your ultimate customers. However, they also tend to work well with radio producers who are looking for stories that will have an immediate reaction from their audiences, such as "You Can't Stop Drunk Drivers."

The Internet is a marketing tool, and like any tool it must be used as intended in order to be most effective. It has brought many unique benefits to marketing, not the least of which are lower information distribution costs and instant, global audiences. The interactive nature of Internet marketing, both in terms of providing vast amounts of information and eliciting responses, is a unique quality of the medium. Use it to interact and network with your target audience, build your reputation as the expert on your topic, make your products easy to purchase, and look for potential buyers in new market segments.

Use a combination of the promotional strategies discussed in this chapter for best results. Exercise trial and error to find the ones with which you are most comfortable and have the most success. And do not be afraid to try something a little outside your typical comfort zone. Growth comes from taking risks. If you put together a budget-friendly promotional mix using the information in this chapter and target it toward the right people, you should see an increase in your sales.

Chapter Seven

Putting It All Together

Congratulations. If you have made it this far you have taken a huge step forward in increasing your profit potential. You have armed yourself with information that can give you a tremendous advantage over your competition, and you should feel really good about that. Now, however, you need to sort through and organize that information so you can put it to use and make it work for you.

In this chapter, you will learn how to look at each of your target markets and find a compromise between its buyers' wants and needs and your own. You will also learn the importance of planning your actions before implementing them, and discover how to create a personalized business plan. Subsequently, you will be provided with an example publication timeline; it takes all of the information discussed throughout this book and separates it into timed phases, so you will get a good idea of when, and in what order you should perform different tasks. You will then learn how to prepare yourself mentally for the sometimes difficult and trying world of non-trade sales. Finally, the chapter culminates with three case studies, highlighting how other authors have used the same strategies described in this book to achieve success. These case studies will hopefully clear up any lingering questions, as well as motivate you to know that you, too, can succeed.

44. CREATE A COMPROMISE BETWEEN BUYERS' WANTS AND NEEDS AND YOUR OWN

There is a rift between publishers' and buyers' viewpoints. Publishers want to make a profitable sale, and buyers want to spend as little as possible. Therefore, it is important to come up with a plan that creates a mutually beneficial solution from these mutually exclusive points of view. You can make this happen by creating a matrix that lays out both your needs and buyers' needs, and then reconciling the differences in order to meet in the middle.

CONSTRUCT A MATRIX

Most independent publishers make marketing decisions to facilitate the sales process. They publish, distribute, price, and promote their books in order to make a profit. However, the book-buying public looks at the process differently. From their viewpoint, books are not *sold,* they are *bought,* and publishers should make them cheap and easy to purchase. Consumers are looking for helpful information that, from their perspectives, is easily accessible and priced properly.

Putting together a matrix will force you to plan how you will design and implement promotion and sales strategies that will address both your needs and the needs of buyers. It will require you to think not just about publishing a book, but also about how you can create a positive experience for everyone involved. Construct a matrix like the one shown in Figure 7.1 to stimulate strategy for reaching each of your target segments. Add as many columns across the top as target markets you have. Then for each one of them, list both your needs and the buyers' needs in each of the five categories along the side.

Figure 7.1.   Needs Matrix

	Needs	Market Segment A	Market Segment B	Market Segment C
Product Design	Yours			
	Buyers			
Distribution	Yours			
	Buyers			
Personal Selling	Yours			
	Buyers			
Pricing	Yours			
	Buyers			
Promotion	Yours			
	Buyers			

MEET IN THE MIDDLE

Each of the categories in the matrix may be manipulated in an unlimited number of combinations. For example, the product could take various forms, such as a book, a DVD, or a booklet, among many other manipulative variables. The product decisions are under your control, but they directly affect buyers' purchasing decisions. So, it is important to strongly consider their needs. Does your book look appealing? Is it easy to use for its intended purpose? Are its size, weight, and shape conducive to minimal delivery costs and handling aggravation?

Similarly, publishers think about distribution in terms of whether or not they should use a distribution partner or handle all of the selling responsibilities on their own, while consumers do not care. When they want to buy a book, they seek it according to habit. This may be from an online source, or it may be at their local supermarket. Find a way to take care of your distribution needs and meet your customers' demands simultaneously.

In many cases, publishers price their books as a function of their printing costs. However, readers do not care about your costs; they are interested in what the price is to them. The most important result of your pricing decision is the perceived value the readers get from your book. If they feel the information or entertainment it provides is worth the price, they will buy it. And if it lives up to their expectations, you will be rewarded with positive word-of-mouth advertising and additional purchases.

Finally, promotion strategy is dependent upon the buying process. Choose cost effective techniques that maximize the reach and frequency of your message, while at the same time, appeal to your potential buyers. Since each new combination yields different results under varying market conditions, there may be limitless variables with which you must contend. The goal is to meet your buyers somewhere in the middle and create a mutually beneficial solution.

45. WRITE A BUSINESS PLAN

Imagine you are a team coach who competes against one or more opponents in any given week. You have a basic game strategy based upon your existing players, but each week you create an additional game plan based upon their strengths and weaknesses in relation to the competition. You also make adjustments as the game goes on to adapt to changing circumstances. You do this because you know your chances of success are limited if you have only one strategy and apply it uniformly against each adversary.

This concept is analogous to selling books in non-trade markets. Your book has unique strengths and weaknesses. Its strength in one market—for example, a spiral-bound cookbook sold through a catalog—may actually be a weakness in others—like retail stores and libraries that prefer readable spines. Success in non-trade sales depends on strategic flexibility. You must be able to adapt to changing markets and conditions, and to do that, you need a plan.

THINK OF THE WORD "PLAN" AS A VERB, NOT A NOUN

Do not think of the word "plan" as a noun. Instead, think of it as a verb—a process defining the parameters for the ways in which you do business. Creating a fluid business plan will help you focus on the daily activities you need to accomplish, while still allowing you to remain flexible enough to recognize potentially profitable, unanticipated opportunities as they present themselves. Your business plan sets your overall purpose and direction, guides your thinking, describes your marketing strategies, and organizes your resources for maximum utilization. It is a controlling device and should be used daily to remind you of the actions you need to take in order to ensure the long-term stability of your business.

The act of non-trade planning is simply asking and answering questions that stimulate innovative ideas, and then writing those ideas down on paper. It is a creative process, and you build your plan as you go through it. Refer back to 6. *Ask the Right Questions* (page 29) to help get you started. In itself, your plan has no worth. The value resides in the insight you get from creating the strategies you will use, and the results that occur from doing everything you said you would.

As you make your business plan, take a critical look at your budget, products, markets, and competition. Using that information, create ways to improve your book's position in each of your target markets. Then, evaluate the pros and cons of each aspect of your plan, and come up with possible alternative actions, making sure to analyze how any changes will impact the bigger picture.

> **T**
> **I**
> **P**
> Non-trade planning is simply the process of thinking about what you will do before you do it. This process is as easy as PIE: *Planning, Implementing,* and *Evaluating.*

DO NOT MAKE EXCUSES

There are several excuses, but no real reasons for not planning your non-trade efforts. The following list includes three excuses publishers commonly make as to why they should not plan, followed by a discussion about why each cannot be justified:

■ *Planning takes too long. I would rather use that time marketing.* A proverb tells us that a journey of a thousand miles begins with one step. But what if that step is in the wrong direction? The traveler would waste unnecessary time, energy, and money going the wrong way. There is a difference between the words "action" and "accomplishment." You can be busy doing something without accomplishing anything. Planning actually *saves* time by directing your actions to accomplishing your objective.

■ *Why should I plan for the future when I can't predict everything that will happen?* Does the marketplace change? Of course it does. The only constant in today's publishing industry is that change is inevitable. But that does not render worthless the time you spend planning. Planning is not fortune telling. It is simply thinking about what might happen in the marketplace or among your competitors, and then deciding in advance what options could be available. Change is the nemesis of independent publishers who are not aware of—or do not acknowledge and adjust to—the constant, subtle ebb and flow of the market. Planning helps you prepare alternative courses of action that are most likely to succeed in various situations. It enables you to be in command of your actions and negates the need to act under pressure when the changing market situation warrants an immediate response.

■ *I already know what I will do, so why write it down?* This is like asking why you should consult a map, since you already know how to drive from coast to coast. But consulting a map makes you aware of detours or new routes that were not there the last time you made the trip, and it may reveal shortcuts or landmarks to help you evaluate your progress. Your business plan performs similar functions that facilitate your trip to non-trade success.

Planning is a process that helps you deal with changing circumstances you cannot control, such as a recession or competitive actions. It also helps you properly utilize the actions you can control, such as your book, budget, employees, and creativity, and allows you to respond to the evolving external environment. Your plan is not a static document; rather, it is a dynamic tool that guides your strategies and actions toward the attainment of your business goals in an environment that is not always favorable or predictable.

WRITE DOWN EVERYTHING

Have you ever thought of the world's best idea at 3:00 in the morning only to forget it by the time you woke up? Had you taken the time to write it down, you would have had an indelible record of your innovation. Similarly, unless you write a formal plan or a series of actions, your new ideas will quickly be burned out of your memory by the daily fires you face.

So, what is the best form for a written plan? Form follows function. The best form is one which works for you. Prepare your plan as a personal document that is not to be seen or judged by anyone else. Do not get so hung up on the way your plan looks that you forget what it is supposed to do. Concentrate on creating a tool that will guide, direct, and remind you of the actions you must take to achieve your goals.

Committing your ideas to paper creates a roadmap of what you should do next. When you find yourself with free time, you can easily consult your plan and perform an action that you might have otherwise forgotten. Additionally, writing down your initial ideas may stimulate new ones as you proceed. Moreover, you will ignite the enthusiasm that comes from experiencing positive, forward progress, and that enthusiasm will permeate into all the work you do.

WHAT TO INCLUDE

Business plans are typically divided into two sections. The first section sets direction. It states your mission and objectives, and describes the current market situation. The second section describes action and is both strategical and tactical. It states what you are going to do and how you are going to do it.

In the first section, describe the end results for which you will be working. First, create a mission statement. Your mission statement should be comprised of who you are, what you have to offer, your business philosophy, your self-concept, and your public image. Then, clearly and concisely state your objectives—personal, financial, marketing, and overall. They will help keep you focused and give you direction.Refer to your objectives and your mission statement often so you never lose sight of why you began non-trade selling in the first place.

The second section of your business plan is dynamic and, as previously mentioned, should be strategical and tactical. There may appear to be little difference between strategies and tactics, but each serves a dissimilar and necessary function. Strategies define the path you will take to get to your objectives, while tactics describe the steps you will take on the path. Divide this second section into four parts: product packaging, pricing, distribution, and promotion. Then, come up with strategies and tactics for each using the wealth of information you have accumulated in this book and throughout your previous experiences.

While this business plan outline has proven itself to work effectively, remember the most important thing is to put your ideas into a form that works for you. Do not dismiss planning by making excuses, write everything down, and coherently organize your thoughts into a personalized business plan. Then, refer to it regularly—every time you have a spare moment—so you avoid wasting any time and remain focused on the finish line.

46. SET UP A PUBLICATION TIMELINE

Have you ever watched experienced workers build a house? They create and consult their blueprints to direct the order and timing of events, beginning with the foundation upon which they erect the structure. If their actions are not performed in the proper sequence, the process could take longer than necessary, cost more than anticipated, and require duplication of effort to correct mistakes and oversights. The same is true for book publishing. Unless you perform certain actions at the right time and in the proper sequence, the publishing process could cost you time, money, and wasted effort.

This section contains an example of a book-production timeline you can draw from to successfully launch your own title. It lists the steps you will need to perform in their relative sequence. The steps have all been thoroughly discussed in the earlier chapters of this book. The difference here is that they are organized into seven phases, and you will learn at which times during the publication process they should be performed. Roughly following the timing and order of these phases will help you establish a foundation upon which you can methodically build momentum to release your title on time, on budget, and with "legs."

○ You can find an Excel spreadsheet that will automatically calculate and create a personalized publication timeline for you based on various publication dates at www.bookmarketingworks.com/shopcart/default.asp?catid=4

SIX TO TWELVE MONTHS BEFORE PUBLICATION

The first two phases of the publication process should be performed six to twelve months before the publication date. They are devoted to research and strategic planning.

1. Research Phase

A full year before your publication date, research your target audience, your target markets, and your competition. Few statements kill a book more quickly than when an author says, "My book is for everyone." Therefore, make sure you know exactly who your target audience is, including where they are located, what their buying habits are, and why they would be interested in your book. After you decide who is in your target audience, you need to learn more about the markets in which they can be found. Evaluate each market to make sure it is worth your time and resources. Is the industry in a growth phase? Does your book fill a market need? Finally, before you decide to release your book and market it to a particular market segment, you need to know what other titles are available to the buyers, as well as what they offer. Additionally, you need to be prepared to explain why yours is the best.

Doing adequate research will help you decide if your book should be released as planned, or if some modifications in content, positioning, or timing are necessary. It will also ensure you are completely knowledgeable about your book, your target audience, and your target markets so you do not ruin any first impressions. For much more detailed information about the work that goes into this research phase, refer back to *Chapter Four. Do Your Homework before You Start Selling* (page 197).

2. Strategy Phase

Six months before your publication date, define the strategies that will guide your production efforts, distribution channels, pricing policies, and promotional tools. During this phase, you are essentially creating your business plan (see page 307). Do not jump right into action or you will undoubtedly miss something or misuse valuable resources. Instead, think about the forms in which you could deliver your content, whether you will attempt to secure foreign rights, how you will promote your title, what methods of distribution you will employ, and more. The more you plan, the more prepared you will be to take action and complete the necessary tasks in the following phases. *Chapter Four. Do Your Homework before You Start Selling* (page 197), *Chapter Five. Start Selling* (page 233), and *Chapter Six. Promoting to Non-Trade Buyers* (page 259) all contain more detailed information about what goes into the strategy phase.

TWO TO SIX MONTHS BEFORE PUBLICATION

The next three phases involve producing, promoting, and distributing your book. This is when you begin putting your research and plans into action. As you will see, there are several events that need to be completed at various times during the two to six months before publication.

3. Production Phase

This phase is devoted to the production process. Finish all rewriting, editing, and indexing of your book. Complete the internal layout, as well as the front and back cover designs. Essentially, finish all the work surrounding your actual product, making sure to comply with all registration details including copyright, ISBN, and CIP data.

- Five Months before Publication:
  - Copyright your manuscript
  - Decide on the title
  - Ask a celebrity or expert to write the introduction

- Four Months before Publication:
  - Complete illustrations and photographs
  - Produce cover art for test marketing
  - Arrange for text layout
  - Send requests for price quotes to printers

- Three Months before Publication:
  - Obtain an ISBN
  - Complete the CIP data application
  - Decide the retail price
  - Write back cover copy
  - Complete bound galleys

4. Promotion Phase

This phase involves implementing the general promotion strategies you planned for during the strategy phase. *Chapter Six Promoting to Non-Trade Buyers* (page 259) will help you a great deal throughout this process.

■ Four Months before Publication

- Construct or update your website
- Contact relevant book clubs and catalogs
- Decide which trade shows you will attend

■ Three Months before Publication

- Develop a list of appropriate niche publications, reviewers, and media outlets
- Create your sales-promotional literature
- Send bound galleys to reviewers
- Prepare and place pre-publication announcement advertisements

■ Two Months before Publication

- Prepare and send direct mail packages
- Take media training courses
- Contact major television and radio shows and send your media kit to those that are interested
- Make follow-up phone calls or emails to media outlets
- Plan author events and personal presentations
- Create your personal sales kit
- Contact magazines about periodical rights for excerpts

5. Distribution Phase

During this phase, use your plan and establish distribution channels. Research and contact relevant wholesalers and distributors, knowing that separate channels may be required for sales to different marketplaces.

■ Two Months before Publication:

- Put together a submission package
- Contact and evaluate potential wholesalers and distributors

PUBLICATION

The publication of your book occurs in Phase Six, which encompasses the month leading up to your publication date and the publication itself. The release of your book is the culmination of all your efforts to this point. Your diligence and attention to detail in the earlier phases will pay off when your book becomes available for purchase to the general public.

6. Introduction Phase

The final month before publication is devoted to following up with everyone with whom you have worked, catching up on actions that still need to be completed, and tying up any loose ends. Coordinate your launch with your printer, distribution partners, potential buyers, the media, and reviewers, and finish up all the miscellaneous tasks that are required to meet your ultimate deadline. When your publication date arrives and your book is finally released, you should be excited and relieved. But know your job is not done. The real work of building and sustaining your book's momentum begins at this point.

AFTER PUBLICATION

The final phase of the publication timeline occurs post-publication. It involves managing your book through its life-cycle stages. Evaluate your efforts and make any necessary changes in strategy or implementation as this cycle unfolds.

7. Evaluation Phase

As the results of your hard work emerge, you may decide to change some of the things you are doing, or the way you are doing them. Evaluate all your previous actions to determine if they were successful, and if they were not, figure out why not. Make alterations as required to increase your effectiveness now, and in the future.

Sometimes, independent publishers are so embroiled in their day-to-day activities that they do not take the time to step back and evaluate their relative progress. If you do not make time for evaluation, though, you will end up wasting time, money, and energy. It is important to constantly ask yourself what is working, what is not working, and what it would take to increase your business and profits.

If you use this publication timeline as a guide, you will efficiently and successfully arrive at your publication date on time. You will still have to put in a lot of hard work, but you will avoid the stress of having to back-peddle in order to finish tasks you forgot about along the way. However, do not let this timeline blind you. Keep your eyes open as you move forward and if a great opportunity arises, do not be afraid to jump on it even if it may veer you slightly off course.

47. PREPARE YOURSELF MENTALLY

The trek to non-trade sales success can be long and arduous. Maintaining a strong and determined attitude along the way will greatly improve your chances of reaching your goals. Prepare yourself for some disappointments, but through it all, remain focused and keep your head held high.

PREVENT NEGATIVE REACTIONS

There are several basic axioms in book marketing in general—non-trade in particular—that may have a negative effect on your attitude. If you know in advance that certain things are going to occur, though, the negative impact on your attitude may be reduced. Therefore, keep the following in mind during your sales efforts:

■ *Rejection is a way of life.* Be forewarned that you will be rejected far more times than you will be accepted. Do not take rejection personally or allow it to wear away at your attitude, though. That of course is easy to say, but it can actually be done if you accept rejection as a challenge. Use it to improve your strategies and tactics, thereby increasing your likelihood of acceptance the next time.

■ *People make decisions on their schedules, not on yours.* One of the problems with setting sales objectives is that they are based on *your* forecasts and *your* presumptions of what and when people will buy. However, potential buyers do not know, or care about your predictions. They only know what and when *they* want things, and their needs and deadlines may not coincide with yours. For example, a buyer may have a promotion planned for next year with which your book will fit nicely, but they will not buy it until next year regardless of *your* goal. Therefore, it is important to keep your predictions and goals flexible to avoid discouragement.

■ *The order is rarely as much as you had hoped.* Again, buyers purchase what they need, not what you forecast. And since many buy on a non-returnable basis, they will not commit to a large quantity until your book has proven to be successful.

Think of non-trade marketing as a marathon, not a sprint, and commit to the long run. Do not expect large, short-term sales. They could happen, but more often than not buyers will proceed carefully until they develop trust for you and your book. So, work with them and accept even the smallest orders with a smile. Do your best to stay positive, persistent, and productive.

THE SEVEN "C'S"

Having a positive attitude enables you to remain competent, professional, enthusiastic, and successful throughout your non-trade sales efforts. The following list includes seven "C's" that will help you along the way:

■ *Commitment.* According to motivational speaker Brian Tracy, commitment is the knowledge that "If it's to be, it's up to me." If you do not take an active role in marketing your books, no one else will, either. It is also the ability to devote your entire focus to the attainment of your objectives, and the discipline to continue trying in the face of adversity and rejection. Understand that you are not perfect, and therefore, you must commit yourself to evaluating your results and trying different tactics on a continual basis, using trial-and-error, and learning from your mistakes.

■ *Competition.* Competition does not always have to be against other people. In fact, you may be more successful if you consider yourself—rather than others—

the competition. Compete with yourself to contact one more person per day this week than you did last week. Look for ways to make your selling skills better than they were yesterday, but not as good as they will be tomorrow. Seek one more idea to solve a problem. Attempt to improve yourself in some way everyday, and you are more likely to become successful more quickly.

■ *Concentration.* Progress in non-trade sales has less to do with speed than it does with direction and concentration. In football games, the most points are scored in the last two minutes before the end of each half, because the players are concentrated on getting points on the board before time runs out. They are not thinking about what happens if they lose, but on scoring the points necessary to win. You have to play the non-trade sales game as if you are always in the last two minutes of the half. Concentrate on the rewards of success, not the consequences of failure.

■ *Confidence.* Confidence is the ability to entrust yourself with your future. Having a high level of self-confidence will bolster your courage to perform all the tasks you may be reluctant to do, including personal visits to buyers or picking up that "200-pound telephone" to make sales calls.

■ *Control.* Some people define control as a restraining act—the need to hold back or curb something. But control is really a dynamic process. It is the ability to recognize an opportunity that comes to you on the spur of the moment, then evaluate and pursue it even though it was not part of your original plan. Control requires adjustments to compensate for unpredicted circumstances that will undoubtedly occur as you move toward your ultimate objective.

Additionally, control will allow you to apply your creativity professionally. It will direct your commitment so you can pursue your goals, and help you use your confidence for productive means. Furthermore, a controlled grip on your anxiety will give you the courage to continue with your efforts even after several rejections. And finally, it will ensure that you maintain your competitive edge.

■ *Courage.* It takes a little bravery to start selling directly to non-trade markets. Leaving your comfort zone is never easy, but sometimes it must be done so have the courage to do so. Also, have the courage to accept responsibility for your situation—whatever it may be. Blaming unresponsive buyers for lost sales will not solve anything. Discover what went wrong and then correct it the next time.

Have the courage to be assertive during negotiations. At times you may feel as if you have lost control and that the potential customer holds all the cards. If you relinquish control of your actions, you will end up either losing the sale, or coming out of it with less than favorable terms. Additionally, have the courage to try out different approaches. It takes valor to attempt something new, but sometimes it is necessary to shake up your thinking and be creative in the actions you take.

Finally, keep in mind that you do not have to go through all of this alone. Have the courage to seek assistance.

■ *Creativity.* If you are to be successful in non-trade marketing, you must use your creativity to make things happen. There will be cases in which your potential buyers have never used books as a premium or sold books in their stores. In these instances, your creativity will serve you well and allow you to convince them explore new opportunities with your book. Find new ways to make sales happen.

Too often we get caught up in talking about products and markets and forget that we are selling to people. Non-trade marketing is a *people* business. Its foundation is based upon making and maintaining relationships with other people, most of whom like to be associated with others who are positive and passionate about what they are doing. Not only must you believe in your book, but you must make others believe in it—and in you—as well. If you can create and maintain an attitude that will sustain you through the short-run delays and negativity, you will cross the finish line with arms raised in triumph.

48. CASE STUDIES

Throughout the earlier chapters in this book you learned a lot of information about, and strategies for, successfully selling more books to non-trade market buyers. Oftentimes people learn best by example, though, so hopefully the following case studies will help clear up any questions you may still have. Each of them is different, but as you will see, they all demonstrate instances in which people successfully sold books to non-trade markets using the same concepts described throughout this book.

CASE STUDY ONE

Connie Bennett, C.H.H.C. wrote *Sugar Shock: How Sweets and Simple Carbs Can Derail Your Life—and How You Can Get it Back on Track,* with Stephen T. Sinatra, M.D. "*Sugar Shock* is the first book to give a complete, up-to-date picture of how eating too many sweets and refined carbohydrates could adversely affect people's physical and emotional well being. It reveals groundbreaking information about the negative effects of refined sugars and carbohydrates on the human body," Connie said. The following information walks you through the process Connie used to achieve a sale with Whole Foods, all the way from how she differentiated her title, to her book submission and final acceptance.

Differentiating *Sugar Shock* from its Competition

A competitive analysis demonstrated that *Sugar Shock* is different from other, related books, because it tells the full sugar story and helps readers break free of their habits. As Connie said, "It is the first book in its category to highlight recent groundbreaking studies, include interviews with some 250 medical experts worldwide, reveal revolutionary research studies documenting that readers could become dependent on sweets much as an alcoholic or drug addict gets hooked on their substance of choice, and explore whether or not 'Big Sugar' is the next 'Big Tobacco.'"

As discussed in *25. Understand Your Competition and Differentiate Your Title* (page 207), buyers do not want more of what they already have. They want something new—something different. They want something that will make their customers take notice and say "Wow!" If your book does not offer something fresh and original, you will lose those who want a new voice or a new perspective on an old problem. Thus, like Connie, figure out how and why your book is better than all the others on the market. Then, show that to buyers through your sales-promotional materials and conversations.

Defining Target Buyers

The target market for *Sugar Shock* is enormous. There are millions of Americans suffering from a large assortment of ailments, including mood swings, depression, memory problems, infertility, severe PMS, fatigue, sexual dysfunction, cancer, heart disease, and skin problems, all brought on by overconsumption of soda, cookies, candies, and chips. Knowing who can benefit from—and may therefore be interested in—your book will help you decide which groups of people to target. This concept is discussed in *23. Define Your Target Buyers* (page 198).

Segmenting the Mass Market and Prioritizing Potential Buyers

Connie created a market map for *Sugar Shock*, defining potential segments in which her book could be sold. The obvious targets were the health-food stores—ranging from the thousands of mom and pop stores to the national Whole Foods chain. Additional prospects included health food associations, clinics, nutritionists, obesity clinics, and support groups. Once all these—and many others—were qualified and prioritized, Whole Foods appeared as the number-one prospect. This demonstrates how dividing your opportunities into manageable segments can make your marketing activities more efficient. As you study each segment more carefully, those most likely to buy your books percolate to the top. See *24. Segment the Mass Market* (page 201) and *29. Qualify, Classify, and Prioritize Your List of Potential Buyers* (page 225) for more detailed discussions about these topics.

Conducting Market Research

Initial research showed that Whole Foods has eleven regions, each with a buyer for its stores' selection of life-style products. However, Whole Foods' buyers do not purchase directly from publishers; they purchase through Nutri-Books, a distribution partner that works with natural-products stores. Further research pointed out some interesting facts that were important to consider before attempting sales to Nutri-Books.

First, Nutri-Books seeks books with general information on healthy living, not mainstream medical books. Furthermore, according to Michael Van Meter, a buyer at Nutri-Books, "Too many authors spoil their objective message with subjective, personal information that we do not want. Tell them to stick to the facts and keep their books on a professional level." And as a rule, fiction does not sell in natural-products stores, and softcover books are preferred over case-bound books.

Furthermore, Connie's research showed that certain books sell better depending on the season, so it is important to know when buyers make their decisions for each season's products. According to Michael, "Our representatives meet with buyers in all eleven of Whole Foods' regions every week to bring them new titles on topics that will be in their stores six to eight months in the future. For example, weight-control topics sell well in January, but the buyers seek those books in May or June."

Finally, Michael said he prefers finished books to manuscripts, "However, I will look at a BLAD or a galley." As discussed in *26. Conduct Simple Market Research* (page 210), and as you can see from this case study, conducting market research is a necessity. How many times could you hit the bullseye on a target if you were blindfolded? Probably none. Research helps remove your blindfolds so you can get a clear view of your buyers and what they need.

Matching Benefits to Buyers

When selling to Nutri-Books buyers, the benefit Connie chose to emphasize was value. She convinced them that her book would bring customers into their stores and would, therefore, be a profitable investment. Connie's book provides several benefits, but she took the time to properly match the correct one with this buyer. This process is discussed in greater detail in *30. Match Benefits to Buyers* (page 228).

Submitting The Book

Sugar Shock was submitted to, and accepted by Michael. Part of his decision to take on this title was the way it was sent to him. The submission package demonstrated the book's competitive advantages, the co-authors' credentials, and a promotion plan demonstrating Connie's willingness to go into stores to conduct signings and events. Reviews and endorsements from industry experts were also included, and they provided the independent testimonials Michael likes to see. "It proved this was not just their story, but that they really knew what they were talking about," he said. Creating professional sales-promotional literature and obtaining promotional materials such as reviews and endorsements is discussed in *Chapter Six. Promoting to Non-Trade Markets* (page 259).

CASE STUDY TWO

Jennifer and Dave Marx created a business selling travel books to a very specific market—people vacationing at the two Disney parks and on the Disney Cruise Line. Their business demonstrates their understanding of several major principles of non-trade marketing, including creating line extensions by focusing on content, promoting through various outlets, and selling books for use as premiums.

Selling Content

The foundation for Jennifer and Dave's business is built upon *PassPorter* guides—unique travel books that offer expert advice, comprehensive information, vacationer tips, and original photos to help people plan their trips to Disney parks and cruises. Over the years, Jennifer and Dave built upon this base and extended the *PassPorter* product line to include guidebooks, destination overviews, treasurehunter books, trip planners, eBooks, worksheets, charts, journals, message boards, and more. They used their content and adapted it into forms buyers demanded. Be willing to think outside the box and do not get stuck on the idea of a traditional book. See *4. Content is King* (page 26) for more information.

Promoting

Jennifer and Dave promote their *PassPorter* products through conventional and niche media. They conduct author events, appear on television and radio shows, and send books to Disney and Disney-fan websites for online reviews and publicity. Additionally, Jennifer and Dave conduct regular contests and use their products as cross-promotional items and giveaways. They advertise in Disney-related newsletters and track their relative success with special discount codes. All of their sales-literature cross-sells the other items in their line, as well.

The *PassPorter* website not only serves as a community for fans, but also as an online store. Other people may register and sell their products through the website, which generates additional traffic and followers. Consequently, Jennifer and Dave are able to reach more people with their own *PassPorter* products. Furthermore, the website generates substantial annual revenue from advertising, links to related websites, and sponsorships on the message board.

Finally, Jennifer and Dave implemented an innovative idea for selling their remainders, because as you might expect, their travel guides become outdated each year. Since some of the information contained in them does remain accurate, though, they can still be useful. Jennifer and Dave realized this and began selling them for one dollar, plus shipping and handling on their website; thereby still reaping the benefits of word-of-mouth advertising from these additional sales. Learn more about these, and other promotional tactics in *Chapter Six: Promoting to Non-Trade Buyers* (page 259).

CASE STUDY THREE

Carl R. Sams II and Jean Stoick are professional wildlife photographers. They exemplify the definitive non-trade marketing team. Together they created a varied product line including picture books, board books, movies, CDs, DVDs, curriculum guides, prints, plush toys, and posters, which they sell in bookstores, gift shops, birdseed stores, galleries, art fairs, pharmacies, associations, parks, online, and through direct marketing.

Selling through Gift Shops

Carl spends a lot of time every year attending gift shows all across the country, but according to him, it has to be done. The time he puts in has paid off—he has found great success in the gift store marketplace. Carl likes gift shops because they allow him to sell all of his various products in the same place. In fact, "Some gift shops show the movie in the stores as a promo for everything else," he said. See *13. Gift Shops* (page 83) for more information about this market segment. And keep in mind that successful book marketing requires commitment and a long-term perspective. Put in the time required to find new buyers and give them suggestions for using your products in creative ways.

Selling to the K–5 Market

Two of Carl and Jean's products provide starting points for many elementary classroom activities. Furthermore, EDCO Publishing, Inc. has worked with them to develop special *Connect-It K–5 Curriculum Guides* containing activity pages and project cards with more great ideas. The challenging activities were all developed to meet the Michigan Education Assessment Program's requirements in Language Arts, Science, Math, Music, and Art. This market segment is discussed in *19. The Academic Market* (page 137). The key here is to know that you do not have to create entirely new products for new market segments. You just have to deliver your existing content in a way that is useful to each of your target audiences, and be willing to listen to, and appease their requests.

Cause Marketing

Carl and Jean donate a percentage of their sales to specific non-profit organizations including the Rainbow Connection, the Grand Traverse Nature Conservancy, and Wishes 4 Kids. Their contributions have totaled as much as $50,000 in a single year. Additionally, they have also printed books especially for the Cincinnati Children's Hospital. People may be more willing to buy more books from you if they know that part of their money is going to a worthy cause—particularly if it is one in which they believe. Cause marketing can be a strong buying motivator that can increase your revenue. For more about cause marketing, see *18. Associations* (page 127).

Direct Marketing

Over the years, Carl and Jean have built a mailing list that now contains over 40,000 names. This enables them to launch new products quickly and effectively. You should also develop and maintain a clean mailing list using the information in *28. Find Potential Buyers* (page 220) so you can introduce each new title with some level of guaranteed sales. This will help you forecast demand and have a more accurate initial print run.

Winning Awards

One of Carl and Jean's series that includes two picture books, two DVDs, and two soundtrack CDs has garnered fifty-six awards including those for Best Children's Picture Book and the 2006 Wildscreen Panda Award. Awards can help you overcome buyer inertia by acting as a surrogate indicator. They give you third-party credibility and help reassure buyers that their money will not be wasted. See *38. Participate in Award Competitions* (page 271) for more information.

You, too, can succeed in non-trade sales. Use these case studies to enhance what you have learned in this book, and as motivation moving forward. If they can do it, so can you. By combining and utilizing all of your new knowledge, you can increase your sales in ways and amounts you may have never thought possible.

Conclusion

Over two thousand years ago, Greek writer and philosopher Aristotle said, "First, have a definite, clear, practical ideal; a goal, an objective. Second, have the necessary means to achieve your ends: wisdom, money, materials, and methods. Third, adjust all your means to that end." Regardless of your background and past experiences, if you use the tools provided in this book, set achievable goals, and believe that you can succeed, you will.

Selling to non-trade markets is not always easy. In fact, it can oftentimes be confusing, frustrating, and intimidating. Too many people are disillusioned by visions of immediate, large-scale success, but the majority of the time those dreams will only lead to disappointment. The truth of the matter is that book marketing is hard work. It requires research, planning, trial and error, confidence, and above all, determination and persistence.

Have you ever thought about how an airplane gets from departure to landing? The pilots' mission is to have a safe and timely flight even though for 99 percent or more of the time they cannot see their final destination. But they know it is there. They follow their written flight plan, listen to feedback from controllers along the way, and check their instruments regularly to make sure they stay on the proper flight path. As necessary, they make course corrections.

This metaphorically applies to selling your books. Even though you cannot see your final destination, setting goals will help you keep it in mind as your book takes flight, and will also serve as the standard against which you can gauge your progress along the way. Your goals should be purposeful, clear, measurable, motivating, specific, and time-oriented. Then, do whatever is necessary to achieve them, because if you do not, they will simply remain good intentions. Dynamic aspirations become the inspiration for work and achievement, and will help you allocate your money, effort, attitude, and time.

I have done my best to fill this book with comprehensive information about the non-trade book sales process from start to finish. My hope is that I have addressed all of your concerns and questions, or at least directed you to resources that can provide the answers for which you are looking. Work with the ideas presented throughout each of the earlier chapters to increase your sales and profitability in non-trade markets. Try out several different strategies in order to find out what is best for you and your title. Keep an open mind, look for new opportunities, and make it happen. It is all up to you now—your profitable future is waiting!

One last thought: The information contained in this book will undoubtedly change as time goes on and the industry continues to evolve. Although complete and accurate at the time of publication, it is a work in progress and will be updated and revised as needed. In the meantime, should you have any comments or suggestions you would like to offer, please contact me.

Brian Jud
Book Marketing Works, LLC
P. O. Box 715
Avon, CT 06001-0715

Website: www.bookmarketingworks.com
Phone: 860-675-1344
Fax: 860-270-0343
Email: BrianJud@bookmarketing.com

Appendices

Included in these appendices are four marketing materials that should typically be included in your submission packages to both retail and non-retail market buyers. The first item is a generic cover letter. An example sell sheet, a sample press release, and an outline of a summary marketing plan follow it. All of these items—aside from the summary marketing plan—use *How To Make Real Money Selling Books* as their subject, and they should give you a good model off of which to base your own materials.

Cover Letter

August 2009

Dear Sir/Madam:

Square One Publishers is very pleased to announce the publication of *How To Make Real Money Selling Books (Without Worrying About Returns)*. This brand-new book has been written by award-winning author Brian Jud, whose experience with non-trade book sales makes him one of the strongest experts on the topic of niche market bookselling in the world. A review copy has been enclosed for your reference.

How To Make Real Money Selling Books provides everything a book publisher needs to know about taking advantage of marketing opportunities beyond the bookstore. It opens your eyes to a wealth of solid, often surprising outlets—from book fairs and specialty shops to specialized libraries and companies that offer premium sales. Unlike bookstores, these are markets that never or rarely return titles. But that's only the beginning. You will also learn how each market works, how to locate key contacts, and how to successfully negotiate a deal. Rounding out this book is invaluable information on print runs, discounts, contracts, and distributors, as well as a heads-up on common marketing pitfalls and how to avoid them. By the time you finish reading this book, you'll wonder how you ever managed to sell books without it.

We here at Square One Publishers feel that this book will become a year-in, year-out aid to first-time book publishers and seasoned veterans alike. This book can also act as a crucial primary text in college-level publishing courses or as a primer for those within the book publishing industry who seek a deeper understanding of specialty and/or niche market sales.

How To Make Real Money Selling Books ($24.95 US / $27.50 CAN) is available to your organization at the following special bulk-rate discounts:

25–49 copies	(30% discount)
50–249 copies	(40% discount)
250–499 copies	(45% discount)
500–999 copies	(50% discount)

If you would like to order copies, feel free to contact our business office directly at 1-516-535-2010 or fax us at 1-516-535-2014. We look forward to hearing from you, and wish you and your colleagues a pleasant and successful publishing season.

Best regards,

Anthony Pomes
Square One Publishers
516-535-2010 x 105
www.squareonepublishers.com

Enc.

Sell Sheet

AUGUST

$24.95 US

384 pages

6 x 9-inch quality paperback

Business/Marketing/Publishing

ISBN 978-0-7570-0213-7

BUSINESS/PUBLISHING

HOW TO MAKE REAL MONEY SELLING BOOKS
(WITHOUT WORRYING ABOUT RETURNS)

A Complete Guide to the
Book Publishers' World of Solid Sales

Brian Jud

No matter what size publisher you are—even if you self-publish—you have the ability to sell hundreds of thousands of books to markets that are entirely outside the bookstore environment. For years, large publishing houses (and savvy independent publishers) have zeroed in on these lucrative markets, satisfied their constant need for new books, and quietly profited from these "special sales" venues. Now, marketing expert Brian Jud has unlocked the secret to the world of non-trade sales through his practical, easy-to-follow guide *How To Make Real Money Selling Books (Without Worrying About Returns)*.

This comprehensive work provides everything a book publisher needs to know about taking advantage of marketing opportunities beyond the bookstore. It opens your eyes to a wealth of solid, often surprising outlets—from book fairs and specialty shops, to specialized libraries and companies that offer premium sales. Unlike bookstores, these are markets that never or rarely return titles. But that's only the beginning. You will also learn how each market works, how to locate key contacts, and how to successfully negotiate a deal. Rounding out this book is invaluable information on print runs, discounts, contracts, and distribution partners, as well as a "heads-up" on common marketing pitfalls and how to avoid them. By the time you finish reading this book, you'll wonder how you ever managed without it.

Each year, many millions of books are sold through these valuable outlets. Isn't it time you took advantage of these special opportunities? With *How To Make Real Money Selling Books* in hand, you can widen your horizon to success.

ABOUT THE AUTHOR

Brian Jud is president of Book Marketing Works, a marketing consultancy firm. Established in 1996, the company's goal is to help independent publishers market their titles more effectively. Brian is an award-winning author, whose titles have included the best-selling *Job Search 101*. In addition to hosting the television series *The Book Authority*, he has appeared as a guest on numerous television and radio talk shows and speaks regularly on marketing topics at seminars and workshops throughout North America. Currently, Brian and his family reside in central Connecticut.

Press Release

FOR IMMEDIATE RELEASE

Contact Info: Anthony Pomes, Marketing/PR Director
                  Square One Publishers (www.squareonepublishers.com)
                  Phone: 516-535-2010 x 105

Increase Your Sales and Profits by Selling "Outside" the Bookstore

Special Sales Publishing Expert Brian Jud Shares His Simple Yet Effective Tips for Making Sure You Strike Gold with Books Sold—New and Old

Garden City Park, New York—Book publishers need to find new places to sell their books if they want to increase their sales and profits in an increasingly competitive marketplace. With an average of more than 250,000 new titles published every year, is it any wonder so many of these books never find their way into bookstores? And if they do, how well do they sell before being returned to the publisher? No matter what size publisher you are—even if you self-publish—you have the ability to sell hundreds of thousands of your books to markets that are entirely outside the bookstore environment. And for years, large publishing houses (and savvy independent publishers) have zeroed in on these lucrative markets, satisfied their constant need for new books, and quietly profited from these special-sales venues. Now, marketing expert Brian Jud has unlocked the secret to the world of special sales through his practical, easy-to-follow guide, *How To Make Real Money Selling Books (Without Worrying About Returns)*.

This comprehensive work provides everything a book publisher needs to know about taking advantage of marketing opportunities in non-bookstore markets. It opens your eyes to a wealth of solid, often surprising outlets—from book fairs and specialty shops to specialized libraries and companies that offer premium sales. Unlike bookstores, these are markets that never or rarely return titles. But that's only the beginning. You will also learn how each market works, how to locate key contacts, and how to successfully negotiate a deal. Rounding out this book is invaluable information on print runs, discounts, contracts, and distributors, as well as a heads-up on common marketing pitfalls and how to avoid them. By the time you finish reading this book, you'll wonder how you ever managed without it.

Each year, many millions of books are sold through these valuable outlets. Isn't it time you took advantage of these special opportunities? *With How To Make Real Money Selling Books* in hand, you can widen your horizon to success.

If you would like to order *How To Make Real Money Selling Books*, our titles are available through any number of book distributors nationwide. Or, you can order books from Square One Publishers directly at 516-535-2010 or 1-877-900-BOOK (for callers outside the New York metropolitan area only). You can also fax us at 516-535-2014. Thank you.

BOOK SPECS: $24.95 US / $27.50 CAN / 384 PAGES / ISBN 978-0-7570-0213-7 / 6 x 9-INCH QUALITY PAPERBACK

115 HERRICKS ROAD   GARDEN CITY PARK   NEW YORK 11040

Summary Marketing Plan

Summary Marketing Plan for (Title), by (Author) to (Distribution Company or Potential Buyer)

Publisher name, Address, Contact information

Content: (50-word description)
Author's Credentials: (50-word description)
Target Audience: (50-word description)

COMPETITION:

Competitive Titles: (List your book's competition)
(Title)'s Competitive Advantages: (Summarize your book's major sales handles and describe how your book is different from, and better than its competitors.)

NON-TRADE SALES OPPORTUNITIES:

(Discuss the non-trade outlets in which you think your book will sell well.)

PROMOTION:

Promotional budget: (Include the amount of money you have at your disposal for promotional purposes.)

OVERALL PROMOTION STRATEGY:

Publicity: (Discuss any reviews you have obtained, any tours you have planned, and any print and/or broadcast coverage you have sought or expect; also state the publicity firm with which you are working if applicable, and describe what is included in your press kit.)
Advertising: (State where you are planning to advertise and whether you are willing to participate in cooperative advertisements with the company if applicable.)
Sales Promotion: (Establish which sales-promotional tools you will use and why, as well as whether you are pursuing any rights sales.)
Personal Selling: (Discuss your availability and willingness to conduct author events, book signings, and other personal appearances and presentations.)

About the Author

Brian Jud is an author, book-marketing consultant, seminar leader, television host, and the president of Book Marketing Works, LLC. He is also a partner in Premium Book Company, which sells books on a non-returnable, commission-only basis to non-trade buyers. Additionally, Brian developed and introduced the Special-Sales Profit Center, which is a web-based, targeted marketing system that helps deliver incremental sales and profits to publishers worldwide. He is a prolific writer of book publishing and marketing articles, as well as a syndicated columnist and a regular contributor to industry publications.

Brian authored the *Publishers Weekly* title *Beyond the Bookstore* , the CD-ROM *Marketing Planning*, and eight e-booklets with proven tips for publishing success. He also created a series of automated book marketing wizards and wrote and self-published five books on career transition, which are internationally distributed. Furthermore, Brian hosts the television series *The Book Authority*, which has aired over 650 shows, and he is the author, narrator, and producer of the media-training video program *You're on the Air*. In addition, he wrote and published *It's Show Time* and *Perpetual Promotion*, which describe techniques authors can use to appear and perform on television and radio shows.

Brian is the founder of the Connecticut Authors and Publishers Association. He is also an adjunct lecturer of sales and marketing courses for undergraduate and graduate students at the University of Hartford in West Hartford, Connecticut, and the University of Connecticut in Storrs, Connecticut. He regularly speaks on marketing topics at IBPA's Publishing University, as well as for other publishing groups around the country.

You can visit Brian's website at www.bookmarketingworks.com.

Resources

This section contains a categorized list of the extensive resources mentioned throughout this book. The book industry is continuously growing, changing, and evolving, though, so you may want to double check the accuracy of this information before using it. The following list outlines how the information is organized:

1. BOOK INDUSTRY RESOURCES

Book Industry Publications

Cataloging in Publication (CIP) Resource

Internet Tools

International Standard Book Number (ISBN) Resource

Library of Congress Catalog Number (LCCN) Resource

Minority- or Women-Owned Business Certifying Organizations

Point-of-Purchase Display Manufacturers

Print on Demand (POD) Companies

Publication Timeline

Publishing Associations and Workshops

Sales Representative Groups

Trade Shows

Uniform Code Council (UCC)

2. PROMOTIONAL RESOURCES

Award Competitions

Celebrity Endorsements

Direct Mail Resources

Magazine Listings

Market Research Companies

Media Contacts

Promotional Date Directory

Promotional Event Markets

Speaking Engagement Resources/Training

3. TRADE BOOK MARKETS

Airport Bookstores

Book Clubs

Discount Stores and Warehouse Clubs

Display Marketing Companies

Gift Shop Markets

Supermarket and Drug Store Associations

1. BOOK INDUSTRY RESOURCES

The following book industry resources can teach you about the book industry as a whole, and help you package, print, and publish your book. They include everything from where to obtain an ISBN, to a list of print on demand printers, to publishing associations and workshops.

BOOK INDUSTRY PUBLICATIONS

Books

For a comprehensive list of books related to book writing, publishing, and marketing, go to www.bookmarketing works.com/bookstore/bookstore.htm

Magazines

Book Business:
www.bookbusinessmag.com

Publishers Weekly:
www.publishersweekly.com

Publishing Executive: www.pubexec.com

Newsletters

Book Marketing Matters:
www.bookmarketingworks.com

John Kremer's Book Marketing Tip of the Week: www.bookmarket.com

Publishers Lunch:
www.publishersmarketplace.com/lun ch/subscribe.html

Publishing Basics:
www.publishingbasics.com

Publishing Poynters:
www.parapublishing.com

PW Daily: www.publishersweekly.com/ enewsletter/CA6629030/2286.html

Shelf Awareness: www.shelf-awareness. com

CATALOGING IN PUBLICATION (CIP) RESOURCE

You can apply for Cataloging in Publication (CIP) data at http://cip.loc.gov/cip

INTERNET TOOLS

Blogs

Book-marketing blog:
www.blog.bookmarketing.com

Directory of blogs: www.blogtoplist.com

Discussion Groups

Find discussion groups at
www.groups.yahoo.com

For a list of discussion groups, go to
http://groups.yahoo.com

Email Marketing Support

Constant Contacts offers services that can help you ensure your emails will not show up as spam, create email campaigns, build your list of contacts, track your emails, and more.

Website: www.constantcontacts.com

Podcast Directories

www.podcastcentral.com

www.podcastdirectory.com

www.podcastingnews.com

www.podcast.net

www.podcastpickle.com

www.podscope.com

Search Engine Collaboration Software

Copernic software will save you time by making your online searches more efficient.

Website: www.copernic.com

Social Networking Websites

www.facebook.com

www.linkedin.com

www.myspace.com

www.squidoo.com

www.twitter.com

www.youtube.com

Webrings

You can find a directory of webrings at http://dir.webring.com/rw

INTERNATIONAL STANDARD BOOK NUMBER (ISBN) RESOURCE

Purchase International Standard Book Numbers (ISBN) at www.bowker.com

LIBRARY OF CONGRESS CATALOG NUMBER (LCCN) RESOURCE

A free Library of Congress Catalog Number (LCCN) is easily obtained online at http://pcn.loc.gov

MINORITY- OR WOMEN-OWNED BUSINESS CERTIFYING ORGANIZATIONS

National Minority Suppliers Development Council
15 W. 39th St.
New York, NY 10018
Tel: 212-944-2430
Website: www.nmsdc.org

Women's Business Enterprise National Council
1710 H St., N.W., 7th Fl.
Washington, DC 20006
Tel: 202-872-5515
Website: www.wbenc.org

POINT-OF-PURCHASE DISPLAY MANUFACTURERS

City Diecutting, Inc.
One Cory Rd.
Morristown, NJ 07960
Tel: 973-270-0370
Website: www.bookdisplays.com

George Patton Associates, Inc.
55 Broadcommon Rd.
Bristol, RI 02809
Tel: 800-572-2194
Website: www.displays2go.com/
    counter_displays.htm

Merchandising Systems, Inc.
2951 Whipple Rd.
Union City, CA 94587
Tel: 510-477-9100
Website: www.wireline.net/index.aspx

PRINT ON DEMAND (POD) COMPANIES

Amazon.com's BookSurge:
    www.booksurge.com
Infinity Publishing:
    www.infinitypublishing.com
Ingram's Lightning Source:
    www.ingrampublisherservices.com
Lehigh Phoenix: www.phoenixcolor.com
Lulu: www.lulu.com
Tri-Ad Litho, Inc.: www.triadlitho.com

For a more complete list of POD printers and publishers, go to www.bookcentralstation.com

PUBLICATION TIMELINE

You can find an Excel spreadsheet that will automatically calculate and create a personalized publication timeline for you based on various publication dates at www.bookmarketingworks.com/
shopcart/default.asp?catid=4

PUBLISHING ASSOCIATIONS AND WORKSHOPS

Associations

Association of American Publishers (AAP): www.publishers.org

Independent Book Publishers Association (IBPA): www.ibpa-online.org

Small Press Association of North America (SPAN): www.spannet.org

Workshops

IBPA Publishing University: www.thepublishinguniversity.com

A list of writers' workshops and conferences may be found at http://writing.shawguides.com

SALES REPRESENTATIVE GROUPS

Andrews McMeel Publishing: www. andrewsmcmeel.com/find_rep.html

Gift Shops of America Vendor/Representative Directory: www.giftshopsofamerica.com

Manufacturers Representative Profile: www.mrpusa.com

Manufacturers Representatives Wanted: www.manufacturers-representatives.com

Rep Hunter: www.rephunter.net

TRADE SHOWS

Calculating Your Break-Even Point

For a spreadsheet that will help you calculate your break-even point for any trade show, go to www.book marketingworks.com/shopcart/ default.asp?catid=4

Largest Book Industry Trade Show

BookExpo America (BEA): www.bookexpoamerica.com

Niche Trade Show Examples

Bologna Children's Book Fair: www.bolognachildrensbookfair.com

Gourmet Housewares Show: www.thegourmetshow.com

Natural Products Expo West: www.expowest.com

Wine Expos: www.wine-expos.com

Purchasing/Renting Trade Show Exhibits

Exhibitor Trader: www.exhibittrader.com

Impact Marketing Displays: www.used-trade-show-booths.com

World Exhibit Brokers: www.webisales.com

Trade Show Listings

www.biztradeshows.com/usa/usa-tradeshows.mp?industry=printing

www.bookcentralstation.com

www.greatrep.com/trade_shows.asp

UNIFORM CODE COUNCIL (UCC)

Uniform Code Council
GS1 US
Princeton Pike Corporate Center
1009 Lenox Dr., Ste. 202
Lawrenceville, NJ 08648
Tel: 609-620-0200
Website: www.uc-council.org

2. PROMOTIONAL RESOURCES

There are a variety of different ways to promote books. This section includes the contact information for companies and organizations that can facilitate your promotional activities.

AWARD COMPETITIONS

Major Awards

Lambda Literary Awards: www.lambdaliterary.org/awards/guidelines.html

National Book Awards: www.nationalbook.org/nba.html

Pulitzer Prize: www.pulitzer.org

Niche Award Examples

800-CEO-READ Business Book Awards: http://800ceoread.com/bookawards

Benjamin Franklin Awards: www.ibpa-online.org/pubresources/benfrank.aspx

Edgar Awards: www.mysterywriters.org/?q=AwardsPrograms

Eric Hoffer Award: www.hofferaward.com

Mom's Choice Awards: www.momschoiceawards.com

National Best Book Awards: www.usabooknews.com

National Indie Excellence Book Awards: www.indieexcellence.com

National Jewish Book Awards: www.jewishbookcouncil.org/page.php?7

National Outdoor Book Awards: www.noba-web.org/policy.htm

Scott O'Dell Historical Fiction Award: www.scottodell.com/odellaward.html

CELEBRITY ENDORSEMENTS

Use the following resource to find celebrities to endorse and/or write the introduction for your book:

Celeb Fan Mail
Website: www.celebfanmail.com

Contact Any Celebrity
8721 Santa Monica Blvd. #431
W. Hollywood, CA 90069
Tel: 310-691-5466
Website: www.contactanycelebrity.com

Reel Classics
Website: www.reelclassics.com/Address/address-list.htm

Screen Actors Guild
5757 Wilshire Blvd.
Los Angeles, CA 90036
Tel: 323-954-1600
Website: www.sag.org

Screen Actors Guild
360 Madison Avenue, 12th Fl.
New York, NY 10017
Tel: 212-944-1030
Website: www.sag.org

DIRECT MAIL RESOURCES

Companies that Sell Mailing Lists

American Student List: www.studentlist.com

Amity Direct: www.amitydirectinc.com

CAS: www.cas-online.com

InfoUSA: www.infousa.com

National Mail Order Association: www.nmoa.org

USAData: www.usadata.com

Software that Allows You to Create Your Own Mailing Lists

NAICS Association
129 Lakeshore Dr.
Rockaway, NJ 07866
Tel: 973-625-5626
Website: www.naics.com

MAGAZINE LISTINGS

Find lists of magazines at
http://en.wikipedia.org/wiki/List_of_
United_States_magazines

MARKET RESEARCH COMPANIES

Cap Ventures, Inc.
600 Cordwainer Dr.
Norwell, MA 02061
Tel: 781-871-9000
Website: www.capv.com

ICv2 Publishing
448 W. Washington Ave.
Madison, WI 53703
Tel: 608-284-9400
Website: www.ICv2.com

Market Data Retrieval
One Forest Pkwy., P.O. Box 907
Shelton, CT 06484
Tel: 800-333-8802
Website: www.schooldata.com

Outsell, Inc.
330 Primrose Rd., Ste. 510
Burlingame, CA 94010
Tel: 650-342-6060
Website: www.outsellinc.com

Subtext/Open Book Publishing, Inc.
P.O. Box 2228, Darien, CT 06820
Tel: 203-316-8008
Website: www.subtext.net/founders/
    founders.htm

MEDIA CONTACTS

Lists of Niche Reviewers

Book Central Station:
    www.bookcentralstation.com
Midwest Book Review:
    www.midwestbookreview.com

Lists of Niche Media Outlets

All-In-One Directory
Gebbie Press, Inc.
P.O. Box 1000
New Paltz, NY 12561
Tel: 845-255-7560
Website: www.gebbieinc.com

Broadcast Interview Source
2233 Wisconsin Ave. NW
Washington, DC 20007
Tel: 800-932-7266
Website: www.expertclick.com

Radio and Television News Directors
    Association
1025 F St. NW, 7th Fl.
Washington, DC 20004
Tel: 202-659-6510
Website: www.rtnda.org

PROMOTIONAL DATE DIRECTORY

Learn about different possibilities for
associating your book with a national
event at www.ideacalendar.com

PROMOTIONAL EVENT MARKETS

Extra Mile Marketing
8655 E. Via de Ventura, Ste. E-130
Scottsdale, AZ 85258
Tel: 480-443-6806
Website: www.extra-mile-marketing.com

Site Systems
5855 Green Valley Circle, Ste. 108
Culver City, CA 90230
Tel: 310-649-0900
Website: www.sitesystems.com

SPEAKING ENGAGEMENT RESOURCES/TRAINING

Professional Speakers

You can locate speakers and their contact information through the National Speakers Association: www.nsaspeaker.org

Training

Learn how to improve your own speaking skills through the following organizations:

Dale Carnegie: www.dalecarnegie.com

National Speakers Association:
   www.nsaspeaker.org

Toastmasters International:
   www.toastmasters.org

Speakers Bureau Examples

If you are an experienced public speaker, a speakers bureau may take you on and book speaking engagements for you. The following list contains only a sampling of the many that exist:

Aviation Speakers Bureau:
   www.aviationspeakers.com

Executive Speakers Bureau:
   www.executivespeakers.com

Hospice, Palliative, and Home Care
   Speakers Bureau: www.nhphc.org

Humorous Speakers Bureau:
   www.humorbureau.com

Latino Speakers Bureau:
   www.latinospeakers.com

3. TRADE BOOK MARKETS

This section provides the resources you will need to successfully sell your trade book to markets other than traditional bookstores. Airport bookstores, book clubs, discount stores, warehouse clubs, display marketing companies, gift shops, supermarkets, and drug stores are all great places to sell trade books, and everything you need to successfully locate and sell to them is included here.

AIRPORT BOOKSTORES

Borders Airport Stores
New Vendor Acquisitions
Borders Group, Inc.
100 Phoenix Dr.
Ann Arbor, MI 48108
Tel: 800-770-7811
Website: www.bordersstores.com

Discovery Channel Airport Stores
P.O. Box 869011
Plano, TX 75086
Tel: 800-627-9399
Website:
   www.discoverychannelstore.com

HMSHost
Book Buyer
6600 Rockledge Dr.
Bethesda, MD 20817
Tel: 866-467-4671
Website: www.hmshost.com

Hudson Booksellers
Sr. Book Buyer
1521 Johnson Ferry Rd., Ste. 250
Marietta, GA 30062
Tel: 201-939-5050, 800-326-7711
Website: www.hudsongroupusa.com

Paradies Shops
5950 Fulton Industrial Blvd.
Atlanta, GA 30336
Tel: 404-344-7905
Website: www.theparadiesshops.com

BOOK CLUBS

Largest National Book Club

Bookspan/Direct Brands, Inc.
501 Franklin Ave.
Garden City, NY 11530
Tel: 516-490-4561
Website: www.directbrands.com

Lists of Smaller, Niche Book Clubs

www.bookclubdirectory.com
www.book-clubs.com
www.booksonline.com
www.freebookclubs.com

DISCOUNT STORES AND WAREHOUSE CLUBS

Best Buy
P.O. Box 9312
Minneapolis, MN 55440
Tel: 612-291-1000
Website: www.bestbuy.com

BJ's Wholesale Club
Book Buyer
P.O. Box 9601
Natick, MA 01760
Phone: 800-257-2582
Website: www.bjs.com

Cost-U-Less
8160 304th Ave., S.E., Bldg. 3, Ste. A
Preston, WA 98050
Tel: 425-222-5022
Website: www.costuless.com

Costco Canada
415 W. Hunt Club Rd.
Ottawa, ON, K2E 1C5, Canada
Tel: 800-463-3783
Website: www.costco.ca

Costco Wholesale Corporation
P.O. Box 34331
Seattle, WA 98124
Tel: 613-221-2000, 800-607-6861
Website: www.costco.com

Kmart
Sears Holdings Corporation
3333 Beverly Rd.
Hoffman Estates, IL 60179
Tel: 847-286-2500
Websites: www.kmart.com,
  www.searsholdings.com

PriceSmart
4649 Morena Blvd.
San Diego, CA 92117
Tel: 858-581-4530
Website: www.pricesmart.com/
  Corporate/Buying-Team.aspx

Sam's Club
608 S.W. 8th St.
Benonville, AR 72716
Tel: 888-746-7726
Website: www.samsclub.com

Target Corporation
777 Nicollet Mall
Minneapolis, Minnesota 55402
Tel: 612-304-6073
Website: www.targetcorp.com

Toys"R"Us, Inc. Headquarters
One Geoffrey Way
Wayne, NJ 07470
Tel: 973-617-3500
Website: www.toysrusinc.com

Wal-Mart Stores, Inc
Book Buyer
702 S.W. 8th St.
Bentonville, AR 72716
Tel: 501-273-4000
Website: www.walmarstores.com

DISPLAY MARKETING COMPANIES

A+ Book Fairs
419 E. Juanita Ave., Ste. 104
Mesa, AZ 85204
Tel: 888-966-2665, 480-632-0440
Website: www.aplusbookfairs.com

A+ Book Fairs
100 N. 700 W.
North Salt Lake, UT 84054
Tel: 888-966-2665, 801-599-6944
Website: www.aplusbookfairs.com

Adventure Land Book Fairs
4550 S. Wayside, Ste. 100
Houston, TX 77087
Tel: 713-644-1177
Website:
    www.adventurelandbookfairs.com

A.G. City Wholesale Ltd.
760 Technology Dr.
Petersborough, Ontario, Canada
    K9J 6X7
Tel: 705-741-1385
Website: www.agcity.com

Allbook, Inc.
50 Division Ave., Bldg. 1N, Ste. 2
Millington, NJ 07946
Tel: 908-542-0366
Website: www.allbookinc.com

Imagine Nation Books Ltd./Books
    Are Fun
4601 Nautilus Court South
Boulder, CO 80301
Tel: 303-516-3400, 888-293-8114
Website: www.imaginenationbooks.com
    Submit books to:
Tim McCormick, Senior Buyer
3628 W. Chicago St.
Chandler, AZ 85226
Tel: 480-838-4309
Fax: 480-820-1011

Reader's World Wholesale
1201 Jacobson Ave.
P.O. Box 129
Ashland, OH 44805
Tel: 419-281-5952
Website: www.readersworldwholesale.com

Smart Start Book Fairs
1416 Dunn Cove Dr.
Apopka, FL 32703
Tel: 407-257-3827
Website: http://book-fairs.net

GIFT SHOP MARKETS
Cooperative Gift Catalogs
Gift Creations Concepts:
    www.gcccatalog.com
Ideation: www.ideationgifts.com

Gift Industry Publications
Giftware News
20 W. Kinzie, 12th Fl.
Chicago, IL 60610
Tel: 312-849-2220
Website: www.giftwarenews.com

Gifts & Decorative Accessories
360 Park Ave. South
New York, NY 10010
Tel: 646-746-6400
Website: www.giftsanddec.com

Gift Shop Chain Store Examples
1-800-Flowers.com, Inc.
1 Old Country Rd.
Carle Place, NY 11514
Tel: 516-237-6000, 800-356-7474
Website: www.1800flowers.com

Aramark Sports and Entertainment
    Services, Inc.
Aramark Tower
1101 Market St.
Philadelphia, PA 19107
Tel: 215-238-3000, 800-999-8989
Website: www.ps.aramark.com

Bed, Bath and Beyond
650 Liberty Ave.
Union, NJ 07083
Tel: 908-688-0888, 800-462-3966
Website: www.bedbathandbeyond.com

Franklin Covey Co.
2200 W. Parkway Blvd.
Salt Lake City, UT 84119
Tel: 801-975-1776, 800-819-1812
Website: www.franklincovey.com

Hallmark Cards, Inc.
2501 McGee St.
Kansas City, MO 64108
Tel: 816-274-5111, 800-425-5627
Website: www.hallmark.com

IKEA North America
1000 IKEA Dr.
Elizabeth, NJ 07202
Tel: 908-352-3270
Website: www.ikea-usa.com

Pier 1 Imports, Inc.
100 Pier 1 Pl.
Fort Worth, TX 76102
Tel: 817-252-8000, 800-245-4595
Website: www.pier1.com

Pottery Barn, Inc.
3250 Van Ness Ave.
San Francisco, CA 94109
Tel: 415-421-7900, 888-779-5176
Website: www.potterybarn.com

Spencer's Gifts
6826 Black Horse Pke.
Egg Harbor Township, NJ 08234
Tel: 609-645-3300
Website: www.spencergifts.com

Successories, Inc.
2520 Diehl Rd.
Aurora, IL 60504
Tel: 630-820-7200, 800-535-2773
Website: www.successories.com

Yankee Candle Company, Inc.
16 Yankee Candle Way
South Deerfield, MA 01373
Tel: 413-665-8306; 800-243-1776
Website: www.yankeecandle.com

Hospital Gift Shops

Linda Williams, Advantage Program
1 Hilldale Dr.
Endicott, NY 13760
Tel: 607-725-7386
Website: www.advantageprogram.com

Lori's Hospital Gift Shops
New Product Review
2125 Chenault Dr., Ste. 100
Carrollton, TX 75006
Tel: 972-759-5000 ext. 1823
Website: www.lorishospitalgiftshops.com/
default1.htm

List of Gift Shows

www.greatrep.com/trade_shows.asp

Online Gift Store

Parade of Gifts: www.paradeofgifts.com

**SUPERMARKET AND DRUG
STORE ASSOCIATIONS**

National Association of Chain Drug
Stores
413 N. Lee St.
P.O. Box 1417-D49
Alexandria, VA 22313
Tel: 703-549-3001
Website: www.nacds.org

National Grocers Association
1005 N. Glebe Rd., Ste. 250
Arlington, VA 22201
Tel: 703-516-0700
Website: www.nationalgrocers.org

National Supermarkets Association
30-50 Whitestone Expy, Ste. 301
Flushing, NY 11354
Tel: 718-747-2860
Website: www.nsany.org

SUPERMARKET AND DRUG STORE CHAIN STORE EXAMPLES

Albertson's, Inc.
Supervalu
11840 Valley View Rd.
Eden Prairie, MN 55344
Tel: 952-828-4000
Website: www.supervalu.com

CVS Corporation
1 CVS Dr.
Woonsocket, RI 02895
Tel: 401-765-1500, 800-666-0500
Website: www.cvs.com

Giant Food Stores
300 E. Baltimore Ave.
Lansdowne, PA 19050
Tel: 717-240-1566
Website: www.giantpa.com

Great Atlantic and Pacific Tea Company
2 Paragon Dr.
Montvale, NJ 07645
Tel: 201-573-9700, 800-927-7368
Website: www.aptea.com

Kroger Co.
Book Buyer
1014 Vine St.
Cincinnati, OH 45202
Tel: 866-221-4141
Website: www.kroger.com

Marsh Supermarkets, Inc.
9800 Crosspoint Blvd.
Indianapolis, IN 46256
Tel: 317-594-2100, 800-382-8798
Website: www.marsh.net

Meijer, Inc.
2929 Walker Ave. N.W.
Grand Rapids, MI 49544
Tel: 616-453-6711, 800-543-3704
Website: www.meijer.com

Pathmark Stores, Inc.
200 Milik St.
Carteret, NJ 07008
Tel: 732-499-3000
Website: www.pathmark.com

Rite Aid Corporation
30 Hunter Ln.
Camp Hill, PA 17011
Tel: 717-761-2633, 800-748-3243
Website: www.riteaid.com

Safeway, Inc.
Book Buyer
5918 Stoneridge Mall Rd.
Pleasanton, CA 94588
Tel: 925-520-8000, 877-723-3929
Website: www.safeway.com

Shaw's
P.O Box 600
East Bridgewater, MA 02333
Tel: 508-313-4000
Website: www.shaws.com

Stop and Shop, Inc.
1385 Hancock St.
Quincy, MA 02169
Tel: 617-770-8743
Website: www.stopandshop.com

Walgreens Co.
200 Wilmot Rd.
Deerfield, IL 60015
Tel: 847-940-2500
Website: www.walgreens.com

WHOLESALERS AND DISTRIBUTORS TO TRADE BOOK MARKETS

Alliance Entertainment, LLC
4250 Coral Ridge Dr.
Coral Springs, FL 33065
Tel: 800-329-7664
Website: www.aent.com
Market: Airport Stores

Anderson Merchandisers
Book Purchasing Dept.
421 E. 34th St.
Amarillo, TX 79103
Tel: 806-376-6251
Website: www.amerch.com/index.html
Market: Discount Stores and Wholesale
Clubs

Anderson News Co.
Purchasing Division
6016 Brookvale Ln., Ste. 151
Knoxville, TN 37919
Tel: 865-584-9765
Website: www.andersonnews.com
Market: Airport Stores, Drug Stores,
Supermarkets, Military

Andrews McMeel Publishing, LLC
100 Front St.
Riverside, NJ 08075
Tel: 800-851-8923
Website: www.andrewsmcmeel.com
Market: Bookstores, Gift Shops

Atlas Books
30 Amberwood Pkwy.
Ashland, OH 44805
Tel: 419-281-1802, 800-266-5564
Website:
www.atlasbooksdistribution.com
Market: Airport Stores

Baker and Taylor
1120 Rte. 22 E.
Bridgewater, NJ 08807
Tel: 908-541-7460; 800-775-1800
Website: www.btol.com
Market: Airport Stores, Bookstores,
Libraries

Bookazine
75 Hook Rd.
Bayonne, NJ 07002
Tel: 201-339-7777, 800-221-8112
Website: www.bookazine.com
Market: Airport Stores, Bookstores

Distributors, The
702 S. Michigan
South Bend, IN 46601
Tel: 574-232-8500
Website: www.thedistributors.com
Market: Airport Stores, Bookstores

Greenleaf Book Group
P.O. Box 91869
Austin, TX 78709
Tel: 800-932-5420
Website: www.greenleafbookgroup.com
Market: Airport Stores

Hudson News Co.
Sr. Book Buyer
1521 Johnson Ferry Rd., Ste. 250
Marietta, GA 30062
Tel: 201-939-5050, 800-326-7711
Website: www.hudsongroupusa.com
Market: Airport Stores, Drug Stores,
Supermarkets

Ingram Book Co.
1 Ingram Blvd.
LaVergne, TN 37086
Tel: 800-937-8000
Website: www.ingrambook.com
Market: Airport Stores, Bookstores,
Libraries

Levy Home Entertainment
Book Buyer
4201 Raymond Dr.
Hillside, IL 60162
Tel: 708-547-4400
Website: www.levybooks.com
Market: Discount Stores and Wholesale
Clubs

News Group
(See website for regional addresses)
Tel: 866-466-7231
Website: www2.thenewsgroup.com/US
Market: Airport Stores, Drug Stores,
Supermarkets

Partners Publishers Group
2325 Jarco Dr.
Holt, MI 48842
Tel: 517-694-3205
Website:
  www.partnerspublishersgroup.com
Market: Airport Stores, Bookstores

Sourcebooks, Inc.
1935 Brookdale Rd., Ste. 139
Naperville, IL 60563
Tel: 630-961-3900
Website: www.sourcebooks.com
Market: Gift Shops

Southern Book Service
5154 N.W. 165th St.
Miami Lakes, FL 33014
Tel: 305-624-4545
Website: www.southernbook.com
Market: Airport Stores

Sunbelt Publishing
1256 Fayette St.
El Cajon, CA 92020
Tel: 619-258-4911, 800-626-6579
Website: www.sunbeltpub.com
Market: Airport Stores

Symak Sales Co.
4747 Cote Vertu
Saint-Laurent, QC, H4S 1C9
Tel: 514-336-8780
Website: www.symaksales.com
Market: Dollar Stores

Workman Publishing Company
225 Varick St.
New York, NY 10014
Tel: 212-254-5900
Website: www.workman.com
Market: Bookstores, Gift Shops

4. SPECIALTY MARKETS

This section encompasses the markets that are interested in a wide variety of specialty books. The following resources will help you get in touch with the right people and find the information you need to successfully sell in these markets.

ASSOCIATION DIRECTORIES AND RESOURCES

Fundraising Groups through which You Can Sell Your Book to Associations

American Marketing Association:
  www.marketingpower.com

Association of Fundraising
  Professionals: www.afpnet.org

Do-It-Yourself Fundraising Ideas:
  www.fundraising-ideas.org/DIY

Fundraising Web:
  www.fundraisingweb.org

Fundrasing.com:
  www.fundraising.com

USA Fundraising:
  www.usafundraising.com

Lists of Associations

AssociationExecs.com
Website: www.associationexecs.com

Directory of Associations
Concept Marketing Group, Inc.
8655 E. Via de Ventura, Ste. G-200
Scottsdale, AZ 85258
Tel: 800-575-5369

Website: www.marketingsource.com/
associations

Encyclopedia of Associations
Website: www.galegroup.com

National Trade and Professional
Associations of the United States
Website: www.columbiabooks.com

Weddles Association Directory
2052 Shippan Ave.
Stamford, CT 06902
Tel: 203-964-1888
Website: www.weddles.com/
associations/index.cfm

BUSINESS/CORPORATE SALES

Lists of Corporations

Chief Executive Officers Club, Inc.
4 West 22nd St., 10th Fl.
New York, NY 10010
Tel: 212-925-7911
Website: www.ceoclubs.org

Fortune Magazine
Website: http://money.cnn.com/
magazines/fortune/rankings
Vistage International
11452 El Camino Real, Ste. 400
San Diego, CA 92130
Tel: 858-523-6800
Website: www.vistage.com

Network Marketing Companies

Direct Selling Association: www.dsa.org
For a list of more network marketing
companies, go to http://en.wikipedia.org/
wiki/List_of_network_marketing_companies

Retail Sourcing Company

Siennax Sourcing Services
171 Saxony Rd.
Encinitas, CA 92024
Tel: 858-385-8900, 800-717-4565
Website: www.siennax.com

CABLE TELEVISION SHOPPING NETWORKS

Home Shopping Network
New Business Development
1 HSN Dr.
St. Petersburg, FL 33729
Tel: 727-872-1000
Website: www.hsn.com

ShopNBC
New Vendor Department
6740 Shady Oak Rd.
Eden Prairie, MN 55344
Tel: 800-676-5523
Website: www.shopnbc.com

QVC
1200 Wilson Dr., Mail Code: 128
West Chester, PA 19380
Tel: 484-701-8282
Website: www.qvc.com

CATALOG MARKETS

CatalogLink
Tel: 831-647-6024, 866-746-7005
Website: www.cataloglink.com
Google Catalogs
Website: http://catalogs.google.com

Catalogs.com
318 Indian Trace, Ste. 330
Ft. Lauderdale, FL 33326
Tel: 954-659-9005
Website: www.catalogs.com

National Directory of Catalogs
Website: www.nmoa.org/catalog/
mailorderdir.htm

National Mail Order Association
Website: www.nmoa.com

GOVERNMENT AGENCY MARKETS AND RESOURCES

Federal Government Agencies

Department of Defense: www.acq.osd.
mil/osbp/doing_business/DoD_
Contracting_Guide.htm

Department of Health and Human
Services: www.os.dhhs.gov/grants/
index.shtml#contract

Department of Housing and Urban
Development: www.hud.gov/offices/
cpo/index.cfm

Department of Interior:
www.doi.gov/osdbu

Department of Justice:
www.usdoj.gov/jmd/pe/

Department of State:
www.statebuy.state.gov/

Department of Transportation:
www.dot.gov/ost/m60/

Department of Treasury: www.ustreas.
gov/offices/management/dcfo/
procurement/

Department of Veterans Affairs:
www1.va.gov/oamm

Federal Government Sales and Informational Resources

Association of Procurement Technical
Assistance Centers

P.O. Box 1607, 405 N 3rd St.

Orange, TX 77631

Tel: 409-886-0125

Website: www.aptac-us.org

Acquisition Central: www.acquisition.gov

Business Partner Network: www.bpn.gov

FedBizOpps.gov: www.fedbizopps.gov

Federal Acquisition Jumpstation: http://
nais.nasa.gov/fedproc/home.html

FedWorld.gov: www.fedworld.gov

General Services Administration:
www.gsa.gov

Google's government search engine:
www.Google.com/ig/usgov

Mark Amtower's "Off Center" radio
show: www.federalnewsradio.com

The United States Government's online
bookstore: http://bookstore.gpo.gov

USA.gov: www.usa.gov

Government Contractor Mark Amtower's Free, Informational Websites

www.governmentexpress.com

www.governmentmarketingbest
practices.com

Learning How to Become A Government Contractor

Register as a contractor at www.business.
gov/guides/contracting/register.html

Find federal contracting opportunities
and learn how to locate and bid on them
at www.business.gov/guides/
contracting/register.html

Learn the rules, regulations, and standards
that govern the federal procurement
process at www.business.gov/guides/
contracting/far.html

Fedmarket.com
3 Bethesda Metro Center, Ste. M010
Bethesda, MD 20814
Tel: 301-652-9504, 866-519-4482
Website: www.fedmarket.com

Local, City, and State Government Resources

Official City Sites' is an online resource for local, city, and state information. On its website you will find contact information and procedures to follow when dealing with government agencies in each different state: www.officialcitysites.org

Resources Needed to Register Your Business for Federal Government Sales

To register for a DUNS number, call 866-705-5711, or go to www.dnb.com/US/duns_update

Find your NAICS Code at www.census.gov/epcd/www/naics.html

Central Contractor Registration database: www.ccr.gov

Central Contractor Registration Handbook: www.ccr.gov/doc/CCR_Handbook.pdf

Online Representations and Certifications Application: https://orca.bpn.gov

Small Business Resources

A Small Business Guide to Federal Contracting can be found at www.business.gov/guides/contracting/small_biz.html

Small Business Association's (SBA) Procurement Marketing and Access Network: www.pronet.sba.gov

To find a Small Business Development Center (SBDC) near you, go to www.sba.gov/aboutsba/sbaprograms/sbdc/sbdclocator/SBDC_LOCATOR.html

United States Small Business Administration
409 3rd St., SW
Washington, DC 20416
Tel: 800-827-5722
Website: www.sba.gov

INCENTIVE/PREMIUM SALES RESOURCES

Agencies

Incentive Manufacturers and Representatives Alliance
Executive Director
1601 N. Bond St., Ste. 303
Naperville, IL 60563
Tel: 630-369-7786
Website: www.imraorg.net

Lifestyle Vacation Incentives
220 Congress Park Dr.
Delray Beach, FL 33445
Tel: 800-881-1900
Website: www.lifestylevacations.com

Maritz, Inc.
1375 North Hwy Dr.
Fenton, MO 63099
Tel: 877-462-7489, 636-827 4000
Website: www.maritz.com

Premium Book Company
1320 Toronita St.
York, PA 17402
Tel: 800-562-4357
Website: www.premiumbookcompany.com

Associations

Incentive Federation
Website: www.incentivefederation.org

Incentive Marketing Association
1601 N. Bond St., Ste. 303
Naperville, IL 60563
Tel: 630-369-7780
Website: www.incentivemarketing.org

National Association of Retail Marketing Services
Website: www.narms.com

Promotion Marketing Association
Website: www.pmalink.org

Promotional Products Association
  International
Website: www.ppa.org

Society of Incentive Travel Executives
Website: www.site-intl.org

Incentive Program

Hallmark Insights Program
Website: www.hallmarkinsights.com/
  corp/mp.html

Publications

Brandweek: www.brandweek.com

Incentive: www.incentivemag.com

Occupational Health & Safety:
  http://ohsonline.com/home.aspx

Promo Marketing: http://magazine.
  promomarketing.com

Selling Power: www.sellingpower.com

MILITARY MARKETS

Associations

American Logistics Association
1133 Fifteenth St., Ste. 640
Washington, DC 20005
Tel: 202-466-2520
Website: www.ala-national.org

Gold Star Wives of America
5510 Columbia Pike, Ste. 205
Arlington, VA 22204
Tel: 888-479-9788
Website: www.goldstarwives.org

National Military Family Association
6000 Stevenson Ave., Ste. 304
Alexandria, VA 22304
Tel: 703-823-6632
Website: www.nmfa.org

The Retired Officers Association
201 N. Washington St.
Alexandria, VA 22314
Tel: 800-245-8762
Website: www.troa.org

Veterans of Foreign Wars
406 West 34th St.
Kansas City, MO 64111
Tel: 816-756-3390
Website: www.vfw.org

A website with a list of most military
associations may be found at www.
military. com/benefits/resources/
military-and-veteran-associations

Chat Rooms and Forums

Military Brats Online: www.military
  brats.com

Military City: www.militarycity.com/
  forums

Clubs and Organizations

For an exhaustive list of military
organizations go to www.military.com/
benefits/resources/ military-and-
veteran-associations#sf

Exchange Services

Army and Air Force Exchange Service
3911 S. Walton Walker Blvd.
Dallas, TX 75236
Tel: 214-312-2011
Website: www.aafes.com

Coast Guard Exchange System
  Headquarters
870 Greenbrier Cir., Tower II, Ste. 502
Chesapeake, VA 23320
Tel: 804-734-8253
Website: www.cg-exchange.com

Marine Corps Exchange Service
MWR Support Activity
3044 Catlin Ave.
Quantico, VA 22134
Tel: 703-784-6331
Website: www.usmc-mccs.org/
  buspartners/index.cfm

Navy Exchange Service Command
3280 Virginia Beach Blvd.
Virginia Beach, VA 23452
Tel: 757-631-3906
Website: www.navy-nex.com

Military Department Websites

Air Force: www.selltoairforce.org

Army Corps of Engineers:
www.usace.army.mil/business.html

Army Security Assistance Command:
www.usasac.army.mil/Business/main
biz.htm

Department of Defense: www.defenselink.
mil/other_info/business.html

Department of Veterans Affairs:
www1.va.gov/oamm/

Navy: www.donhq.navy.mil/OSBP/

Military Media

Armed Forces Journal
6883 Commercial Dr.
Springfield, VA 22159
Tel: 703-750-9000
Website: www.afji.com

Army Times Publishing Company
6883 Commercial Dr., Springfield, VA
22159
Websites: www.armytimes.com,
www.navytimes.com,
www.airforcetimes.com,
www.marinecorpstimes.com

Family Magazine
370 Old Country Rd., Ste. C20
Garden City, NY 11530
Tel: 516-746-2000
Website: www.familymedia.com

Military Living
P.O. Box 2347
Falls Church, VA 22042
Tel: 703-237-0203
Website: www.militaryliving.com

Salute Magazine
370 Old Country Rd., Ste. C20
Garden City, NY 11530
Tel: 516-746-2000
Website: www.familymedia.com

Stars and Stripes
529 14th St. NW, Ste. 350
Washington, DC 20045
Tel: 202-761-0900
Website: www.estripes.com/index.asp

Museums

Fort Huachuca Historical Museum
Museum Director
U.S. Army Garrison, ATTN: ATZS-TDO-M
Fort Huachuca, Arizona 85613
Tel: 520-533-5736
Website: http://huachuca-
www.army.mil/
HISTORY/museum.htm

General Sweeney's Museum of Civil War
History
Tom Sweeny
5228 South State Hwy. ZZ
Republic, MO 65738
Tel: 417-732-1224
Website: www.civilwarmuseum.com

National Museum of the United States
Air Force
1100 Spaatz St.
Wright-Patterson AFB, OH 45433
Tel: 937-255-3286
Website: www.nationalmuseum.af.mil

Representative Group

Jagco and Associates, Inc.
598 Indian Trail Rd. South #227
Indian Trail, NC 28079

Tel: 704-684-0399

Sales Opportunities On Bases and Posts

Defense Commissary Agency
38th St. and East Ave., Bldg. 11200
Ft. Lee, VA 23801
Tel: 757-483-8515
Website: www.commissaries.com

Defense Department Child Development
  Program
Website: www.allmilitary.com/spouse
  andfamily/daycare/CDS.html

Employee Assistance Program
Website: www.uscg.mil/WORKLIFE/
  employee_assistance.asp

Life Skills Educational Programs
Website: www.milspouse.org/Educ/

National Guard Family Program
1411 Jefferson Davis Hwy.
Arlington, VA 22202
Tel: 703-607-5414
Website: www.guardfamily.org

Relocation Assistance
Website: www.milspouse.org/Relocate/

Special-Needs Family Member
  Assistance Programs
Website: www.milspouse.org/Benefits/
  SpChild/

Spouse Clubs
Website: www.milspouse.org

Selling Aboard Ships

Ship Stores Program
NEXCOM
3280 Virginia Beach Blvd.
Virginia Beach, VA 23452

Tel: 757-502-7473/7474, 800-628-3924
Website: www.navy-nex.com

Small Business Assistance

Defense Logistics Agency
Website: www.dla.mil/facts.aspx

Office of Small Business Programs
Crystal Gateway North
Ste. 406 West Tower, 201 12th St. South
Arlington, VA 22202
Tel: 703-604-0157
Website: www.acq.osd.mil/osbp

Websites

www.military.com
www.militarybookclub.com;
  www.militarybookclub.co.uk
www.militaryclothing.com
www.militaryfamily.com
www.militaryfamilybooks.com
www.militaryonesource.com
www.militaryspot.com
www.onmilitarymatters.com

MUSEUM, PARK, ZOO, AND AQUARIUM ASSOCIATIONS

Museum Association General Listings

American Association of Museums
1575 Eye St. NW, Ste. 400
Washington DC 20005
Tel: 202-289-1818
Website: www.aam-us.org/index.cfm

International Council of Museums
Maison de I'UNESCO, 1, rue Miollis
75732 Paris Cedex 15, France
Tel: +33-0-1-47-34-05-00
Website:
  http://icom.museum/museum_
  directories.html

Museum Store Association
4100 E. Mississippi Ave., Ste. 800
Denver, CO 80246
Tel: 303-504-9223
Website: www.museumdistrict.com

Museum Association Regional Listings

American Association for State &
  Local History
1717 Church St.
Nashville, TN 37203
Tel: 615-320-3203
Website: www.aaslh.org/hhouses.htm

Association of Midwest Museums
P.O. Box 11940
St. Louis, MO 63112
Tel: 314-746-4557
Website: www.midwestmuseums.org

Canadian Museums Association
280 Metcalfe St., Ste. 400
Ottawa, Ontario, Canada K2P 1R7
Tel: 613-567-0099
Website: www.museums.ca

Mid-Atlantic Association of Museums
2300 N St., NW, Ste. 710
Washington DC, 20037
Tel: 202-452-8040
Website: www.midatlanticmuseums.org

Mountain-Plains Museum Association
7110 W. David Dr.
Littleton, CO 80128
Tel: 303-979-9358
Website: www.mpma.net

New England Museum Association
22 Mill St., Ste. 409
Arlington, MA 02476
Tel: 781-641-0013
Website: www.nemanet.org

Southeastern Museums Conference
P.O. Box 9003

Atlanta, GA 31106
Tel: 404-378-3153
Website: www.semcdirect.net

Western Museums Association
P.O. Box 8367
Emeryville, CA 94662
Tel: 510-665-0700
Website: www.westmuse.org

Museum Association Specialty Listings

American Public Gardens Association
100 W. 10th St., Ste. 614
Wilmington, DE 19801
Tel: 302-655-7100
Website: www.publicgardens.org

Association of African American
  Museums
P.O. Box 427
Wilberforce, OH 45384
Tel: 937-376-4944 ext. 123
Website: www.blackmuseums.org/
  memberlinks/institutional.htm

Association of Children's Museums
1300 L St. NW, #975
Washington, DC 20005
Tel: 202-898-1080
Website: www.childrensmuseums.org

Association of Railway Museums
1016 Rosser St.
Conyers, GA 30012
Tel: 770-278-0088
Website: www.railwaymuseums.org

Association of Science-Technology
  Centers
1025 Vermont Ave., NW, Ste. 500
Washington, DC 20005
Tel: 202-783-7200
Website: www.astc.org/sciencecenters/
  find_scicenter.htm

Association of Zoos and Aquariums
8403 Colesville Rd., Ste. 710
Silver Spring, MD 20910
Tel: 301-562-0777
Website: www.aza.org

Council of American Jewish Museums
Executive Director
Center for Judaic Studies
University of Denver
2000 E. Asbury Ave., Ste. 157
Denver, CO 80208
Tel: 303-871-3015
Website: http://www2.jewishculture.
   org/?pid=cajm

Council of American Maritime Museums
Website: www.councilofamerican
   maritimemuseums.org

Fire Museum Network
Website: www.firemuseumnetwork.org/
   directory/index.html

Parks Association

National Recreation and Park
   Association
22377 Belmont Ridge Rd.
Ashburn, VA 20148
Tel: 703-858-0784
Website: www.nrpa.org

**NATIONAL RETAIL
ASSOCIATIONS**

National Association for Retail
   Marketing Services
P.O. Box 906
Plover, Wisconsin 54467
Tel: 715-342-0948
Website: www.narms.com

National Retail Federation
325 7th St., N.W., Ste. 1100
Washington, DC 20004

Tel: 202-783-7971, 800-673-4692
Website: www.nrf.com

National Retail Hardware Association
5822 W. 74th St.
Indianapolis, IN 46278-1787
Tel: 317-290-0338, 800-772-4424
Website: www.nrha.org

Retail Merchants Association
5101 Monument Ave.
Richmond, Virginia 23230
Tel: 804-662-5500, 866-750-2532
Website: www.retailmerchants.com

**WHOLESALERS AND
DISTRIBUTORS TO SPECIALTY
MARKETS**

Anderson News Co.
Purchasing Division
6016 Brookvale Ln., Ste. 151
Knoxville, TN 37919
Tel: 865-584-9765
Website: www.andersonnews.com
Market: Airport Stores, Drug Stores,
   Supermarkets, Military

Coutts
1823 Maryland Ave., P.O. Box 1000
Niagara Falls, NY 14302
Tel: 800-263-1686
Website: www.couttsinfo.com
Market: Libraries, Military

Eastern National
Purchasing Manager
470 Maryland Dr., Ste. 1
Ft. Washington, PA 19034
Tel: 215-283-6900 ext. 129
Website: www.easternnational.org
Market: National Park System

Event Network, Inc.
Purchasing Department
1010 Turqoise St., Ste. 325

San Diego, CA 92109
Tel: 858-488-7507
Website: www.eventnetwork.com
Market: Aquariums, Botanical Gardens,
Museums, Science Centers, and Zoos

Harrisburg News
Military Book Buyer
980 Briarsdale Rd.
Harrisburg, PA 17109
Tel: 717-561-8377, 800-676-6397
Website: www.harrisburgnewsco.com
Market: Military

Home Design Alternatives
944 Anglum Rd.
St. Louis, MO 63042
Tel: 314-770-2222
Website: www.hdainc.com
Market: Specialty Stores

Hudson News Group
Military Book Buyer
One Meadowlands Plaza, Ste. 902
East Rutherford, NJ 07073
Tel: 201-867-3600 ext. 1018
Website: www.hudsongroup.com
Market: Military

PMG International
Military Book Buyer

1011 N Frio St.
San Antonio, TX 78207
Tel: 404-363-6669 ext. 20
Website: www.pmg-intl.com
Market: Military

Select Media
Attn: Book Buyer for (your topic)
1685 Boggs Rd., Ste. 400
Duluth, GA 30096
Tel: 678-380-9880, 888-236-9457
Website: www.selectmediaservices.com
Market: Specialty Stores

Source Interlink Companies
27500 Riverview Center Blvd.
Bonita Springs, FL 34134
Tel: 239-949-4450
Website: www.sourceinterlink.com
Market: Specialty Stores

Source Interlink/Chas Levy
1200 N North Branch St.
Chicago, IL 60622
Tel: 312-440-4400
Website: www.chaslevy.com,
www.sourceinterlink.com
Market: Military

5. LIBRARY MARKETS AND RELATED SERVICES

This section includes resources for selling to all different types of libraries—hospital, military, niche, prison, and professional. It also includes library associations, review publications, and trade shows, as well as information about getting Spanish-language materials into libraries.

ASSOCIATIONS

American Library Association
50 E. Huron
Chicago, IL 60611
Tel: 800-545-2433
Website: www.ala.org

Independent Book Publishers
 Association
627 Aviation Way
Manhattan Beach, CA 90266
Tel: 310-372-2732
Website: www.pma-online.org

For a more complete list of library associations, go to www.acqweb.org/assn.html

HOSPITAL LIBRARY RESOURCES

Hardin Library for the Health Sciences
600 Newton Rd.
Iowa City, IA 52242
Tel: 319-335-9151
Website: www.lib.uiowa.edu/hardin/
 hslibs.html

J.A. Majors Company
530 E. Corporate Dr., Ste. 600
Lewisville, TX 75057
Tel: 972-353-1100, 800-633-1851
Website: www.majors.com

National Library of Medicine
8600 Rockville Pike, Bldg. 38, Rm. B1-E03
Bethesda, MD 20894
Tel: 800-338-7657
Website: http://nnlm.gov

MILITARY LIBRARY RESOURCES

Department of Defense Library System:
 www.dod.mil/other_info/libraries.html
Joint Forces Staff College:
 www.jfsc.ndu.edu/library/default.asp
Military Librarians Division:
 www.sla.org/division/dmil
National Defense University Library:
 www.ndu.edu/Library
National Library of Medicine:
 http://locatorplus.gov
Pentagon Library:
 www.hqda.army.mil/library

For a listing of Service Academy and post and base libraries, go to www.defense link.mil/other_info/libraries.html

NICHE LIBRARY RESOURCES

Children

Books for Kids Foundation
225 W. 35th St., 3rd Fl.
New York, NY 10001
Tel: 212-252-9168
Website: www.booksforkidsfoundation.
 org

Students With Disabilities

Bookshare
Publisher Liaison
480 S. California Ave.
Palo Alto, CA 94306
Tel: 650-644-3412
Website: www.bookshare.org

PRISON LIBRARY RESOURCES

Amherst Prison Book Project
Website: http://prisonbooks.org

Books through Bars
4722 Baltimore Ave.
Philadelphia, PA 19143
Tel: 215-727-8170
Website: www.booksthroughbars.org

Books to Prisoners
Website: www.bookstoprisoners.net
Boston Prison Book Program
Website: www.prisonbookprogram.org

Chicago Books to Women in Prison
Website: http://chicagobwp.org

Federal Bureau of Prisons Library
500 First St., NW, 7th Fl.
Washington, DC 20534
Tel: 202-307-3029
Website: http://bop.library.net

Ohio Books to Prisoners
Website:
    www.freewebs.com/books4prisoners

Women's Prison Book Project
Website: www.wpbp.org

PROFESSIONAL LIBRARY RESOURCES

American Association of Law Libraries
53 W. Jackson, Ste. 940
Chicago, IL 60604
Tel: 312-939-4764
Website: www.aallnet.org

Medical Library Association
65 E. Wacker Pl., Ste. 1900
Chicago, IL 60601
Tel: 312-419-9094
Website: www.mlanet.org

For a list of Medical and Health Sciences
Libraries, go to www.lib.uiowa.edu/
hardin/hslibs.html

REVIEW PUBLICATIONS

Major Review Publications

Booklist: www.booklistonline.com

Kirkus: www.kirkusreviews.com

Library Journal:
    www.libraryjournal.com

Publishers Weekly:
    www.publishersweekly.com

Niche Review Publications

For a list of niche reviewers, go to
www.bookcentralstation.com

SPANISH-LANGUAGE MATERIAL RESOURCES

Book Fairs

Guadalajara Book Fair:
    www.fil.com.mx/ingles/i_index.asp

Miami Book Fair International:
    www.miamibookfair.com

Reforma National Conference:
    www.reforma.org

Example Translations

For examples of good translations, go to
www.csusm.edu/csb/english/lists/cald
ecot.htm where you will find Caldecott
Medal winners translated into Spanish

Publication

Criticas Magazine:
    www.criticasmagazine.com

TRADE SHOWS

Dates and locations for library trade
shows can be found by clicking on the
"Conferences and Events" link at
www.ala.org

WHOLESALERS AND DISTRIBUTORS TO LIBRARY MARKETS

Baker and Taylor
1120 Rte. 22 E.
Bridgewater, NJ 08807
Tel: 908-541-7460; 800-775-1800
Website: www.btol.com
Market: Airport Stores, Bookstores, Libraries

Big River Distribution
8214 Exchange Way,
St. Louis, MO 63144
Tel: 314-918-9800
Website: www.bigriverdist.com
Market: Libraries (Midwest Region)

Blackwell North America, Inc.
6024 SW Jean Rd., Bldg. G
Lake Oswego, OR 97035
Tel: 503-684-1140, 800-547-6426
Website: www.blackwell.com
Market: Libraries (College and University)

Book Distribution Partners, Inc.
1847 Mercer Rd.
Lexington, KY 40511
Tel: 859-231-9789, 800-888-4478
Website: www.bwibooks.com/index.php
Market: Libraries

Brodart Books
500 Arch St.
Williamsport, PA 17705
Tel: 800-233-8467
Website: www.brodart.com
Market: Libraries (English- and Spanish-Language)

Coutts
1823 Maryland Ave., P.O. Box 1000
Niagara Falls, NY 14302
Tel: 800-263-1686
Website: www.couttsinfo.com
Market: Libraries, Military

EBSCO Book Services
Division Headquarters
5724 Hwy. 280 E.
Birmingham, AL 35242
Tel: 205-980-5623
Website: www.ebscobooks.com
Market: Libraries

Emery-Pratt Company
1966 W. Main St.
Owosso, MI 48867
Tel: 517-723-5291, 800-248-3887
Website: www.emery-pratt.com
Market: Libraries

Follett Library Resources
1340 Ridgeview Dr.
McHenry, IL 60050
Tel: 815-759-1700, 888-511-5114
Website: www.flr.follett.com
Market: Libraries (K–12)

Follett Educational Services
1433 International Pkwy.
Woodridge, IL 60517
Tel: 800-621-4272
Website: www.fes.follett.com
Market: Libraries (College and University)

Lectorum Publications, Inc.
205 Chubb Ave.
Lyndhurst, NJ 07071
Tel: 800-853-3291
Website: www.lectorum.com
Market: Libraries (Spanish-Language)

Mackin Library Media Services
14300 W. Burnsville Pkwy.
Burnsville, MN 55306
Tel: 952-895-9540
Website: www.mackin.com
Market: Libraries (K–12)

Matthews Medical Book Company
11559 Rock Island Ct.
Maryland Heights, MO 63043
Tel: 314-432-1400, 800-633-2665

Website: www.mattmccoy.com
Market: Libraries

NACSCORP
528 East Lorain St.
Oberlin, OH 44074
Tel: 440-775-7777
Website: www.nacscorp.com
Market: Libraries (College and
  University)

Quality Books, Inc.
Manager, Publisher Relations Dept.
1003 W. Pines Rd.
Oregon, IL 61061
Tel: 800-323-4241
Website: www.quality-books.com
Market: Libraries

Rittenhouse Book Distributors
511 Feheley Dr.
King of Prussia, PA 19406
Tel: 800-345-6425
Website: www.rittenhouse.com
Market: Libraries

Spanish Book Distributor, Inc.
6706 Sawmill Rd.
Dallas, TX 75252
Tel: 800-609-2113
Website: www.sbdbooks.com
Market: Libraries (Spanish-Language)

Unique Books
5010 Kemper Ave.
St. Louis, MO 63139
Tel: 314-776-6695; 800-533-5446
Website: www.uniquebooksinc.com
Market: Libraries

YBP Library Services
999 Maple St.
Contcoocook, NH 03229
Tel: 603-746-3102, 800-258-3774
Website: www.ybp.com
Market: Libraries (College and
  University)

6. ACADEMIC MARKETS, ASSOCIATIONS, AND RELATED SERVICES

This section contains all of the resources related to the academic market discussed in this book. It includes everything from direct mail lists, to homeschool resources, to a company that can determine your book's reading level—and everything in between.

COLLEGE AND UNIVERSITY RESOURCES

Conferences
Find lists of state college conferences at www.allconferences.com/Regional/State_College/

School Supply Stores
ABC School Supply, Inc.
3312 N. Berkeley Lake Rd.
Duluth, GA 30096
Tel: 800-669-4222
Website: www.abcschoolsupply.com

University Book Store
711 State St.
Madison, WI 53703
Tel: 608-257-3784
Website: www.univbkstr.com

Trade Show
Collegiate Marketing Expo:
  www.camex.org

DIRECT MAIL LISTS

Market Data Retrieval
6 Armstrong Rd.
Shelton, CT 06484
Tel: 800-333-8802
Website: www.schooldata.com

Quality Education Data
1625 Broadway, Ste. 250
Denver, CO 80202
Tel: 800-525-5811
Website: www.qeddata.com

GOVERNMENT SCHOOL RESOURCES

Department of Defense Education
  Activity (DoDEA)
4040 N. Fairfax Dr., Webb Bldg.
Arlington, VA 22203
Tel: 703-588-3104
Website: www.dodea.edu

A current list of DoDEA schools may be
obtained by writing:

Department of Defense Dependent
  Schools
Hoffman I, Rm. 152, 2461 Eisenhower Ave.
Alexandria, VA 22331

HOMESCHOOL RESOURCES

Book Fairs and Conventions

Homeschool Fair:
  www.homeschoolfair.com

Southern California Catholic Home
  Educators: www.scchehomepage.com

For a state-by-state list of homeschool
conventions, go to www.thehomeschool
mom.com/states/conventions.php

Categorical Association Examples

Jewish Home Educator's Network:
  www.snj.com/jhen

National African-American Homeschoolers Alliance: www.naaha.com

International Associations

Alternative Education Resource
  Organization:
  www.educationrevolution.org

Alternative Learning Organization:
  www.alternative-learning.org

Education Otherwise: www.education-
  otherwise.org

Home Education Advisory Service:
  www.heas.org.uk

HomeLearning Canada:
  www.homelearningcanada.ca

National Associations

American Homeschool Association: www.
  americanhomeschoolassociation.org

Association for Experiential Education:
  www.aee.org

Home School Legal Defense Association:
  www.hslda.org

Online Directory

Homeschool.com:
  www.homeschool.com

Publications

Home Education Magazine:
  www.homeedmag.com

Homeschooling Today:
  www.homeschooltoday.com

LINK Homeschool Newspaper:
  www.homeschoolnewslink.com

Old Schoolhouse Magazine:
  www.thehomeschoolmagazine.com

State Association Examples

California Homeschool Network:
  www.californiahomeschool.net

Florida Parent Educators Association:
  www.fpea.com

Smoky Mountain Home Education
  Association: www.smhea.org

Washington Homeschool Organization:
www.washhomeschool.org

K–12 PUBLIC SCHOOL RESOURCES

To find the contact information for
any public school in any state, go to
http://nces.ed.gov/ccd/schoolsearch/

To find state Departments of Education,
use the map at www.ed.gov/about/
contacts/state/index.html?src=ln

MEASURING READING LEVEL

You can send your book to MetaMatrics
and they can tell you its reading level:

MetaMatrics, Inc.
1000 Park Forty Plaza Dr., Ste. 120
Durham, NC 27713
Tel: 919-547-3400, 888-539-4537
Website: www.lexile.com

PROFESSIONAL PUBLICATION DIRECTORY

Ulrich's Periodicals Directory
Serials Solutions
501 N. 34th St. #400
Seattle, WA 98103
Tel: 206-545-9056, 866-737-4257
Website: www.ulrichsweb.com

STUDY SOFTWARE

VitalSource Bookshelf can convert your
book into a form that will allow students
to download it directly to their personal
computers.

VitalSource Bookshelf:
www.vitalsource.com

WHOLESALERS AND DISTRIBUTORS TO ACADEMIC MARKETS

Follet College Stores Co.
400 W. Grand Ave.
Elmhurst, IL 60126
Tel: 630-279-2330
Website: www.follett.com
Market: Academic (College and
University)

Ingram Digital Group
Website: www.ingramdigital.com
Market: E-content textbooks

J.R. Holcomb Educational Materials
3205 Harvard Ave.
Cleveland, OH 44105
Tel: 216-341-3000
Website: www.holcombs.com
Market: Academic (College and
University)

Nebraska Book Company, Inc.
4700 S. 19th St.
Lincoln, NE 68501
Tel: 402-421-7300
Website: www.nebook.com
Market: Academic (College and
University)

7. WHOLESALERS AND DISTRIBUTORS

This section includes all of the wholesalers and distributors discussed throughout this book. While this is not a comprehensive list of every distribution partner that exists, it contains the majority of the major players and the markets they serve.

Alliance Entertainment, LLC
4250 Coral Ridge Dr.
Coral Springs, FL 33065
Tel: 800-329-7664
Website: www.aent.com
Market: Airport Stores

Anderson Merchandisers
Book Purchasing Dept.
421 E. 34th St.
Amarillo, TX 79103
Tel: 806-376-6251
Website: www.amerch.com/index.html
Market: Discount Stores and Wholesale
   Clubs

Anderson News Co.
Purchasing Division
6016 Brookvale Ln., Ste. 151
Knoxville, TN 37919
Tel: 865-584-9765
Website: www.andersonnews.com
Market: Airport Stores, Drug Stores,
   Supermarkets, Military

Andrews McMeel Publishing, LLC
100 Front St.
Riverside, NJ 08075
Tel: 800-851-8923
Website: www.andrewsmcmeel.com
Market: Bookstores, Gift Shops

Atlas Books
30 Amberwood Pkwy.
Ashland, OH 44805
Tel: 419-281-1802, 800-266-5564
Website: www.atlasbooksdistribution.com
Market: Airport Stores

Baker and Taylor
1120 Rte. 22 E.
Bridgewater, NJ 08807
Tel: 908-541-7460; 800-775-1800
Website: www.btol.com
Market: Airport Stores, Bookstores,
   Libraries

Big River Distribution
8214 Exchange Way,
St. Louis, MO 63144
Tel: 314-918-9800
Website: www.bigriverdist.com
Market: Libraries (Midwest Region)

Blackwell North America, Inc.
6024 SW Jean Rd., Bldg. G
Lake Oswego, OR 97035
Tel: 503-684-1140, 800-547-6426
Website: www.blackwell.com
Market: Libraries (College and
   University)

Book Distribution Partners, Inc.
1847 Mercer Rd.
Lexington, KY 40511
Tel: 859-231-9789, 800-888-4478
Website: www.bwibooks.com/index.php
Market: Libraries

Bookazine
75 Hook Rd.
Bayonne, NJ 07002
Tel: 201-339-7777, 800-221-8112
Website: www.bookazine.com
Market: Airport Stores, Bookstores

Brodart Books
500 Arch St.

Williamsport, PA 17705
Tel: 800-233-8467
Website: www.brodart.com
Market: Libraries (English- and Spanish-
Language)

Coutts
1823 Maryland Ave., P.O. Box 1000
Niagara Falls, NY 14302
Tel: 800-263-1686
Website: www.couttsinfo.com
Market: Libraries, Military

Distributors, The
702 S. Michigan
South Bend, IN 46601
Tel: 574-232-8500
Website: www.thedistributors.com
Market: Airport Stores, Bookstores

Eastern National
Purchasing Manager
470 Maryland Dr., Ste. 1
Ft. Washington, PA 19034
Tel: 215-283-6900 ext. 129
Website: www.easternnational.org
Market: National Park System

EBSCO Book Services
Division Headquarters
5724 Hwy. 280 E.
Birmingham, AL 35242
Tel: 205-980-5623
Website: www.ebscobooks.com
Market: Libraries

Emery-Pratt Company
1966 W. Main St.
Owosso, MI 48867
Tel: 517-723-5291, 800-248-3887
Website: www.emery-pratt.com
Market: Libraries

Event Network, Inc.
Purchasing Department
1010 Turqoise St., Ste. 325
San Diego, CA 92109

Tel: 858-488-7507
Website: www.eventnetwork.com
Market: Aquariums, Botanical Gardens,
Museums, Science Centers, and Zoos

Follet College Stores Co.
400 W. Grand Ave.
Elmhurst, IL 60126
Tel: 630-279-2330
Website: www.follett.com
Market: Academic (College and
University)

Follett Educational Services
1433 International Pkwy.
Woodridge, IL 60517
Tel: 800-621-4272
Website: www.fes.follett.com
Market: Libraries (College and
University)

Follett Library Resources
1340 Ridgeview Dr.
McHenry, IL 60050
Tel: 815-759-1700, 888-511-5114
Website: www.flr.follett.com
Market: Libraries (K–12)

Greenleaf Book Group
P.O. Box 91869
Austin, TX 78709
Tel: 800-932-5420
Website: www.greenleafbookgroup.com
Market: Airport Stores

Harrisburg News
Military Book Buyer
980 Briarsdale Rd.
Harrisburg, PA 17109
Tel: 717-561-8377, 800-676-6397
Website: www.harrisburgnewsco.com
Market: Military

Home Design Alternatives
944 Anglum Rd.
St. Louis, MO 63042
Tel: 314-770-2222

Website: www.hdainc.com
Market: Specialty Stores

Hudson News Co.
Sr. Book Buyer
1521 Johnson Ferry Rd., Ste. 250
Marietta, GA 30062
Tel: 201-939-5050, 800-326-7711
Website: www.hudsongroupusa.com
Market: Airport Stores, Drug Stores,
  Supermarkets

Hudson News Group
Military Book Buyer
One Meadowlands Plaza, Ste. 902
East Rutherford, NJ 07073
Tel: 201-867-3600 ext. 1018
Website: www.hudsongroup.com
Market: Military

Ingram Book Co.
1 Ingram Blvd.
LaVergne, TN 37086
Tel: 800-937-8000
Website: www.ingrambook.com
Market: Airport Stores, Bookstores,
  Libraries

Ingram Digital Group
Website: www.ingramdigital.com
Market: E-content textbooks

J.R. Holcomb Educational Materials
3205 Harvard Ave.
Cleveland, OH 44105
Tel: 216-341-3000
Website: www.holcombs.com
Market: Academic (College and
  University)

Lectorum Publications, Inc.
205 Chubb Ave.
Lyndhurst, NJ 07071
Tel: 800-853-3291
Website: www.lectorum.com
Market: Libraries (Spanish-Language)

Levy Home Entertainment
Book Buyer
4201 Raymond Dr.
Hillside, IL 60162
Tel: 708-547-4400
Website: www.levybooks.com
Market: Discount Stores and Wholesale
  Clubs

Mackin Library Media Services
14300 W. Burnsville Pkwy.
Burnsville, MN 55306
Tel: 952-895-9540
Website: www.mackin.com
Market: Libraries (K–12)

Matthews Medical Book Company
11559 Rock Island Ct.
Maryland Heights, MO 63043
Tel: 314-432-1400, 800-633-2665
Website: www.mattmccoy.com
Market: Libraries

NACSCORP
528 East Lorain St.
Oberlin, OH 44074
Tel: 440-775-7777
Website: www.nacscorp.com
Market: Libraries (College and
  University)

Nebraska Book Company, Inc.
4700 S. 19th St.
Lincoln, NE 68501
Tel: 402-421-7300
Website: www.nebook.com
Market: Academic (College and
  University)

News Group
(See website for regional addresses)
Tel: 866-466-7231
Website: www2.thenewsgroup.com/US
Market: Airport Stores, Drug Stores,
  Supermarkets

PMG International
Military Book Buyer
1011 N Frio St.
San Antonio, TX 78207
Tel: 404-363-6669 ext. 20
Website: www.pmg-intl.com
Market: Military

Partners Publishers Group
2325 Jarco Dr.
Holt, MI 48842
Tel: 517-694-3205
Website: www.partnerspublishersgroup.
  com
Market: Airport Stores, Bookstores

Quality Books, Inc.
Manager, Publisher Relations Dept.
1003 W. Pines Rd.
Oregon, IL 61061
Tel: 800-323-4241
Website: www.quality-books.com
Market: Libraries

Rittenhouse Book Distributors
511 Feheley Dr.
King of Prussia, PA 19406
Tel: 800-345-6425
Website: www.rittenhouse.com
Market: Libraries

Select Media
Attn: Book Buyer for (your topic)
1685 Boggs Rd., Ste. 400
Duluth, GA 30096
Tel: 678-380-9880, 888-236-9457
Website: www.selectmediaservices.com
Market: Specialty Stores

Source Interlink Companies
27500 Riverview Center Blvd.
Bonita Springs, FL 34134
Tel: 239-949-4450
Website: www.sourceinterlink.com
Market: Specialty Stores

Source Interlink/Chas Levy
1200 N North Branch St.
Chicago, IL 60622
Tel: 312-440-4400
Website: www.chaslevy.com,
  www.sourceinterlink.com
Market: Military

Sourcebooks, Inc.
1935 Brookdale Rd., Ste. 139
Naperville, IL 60563
Tel: 630-961-3900
Website: www.sourcebooks.com
Market: Gift Shops

Southern Book Service
5154 N.W. 165th St.
Miami Lakes, FL 33014
Tel: 305-624-4545
Website: www.southernbook.com
Market: Airport Stores

Spanish Book Distributor, Inc.
6706 Sawmill Rd.
Dallas, TX 75252
Tel: 800-609-2113
Website: www.sbdbooks.com
Market: Libraries (Spanish-Language)

Sunbelt Publishing
1256 Fayette St.
El Cajon, CA 92020
Tel: 619-258-4911, 800-626-6579
Website: www.sunbeltpub.com
Market: Airport Stores

Symak Sales Co.
4747 Cote Vertu
Saint-Laurent, QC, H4S 1C9
Tel: 514-336-8780
Website: www.symaksales.com
Market: Dollar Stores

Unique Books
5010 Kemper Ave.
St. Louis, MO 63139
Tel: 314-776-6695; 800-533-5446

Website: www.uniquebooksinc.com
Market: Libraries

Workman Publishing Company
225 Varick St.
New York, NY 10014
Tel: 212-254-5900
Website: www.workman.com
Market: Bookstores, Gift Shops

YBP Library Services
999 Maple St.
Contcoocook, NH 03229
Tel: 603-746-3102, 800-258-3774
Website: www.ybp.com
Market: Libraries (College and
  University)

Index

THE SQUARE ONE® WRITERS GUIDES

If you've been wondering how to get your writing into publication or your screenplay produced, we believe we have the right books for you. The following titles described in these pages focus on how you can find an appropriate book publisher, magazine editor, or producer for your work. Each of these guides has been proven to work—time and time again. Each title has been written by an expert in his or her own field. I should know, because I selected them.

"...THOSE WHO WANT TO SEE THEIR POEMS BETWEEN
COVERS WILL WELCOME [CIARAVINO'S] GUIDANCE"
–BOOKLIST
(REGARDING HOW TO PUBLISH YOUR POETRY)

"THE ONLY THING THE BOOK DOESN'T DO IS PREPARE
THE PACKAGE FOR YOU"
–WRITEDIRECTION.COM
(REGARDING HOW TO PUBLISH YOUR NONFICTION BOOK)

"NOT ONLY LETS YOU IN ON THE RULES, IT LET'S YOU IN
ON THE SECRETS OF WINNING THE GAME"
–SCR(I)PT MAGAZINE
(REGARDING HOW TO SELL YOUR SCREENPLAY)

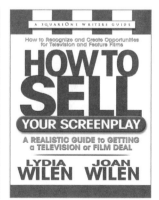

$16.95 • 252 pages
7.5 x 9-inch quality paperback
ISBN 978-0-7570-0000-3

$15.95 • 192 pages
7.5 x 9-inch quality paperback
ISBN 978-0-7570-0001-0

$17.95 • 320 pages
7.5 x 9-inch quality paperback
ISBN 978-0-7570-0002-7

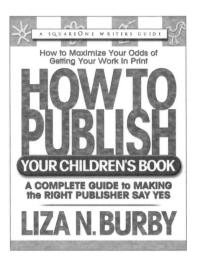